Transnational Food Security

Transnational Food Security addresses food security from an international relations, political economy and legal perspective analysing the relationship between food security and the environment and climate change, trade, finance and contracts, and the intersection between food and human rights.

The topic of food concerns one of the most basic and profound aspects of human survival. Universal and equal access to food is, at the same time, ridden with problems of power, inequality, distribution and implicated in old and new geopolitical conflicts. As such, 'food' and food security are central to conditions of poverty and hunger, development and 'modernization', transitional justice and rule of law reform around the world. As a problem of critique and scholarly inquiry, food prompts an inter-disciplinary assessment of the nature of food security in the modern world. The contributors to this book take us deep into the complexity of food and illustrate the challenges of adequately understanding and approaching questions of food security and food sovereignty in a globally interconnected world.

Transnational Food Security will be of great interest to scholars of international relations, political economy, and transnational law.

The chapters were originally published as a special issue of *Transnational Legal Theory* Journal.

Emily Webster is a Senior Research Fellow at the Transnational Law Institute at King's College London, UK, with an LLM in Transnational Law from King's College London, UK, and an LLB from Bournemouth University, UK.

Ankita Gupta is an Aspiring Lawyer in Toronto, with a JD from Osgoode Hall Law School, Canada, and BBA from the University of Toronto, Canada.

Ruth Ambros is a Mother and Aspiring Lawyer in Toronto, with a JD from Osgoode Hall Law School, Canada, and a BA from the University of Waterloo, Canada.

I0894949

Transnational Food Security

Edited by
Emily Webster, Ankita Gupta
and Ruth Ambros

Routledge
Taylor & Francis Group
LONDON AND NEW YORK

First published in paperback 2024

First published 2020
by Routledge
4 Park Square, Milton Park, Abingdon, Oxon OX14 4RN

and by Routledge
605 Third Avenue, New York, NY 10158

Routledge is an imprint of the Taylor & Francis Group, an informa business

British Library Cataloguing-in-Publication Data
A catalogue record for this book is available from the British Library

ISBN: 978-0-367-46564-3 (hbk)
ISBN: 978-1-03-283925-7 (pbk)
ISBN: 978-1-00-302963-2 (ebk)

DOI: 10.4324/9781003029632

Typeset in Minion Pro
by codeMantra

Contents

Trade and the Financialisation of Food

Food Security/Sovereignty: A Challenge for Human Rights

Citation Information

The chapters in this book were originally published in *Transnational Legal Theory*, volume 9, issues 3–4 (October–December 2018). When citing this material, please use the original page numbering for each article, as follows:

Chapter 1
Introduction: transnational food (in)security
Emily Webster and Peer Zumbansen
Transnational Legal Theory, volume 9, issues 3–4 (October–December 2018) pp. 175–190

Chapter 2
At the brink of famine in conflict and natural disaster zones: human rights approach to extreme hunger and malnutrition
Hilal Elver
Transnational Legal Theory, volume 9, issues 3–4 (October–December 2018) pp. 191–217

Chapter 3
Third world sovereignty, indigenous sovereignty, and food sovereignty: living with sovereignty despite the map
Michael Fakhri
Transnational Legal Theory, volume 9, issues 3–4 (October–December 2018) pp. 218–253

Chapter 4
The effects of oil pollution on the marine environment in the Gulf of Guinea—the Bonga Oil Field example
Ifesinachi Okafor-Yarwood
Transnational Legal Theory, volume 9, issues 3–4 (October–December 2018) pp. 254–271

Chapter 5

Compromised collaborations: food, fuel, and power in transnational food security governance
Matthew Canfield
Transnational Legal Theory, volume 9, issues 3–4 (October–December 2018) pp. 272–287

Chapter 6

International law and feeding the world in times of climate change
Anne Saab
Transnational Legal Theory, volume 9, issues 3–4 (October–December 2018) pp. 288–301

Chapter 7

GMO risks, food security, climate change and the entrenchment of neo-liberal legal narratives
Giulia Claudia Leonelli
Transnational Legal Theory, volume 9, issues 3–4 (October–December 2018) pp. 302–315

Chapter 8

Financialisation of the transnational food chain: from threat to leverage point?
Tomaso Ferrando
Transnational Legal Theory, volume 9, issues 3–4 (October–December 2018) pp. 316–342

Chapter 9

The World Trade Organization between law and politics: negotiating a solution for public stockholding for food security purposes
Matias E Margulis
Transnational Legal Theory, volume 9, issues 3–4 (October–December 2018) pp. 343–360

Chapter 10

Transnational legal methodology and domestic markets for food
Amy J. Cohen
Transnational Legal Theory, volume 9, issues 3–4 (October–December 2018) pp. 361–370

Chapter 11

Commodity derivatives, contract law, and food security
Anna Chadwick
Transnational Legal Theory, volume 9, issues 3–4 (October–December 2018) pp. 371–385

Chapter 12

The rise of new rights for peasants. From reliance on NGO intermediaries to direct representation
Priscilla Claeys
Transnational Legal Theory, volume 9, issues 3–4 (October–December 2018) pp. 386–399

Chapter 13

Engendering the right to food? International human rights law, food security and the rural woman
Joanna Bourke Martignoni
Transnational Legal Theory, volume 9, issues 3–4 (October–December 2018) pp. 400–414

Chapter 14

The UN Committee on World Food Security's break from the agricultural productivity trap
Nadia Lambek
Transnational Legal Theory, volume 9, issues 3–4 (October–December 2018) pp. 415–429

Contributors

Joanna Bourke Martignoni is a Senior Research Fellow at the Geneva Academy, Switzerland. Her research areas include the right to food, land commercialization, climate change, the right to education and gender equality. She is a member of the DEMETER (Droits et Egalité pour une Meilleure Economie de la Terre) multidisciplinary research for development project (2015–2020) that is examining land commercialization, gendered agrarian transformation and the right to food, with Cambodia and Ghana as case studies. In addition to her research work, she teaches on the Geneva Academy training courses on economic, social and cultural rights (ESCR). She also teaches a master's level course in ESCR at the University of Fribourg, Switzerland.

Matthew Canfield is an Assistant Professor, Program in Law, Politics, and Society at Drake University, Des Moines, USA. He is a cultural anthropologist who examines the relationship between law and social movements in the context of food and agricultural regulation. Drawing on ethnographic methods, his research explores how new forms of governance shape the prospects and possibilities for a more equitable and sustainable food system on local and global scales. At Drake, he teaches classes on food and law; social movements and global justice; and law, science and technology. In his spare time, he loves traveling, camping and cooking.

Anna Chadwick is a Lord Kelvin Adam Smith Research Fellow in the School of Law at the University of Glasgow, UK. Her research interests lie at the intersection between law and markets. As an LKAS Fellow at the University of Glasgow, UK, Anna is undertaking a new research project that examines the relationship between law and the institutionalization of visions of political economy. She is also part of a joint research initiative on food and finance.

Priscilla Claeys is a Senior Research Fellow in the Centre for Agreocology, Water and Resilience at Coventry University, UK. After several years working for human rights organizations and development NGOs, she decided to become a scholar to better understand the challenges facing social movements and human rights activists working towards more equitable and sustainable food systems. Her approach is multidisciplinary, empirical and inductive, mobilizing concepts from the socio-anthropology of rights, the sociology of social movements, rural sociology, international human rights law and development studies. Her areas of thematic expertise are human rights, food sovereignty, the right to food, land rights, peasant and social movements, agricultural trade and global governance, agricultural policy and food security.

Amy J. Cohen is John C. Elam/Vorys Sater Professor of Law at Ohio State University Moritz College of Law, Columbus, USA. A creative and cross-disciplinary scholar, she brings a range of qualitative and historical research methods to bear on two areas of legal scholarship—alternative dispute resolution (ADR) and law and economic development, including the law and political economy of agriculture and food. She teaches property, mediation, negotiation, international dispute resolution, law and development and global food law and policy.

Hilal Elver is a Global Distinguished Fellow at the Resnick Program for Food Law and Policy, Los Angeles Law School at the University of California, Berkeley, USA. Since 2002, she has been a Visiting Professor at the University of California Santa Barbara, USA, and the Co-Director of the Project on Climate Change, Human Security and Democracy housed at the Orfalea Center, USA. She is a member of the Academic Council of the UN Least Developed Countries (2011–2021), and a member of the official delegation of the Turkey's UN Climate Change Framework Convention. In May 2014, she was appointed by the United Nations Human Rights Council as the Special Rapporteur on the Right to Food.

Michael Fakhri is an Associate Professor at the University of Oregon School of Law, Eugene, USA. He teaches in the areas of international economic law, commercial law and food law. His research focuses on the right to food and agroecology. His theoretical agenda involves investigating law's role in imperial and capitalist adventures. He is a faculty member of the Environmental and Natural Resource Program where he co-leads the Food Resiliency Project.

Tomaso Ferrando is a Research Professor in the Faculty of Law at the University of Antwerp, Belgium. His main line of research focuses on the link between law and food, with particular attention to the international dimension (trade, investments and the human right to food) and the implementation of local practices. His second line of research concerns the socio-legal-financial construction of Green Bonds as a new/old form of financing that combines the instrument of debt with the desire of building sustainable and green futures. Outside of academia, he is the legal advisor of the UN Special Rapporteur on the Right to Food since 2016. He is a member of the Legal Committee of the Global Legal Action Network (glanlaw.org) and the Extraterritorial Obligation Consortium (ETOc).

Nadia Lambek is a Doctor of Juridical Science (SJD) candidate at the University of Toronto, Canada, and a human rights lawyer, researcher and advocate focused on food system transitions and the rights of working people. Her current research explores how the law and legal claims are framed by transnational agrarian movements and how law can (and cannot) be mobilized in the pursuit of more equitable, just and sustainable food systems. She will be a Residential Fellow at Harvard Law School's Institute for Global Law and Policy, Cambridge, USA, during the 2019–2020 academic year. She is an Adjunct Faculty at Vermont Law School where she teaches courses on global food security governance.

Giulia Claudia Leonelli is a Lecturer in Law at Birkbeck University, London, UK, and a Research Fellow at the Transnational Law Institute, King's College London, UK. Her research interests range from risk regulation, environmental law and public health law to legal theory, transnational legal theory and transnational regulatory governance.

Matias E Margulis is a Lecturer in International Political Economy in the School of Social and Political Science at the University of Edinburgh, UK. His research and teaching interests are interdisciplinary and cut across the fields of global development, human rights, international law and global food politics. In addition to his academic research, he is a former Canadian representative to the Organization for Economic Cooperation and Development (OECD), Food and Agriculture Organization (FAO) and World Trade Organization (WTO). He has also advised the UN Special Rapporteur on the Right to Food and the Scottish Parliament and consulted for international NGOs and the Brookings Institution.

Ifesinachi Okafor-Yarwood is a PhD student in the African Leadership Centre at King's College London, UK. Her research seeks to explore the interaction between illegal, unreported and unregulated fishing (IUUF) and other maritime threats in the Gulf of Guinea. She also analyses the possible (human security) implications of the prevalence of IUUF.

Anne Saab is an Assistant Professor in International Law at the Graduate Institute of International and Development Studies, and the Co-Director of the LLM programme. Her areas of interest and expertise include food and agriculture, climate change, intellectual property law and, more recently, emotions and international law. Prior to entering academia, she worked as a legal advisor and policy officer at the Ministry of Agriculture and Economic Affairs and at the Foreign Office in The Hague.

Peer Zumbansen joined The Dickson Poon School of Law, King's College London, UK, in 2014 as the inaugural Professor of Transnational Law and Founding Director of The Dickson Poon Transnational Law Institute. His research is focused on private law theory, comparative and transnational law. He has supervised major research theses, LLM and PhD projects in corporate governance, international law and transnational private regulatory governance. One of his long-standing research interests has been in legal education and legal curriculum reform, with a particular emphasis on the enhancement of a more foundational as well as practice-oriented law training.

Introduction: transnational food (in)security

Emily Webster and Peer Zumbansen

ABSTRACT

Serving as introduction to the first Annual Transnational Legal Theory Symposium —with a focus on Transnational Food (In)Security—this essay provides an overview of the themes that stood at the centre of the conference and which pervade the symposium contributions. The topic of food concerns one of humanity's basic and profound aspects of survival. Universal and equal access to food is, at the same time, ridden with problems of power, inequality, distribution and implicated in old and new geopolitical conflicts. As such, 'food' has ties and is central to conditions of poverty and hunger, development and 'modernisation', transitional justice and rule of law reform around the world. As a problem of critique and scholarly inquiry, food prompts an inter-disciplinary assessment of the nature and different aspects of what is at issue here. The contributors to this symposium take us deep into the complexity of food and illustrate the challenges of adequately understanding and approaching questions of food security and food sovereignty in a globally interconnected world.

> The concept of food security is deceptively simple …
> [e]nsuring global food security is, however, not simple.[1]
> Food and nutritional anthropology in particular, and food studies generally, manage to rise above the dualisms that threaten to segment most fields of study. This field resists separating biological from cultural, individual from society, and local from global culture, but rather struggles with their entanglements.[2]

A crisis of global proportions

There are currently 815 million people suffering from chronic hunger and 52 million children suffering from acute malnourishment in the world.[3] A decade

---

[1] Rosemary Rayfuse and Nicole Weisfelt, 'The International Policy and Regulatory Challenges of Food Security: An Overview', *The Challenge of Food Security: International Policy and Regulatory Frameworks* (Elgar, 2012) 3.

[2] Carole Counihan and Penny Van Esterik, 'Why Food? Why Culture? Why Now?' Introduction to the Third Edition, in: Carole Counihan and Penny Van Esterik (eds.), *Food and Culture. A Reader* (Routledge, 3rd edn, 2013), 1.

[3] FAO, 'What We Do' (*Food and Agriculture Organization of the United Nations*, 2018) online: <http://www.fao.org/about/what-we-do/en/> accessed 27 May 2018.

after the devastating world food crisis of 2007–2008[4] which triggered food riots in several countries and starkly demonstrated the fragilities and interconnectedness of modern global food production, food insecurity continues to increase.[5] There are several factors that have contributed to this, including but not limited to, armed conflict, the globalisation and financialisation of the food system and climate change. Indeed, climate change is fast becoming an issue of grave and overriding concern due to its global and complex nature and its devastating impacts upon food production—hitting the most vulnerable populations with the greatest severity.[6] It is within this context that the increasingly urgent question of *how* to feed the world in an equitable and sustainable way, has given rise to lively debate and deep contestation.

Access to food has always been an issue of central importance to humanity. 'Achieving food security has ... been a project of international institutions throughout the twentieth century, and a transnational project long before that'.[7] The establishment of the Food and Agriculture Organization (FAO) in 1945 and the subsequent proliferation of international instruments, have emanated from concerted attempts to address this problem.[8] Nevertheless, there is little consensus regarding the root causes of food insecurity nor how this problem can, and should, be remedied.[9] There are broadly two different perspectives regarding the causes of and answers to food insecurity. According to the first set of arguments, more food must be produced to feed the world's growing population through, for example, technological innovation or agricultural expansion.[10] The competing view holds that sufficient food to meet the world's needs is already being produced but that it is inadequately and unequally distributed.[11] Under these larger umbrellas, the debate

---

[4] 'Global Food Crisis 2008—Global Issues' (*Global Issues*, 8 October 2008) online: <http://www.globalissues.org/article/758/global-food-crisis-2008>.

[5] FAO and others, 'The State of Food Security and Nutrition in the World 2018: Building Resilience for Peace and Food Security' (2018) online: <https://docs.wfp.org/api/documents/WFP-0000074343/download/?_ga=2.194982701.1690239477.1548006449-382277349.1548006449>.

[6] *Ibid.*

[7] Anne Orford, 'Food Security, Free Trade, and the Battle for the State' (2015) 11(2) *Journal of International Law and International Relations* 1, 5; United Nations, 'Transforming Our World: The 2030 Agenda for Sustainable Development' (2015) A/RES/70/1 online: <https://sustainabledevelopment.un.org/content/documents/21252030%20Agenda%20for%20Sustainable%20Development%20web.pdf>; 'World Food Summit, Rome Declaration and Plan of Action' (1996) online: <http://www.fao.org/wfs/index_en.htm> accessed 27 May 2018; 'Ministerial Declaration: Action Plan on Food Price Volatility and Agriculture, Meeting of G20 Agriculture Ministers' (Paris, 22 and 23 June 2011) online: <http://www.oecd.org/site/agrfcn/48479226.pdf>.

[8] Lucy Jarosz, 'Comparing Food Security and Food Sovereignty Discourses' (2014) 4(2) *Dialogues in Human Geography* 168; Orford (n 7).

[9] Orford (n 7) 2.

[10] Jarosz (n 8) 169.

[11] Hilal Elver, 'Rising Hunger and Malnutrition in conflict and natural disaster zones' (2019) 9(3–4) *Transnational Legal Theory*, 1, 3 (this issue); Olivier de Schutter, 'International Trade in Agriculture and the Right to Food' Dialogues in Globalization (No 46/November 2009) 46 online: https://www.researchgate.net/publication/238704700_International_Trade_in_Agriculture_and_the_Right_to_Food; Oxfam, 'There Is Enough Food to Feed the World' (*Oxfam Canada*) online: https://www.oxfam.ca/there-enough-food-feed-world.

unfolds around more specific issues, a central one of which concerns the relationship between poverty and access to food.[12] Another, scrutinises the relationship between food insecurity and the global dominance of the economic liberalism paradigm.[13] In that regard, Anne Orford has argued:

> Something in the routine operation of international economic life, organised around global value chains, free trade, and open markets, produces a system of compulsion such that food is exported to foreign lands while the people who grow it are undernourished.[14]

The foregoing provides an important perspective on the role that history plays in the present-day production of food insecurity. This also implies that 'answers' to the current situation have to acknowledge the historical creation of conditions that cannot, by themselves, be easily set aside or undone. While a historical perspective on food insecurity must include an in-depth engagement with the colonial and post-colonial realities of the international economic and legal system, the closer scrutiny of governance arrangements over the second half of the twentieth century also reveals important shifts in the institutional arrangements that we, as lawyers, tend to take for granted. In that regard, the growing and intensifying internationalisation and transnationalisation of regulatory arrangements point to the need to take a fresh look at the idea that policy programmes are the prerogative and within the exclusionary competence of nation states.[15]

In recognition of its border-crossing dimensions, the concept of 'food security' emerged as the basis of the various food-related programmes as they were introduced by international organisations.[16] According to the *communiqué* issued at the World Food Summit in 1996: 'Food security exists when all people, at all times, have physical and economic access to sufficient, safe and nutritious food that meets their dietary needs and food preferences for an active and healthy life'.[17] It is important to highlight how closely this

---

[12] 'World Food Summit, Rome Declaration and Plan of Action' (n 7).

[13] Orford (n 7) 2.

[14] *Ibid*, 16.

[15] See again Orford (n 7) 4, who argues that 'in a transnational food system characterised by economic interdependence and shared vulnerability, states can no longer (if they ever could) guarantee access to food for their populations through domestic means alone'.

[16] For an overview of the history of food security as an international project see, eg, Orford (n 7); Rosemary Rayfuse and Nicole Weisfelt (eds), *The Challenge of Food Security: International Policy and Regulatory Frameworks* (Edward Elgar, 2012); Robin Sharp, *The Struggle for Food Security* (FAO, 1979); Daniel J Gustafson and John Markie, 'A Stronger Global Architecture for Food and Agriculture: Some Lessons from FAO's History and Recent Evaluation' in Jennifer Clapp and Marc J Cohen, *The Global Food Crisis: Governance Challenges and Opportunities* (Wilfred Laurier University Press, 2009); Baris Karapinar and Christian Häberli (eds), *Food Crises and the WTO* (Cambridge University Press, 2010); Joseph A McMahon and Melaku Geboye Desta (eds), *Research Handbook on the WTO Agriculture Agreement* (Edward Elgar, 2012); Eugenio Diaz-Bonilla, On Food Security Stocks, Peace Clauses, Permanent Solutions After Bali (IFPRI Discussion Paper, November 2014); S Ryan Isakson, 'Food and Finance: The Financial Transformation of Agro-Food Supply Chains' (2014) 41(5) *The Journal of Peasant Studies* 749; Robert Wolfe, *Farm Wars: The Political Economy of Agriculture and the International Trade Regime* Macmillan, 1998);

[17] World Food Summit (n 7) s1.

approach to food security has in fact been related to market-oriented approaches to food production and food distribution, firmly grounded in a liberal concept of global market dynamics[18] against the background of 'neo-liberal development discourses'.[19] This particular, and for a long time dominating, food security narrative has prompted a great deal of scholarly debate over the last few years.[20] These efforts, for better or worse, helped to carve out more specifically that a liberal market-based approach to food *security* had to rest on the working assumption that food *insecurity* exists because 'food production and its distribution do not meet the needs of the world's population'.[21] Therefore, the dominating argument held that more and better food production[22] and, importantly, *access* to food[23] was required, utilising existing technologies, liberalised trade, and global finance.[24]

This approach has been challenged by the emergence of the 'food sovereignty' discourse, which is generally associated with the social movement La Via Campesina.[25] The Declaration of Nyéléni 2007 states that: 'Food

---

[18] Orford (n 7) 6.

[19] Jarosz (n 8) 169.

[20] Eg, see: *ibid*; Orford (n 7); Rayfuse and Weisfelt (n 16); Jennifer Clapp and Sophia Murphy, The G20 and Food Security: a Mismatch in Global Governance? (2013) 4(2) Global Policy 129; Carmen G Gonzalez, Trade Liberalization, Food Security and the Environment: The Neoliberal Threat to Sustainable Rural Development (2004) 14 Transnational Law and Contemporary Problems 419; Carmen G Gonzalez, Climate Change, Food Security, and Agrobiodiversity: Toward a Just, Resilient, and Sustainable Food System (2011) Fordham Environmental Law Review 493; Olivier de Schutter, The Right to Food: Fighting for Adequate Food in a Global Crisis (2009) 31(2) Harvard International Law Review 38;

[21] Craig Pearson, 'A fresh look at the roots of food insecurity' in Rosemary Reyfuse and Nicole Weisfelt (eds) *The challenge of food security: international policy and regulatory frameworks* (Elgar, 2012).

[22] For a critique of this approach: Jennifer Clapp and Sophia Murphy, The G20 and Food Security: a Mismatch in Global Governance? (2013) 4(2) *Global Policy* 129; Jennifer Clapp, Hunger and the global economy: strong linkages, weak action (2014) 67(2) *Journal of International Affairs* 1.

[23] Amartya Sen, *Poverty and Famines: An Essay on Entitlement and Deprivation* (Oxford University Press, 1981); Jean Drèze and Amartya Sen, *Hunger and Public Action* (Oxford University Press, 1989); Clapp (n 22); FAO, The State of Food Insecurity in the World 2001 (FAO 2001) online: http://www.fao.org/docrep/003/y1500e/y1500e00.htm.

[24] Eg, see: The World Bank, Food Security (The World Bank 2018) online: https://www.worldbank.org/en/topic/food-security; TAD, *Trade and Environment Review 2013: Wake Up Before It Is Too Late* (UNCTAD, 2013); Orford (n 7) 12–13; Jarosz (n 8); Clapp (n 23); Kim Burnett and Sophia Murphy, 'What place for international trade in food sovereignty?' (2014) 41(6) *The Journal of Peasant Studies* 1065; Lucy Jarosz, 'Defining World Hunger: scale and neoliberal ideology in international food security policy discourse' (2011) 14(1) *Food, Culture and Society: An International Journal of Multidisciplinary Research* 117; Matias E Margulis, 'The World Trade Organization between law and politics: negotiating a solution for public stockholding for food security purposes' (2019) 9(3–4) *Transnational Legal Theory* 1 (this issue); Matias E. Margulis, 'Regulating Food-based Agrofuels: The Prospects and Challenges of International Trade Rules' (2015) 2(2) *Canadian Food Studies* 97; Matias E. Margulis, 'Trading Out of the Global Food Crisis? The WTO and the Geopolitics of Agro-Power' (2014) 19(2) *Geopolitics* 322; Anna Chadwick, 'Gambling on hunger? The right to adequate food and commodity derivatives trading' (2018) 18(2) *Human Rights Law Review* 233.

[25] Eg, see: Hannah Wittman, 'Food Sovereignty: A New Rights Framework for Food and Nature?' (2011) 2 *Environment and Society: Advances in Research* 87, 96–97; Annette Aurélie Desmarais, Marta G Rivera-Ferre and Beatriz Gasco, 'Building Alliances for Food Sovereignty: La Vía Campesina, NGOs, and Social Movements' in Douglas H Constance, Marie-Christine Renard and Marta G Rivera-Ferre (eds), *Research in Rural Sociology and Development*, vol 21 (Emerald Group Publishing Limited, 2014) 92; Marc Edelman and Saturnino M Borras, *Political Dynamics of Transnational Agrarian Movements* (Fernwood Publishing, 2016); Maryam Rahmanian, 'Food sovereignty—A critical dialogue' (*TNI*, 21 February 2014) online:

sovereignty is the right of peoples to healthy and culturally appropriate food produced through ecologically sound and sustainable methods, and their right to define their own food and agriculture systems'.[26] The definition incorporates wider considerations than the traditional interpretation of food security, including that of inter-generational equity, resistance to and dismantling of corporate domination of food production and trade, rights to decision-making regarding land use and food production, and notions of equality.[27] According to Lucy Jarosz, these discourses, developed by civil society and NGOs, build on Marxist political economy and promote ecology discourses that 'stress the importance of analyzing power relations and capitalist development's impacts upon agricultural development, local ecologies, hunger, and poverty'.[28]

The food sovereignty movement aims to bring together those most affected by food insecurity in order to form and mobilise transnational networks that articulate new rights to food and food production though the struggles of peasants, farmers, and Indigenous peoples. This is achieved, for example, through the identification of the negative effects of biofuels and monocultures for food production and the environment and by opposing the neoliberal agribusiness interests that dominate global food supply chains.[29] These social movements have utilised international human rights law and worked with international institutions to promote food security through the development of peasants rights.[30] Yet, according to Priscilla Claeys, this has been done *without* using the traditional conceptions of human rights or the right to adequate

---

<www.tni.org/en/multimedia/maryam-rahmanian-food-sovereignty-critical-dialogue≥ accessed 14 December 2018; Priscilla Claeys, 'The Creation of New Rights by the Food Sovereignty Movement: The Challenge of Institutionalizing Subversion' (2012) 46(5) *Sociology* 844. Josh Brem-Wilson, 'La Vía Campesina and the UN Committee on World Food Security: Affected publics and institutional dynamics in the nascent transnational public sphere' (2016) 43(2) *Review of International Studies* 302; Hannah Kay Wittman, Annette Aurelie Desmarais and Nettie Wiebe, 'The Origins & Potential of Food Sovereignty' in Hannah Wittman, Annette Aurelie Desmarais and Nettie Wiebe (eds), *Food Sovereignty: Reconnecting Food, Nature and Community* (Food First Books, 2010); Jessica Duncan, *Global Food Security Governance: Civil Society Engagement in the Reformed Committee on World Food Security* (Routledge, 2015); Josh Brem-Wilson, 'Towards Food Sovereignty: Interrogating Peasant Voice in the United Nations Committee on World Food Security' (2015) 42(1) *The Journal of Peasant Studies* 73; Ingeborg Gaarde, *Peasants Negotiating a Global Policy Space: La Vía Campesina in the Committee on World Food Security* (Routledge, 2017); Raj Patel, 'Food Sovereignty' (2009) 36(3) *The Journal of Peasant Studies* 663.

26 'Declaration of Nyéléni' (2007) online: <https://nyeleni.org/IMG/pdf/DeclNyeleni-en.pdf>.

27 *Ibid.*

28 Jarosz (n 8) 170.

29 La Via Campesina, Food Sovereignty (*La Via Campensina*, 2003) online: https://viacampesina.org/en/food-sovereignty/; FIAN International, Beyond Food Security, towards Food Sovereignty (*FIAN*, 2016) online: https://www.fian.org/en/news/article/beyond_food_security_towards_food_sovereignty/; Jasorz (n 8).

30 Eg, see: The Committee on World Food Security, About (*CFS*, 2017) online: http://www.fao.org/cfs/home/about/en/; Boaventura Monjane, 'The right to adequate food is the right to dignity and life' (La Via Campesina, 2018) online: https://viacampesina.org/en/the-right-to-adequate-food-is-the-right-to-dignity-and-life/; Draft United Nations declaration on the rights of peasants and other people working in rural areas A/HRC/WG. 15/5/3 (2018) online: https://www.ohchr.org/Documents/HRBodies/HRCouncil/WGPleasants/Session5/A_HRC_WG.15_5_3-English.pdf; Priscilla Claeys, *Human rights and the food sovereignty movement: reclaiming control* (Routledge, 2015); Patel (n 25).

food.[31] At the same time, the food sovereignty movement has had a heavy influence on the way in which international institutions working to alleviate hunger and provide access to food, develop responses to this issue.[32]

These discourses have been crucial in drawing attention to the causes of and possible solutions to food insecurity in widely divergent and contrasting ways.[33] Nevertheless, there is some concern that they remain too closely moored to that part of the international law regime which is tied into the prevailing international trade order and therefore may too readily buy into some of the neoliberal assumptions that underlie that system.[34] In that vein, Jennifer Clapp has taken issue with views that frame 'food security' and 'food sovereignty' as oppositional, arguing, instead, for a more constructive approach 'on how best to address hunger and other pressing issues facing the global food system'.[35] Similarly, other scholars recognise a movement within the literature away from a dichotomous understanding of food security and food sovereignty towards a more nuanced understanding of the relationship between the two. Christina Schiavoni advocates an approach that moves beyond strict binaries to more effectively 'examine the extent to which these two approaches are clashing, converging and mutually shaping each other'.[36]

In practice, we have witnessed the evolution of a system of food governance, which consists of an array of state and non-state actors, international organisations, networks, and political and legal mechanisms.[37] The sheer institutional complexity of these arrangements has prompted a plethora of work in governance and regulation theory geared towards, but not limited to, the emergence of complex global supply chains,[38] and what has been described as 'a distinct shift from the national to the international governmental level and from public to private governance'.[39] The growing tensions, but also overlaps, between public and private governance mechanisms against the background of a deeply contested normative divide over the liberal and redistributive dimensions of food security/sovereignty, further illuminate the need for an integrative, critical approach that acknowledges, at the outset, the

[31] Claeys (n 30); United Nations, The Right to Adequate Food, Human Rights Fact Sheet No. 24 (United Nations Human Rights Office of the Hugh Commissioner for Human Rights) online: https://www.ohchr.org/documents/publications/factsheet34en.pdf.

[32] Patel (n 25).

[33] Jarosz (n 8) 169.

[34] Anne Saab, International law and feeding the world in times of climate change (2019) 9(3–4) *Transnational Legal Theory* 1, 3 (this issue).

[35] Jennifer Clapp, 'Food Security and Food Sovereignty: Getting Past the Binary' (2014) 9(2) *Dialogues in Human Geography* 206; Bina Agarwal, 'Food sovereignty, food security and democratic choice: critical contradictions, difficult conciliations' (2014) 41(6) *The Journal of Peasant Studies* 1247; Patel (n 25).

[36] Christina M Schiavoni, 'The Contested Terrain of Food Sovereignty Construction: Toward a Historical, Relational and Interactive Approach' (2016) 44(1) *The Journal of Peasant Studies* 1, 15.

[37] Tetty Havinga, Donal Casey and Frans van Waarden, 'Changing Regulatory Arrangements in Food Governance', *The Changing Landscape of Food Governance* (Edward Elgar, 2015) 3.

[38] *Ibid.*

[39] *Ibid.*

interconnected but infinitely locally rooted nature of global food supply chains on the one hand, and financial and trade systems on the other.[40] These tensions pervade the competing discourses with regard to food security/sovereignty. As for food security, there is primary emphasis on technological development, the alleged merits of further privatisation and the use of financial instruments in structuring global food markets. Meanwhile, for those arguing for the need to reframe the problem as one of food *sovereignty*, the focus rests on protecting the rights of the most vulnerable stakeholders and on strengthening the transnational agrarian movement, on regaining control of land and production methods, and on ensuring that the voices of the people most affected are heard and taken account of.[41]

Food security as well as its competing, complementing paradigm of food sovereignty, are inextricably linked with issues of, *inter alia*, human rights, development, international trade, investment, biodiversity, access to water, and access to land and sustainability.[42] As such, they are part of the normative and regulatory fabric that is woven, by uncounted hands and through myriad processes, around the world today. The interconnected nature of issues that 'food' exposes, aligns it alongside those problems which are identified as being at the root of climate change today. In both we see, more strikingly than ever, that so-called 'answers' are no longer to be drawn from within an oppositional, dualist framework of liberal v conservative, state v market, local v global. Rather, food—as much as the climate—presents transnational regulatory challenges par excellence, drilling deep into the local foundations of democratic governance and, at the same time, revealing a globe-spanning web of interconnectivities, dependencies and influences.[43] Arguably, food,

[40] For discussions on trade, the connections between finance and food security see Margulis (n 23), Tomaso Ferrando, 'Financialisation of the Transnational Food Chain: From Threat to Leverage Point?' (2019) 9(3–4) *Transnational Legal Theory* 1 and Anna Chadwick, 'Commodity derivatives, contract law, and food security' (2019) 9(3–4) *Transnational Legal Theory* 1, both in this issue.

[41] Eg, La Via Campesina (n 29); Claeys (n 30); Peter Oosterveer, 'Promoting Sustainable Food Provision; the Role of Networks in Global Governance' (2017) 12(1) *Agricultural Research & Technology Open Access Journal* 001; Olivier De Scutter, 'Reshaping Global Governance: The Case of the Right to Food' (2012) 3(4) *Global Policy* 480; Jennifer Clapp and Marc J Cohen, *The Global Food Crisis: Governance, Challenges and Opportunities* (Wilfred Laurier University Press and Centre for International Governance (Studies in International Governance series) 2009).

[42] Eg, see: Claeys (n 30); Ferrando (n 40); Chadwick (n 40); Chadwick (n 24); Michael Fakhri, *Sugar and the Making of International Trade Law* (Cambridge University Press, 2014); Anna Chadwick, 'Gambling on hunger? The right to adequate food and commodity derivatives trading' (2018) 18(2) *Human Rights Law Review* 233; Nadia Lambek, 'The Right to Food: Reflecting on the Past and Future Possibilities' (2015) 2(2) *Canadian Journal of Food Studies* 68; Jennifer Clapp, 'The Trade-ification of the food sustainability agenda' (2016) 44(2) *The Journal of Peasant Studies* 335; Margulis (n 24); Margulis (n 24); Joanna Bourke Martignoni, *Research Brief: Gender Equality and the Right to Food* (Geneva Academy of International Humanitarian Law and Human Rights, 2017); Matthew Canfield, 'Compromised Collaborations: Food, Fuel, and Power in Transnational Food Security Governance' (2019) 9(3–4) *Transnational Legal Theory* 1 (this issue); Ifesinachi Okafor-Yarwood, 'The effects of oil pollution on the marine environment in the Gulf of Guinea—the Bonga Oil Field example' (2019) 9(3–4) *Transnational Legal Theory* 1 (this issue); Saab (n 34).

[43] Eg, see: Jennifer Clapp, Peter Newell and Zoe W Brent, 'The global political economy of climate change, agriculture and food systems' (2017) 45(1) *The Journal of Peasant Studies* 80; Marcus Taylor, 'Climate-

too, 'changes everything', to take a cue from Naomi Klein's ground-breaking work on climate change.[44]

The TLT symposium

On 20th January 2018, the *Transnational Legal Theory* Journal hosted a group of leading scholars at its first annual symposium. The event, which took place in the awe-inspiring setting of London's Somerset House, home to King's College London's Dickson Poon School of Law and the Transnational Law Institute,[45] focused on the theme of 'Transnational Food Security'. Three themes dominated the discussion: *The Environment and Climate Change, Trade and the Financialisation of Food*, and *Food Security/Sovereignty: A Challenge for Human Rights.*

The Symposium was bookended by two outstanding keynote addresses. In her written contribution to this Issue, 'At the Brink of Famine in Conflict and Natural Disaster Zones: Human Rights Approach to Extreme Hunger and Malnutrition', Hilal Elver, the current UN Special Rapporteur for Food, discusses right to food violations in the form of hunger and malnutrition caused by conflict and environmental disasters. Hunger and famine, in a variety of combat settings, inflict massive casualties and widespread suffering on the civilian population. Elver critically reviews the implementation of norms and guidelines, the non-compliance of states and other political actors with existing norms, and the prevailing failure to address international criminal behaviour to stop human rights violations with regard to the right to food. She argues: 'If the international community is serious about the imperative character of the right to food and the eradication of massive starvation and famine, steps must be taken to encourage the implementation of existing standards as well as to codify and elaborate new rules'. Elver concludes that this would be best achieved through the introduction of a new, binding international agreement designed to tackle food insecurity specifically in the context of conflict and disaster zones.

The second keynote speaker, Michael Fakhri, in his contribution, 'Third World Sovereignty, Indigenous Sovereignty, and Food Sovereignty: Living With Sovereignty Despite the Map', innovatively employs his personal experiences as a migrant to both situate his own scholarship and investigate and frame the meaning of 'sovereignty' by grounding it in his 'personal history

smart agriculture: what is it good for?' (2017) 45(1) *The Journal of Peasant Studies* 89; Anne Saab, 'Climate-Resilient Crops and International Climate Change Adaptation Law' (2016) 29(2) *Leiden Journal of International Law* 503; FAO, *The State of Food and Agriculture 2016: Climate Change, Agriculture and Food Security* (FAO, 2016). See also Michael Fakhri, 'Food a Matter of Global Governance' (2015) 11(2) *Journal of International Law and International Relations* 68.

44 Naomi Klein, *This Changes Everything* (Simon & Schuster, 2014).

45 King's College London, *The Transnational Law Institute* (2019) online: https://www.kcl.ac.uk/law/tli/index.aspx. See also King's College London, *KTLS* (2018) online: www.transnationallawsummit.org.

and political commitment'. He situates himself in this way to 'learn from those particular struggles and propose insights to others in TWAIL and law more broadly. I am also introducing myself, offering an account of who I am and where I am from, to scholars and activists in those other struggles as an invitation to collaborate with me and my comrades'. He investigates the challenges facing TWAIL scholarship when considering issues of sovereignty, using the lens of Inuit geographical reframing achieved though international law and institutions to ask: 'whether the underlying theoretical concepts that arise from Inuit sovereignty—and the technique of using doctrine to geographically reframe a political argument—could be deployed in other contexts in a way that transforms and debilitates imperial power'. Using the emergence of the social movement La Via Campesina, Fakhri draws on questions, challenges and opportunities raised that may 'propose insights' to TWAIL scholars, and to learn from La Via Campesina's success as a social movement which 'has quickly rearticulated sovereignty in transnational manifold terms while maintaining an ambivalence to the state and empowering millions of people across the world'. Both struggles, he argues, redefine sovereignty in terms of 'transnational solidarity'. As such, any understanding of change in international law that 'counters imperial forces on a global scale', must now embrace solidarity as a central concept.

The relationship between access to food, food production and the environment is a crucial factor in the fight against hunger. Modern forms of industrial food production may create new pressures and severe environmental degradation, including for example, from the impact of agribusiness and the development of genetically modified organisms (GMOs) and their regulation. These narratives and relationships take on a more urgent, global character when climate change and its impacts are considered.

In her contribution to the issue, 'The Effects of Oil Pollution on the Marine Environment in the Gulf of Guinea—the Bonga Oil Field Example', Ifesinachi Okafor-Yarwood, in an analysis grounded in the social sciences, focuses on the legal and political failings apparent in Nigeria in relation to water pollution. She finds a situation in which multinational oil companies are able to avoid their responsibilities and obligations in relation to the prevention and clean-up of oil spills and the compensation of those affected. This results in damage to both the marine environment, including important fish breeding grounds, and fisher folks dependent on fish stocks throughout the Niger Delta region, and potentially the wider Gulf of Guinea, for subsistence. She ends by making certain proposals for policy improvements to ensure that oil companies are held to the same environmental standards as in their home jurisdictions.

Matthew Canfield in 'Comprised Collaborations: Food, Fuel, and Power in Transnational Food Security Governance', highlights the entanglement between agrofuels and agriculture in contributing to the world food crisis and the rise of what he terms *energopolitics*, that is, the power exercised over and through energy. Canfield draws on the concept of energopolitics to demonstrate both how changing the material processes of energy extraction condition the calculative logics through which transnational food governance is constituted, and, how collaborative food governance in fact supresses the conflict between food and fuel that it was developed to mediate. He concludes that '[u]ltimately, as collaboration becomes the *sine-qua-non* for sustainability in an age of climate change, an energopolitical analysis is essential. For as we enter the new geological epoch known as the Anthropocene, new analytical tools are needed to integrate nature back into our accounts of how power operates'.

In 'International Law and Feeding the World in Times of Climate Change', Anne Saab provides an incisive look at the tensions between the neoliberal narrative of eliminating hunger through technological development, privatisation and strong corporate influences, and the food sovereignty narrative which rejects and opposes the neoliberal food regime. Saad claims both narratives highlight wider controversies surrounding how the global food system should be governed and explores these dynamics in the context of climate change through the example of climate-ready seeds. She argues that both narratives are constructed and reinforced by international law and are therefore based on the same underlying assumptions that are consistent with the neoliberal status quo. It is this interaction with international law that ultimately limits the ability of the food sovereignty movement to question and challenge the dominant approach to the governance of food.

In 'GMO Risks, Food Security, Climate Change and the Entrenchment of Neo-Liberal Legal Narratives' Giulia Claudia Leonelli builds on Anne Saab's analysis of the public international law climate change adaptation regime in 'Climate-Resilient Crops and International Climate Change Adaptation Law'.[46] Leonelli, through the lens of a public international law discourse, adopts a transnational legal narrative in response to GMOs. She explores the artificial nature of the neo-liberal legal narratives in this context and argues that the public international law discourse on climate resilient GMOs and the hegemonic transnational legal narrative on GMO safety and food security, turn out in fact to be two sides of the same coin. Ultimately, she argues, '[d]ifferent transnational strategies and solutions are being obscured, neglected or discarded as a result of the entrenchment of artificial —neo-liberal—transnational legal narratives. Legal analysis is thus called upon to give its contribution, deconstructing law's social embeddedness and casting light on the political and socio-economic implications of different regulatory approaches. This will be all the more important, as

[46] Saab (n 43).

globalisation progresses; and indeed, this is the challenge that methodological transnationalism is striving to face'.

Trade, finance and corporate law, and the neoliberal tenants that underlie the global economic system, are often viewed as in conflict with moves to secure the rights of vulnerable people, in this case access to sufficient food. Privatisation, the dominance of big agribusiness and the adherence to trade liberalisation and neoliberal forms of market ordering, as well as the WTO trade regime, ensure that these considerations play a great, if increasingly contested, role in shaping both international and domestic approaches to the production of food.

In his article, 'Financialisation of the Transnational Food Chain: From Threat to Leverage Point?' Tomaso Ferrando examines the financialisation of global food chains in light of the negative consequences often associated with this development, including the world food crisis caused in part, he argues, by financial speculation in the global food market. Through meta-regulation such as the 2014 EU Directive on non-financial reporting, he analyses the potential of legal and quasi-legal approaches to make the food system more sustainable. 'Instead of legitimising finance and its vision of the world', he argues 'a stronger understanding of the financial complexity of the food system would expose the role of finance and financialisation in defining the food system beyond commodity speculation'.

In 'The World Trade Organization Between Law and Politics: Negotiating A Solution for Public Stockholding for Food Security Purposes', Matias E. Margulis examines global responses to public stockholding for food. Taking a political economy perspective, Margulis argues that parties to the World Trade Organization (WTO) engage in politics though its negotiation function to deal with legal uncertainty about public food stockholding rather than turning to 'law' to adjudicate disputes between states. This has resulted in the negotiation of a temporary Peace Clause to avoid developing countries breaching WTO terms in relation to their existing public food stockholding programmes while, at the same time, on-going negotiations attempt to provide a consensus-based solution within the WTO legal framework. The case of public food stockholding he argues, reveals important dynamics about the WTO-food security relationship that are overlooked by approaches primarily concerned with supra-national constraints on national policy and the fragmentation of international law.

In 'Transnational Legal Methodology and Domestic Markets for Food', Amy Cohen uses the lens of supermarket chain regulation in India to explore the tensions and synergies of transnational economic ordering and state power in describing the distribution of authority, resources, and power within the Indian food system. Cohen suggests that food is a generative category for transnational legal analysis, as it supersedes boundaries between public good and private commodity and between national sovereignty and transnational markets. Adopting the transnational legal methodology advocated by Peer Zumbansen[47] as a form of analysis, Cohen argues that the transnational and domestic, like the state and the market, are not opposites but rather are alternatives, even potentially homologous, ways of describing the distribution of authority, resources, and power.

In 'Commodity Derivatives, Contract Law, and Food Security', Anna Chadwick approaches the question of speculation in the food market from the vantage point of contract law and its role in commodity derivatives trading. Identifying a gap in the literature regarding how the norms of contract law have been altered, extended, and even distorted to create a new generation of financial assets linked to food prices, Chadwick examines how the trade in commodity derivatives has disrupted some of the established principles of contract law, and reflects on the significance of her findings for the debate about derivatives regulation. She concludes, that 'ensuring the food security of future generations might require contesting some of the extensive liberties that the financial services industry has been taking with respect to contract law'.

The third part of this special issue focuses on the nexus between human rights, Indigenous peoples, food security, and food sovereignty movements. In this sphere, agrarian movements have been effectively deployed to exert pressure on the international stage, new norms have been developed, human rights have been employed, and language disassociated with the 'traditional' colonial international legal order have been embedded in the discourse.

Priscilla Claeys, in 'The Rise of New Rights for Peasants. From Reliance on NGO Intermediaries to Direct Representation', offers an alternative perspective and analysis of questions of food sovereignty, human rights and social movements in transnational food security from that undertaken by Fakhri. Claeys provides insights into La Via Campesina, through the analysis of certain human rights discourses relating to 'social movements from below'. She uses the 4-step framework developed by Clifford Bob in *The International Struggle for New Human Rights*[48] to analyse the 'development of new human rights by various 'claimants''. She argues that these frameworks 'need to be updated to account for the emergence of transnational social movements representing the affected and capable of engaging, directly and autonomously with states, in the political and technical process of creating new global human rights norms'.

In 'Engendering the Right to Food? International Human Rights Law, Food Security and the Rural Woman', Joanna Bourke Martignoni examines the

---

[47] Peer Zumbansen, 'Transnational Law, *Evolving*' in Jan M Smits (ed), *Elgar Encyclopaedia of Comparative Law* (Elgar, 2nd edn 2012); Peer Zumbansen, *Transnational Legal Pluralism* (Cambridge University Press, 2019) (*forthcoming*).

[48] Clifford Bob, *The International Struggle for New Human Rights* (University of Pennsylvania Press, 2008).

construct of gender in the international legal system, seeking to 'problematise the binary categories of the public and the private spheres, tradition and modernity, local and global spaces and State and non-State forms of normativity that have been deployed in efforts to diagnose and remedy the problem of gendered food insecurity'. Martignoni analyses the discourses of international human rights mechanisms in relation to the rural woman and her right to food through the work of the Committee on the Elimination of Discrimination Against Women. She ultimately argues that international institutions 'should be cognisant of the complexities of gendered power relations in rural communities and be prepared to make recommendations on the right to food that are nuanced, contextualised and informed by quality research'.

Finally, in 'The UN Committee on World Food Security: Creating Space for Transformative Global Food Security Governance', Nadia Lambek investigates the dominant narrative stemming from the world food crisis that reverted to the 'productivity paradigm' despite this not being the cause of the crisis. Lambek investigates the participatory mechanisms implemented by the UN Committee on World Food Security (CFS) and the disparities between its goals and implementation a decade into the project. She argues that by focusing on small-scale producer livelihood, through recommendations on access to productive resources, infrastructure and social protection, rather than productivity rates and availability of food on markets, the CFS has contributed to the normative elaboration of an alternative paradigm to that of productivity.

Food security/sovereignty: an outlook

Last year, the FAO, World Health Organization, UNICEF, International Fund for Agricultural Development and World Food Programme published their latest joint report: '*The State of Food Security and Nutrition in the World*' (SOFI 2018).[49] SOFI 2018 highlights the strong connection between food security and the Sustainable Development Goals (SDGs) and the prominent place that achieving SDG 2, *end hunger, achieve food security and improved nutrition and promote sustainable agriculture*,[50] has within efforts to tackle hunger and food insecurity. SDG 2 demonstrates the traditional food security narrative: the need to increase productivity and production [2.4], to increase investment 'including through enhanced international cooperation, in rural infrastructure, agricultural research and extension services, technology development and plant and livestock gene banks' [2.a], to 'correct and prevent trade restrictions in world agricultural markets'[2.b], and to ensure the proper functioning of the food commodity markets [2.c].[51] While there is

[49] FAO and others (n 5).
[50] *Ibid*, xiii.
[51] United Nations (n 7).

an acceptance of the special situation of women and Indigenous peoples in relation to food insecurity, the character of the SDGs is firmly rooted in the neoliberal influences underpinning the food security narrative and, furthermore, have been embraced by international institutions concerned with alleviating global hunger.[52] It is clear therefore that SDG 2 will be fundamental to the response to food insecurity of international institutions/organisations in the years ahead.

SOFI 2018 focuses on the immediate and growing impacts of climate change and warns that 'the gains made in ending hunger and malnutrition are being eroded by climate variability and exposure to more complex, frequent and intense climate extremes'.[53] This climate variability has been identified as 'a key driver … and one of the leading causes of severe food crises'.[54] It goes on to highlight the different international agreements and organisations promoting climate adaptation, but calls for 'better integration of these global policy platforms and processes to ensure that actions across and within sectors such as environment, food, agriculture and health pursue coherent objectives'.[55] Therefore, it is clear that climate change and the actions of states to implement both mitigation and adaptation policies and measures will be key to food security efforts in the coming years.

On the 17th December 2018 the UN General Assembly adopted the UN Declaration on the Rights of Peasants and Other People working in Rural Areas[56] (UNDROP). UNDROP came after a 17-year long process of development which was spearheaded by a large network of civil society actors around the world, including the transnational agrarian movement, La Via Campesina.[57] Arguably, the adoption of UNDROP will further strengthen the rights of peasants in international law, in that it embraces the idea that sustainable rights development must be bottom-up and driven and articulated by the people themselves.[58] Conversely, food sovereignty movements highlight the need for the establishment, the development and the extension of 'a human rights approach to the heart of decision-making and governance on food security'.[59] Therefore, it is central to any food sovereignty approach that the perspectives of civil society actors—especially those 'from countries

[52] Eg, FAO, *Sustainable Development Goals* (Food and Agriculture Organization of the United Nations) online: http://www.fao.org/sustainable-development-goals/en/; FAO and others (n 5).
[53] *Ibid*, vi.
[54] *Ibid.*
[55] *Ibid.*
[56] Draft United Nations declaration on the rights of peasants and other people working in rural areas A/HRC/WG. 15/5/3 (2018) online: https://www.ohchr.org/Documents/HRBodies/HRCouncil/WGPleasants/Session5/A_HRC_WG.15_5_3-English.pdf.
[57] Finally, UN General Assembly adopts Peasant Rights declaration! Now focus is on its implementation (*La Via Campesina*, 17 December 2018) online: https://viacampesina.org/en/finally-un-general-assembly-adopts-peasant-rights-declaration-now-focus-is-on-its-implementation/.
[58] Claeys (n 30).
[59] Monjane (n 30).

most affected by hunger and malnutrition'[60]—are taken seriously by governments and international institutions.[61] Indeed, in 2018 La Via Campesina highlighted growing calls from civil society organisations for agroecology as 'an alternative form of sustainable agriculture, and food sovereignty as the alternative paradigm to transform the current food system'.[62]

According to Steve Gliessman, agroecology attempts to '[bring] sustainability to all parts of the food system: ecological, economic, and social'.[63] This approach is transdisciplinary, participatory and action-orientated in that 'it confronts the economic and political power structures of the current industrial food system with alternative social structures and policy action. The approach is grounded in ecological thinking where a holistic, systems-level understanding of food system sustainability is required'.[64] Promoted by La Via Campesina and other civil society organisations over the last decade,[65] as well as being a hub of scholarly debate,[66] in 2018 the FAO held its 2nd International Symposium on Agroecology where '[m]ost participants agreed that agroecology was at a critical turning point and the time to accelerate its spread was now'.[67] The current UN Special Rapporteur to the Right to Food, and contributor to this special edition, Hilal Elver further stated at the Civil Society Global Forum 2018,

> [a]groecology will [increasingly] be the only way. When everyone understands this maybe it will be too late. We need to push now to make it an acceptable alternative.[68]

This paradigm is utilised in direct opposition to the current domination of the agro-industrial sector at the international level[69] and is likely to dominate discussions in the food sovereignty movement in the years ahead.

Today, at the time of writing this introduction, hunger and malnutrition are growing, somewhat unabatedly and seemingly exacerbated by political

---

[60] *Ibid.*

[61] *Ibid.*

[62] *Ibid.*

[63] Steve Gliessman, 'Defining Agroecology' (2018) 42(6) *Agroecology and Sustainable Food Systems* 599, 599.

[64] *Ibid.*

[65] Monjane (n 30).

[66] Eg, see: Gliessmann (n 63); Michael M. Bell, 'The Agroecological Imagination: Introduction' (2018) 42(6) *Agroecology and Sustainable Food Systems* 602; Michael M Bell and Stéphane Bellon, 'Generalization without universalization: Towards an agroecology theory' (2018) 42(6) *Agroecology and Sustainable Food Systems* 605; Claire Lamine and Julie Dawson, 'The agroecology of food systems: Reconnecting agriculture, food, and the environment' (2018) 42(6) *Agroecology and Sustainable Food Systems* 629; Eric Holt-Giménez and Miguel A Altieri, 'Agroecology, Food Sovereignty, and the New Green Revolution' (2012) 37(1) *Agroecology and Sustainable Food Systems* 90; V. Ernesto Méndez, Christopher M Bacon and Roseann Cohen, 'Agroecology as a Transdisciplinary, Participatory, and Action-Oriented Approach' (2012) 37(1) *Agroecology and Sustainable Food Systems* 3.

[67] Steve Gliessman, 'Scaling-Out and Scaling up Agroecology' (2018) 42(8) *Agroecology and Sustainable Food Systems* 841.

[68] Monjane (n 30).

[69] *Ibid.*

upheaval, poverty, war and climate change.[70] It is clear that in 2019 and beyond, both paradigms will continue to become further accentuated as their proponents mobilise them in an attempt to oppose the excesses of the neoliberal tenants that have guided the development of international approaches and provide voices for those historically left voiceless. Nevertheless, the impacts of climate change demonstrate that combatting threats to food production requires engagement with climate mitigation and adaptation.[71] Indeed, the rights-based approach advocated by civil society movements will be critical to ensuring that climate change is both mitigated and adapted to in ways that take account of, and react to, the perspectives of those most affected by both mitigation and adaptation and food insecurity. It is in this context that calls to transform the food system in line with agroecology will continue to gain greater momentum while the creation of inclusive and interdisciplinary forums for debate, discussion and cooperation will remain crucial.

Acknowledgements

The authors are grateful for the helpful input received from Ankita Gupta and Ruth Rosenblood.

Disclosure statement

No potential conflict of interest was reported by the authors.

[70] FAO and others (n 5). For example of the effect of conflicts see, eg, FAO, IFAD, UNICEF, WFP and WHO, *The State of Food Security and Nutrition in the World 2017: Building Resilience for Peace and Food Security* (FAO, 2017).

[71] Celia A. Harvey et al, 'Climate-Smart Landscapes: Opportunities and Challenges for Integrating Adaptation and Mitigation in Tropical Agriculture' (2014) 7(2) *Conservation Letters* 77.

At the brink of famine in conflict and natural disaster zones: human rights approach to extreme hunger and malnutrition*

Hilal Elver

ABSTRACT
This article focuses predominantly on conflict and disaster prone places as the major cause of right to food violations in the form of severe hunger and malnutrition. Food insecurity, in its most extreme form of famine, but also in the form of malnutrition, has increased alarmingly in the face of abundant food availability. Hunger and famine in a variety of combat settings inflict massive casualties and widespread suffering on the civilian population. This article will critically review the existing norms and guidelines, the non-compliance of States and other political actors and the failure to address international criminal behaviour to stop human rights violations in conflict and emergency situation.

We are all aware that it is not enough to seek to ensure that all receive their daily bread; rather we have to recognise that everybody has the right to it and should therefore benefit from it. (Pope Francis[1])

1. Point of departure

1.1. Hunger is rising and famine has returned

Despite decades of economic growth and development, the world continues to be haunted by the spectre of mass starvation and malnutrition, and food insecurity remains an unmet challenge for both rich and poor countries. Famine, the most severe form of food insecurity, which caused nearly 75 million deaths in

---

*This article mostly derived from author's two UN reports delivered in the UNGA Third Committee (A/72/188) and the Human Rights Council (A/HRC/37/61).

[1] Food and Agriculture Organization of the United Nations (FAO), *Message of His Holiness Pope Francis* (July 2017), FAO Conference, Rome C 2017/INF/11, online: <www.fao.org/3/a-mu028e.pdf>.

the twentieth century, had virtually disappeared in recent decades. Yet, in an era of declining poverty and hunger worldwide, it has tragically returned. Famine is technically defined by the *Integrated Food Security Phase Classification* (*IPC*) as 'an extreme inaccessibility to food that leads to widespread malnutrition, infectious diseases and death'.[2] There are three characteristics of famine: (i) at least 20% of households in a given group face an extreme food deficit, without the ability to cope; (ii) acute malnutrition prevalence exceeds 30%; and (iii) mortality rates exceed two people per 10,000 of the population per day.[3]

The recent phenomenon of famine in conflict-torn countries has increased the number of hungry people at an alarming rate.[4] This concern has been highlighted by the United Nations Under-Secretary-General of Humanitarian Affairs' official recognition of famine in South Sudan in March of 2017 when he declared that the world is facing the largest humanitarian crises since the creation of the United Nations.[5] On 9 August 2017, the president of the UN Security Council made a statement about the devastating impact on civilians, and the humanitarian consequences of on-going armed conflict and violence in relation to four countries, namely, Yemen, Somalia, South Sudan, and Northeast Nigeria. The president emphasised the links between food scarcity and the increased vulnerability of women, children, and persons with disabilities, as well as a lack of resources for humanitarian emergency.[6]

The most critical countries, Northeast Nigeria, Somalia, South Sudan, and Yemen most likely will deteriorate further without urgent intervention, due to protracted conflict, instability and the breakdown of public and social services. Yemen, the poorest country in the Arab region, has experienced an alarming rise in rates of acute malnutrition since the beginning of the civil war in 2015. A report by the Food and Agriculture Organization (FAO) highlights that 7.3 million Yemenis are facing food emergency status with another 10.2 million in crisis, representing a 21% increase in hunger since June 2016.[7] As of November 2018, at least 85,000 children under the age of 5 have suffered from starvation.[8] Yemen's condition has been described by the Famine Early Warning

[2] Famine Early Warnings System Network (FEWS), 'Overview of the Integrated Phase Classification' (May 2017) online: <http://fews.net/sites/default/files/IPC%20Overview_May_2017_final.pdf>.

[3] *Ibid.*

[4] UN Food and Agriculture Organization (FAO), *The State of Food Security and Nutrition in the World* (2018) online: <www.fao.org/3/I9553EN/i9553en.pdf>.

[5] The 20 million refers to Yemen, Somalia, South Sudan and Nigeria. In Yemen 320,000, Nigeria 220,000, South Sudan 220,000, Somalia 200,000 children are at imminent risk of death from severe acute malnutrition; UN Office for the Coordination of Humanitarian Affairs, UN, *Statement to the Security Council on Missions To Yemen, South Sudan, Somalia and Kenya and an Update on the Oslo Conference on Nigeria and The Lake Chad Region* (2017) online: <https://reliefweb.int/report/yemen/under-secretary-general-humanitarian-affairsemergency-relief-coordinator-stephen-o>.

[6] UNSC, 'Statement by the President of the Security Council' (9 August 2017) UN Doc.S/PRST/2017/14.

[7] FAO, *The State of Food Security and Nutrition in the World* (2018) online: <www.fao.org/3/I9553EN/i9553en.pdf>.

[8] David Beasley, the director of the WFM said in 21 November 2018: 'What I have seen in Yemen this week is the stuff of nightmares, of horror, of deprivation, of misery. And we—all of humanity—have only

System as 'the largest food emergency in the world'.[9] The war is directly responsible for the current humanitarian disaster and massive displacement due to blockades, sieges and a complete collapse of the economic infrastructure.

The fragile food security situation in South Sudan, already impoverished and underdeveloped following decades of war with Sudan, was severely compounded by the outbreak of civil war in 2013. The situation has been described as one of the most acute and nationally widespread food emergencies, with UN agencies estimating that 100,000 people are facing starvation, and another million classified as being on the brink of famine.[10] In February 2017, the South Sudan Government declared famine in two counties in the former Unity State. Over 40% of the South Sudanese population is in need of urgent food, agriculture and nutrition assistance, with imminent risk of severe food insecurity and of death.[11]

Somalia has suffered from enduring conflict and economic crisis, the ongoing presence of the terrorist group Al-Shabab, drought, water shortages and high food prices. Currently 6.2 million people are in desperate need of food aid.[12] In Somalia, as in Syria and Yemen, the situation has been exacerbated by United States (US) counter-terrorism legislation, which has prohibited relief agencies from providing support or resulted in significant delays in the international response to the disaster.[13]

North Eastern Nigeria has been prone to periodic food crises in some of the poorest States within the country. The magnitude of the damage inflicted by a protracted war between the Nigerian army and the extremist group Boko Haram recently became evident after the retreat of Boko Haram. As they fell back, it was discovered that thousands were living in famine-like conditions. While 7 million people are estimated to struggle with food insecurity, there are still areas under the control of Boko Haram, which aid agencies cannot reach. The full extent of the conditions faced by trapped populations is, therefore, unknown.[14]

---

ourselves to blame'. UN News, 'Amid Continued Suffering in Yemen, UN Envoy Welcomes Reports of Reduced Violence' (16 November 2018) online: <https://news.un.org/en/story/2018/11/1025991>.

[9] FEWS, 'World's Largest Food Security Emergency Continues as Conflict Enters its Fifth Year' (2018) online: <http://fews.net/east-africa/yemen>.

[10] UNICEF, 'Famine Hits Parts of South Sudan' (20 February 2017) online: <www.unicef.org/press-releases/famine-hits-parts-south-sudan>.

[11] The Conversation, 'How South Sudan's Warlords Triggered Extreme Hunger in a Land of Plenty' (1 March 2017) online: <http://theconversation.com/how-south-sudans-warlords-triggered-extreme-hunger-in-a-land-of-plenty-73380>.

[12] Michael Snyder, GlobalResearch, 'The Global Famine Begins; UN: World facing greatest humanitarian crisis since 1945' (21 March 2017) online: <www.globalresearch.ca/the-global-famine-begins-un-announces-that-the-worst-food-crisis-since-world-war-ii-is-happening-right-now/5580929>.

[13] Alex De Waal, *Mass Starvation: The History and Future of Famine* (Wiley 2018) 203. Peter Gill, *Today We Drop Bombs, Tomorrow We Build Bridges: How Foreign Aid Became a Casualty of War* (University of Chicago Press 2016).

[14] Oxfam, 'Lake Chad's Unseen Crisis: Voices of Refugees and Internally Displaced People From Niger and Nigeria' (2016) online: <www.oxfam.org.hk/filemgr/5167/bn-lake-chad-refugees-idps-190816-en.pdf>.

As of today, famine affects approximately 32 million people, including more than 2 million children.[15] In 2018, the Global Report of Food Crises added the Democratic Republic of Congo (DRC), the Rohingya people in Myanmar, and the refugee camps in Bangladesh to the list of most severe food crises. Beyond these particularly severe situations, some 70 million people across 45 countries currently require emergency food assistance, comprising a 40% increase from 2015.[16]

Although the exact nature of food crises varies widely, almost all share a common cause: human activity. All of the countries discussed above have been engulfed by war, protracted crises, and/or extreme weather events resulting in a situation in which ongoing efforts to eliminate hunger and malnutrition are significantly undermined. In concert with factors such as demographic growth, shocks to the global food supply and weak governance, as well as lack of sufficient international cooperation, conflict is a leading cause of food emergency. It is the cumulative force of these factors that ultimately results in the emergence of famine.

There has been a dramatic increase in those affected by hunger since 2008.[17] Undernourishment has increased by 11% from 777 million in 2015 to 821 million in 2017. Today, one in nine people in the world go to bed hungry, mostly in countries in Sub- Saharan Africa and the conflict zones of the Middle East.[18] Hunger kills approximately 9 million people every year: more than malaria, tuberculosis, and AIDS combined.[19] Nearly 1.4 million children are at imminent risk of death and 5–6 million children die every year from malnutrition and related diseases.[20] The pervasiveness of malnutrition and hunger in the world today, and the steady increase in those

---

[15] According to Integrated Food Security Phase Classification (IPC) there are five levels of food insecurity. Most severe IPC Phases are: Crisis (Phase 3), Emergency (Phase 4) and Catastrophe/Famine (Phase 5). Famine Early Warning Systems Network, *Integrated Phase Classification*, online: <http://fews.net/IPC>.

[16] Food Security Information Network (FSIN), *Global Report on Food Crises 2018* (2018) online: <https://docs.wfp.org/api/documents/WFP-0000069227/download/?_ga=2.9361586.665297234.1543061199-1129703017.1542597149>. The Global Report on Food Crises has listed the following countries as suffering from widespread or localised food insecurity: Afghanistan, Burundi, Central African Republic, Chad, the Democratic Republic of Congo, Ethiopia, Guatemala, Haiti, Iraq, Kenya, Madagascar, Malawi, Mozambique, Niger, Sudan, Syria (including Syrian refugees in neighbouring countries), Uganda and Zimbabwe.

[17] According to the 2018 State of Food Insecurity in the World Report Global rates of acute malnutrition have been rising since 2008. FAO (n 7).

[18] FAO, *The Global Report on Food Crises 2017* (2017) online: <https://documents.wfp.org/stellent/groups/public/documents/ena/wfp291271.pdf?_ga=2.234763548.36904603.1542597149-1129703017.1542597149> lists the following countries as suffering from widespread or localised food insecurity: Afghanistan, Burundi, Central African Republic, Chad, Democratic Republic of the Congo, Ethiopia, Guatemala, Haiti, Iraq, Kenya, Madagascar, Malawi, Mozambique, Niger, Sudan, Syrian Arab Republic (including Syrian refugees in neighbouring countries), Uganda, Zimbabwe.

[19] World Food Programme (WFP), 'WFP Says Hunger Kills More Than AIDS, Malaria, Tuberculosis Combined' (4 June 2009) online: <www.wfp.org/content/wfp-says-hunger-kills-more-aids-malaria-tuberculosis-combined>.

[20] UNICEF, 'Fighting Famine in a Race Against Time' (16 January 2018) online: <www.unicef.org/emergencies/index_95476.html>.

falling victim to it, raises significant questions regarding *why* this is occurring. In a context of global economic growth and the vast distance between the global rich and poor, how is it that we have reached this point?

1.2. Why are hunger and malnutrition rising, despite global economic growth?

While hunger and malnutrition increase, per capita food availability has also increased from approximately 2220 kcal per person per day in the 1960s to 2790 kcal per person per day in 2006.[21] The world already produces enough food to feed 10 billion people (the population peak that is expected by 2050), and more than 1.5 times what is necessary to feed the current population.[22] But people making less than $2 a day—most of whom are resource-poor farmers cultivating non-viable small plots of land, herders who are living in dry lands, and fisher folks living in the highly vulnerable coastal zones of developing countries—cannot afford to buy the food available to them or produce their own food due to poverty escalated by extreme weather conditions and/or political conflict. Food availability is therefore increasing across the world, except in climate vulnerable and conflict-prone regions.[23]

Advocates of the free-market economy misleadingly use the rhetoric of 'feeding the world' to justify unsustainable excessive food production, that serves to profit large-scale industrial agriculture, but fails to eliminate hunger.[24] Although this article will not focus on the current neo-liberal economic system, and its adverse impact on hunger and poverty, economic and physical accessibility to affordable food is the major reason why efforts to reduce hunger and malnutrition have so far been disappointing. Even in the richest countries, especially those that follow the precepts of neoliberal capitalism, deep pockets of extreme poverty, hunger, suffering and hopelessness exist.[25] For instance, in the US, one of the richest and most powerful countries in the world, 47 million people are food insecure and rely on the SNAP programme (the food stamp system) that is currently in danger of

---

21 Max Roser and Hannah Ritchie, 'Food per Person' *Our World in Data* (2018) online: <https://ourworldindata.org/food-per-person>.

22 Eric Holt-Gimenez and others, 'We Already Grow Enought Food for 10 Billion People … and Still Can't End Hunger' (2012) 36(6) *Journal of Sustainable Agriculture* 595.

23 FAO (n 7).

24 For examples of such rhetoric, see: Chelsea Follett and Marian L Tupy, 'Capitalism is Feeding a Hungry World' *Foundation for Economic Education* (2016) online: <https://fee.org/articles/capitalism-is-feeding-a-hungry-world/>. The Borgen Project, 'Capitalism is Helping End Global Poverty' (2013) online: <https://borgenproject.org/capitalism-is-helping-end-global-poverty/>. The Heritage Foundation, '2018 Index of Economic Freedom' (2018) online: <www.heritage.org/index/?_ga=2.181534759.1007558937.1547822616-953168243.1547822616>.

25 Greg S Garrett, 'Unmasking Hidden Hunger in the Developed World' *Food Sustainability Index* (2016) online: <http://foodsustainability.eiu.com/unmasking-hidden-hunger-in-the-developed-world/>.

significant budgetary reduction.[26] In the UK, after recent austerity measures, the number of food insecure people increased to approximately 5 million.[27] Large families and the unemployed are hit worst by the rising costs and austerity, with 32% of the former and 36% of the latter missing meals[28] and an increasing proportion of the population relying on Food Banks to support those unable to afford basic sustenance.[29] Nevertheless, the reception from the UK Government to these figures was one of intransience and denial; a failure to recognise the links between poverty, austerity and hunger and therefore to tackle the root causes of the problem.[30]

There is a strong connection between poverty and hunger. The World Bank estimates that 10% of the world's population, or 736 million people, lived on less than $1.90 per day in 2015.[31] In poor communities, 60–80% of the family budget is spent on food, as opposed to 6–15% in the developed world.[32] Half of the extremely poor live in the rural areas in Sub-Saharan Africa and South Asia. Employment is mainly found in the agricultural sector with over half of those employed under 18 years of age; yet these areas suffer high unemployment rates.[33] It is unsurprising therefore that 75% of the world's poorest depend on producing their own food using ecosystem resources such as rain-fed agriculture without external inputs.[34] These people have limited savings, depend on agriculture for a living and face increasing exposure to disaster risks as well as conflicts, mostly derived from limited access to natural resources.[35] These conditions cause widespread food insecurity and price volatility in developing countries, as drought,

[26] United Nations Human Rights Office of the High Commissioner (OHCHR), 'Statement on Visit to the USA, by Professor Philip Alston, United Nations Special Rapporteur on Extreme Poverty and Human Rights' (15 December 2017) online: <www.ohchr.org/EN/NewsEvents/Pages/DisplayNews.aspx?NewsID=22533&LangID=E> [20].

[27] FAO, *Voices of the Hungry Technical Report* (August 2016) online: <www.fao.org/3/a-i4830e.pdf> 39.

[28] Patrick Butler, 'Food Insecurity: A Third of Poorest Households Skip Meals, Survey Finds' *The Guardian* (30 January 2018) online: <www.theguardian.com/global-development/2018/jan/30/food-insecurity-a-third-of-poorest-households-skip-meals-survey-finds>.

[29] OHCHR, 'Statement on Visit to the United Kingdom, by Professor Philip Alston, United Nations Special Rapporteur on Extreme Poverty and Human Rights' (16 November 2018) online: <www.ohchr.org/EN/NewsEvents/Pages/DisplayNews.aspx?NewsID=23881&LangID=E> 17.

[30] *Ibid.* However, in February 2019 the current Work and Pensions Secretary, Amber Rudd, upon answering a Ministerial question in the House of Commons 'conceded that the rollout of universal credit has contributed to an increase in food bank use': Peter Walker, 'Universal Credit Rollout Linked to Rising Food Bank Use, Rudd Admits' *The Guardian* (11 February 2019) online: <www.theguardian.com/society/2019/feb/11/universal-credit-rollout-linked-to-rising-food-bank-use-amber-rudd-admits>.

[31] The World Bank (WB), 'Decline of Global Extreme Poverty Continues but Has Slowed: World Bank' (2018) online: <www.worldbank.org/en/news/press-release/2018/09/19/decline-of-global-extreme-poverty-continues-but-has-slowed-world-bank>.

[32] Brad Plumer, 'Maps: How Much Each Country Spends on Food?' *Vox* (19 August 2015) online: <www.vox.com/2014/7/6/5874499/map-heres-how-much-every-country-spends-on-food>.

[33] Jonathan Brooks and others, OECD, *Agricultural Policy and Poverty Reduction* (2012) online: <www.researchgate.net/publication/251237411_Agricultural_Policies_for_Poverty_Reduction> 10.

[34] FAO, *The Future of Food and Agriculture: Trends and Challenges* (2017) online: <www.fao.org/3/a-i6583e.pdf>; Science Direct, *'Rainfed Agriculture'*, online: <www.sciencedirect.com/topics/earth-and-planetary-sciences/rainfed-agriculture>.

[35] FAO (n 35).

climate change and related natural disasters, and food price increases can easily cut off or seriously impair a family's food supply, as well as its nutritional value.

This article will primarily focus on hunger and malnutrition as a violation of the peoples' fundamental human right to food in conflict and natural disaster-prone places. Firstly, the disruption and damage to agriculture and food systems as a result of conflicts and natural disasters will be discussed, including their impact on disadvantaged groups such as women, children, and migrants. Secondly, the effectiveness of the response of the international community in the form of humanitarian aid and food assistance will be critically evaluated. Thirdly, possible legal remedies will be discussed from the perspective of human rights law, humanitarian law and international criminal law. Finally, the paper will be concluded with a discussion on widespread impunity, lack of mandatory accountability, as well as the reluctance to adopt a human rights-based approach to severe food insecurity as elements of the lack of political will of the international community to deal with such severe right to food violations in conflict and disaster zones.

2. Disruption and damage to agriculture and food systems

2.1. Conflicts and protracted crises

Protracted crises are among the most challenging situations in which to fight hunger and malnutrition. In 2016, almost half a billion people in over 20 countries and territories were affected by protracted conflicts and as a direct result suffered from severe undernourishment and emergency levels of food insecurity.[36] The proportion of people who are undernourished is almost three times higher in countries in protracted crisis than in other developing countries.[37] Since 2000, 48% of civil conflicts have been in Africa, where access to rural land underpins the livelihoods of many peoples.[38] Some 2.5 billion people worldwide depend on the agricultural sector—the main source of income for the populations of many of the countries currently suffering from conflict.

Conflict obstructs the enjoyment of the right to food[39] and furthermore may erode societal resilience, impeding society's ability to absorb or recover from other shocks, such as the impacts of climate change, extreme weather

---

[36] FAO, 'Protracted Conflicts Causing Alarming Spikes in Severe Hunger' (29 July 2016) online: <www.fao.org/news/story/en/item/427423/icode/>.

[37] FAO, *The State of Food Insecurity in the World* (2010) online: <www.fao.org/docrep/013/i1683e/i1683e.pdf>.

[38] Twenty-seven out of 30 interstate conflicts in Africa are land related. FAO, *Peace and Food Security: Investing in Resilience to Sustain Rural* (2016) online: <www.fao.org/3/a-i5591e.pdf>.

[39] FAO, *The Right to Food in Practice: Implementation at the National Level* (2006) online: <www.fao.org/3/a-ah189e.pdf>.

events, drought and flood. All these factors contribute toward increases in food prices.[40] It is also important to recognise that food insecurity in turn can contribute to social and political unrest, and thus lead to a negative spiral of conflict and hunger.

Casualties resulting directly from combat usually make up only a small proportion of deaths in conflict zones, with many more people perishing from hunger and diseases. Farmers in conflict zones are often unable to work owing to restrictions on their movement or from forcible recruitment into armed forces or militias. Crops may be plundered or destroyed inflicting serious damage to farming and fishing infrastructures, there may be severe disruption to livestock markets and veterinary services, and migration routes may be block leading to the abandonment or slaughter of animals.[41] In protracted crises, agricultural assets and capacity to cope becomes so severely eroded that households are left incapable of resuming their farming activities, forced to sell their farming equipment under extremely adverse conditions, lose their herds, or are unable to recover abandoned fields. Agricultural assets sometimes create vulnerabilities in the community by attracting looting and violent attacks by militias. Communities sometimes even refuse humanitarian food aid out of fear of provoking an attack.[42]

Conflict also severely affects household income and purchasing power. Mass unemployment and the breakdown of social services limit the ability to gain access to food, while currency devaluation, price inflation, market disruptions and reliance on costly food imports owing to shortages may render basic food items prohibitively expensive and make nutritious food unavailable.[43]

Countries suffering from long-standing conflict tend to be particularly fragile, often aggravated by poor governance and weak infrastructure, hampering the effective coordination and delivery of food assistance.[44] Political interference and cumbersome negotiations can also impede humanitarian responses.

2.2. Natural disasters and emergencies

The obligations of the state and responses of the international community in relation to natural disasters are vastly different from that of conflict. Drought,

---

[40] United Nations Conference on Trade and Development, *Commodities and Development Report 2015: Smallholder Farmers and Sustainable Commodity Development* (2015) online: <http://unctad.org/en/PublicationsLibrary/suc2014d5_en.pdf>; FAO (n 4).

[41] FAO, *Livestock in Protracted Crises: The Importance of Livestock for Resilience-Building and Food Security of Crisis-Affected Populations* (2016) online: <www.fao.org/3/a-i6637e.pdf>.

[42] High-level Expert Forum on Food Insecurity in Protracted Crises, *Agriculture, Conflict and Stability: A Call for Renewed Focus on Protection and Conflict Sensitive Programming in Agriculture and Food and Nutrition Security* (2012) online: <www.fao.org/fileadmin/templates/cfs_high_level_forum/documents/Agriculture-Conflict-Stability Lautze_01.pdf>.

[43] *Ibid.*

[44] FAO, *The Elimination of Food Insecurity in the Horn of Africa: A Strategy for Concerted Government and UN Agency Action (Summary Report)* (2000) online: <www.fao.org/docrep/meeting/023/mb729e.pdf> 4.

desertification and floods, as well as hurricanes, wildfires, tsunamis and earthquakes, all have immediate, direct or indirect, long-term impacts on the right to food and the livelihood of peoples, therefore contributing to hunger, malnutrition, human rights violations and long-term resource depletion.

Climate-related disasters are increasing in frequency and intensity. Their number has almost doubled in the past decade (there are now, on average, 335 events annually).[45] In 2017, Hurricanes Irma and Maria caused significant damage in the Caribbean region, particularly Cuba, Haiti and Puerto Rico. Drought in the Horn of Africa pushed more that 11 million people into severe food insecurity in Ethiopia, Kenya and Somalia. Flooding in Nepal and Bangladesh has left 10 million people food-insecure.[46] The impacts of such natural disasters can be devastating for any State, even wealthy ones. In 2017, overall losses from storms and fires in the US and widespread flooding in South Asia reached $330 billion.[47] Hurricane Harvey in Texas was the most costly natural disaster in 2017, causing $85 billion worth of damage.[48] The impact on agriculture from devastating wildfires in California in 2018, is yet to be calculated.

Strong economies are well prepared for such risks, unlike developing countries and weak economies. Poor infrastructure, a deprived population, compromised building safety standards and under-resourced health services undoubtedly add to the human suffering already caused by severe natural disasters. One study has shown that between 1950 and 2000 the rapid onset of natural disasters significantly increased the risk of violent civil conflict, particularly in low and middle-income countries.[49] Such a combination creates a vicious cycle from natural disasters to violent conflict and vice versa. Somalia is a good example of this deadly combination of impoverishment, bad governance, and conflict.[50]

Natural disasters create large-scale human suffering. Responding properly to disaster situations is therefore challenging. In recent years, 80% of natural disasters were weather-related. As discussed in the 2015 UNHRC report on climate change and the right to food, global warming triggers or prolongs such extreme weather-related disasters, with commensurate effects on food

---

45 United Nations Office for Disaster Risk Reduction (UNISDR), *The Human Cost of Weather Related Disasters (1995–2015)* (2015) online: <www.unisdr.org/files/46796_cop21weatherdisastersreport2015.pdf>.

46 World Food Programme, 'Climate-related Disasters and Food Insecurity in 2017: Preparedness and Response' (October 2017) online: <https://docs.wfp.org/api/documents/WFP-0000023693/download/>.

47 Hiroko Tabuchi, '2017 Set a Record for Losses From Natural Disasters. It Could Get Worse' *The New York Times* (4 January 2017) online: <www.nytimes.com/2018/01/04/climate/losses-natural-disasters-insurance.html>.

48 *Ibid.*

49 Philip Nel and Marjolein Righarts, 'National Disasters and the Risk of Violent Civil Conflict' (2008) 52(1) *International Studies Quarterly* 159. (Cited in Elisabeth Ferris, *Natural Disasters, Conflict and Human Rights: Tracing the Connection* (Brooking 2010).)

50 The Conversation, 'Somalia Conflict and Famine: The Causes Are Bad Governance, Not Climate Change' (4 October 2017) online: <http://theconversation.com/somalia-conflict-and-famine-the-causes-are-bad-governance-not-climate-change-84166>.

security.[51] The same year, the FAO launched its first report on disasters, 'The impact of disasters on agriculture and food safety'.[52] The report showed that a staggering 22% of total damage and losses from natural hazards in developing countries were absorbed by the agriculture sector.[53] According to the 2017 FAO report, this ratio is now 23%.[54] Severe floods in 2017 affected at least 8 million people, causing deaths and injuries, loss of livestock, food supplies, damage to housing and farming infrastructure. Aside from destroying food supplies and sources, such disasters also inflict damage on the food production system as a whole, raising food prices, and causing other harmful effects on the livelihood of individuals and communities. Such situations are likely to continue to affect a wide number of people given that 80% of hungry people currently live in disaster prone and degraded areas.[55] The World Bank reports claim that each year, natural disasters push 26 million people into poverty, eroding development gains and increasing dependency on aid.[56]

Even though the detrimental impacts of climate change are experienced across the planet, from the perspective of agriculture and food systems some areas are more vulnerable than others. For instance, African countries are particularly vulnerable since less than 5% of the continent's cropped area is irrigated.[57] In 2015 and 2016, drought caused by one of the harshest *El Niño* events on record led to significant crop and livestock losses in Sub Saharan Africa, affecting the livelihoods of farmers and agricultural communities. Consecutive failed harvest seasons resulted in wide-scale dependence on food aid, creating high levels of debt and massive depletion of household seed supplies.[58] More than 60 million people were affected by the *El Niño* events, leading 23 countries to apply for international humanitarian assistance.[59] The special envoy stated that the most vulnerable groups; women,

---

[51] Hilal Elver, UN Special Rapporteur on the right to food, *Interim Report* (2015), UN Doc.A/70/287, online: <www.ohchr.org/Documents/Issues/Food/A-70-287.pdf>.

[52] FAO, *The Impact of Disasters on Agriculture and Food Security* (2015) online: <www.fao.org/3/a-i5128e.pdf>.

[53] *Ibid*, 11.

[54] FAO, *The Impact of Disasters on Agriculture: Addressing the Information Gap* (2017) online: <www.fao.org/3/a-i7279e.pdf>.

[55] World Food Programme, 'Infographic: How Disasters Drive Hunger', online: <www.wfp.org/content/how-disasters-drive-hunger>.

[56] Stephane Hallegatte and others, World Bank Group, *Unbreakable: Building the Resilience of the Poor in the Face of Natural Disasters* (2016) online: <http://documents.worldbank.org/curated/en/512241480487839624/Unbreakable-building-the-resilience-of-the-poor-in-the-face-of-natural-disasters> 5.

[57] OECD and FAO, *OECD-FAO Agricultural Outlook 2018–2027* (2018) online: <www.fao.org/3/i9166en/I9166EN.PDF> 68.

[58] FAO, *2015–2016 El Niño Early Action and Response for Agriculture, Food Security and Nutrition* (2016) online: <www.fao.org/3/a-i6049e.pdf> 7.

[59] Special Envoys on El Niño and Climate Change, *Preventing El Niño Southern Oscillation Episodes from Becoming Disasters: A 'Blueprint for Action'* (2016) online: <https://reliefweb.int/sites/reliefweb.int/files/resources/301215-Blueprint_Final.pdf> 2. The affected geographical area included East and Southern Africa, Central America, the Caribbean, and the Pacific.

children, the elderly, the disabled and people living with HIV/AIDS, suffered the most.[60]

2.3. Human rights violations of disadvantaged people in times of conflicts and natural disasters

Conflict and natural disasters tend to exacerbate existing inequalities, leaving already vulnerable segments of society particularly exposed to food insecurity, which often causes massive internal and external displacement of people. Disadvantaged groups, such as children under 5 years of age, orphans, pregnant and lactating women, female-headed households, refugees and internally displaced persons, older persons, persons with disabilities, minorities and already marginalised communities suffering from social exclusion, tend to have less access to resources and the weakest coping capacity, leaving them most vulnerable to the risk of insufficient food and an inadequate diet.[61] This is also true of pastoralists, nomadic peoples, peasants and indigenous communities who are disproportionately impacted by conflict and disasters in their access to land, fishing and hunting resources.[62] Also, access to information on the availability and accessibility of food assistance becomes limited, increasing the risk of exploitation and abuse of the vulnerable groups.

Women and girls worldwide already face many inequalities that are embedded in traditional practices and laws, constraining their access to resources and affecting their food security and nutrition.[63] Extreme food insecurity induces people to turn to detrimental coping mechanisms, including rationing or skipping meals, begging, early marriage, child labour, child recruitment, and transactional sex in exchange for food.[64] Times of conflict and natural disasters triggers gender-based violations, including an increase in sexual violence and diseases.[65] Such risks are heightened if condoms are unavailable or scarce.[66] Mother to child transmission of HIV, including

---

60 *Ibid.*

61 Sisay Alemahu Yeshanew, FAO, *The Right to Adequate Food in Emergency Programmes,* (2014) online: <www.fao.org/3/a-i4184e.pdf> 5; International Federation of Red Cross and Red Crescent Societies, 'Minimum Standards for Protection, Gender and Inclusion in Emergencies' (2018) online: <https://media.ifrc.org/ifrc/wp-content/uploads/sites/5/2018/11/Minimum-standards-for-protection-gender-and-inclusion-in-emergencies-LR.pdf> 5.

62 OHCHR, *The Right to Adequate Food (Fact Sheet no.34)* (2010) online: <www.ohchr.org/Documents/Publications/FactSheet34en.pdf> 10 (fn 27).

63 Global Protection Cluster, 'Briefing Note on Protection Cluster', online: <reliefweb.int/sites/reliefweb.int/files/resources/protection_cluster_briefing_note_october_2015.pdf.FAO> and Asian Development Bank, *Gender Equality and Food Security: Women's Empowerment as a Tool against Hunger* (2013) online: <www.fao.org/wairdocs/ar259e/ar259e.pdf>.

64 UN Special Rapporteur on the Right to Food, *Interim Report* (21 July 2017) UN Doc.A/72/188, online: <https://undocs.org/A/72/188> [38].

65 Fiona Samuels, Paul Harvey and Thobias Bergmann, Overseas Development Institute, *HIV and AIDS in Emergency Situations Synthesis Report* (2008) online: <www.odi.org/sites/odi.org.uk/files/odi-assets/publications-opinion-files/4277.pdf> 7.

66 *Ibid*, 11.

through breastfeeding, tends to increase under the impact of natural disasters.[67]

A total of 65.6 million people around the world have been forced to flee from their homes as a result of natural disasters and conflicts. 22.5 million are now seeking safety across international borders as refugees, which is the highest number since records began.[68] Some 28,300 persons are forced to flee every day from conflict or persecution.[69] A study conducted by the World Food Programme (WFP) found that countries with the highest levels of food insecurity, together with armed conflict, had the highest outward migration of refugees.[70] Those fleeing conflict are often forced to leave behind their property, and their economic independence may be further hampered by the costs of transit, few income opportunities and limited rights in the host state.[71] Host communities may also experience strains on their food supplies from a major influx of deprived people, especially if their societies are already facing economic instability.[72] In situations of massive displacement, humanitarian agencies are often unable to fully meet food needs, leaving displaced communities in dire circumstances.

Subsistence farmers, peasants, and indigenous communities tend to be dependent on the lowest-quality land, including hillsides, arid lands, deserts and flood plains, and often suffer from chronic food insecurity. These groups may also not have any entitlement to formal social safety nets. In the face of natural disasters, individuals and communities that are already vulnerable have less capacity to cope with such challenges and might incur crippling debts and resort to other more extreme measures just to survive.

3. Responsibility of the international community in emergencies: food aid/assistance

3.1. History and structure

Food assistance is one of the oldest forms of international support saving many lives during severe humanitarian crises. It is a remedy for emergency situations, to provide food for those who are caught in the midst of a disaster situation. Although the immediate and primary obligation to provide food, water, shelter and medical aid are the duty of governments, in times of emergency the international community has a residual responsibility to help

[67] *Ibid*, 13.

[68] Adrian Edwards, Office of the United Nations High Commissioner for Refugees (UNHCR), 'Forced Displacement Worldwide at Its Highest in Decades' (19 June 2017) online: <www.unhcr.org/news/stories/2017/6/5941561f4/forced-displacement-worldwide-its-highest-decades.html>.

[69] UNHCR, 'Figures at a Glance', online: <www.unhcr.org/figures-at-a-glance.html>.

[70] World Food Programme, *At the Root of Exodus: Food Security, Conflict and International Migration* (2017) online: <https://docs.wfp.org/api/documents/WFP-0000015358/download/> 33.

[71] *Ibid*, 48.

[72] *Ibid*, 9.

countries faced with dire conditions in accordance with Article 56 of the Charter of the United Nations.[73] Nevertheless, this article does not imply a financial obligation, and makes clear that each State should contribute to this task in accordance with its ability.[74]

In the 1950s, the food aid system was dominated by the US, Canada, and Australia, which together accounted for over 90% of the total aid provided. During the Cold War, international commitments to food aid were only partly about humanitarianism, often driven by high-priority geopolitical and economic interests. These earlier food aid programmes largely provided grain in the form of bulk commodities—often agricultural surpluses that were accumulating in donor countries.[75] In the 1970s, the European Community and Japan also began to provide international food aid. The European Union (EU) is now the second-largest food aid donor[76] as 40% of its annual humanitarian aid budget is allocated to provide emergency food assistance.[77]

Over the last 50 years, the character of food aid policies and practices has changed, in parallel with the global structural changes in agriculture and geopolitical conditions. Firstly, the absolute value and relative importance of food aid has declined dramatically. In the 1960s, food aid represented approximately 20% of all Overseas Development Assistance (ODA). By the early 2000s, that figure had fallen to about 5%.[78] Secondly, in the aftermath of the Cold War, donors began to direct their food aid towards the poorest countries, rather than prioritising geopolitical considerations. However, frequent, severe and longer-lasting man-made and natural disasters worldwide have refocused the agenda of food aid on the challenge of feeding emergency victims. In 2000, over 60% of food aid was provided in response to emergency situations, mostly in response to climate change-related extreme weather events and countries that already suffered from food insecurity, such as those in South Asia, sub-Saharan Africa, the Middle East, and Central America. Thirdly, donor countries have gradually moved from direct transfer of commodity surpluses to sourcing food aid on open markets funded with

---

73 Article 56—All Members pledge themselves to take joint and separate action in co-operation with the Organization for the achievement of the purposes set forth in Article 55. UN, Charter of the United Nations, 24 October 1945, 1 UNTS XVI, online: <www.un.org/en/charter-united-nations/>.

74 OHCHR, *CESCR General Comment 12* (11 August 2000) online: <www.refworld.org/pdfid/4538838d0.pdf> [13].

75 Jennifer Clapp, *Hunger in the Balance: The New Politics of International Food Aid* (Cornell University Press, 2012).

76 World Food Programme, 'EU Contributed Over €1 Billion to WFP in the Fight Against Hunger in 2017' (31 January 2018) online: <www.wfp.org/news/news-release/eu-contributed-over-%E2%82%AC1-billion-wfp-fight-against-hunger-2017>.

77 EU, 'Humanitarian Aid & Civil Protection' *Europa.eu* (2015) online: <https://europa.eu/european-union/topics/humanitarian-aid-civil-protection_en>.

78 Jennifer Clapp, 'Food Aid' in Kenneth A Reinert (ed), *Handbook of Globalisation and Development* (Edward Elgar Publishing, 2017) 394.

cash money.[79] As Oxfam has documented, the transfer of commodity is an out-dated and inefficient method of getting food to people in need.[80] In recent years, several reform efforts have been undertaken in an attempt to correct the structural problems in the provision of food aid.

3.2. The shortcomings of humanitarian aid

In recent decades, the international humanitarian response system has been essential in reducing the negative effects of conflict and natural disasters and lowering death tolls. Concurrently, poorly designed, charity-based food aid can do more harm than good, can have negative effects on small-scale farmers in recipient countries by exerting downward pressure on domestic food prices, and can adversely affect trade, production incentives and labour markets.[81] In some cases, food aid practices might even violate the right to food, if the food aid is distributed unfairly or if the most vulnerable are not prioritised.[82] Food aid should serve the best interests of the recipient country's food and agricultural policy, provide long-term livelihoods for people and uphold environmental best practices. The very simplistic 'if people are hungry, we should simply give them food' argument is an example of an inappropriate use of food aid.[83]

Volunteer provision of food assistance motivated by donor objectives may frequently be manipulated for political gain.[84] Food from supply-driven rather than demand-driven food aid programmes frequently goes to people who do not want to eat it, do not know how to cook it, or have no real use for it.[85] Furthermore, the quality and cultural acceptability of food aid has been often criticised; provided aid often includes genetically modified seeds

---

[79] For instance, the US, as the biggest donor, provides roughly 50% of all food aid worldwide, at an average annual cost of US$2–3 billion, spends more than half of its international food aid budget transporting life-saving commodities through a complex system that is responsive to special interests and hampered by bureaucratic obstructions. For instance, in the case of Africa 70% of the budget is allocated to transportation. Medill-USA Today, 'Hunger Pains: U.S. Food Program Struggles to Move Forward' (26 September 2014) online: <www.usatoday.com/story/news/nation/2014/09/26/hunger-pains-troubled-usaid-food-aid-overseas/16150791/>.

[80] Oxfam, 'Food Aid: A Critical Program, Ripe for Reform', online: <www.oxfamamerica.org/take-action/campaign/food-farming-and-hunger/food-aid/>.

[81] Christopher B Barrett, FAO, *Food Aid's Intended and Unintended Consequences* (2006) 4.

[82] For example, in 2007, after the US government made a commitment to ship $19.5 million of American corn and soya to Malawi as food aid, Malawian farmers suffered as they were not able to sell their local maize. Alex Renton, 'How America is Betraying the Hungry Children of Africa' *The Observer, The Guardian* (27 May 2007) online: <www.theguardian.com/lifeandstyle/2007/may/27/foodanddrink.features7>. For other examples of the effects of food aid programmes in Haiti and Guatemala led by US on the rights of the local populations, see: Saskia Westenberg, 'Feeding Dependency in the Americas: U.S. Food Aid Practices in Haiti and Guatemala' (2013) *Georgetown Journal of International Affairs*, online: <www.georgetownjournalofinternationalaffairs.org/online-edition/feeding-dependency-in-the-americas-u-s-food-aid-practices-in-haiti-and-guatemala-by-saskia-westenberg>.

[83] Christopher B Barrett and Daniel G Maxwell, *Food Aid After Fifty Years: Recasting its Role* (Routledge, 2005) 35.

[84] *Ibid*, 18.

[85] Rob Bailey, Chatham House, cited in Medill-USA Today (n 73).

and fortified foods never tested on large populations[86] with the potential to cause adverse health effects to those it is intended to benefit.

As the humanitarian aid structure consists of autonomous entities such as governments, NGOs, religious organisations, and even the private sector, it suffers from fragmentation of activities.[87] There are three traditionally accepted types of food aid: (i) programme food aid, that is the aid provided by one government to another as a sub-category of foreign aid; (ii) project food aid, that is the aid provided to a government, an international organisation/agency or a non-governmental organisation to be used in development projects or initiatives; and (iii) emergency food aid, provided in response to emergencies.[88] Channels of distribution for food aid can be bilateral (between governments),[89] or through the UN agency WFP. The WFP then may use NGOs for local distribution.[90]

Accountability structures are generally weak or non-existent.[91] This disparate system, which lacks leadership and coordination, is susceptible to inefficiencies, poor communication, bureaucratic restrictions, corruption, and costly duplicative administrative systems that prevent rapid, flexible and effective responses to changing needs.[92]

While budget allocations are greater than ever in terms of financial and human resources, concurrent major emergencies have overstretched humanitarian operational capacity and the ability to meet global demands. Even though donor countries promised to spend 0.7% of their gross national income on international aid, according to OECD records, almost all rich countries have failed to reach their agreed obligations. Besides the funding shortages, almost all foreign aid for food security goes to short term relief operations just to keep people alive, therefore there are no available funds devoted to agricultural investment and rural development that could raise the quality of food security and build resilience in regions vulnerable to climate change and conflict crises.[93]

---

86 Frederic Mousseau, 'Food Aid or Food Sovereignty? Ending World Food Hunger in Our Time' *The Oakland Institute* (2005) online: <www.oaklandinstitute.org/sites/oaklandinstitute.org/files/fasr.pdfwww.theguardian.com/lifeandstyle/2007/may/27/foodanddrink.features>.

87 Barrett and Maxwell (n 86) 13.

88 *Ibid*, 13–14.

89 Although the US is the only donor still distributing on a bilateral basis. *Ibid.*

90 WFP has stated that they work with over 1000 NGOs around the world. World Food Programme, 'Non-governmental Organizations', online: <www1.wfp.org/non-governmental-organizations>.

91 In the current structure of donor state, multilateral aid organisation, and recipient state, the recipient does not have any tools to directly influence 'relevant decision-making processes'. Paolo de Renzio, 'Accountability Dilemmas in Foreign Aid' *ODI* (August 2016) online: <www.odi.org/sites/odi.org.uk/files/resource-documents/10805.pdf> 6.

92 ALNAP, *State of the Humanitarian System* (2015) online: <www.alnap.org/resource/21036.aspx> 10–14.

93 Rosamond L Naylor, 'The Elusive Goal of Global Food Security' (2018) 117(795) *Current History* 3.

3.3. Reform efforts: rights-based approach to food assistance

Although the entire humanitarian emergency landscape is fragmented and uncertain, there have recently been positive moves toward implementing a human rights approach in disaster situations. A human rights approach has crucial advantages in disaster settings: avoiding discrimination, prioritising vulnerable communities, and providing measurable and enforceable obligations through accountability mechanisms. Yet, accountability remains challenging at the national and international levels due to the complexity of the humanitarian system.

Recently, the International Law Commission (ILC) has produced 21 draft articles on subjects ranging from the role of the affected State in coordinating an international disaster response, to the recognition of human rights in the context of a natural disaster.[94] The 2016 draft articles of the ILC on the Protection of persons in the event of disasters, explicitly adopt a rights-based approach, stressing *inter alia*, the respect and protection of human dignity in the event of disasters (Article 4) and the need to address vulnerabilities in emergencies (Article 6).[95] The Commission's Special Rapporteur on the topic commented that debate within the humanitarian community between 'rights-based' and more traditional 'needs-based' approaches were not necessarily mutually exclusive, but complementary.[96] Moreover, while he recognised the primary responsibility of the disaster-affected State, he took a fresh approach by suggesting that human rights responsibilities might be on the verge of being deterritorialised, by declaring and establishing an international duty of cooperation.[97] Concurrently, the draft articles primarily cover the rights and obligations of States (Articles 7–17), as opposed to non-State actors,[98] while invoking the phrase 'external assistance' to describe the assemblage of relevant actors that offer humanitarian assistance to the State in question (Article 12).

Nevertheless, and contrary to the approach adopted by the ILC draft articles, the current dominant view for international community disaster relief is still based on voluntarism and assumes that disaster-affected people remain dependent on the vagaries of altruism, which is often unreliable, politically partisan and arbitrary.[99]

---

[94] International Law Commission, *Draft Articles on the Protection of Persons in the event of Disasters, with Commentaries* (2016) A/71/10 Yearbook of the International Law Commission 2016, vol II, part two, online: <http://legal.un.org/ilc/texts/instruments/english/commentaries/6_3_2016.pdf>.

[95] UN, *Report of the International Law Commission* (June and August 2016) 68th session, UN doc.A/71/10, [48].

[96] *Ibid*, 19.

[97] Therese O'Donnell and Craig Allan, 'Identifying Solidarity: The ILC Project on the Protection of Persons in Disasters and Human Rights' (2016) 49(1) *George Washington International Law Review* 53.

[98] Dug Cubie and Marlies Hesselman, 'Accountability for the Human Rights Implications of Natural Disasters: A Proposal for Systemic International Oversight' (2015) 33(1) *Netherlands Quarterly of Human* 18; ILC (n 97).

[99] O'Donnell and Allan (n 100).

4. Legal approaches to right to food violations in times of conflict and disaster

Emergency aid plays a critical role in situations where States themselves are unable or unwilling to meet the basic needs of their populations. In many of today's conflicts, the humanitarian system is, in essence, asked to take over basic functions from States and parties to the conflict. Yet it is essential to reemphasise that it is first and foremost the obligation of the States, and the parties to the conflict to uphold their responsibilities under the applicable legal frameworks to ensure the right to food in contexts of acute food insecurity. Several branches of international law, including human rights law, international humanitarian law, international criminal law and disaster response law contain norms that apply to the right to adequate food in conflict, disaster and emergency situations.

4.1. International human rights law

Traditionally, the main distinction between international human rights law and international humanitarian law was that the former applied to situations of normality and peace and the latter to situations of conflict. It is now widely recognised that this distinction is misleading, and international human rights law applies at all times, in peace and in war.[100]

The Universal Declaration of Human Rights (UDHR) Article 25(1)[101] in general terms, and after 18 years, the International Covenant on Economic, Social and Cultural Rights (ICESCR) Article 11,[102] define the obligation of all states to eliminate hunger and malnutrition and realise the right to food for all. Severe malnutrition and hunger that causes starvation and famine are clear violations of the right to food. States are obligated to take appropriate steps to prevent starvation. If Article 11 was properly implemented, it would prevent famines from arising.[103]

While the International Covenant on Civil and Political Rights[104] (ICCPR) contains a derogation clause permitting States to limit the enjoyment of certain rights in situations of public emergency, ICESCR does not.[105]

[100] OHCHR, *International Legal Protection of Human Rights in Armed Conflict* (2011) online: <www.ohchr.org/Documents/Publications/HR_in_armed_conflict.pdf>.

[101] 'Everyone has the right to a standard of living adequate for the health and well being of himself and of his family, including food, clothing, housing and medical care ... ' Universal Declaration of Human Rights (adopted 10 December 1948 UNGA Res 217 A(III) (UDHR) Art 25(1).

[102] (Adopted 16 December 1966, entered into force 3 January 1976) United Nations, Treaty Series, vol 993, 3.

[103] Eide Asbjørn, 'Famine' in DL Shelton (ed), *Encyclopedia of Genocide and Crimes Against Humanity* (Macmillan Reference USA, 2005) 343.

[104] (Adopted 16 December 1966, entered into force 23 March 1976) United Nations, Treaty Series, vol 999, 171.

[105] UN Human Rights Committee (HRC), 'CCPR General Comment No. 29 (2001) on Derogations from Provisions of the Covenant During a State of Emergency' (31 August 2001) UN Doc. CCPR/C/21/Rev.1/

Moreover, freedom from hunger is accepted as part of customary international law, rendering it binding on all States regardless of whether they are a party to the Covenant or not.[106] Even though the enforcement mechanism of the ICESCR is weaker in comparison to the mechanism of the ICCPR, the deliberate act of blocking access to food and water in case of emergency or in a conflict situation could constitute a criminal act, as a violation of other international obligations. For instance, where the denial of food would threaten the lives of the affected population, the State would be in violation of the right to life.[107]

The obligations of States with regard to the right to food and other economic, social and cultural rights fall into three categories: the obligations to respect, protect and fulfil such rights.[108] States have an obligation to refrain from interfering with individuals' enjoyment of their economic and social rights, including the right to food, and are also obliged to protect those rights from interference by third parties, including armed groups. In terms of the fulfilment and progressive realisation of rights, States must continue to take deliberate and targeted steps in times of conflict and disaster using all appropriate means to fully implement them. Although the ICESCR Article 2 obliges 'states [to] take steps to the maximum of its available resources, … to [achieve] progressively the full realization of the rights', regressive measures may be prohibited in times of natural and other disasters.[109]

The prohibition against discrimination also remains applicable in times of emergencies. In fact, the principle of non-discrimination becomes even more essential when there exists an increased risk of regressive measures in emergency situations. In particular, states are required to eliminate discriminatory laws and practices relating to food policy and adopt measures to protect those most at risk by treating their needs as a priority.[110]

Add.11, [3]; OHCHRC, *Report of the High Commissioner for Human Rights* (19 May 2015) UN Doc.E/2015/59, [12].

[106] For a comprehensive analysis of the customary nature of the right to be free from hunger, see: Smita Narula, 'The Right to Food: Holding Global Actors Accountable Under International Law' (2006) 7 *Center for Human Rights and Global Justice Working Papers*, online: <www.etoconsortium.org/nc/en/main-navigation/library/documents/?tx_drblob_pi1%5BdownloadUid%5D=17> 1,62.

[107] In fact, in 2008, when Cyclone Nargis struck Myanmar, the military regime initially rejected all offers of international humanitarian assistance. This reignited a debate over the apparent conflict between the right of a sovereign State to refuse assistance and the right of people to receive humanitarian relief in the context of natural disasters. See: Matias Thomsen, 'The Obligation Not to Arbitrarily Refuse International Disaster Relief: A Question of Sovereignty' (2015) 16 *Melbourne Journal of International Law* 28.

[108] UN Committee on Economic, Social and Cultural Rights (CESCR), *General Comment No. 12: The Right to Adequate Food (Art.11)* (12 May 1999) UN Doc.E/C.12/1999/5, online: <https://tbinternet.ohchr.org/_layouts/treatybodyexternal/Download.aspx?symbolno=E%2fC.12%2f1999%2f5&Lang=en>.

[109] *Ibid.*

[110] OHCHR, *Protection of Economic, Social and Cultural Rights in Conflict* (2015), UN Doc.E/2015/59, [31–32].

In addition to legally binding principles, several non-binding principles highlight the responsibility of the State and the international community to maintain food security in situations of conflict and emergency:

(i) *General Comment No. 12* (1999) on the right to adequate food, the Committee on Economic, Social and Cultural Rights distinguishes between the *inability* and the *unwillingness* of State parties to comply. This is a useful distinction especially in situations of conflict and emergency.[111] For a State party to claim that it is unable to fulfil the right to food, the burden falls on the State to demonstrate both that internal resource constraints make it impossible to provide access to food, and that every effort has been made to seek international support. Failures along these lines are a strong indication of unwillingness and therefore constitute a violation of international humanitarian law, in some specific cases international criminal law, as well as the ICESCR. 'The prevention of access to humanitarian food aid in internal conflicts or other emergency situations'[112] through the direct action of states or other entities insufficiently regulated by States is considered a violation of the right to adequate food.

(ii) *The Voluntary Guidelines to Support the Progressive Realization of the Right to Adequate Food in the Context of National Food Security* (2004) refer to humanitarian law and assert clearly that food should never be used as an instrument of political and economic pressure, and that States should provide for the needs of their civilian population, including providing access to food in situations of armed conflict and occupation.[113] Voluntary Guidelines elaborate the concept of international food aid in times of emergency, regardless of whether the emergency is a result of conflict or natural disaster. In this context, donor States should ensure that their food aid policies support national efforts by the recipient States to achieve food security, and that assistance is provided in a manner that takes into account food safety. Not disrupting local food production and the nutritional and dietary needs and cultures of recipient populations is of great importance. The provision of food aid should be accompanied by a clear exit strategy, in order to ensure that it will not result in relationships of dependency. Donors should promote increased use of local and regional commercial markets to meet food needs in famine-prone situations, thereby helping to reduce dependence on food aid.[114]

(iii) In 2015, *the Framework for Action for Food Security and Nutrition in Protracted Crises* was endorsed by the Member States of the FAO in

---

[111] CESCR (n 93) [19].

[112] *Ibid.*

[113] FAO, *Voluntary Guidelines – to Support the Progressive Realization of the Right to Adequate Food in the Context of National Food Security* (2005) online: <www.fao.org/3/a-y7937e.pdf>.

[114] International food-aid transactions should be carried out in a manner consistent with the FAO Principles of Surplus Disposal and Consultative Obligations, the Food Aid Convention and the Agreement on Agriculture. See: *Ibid*, no. 15.

recognition of the fact that protracted crises require special attention, and that appropriate responses in such contexts differ from those appropriate in a short-term crisis or in non-crisis development contexts.[115] While the Framework is voluntary and non-binding, it draws on widely endorsed and influential international and regional instruments and global frameworks, including the Sustainable Development Goals. It is the first instrument of consensus aiming to mitigate threats to food security and nutrition during protracted crises. It is intended to improve the conditions of populations affected by or at risk of a protracted crisis by building resilience, adapting to specific challenges and helping to address underlying causes.

The Framework is based on eleven principles including: meeting immediate humanitarian needs and building resilient livelihoods, empowering women and girls and promoting gender equality, strengthening country ownership, participation, coordination and accountability, contributing to resolving underlying causes and peace-building through food security and nutrition.[116]

4.2. International humanitarian law

Throughout history, starvation and famine were used as tactics of warfare by states or armed rebels. Current conflicts in Afghanistan, the Central African Republic, Iraq, South Sudan, Somalia, the Syrian Arab Republic and Yemen, as well as several other countries, are examples of such tactics, undermining food security and the right to food on a daily basis.[117] In some cases, States and their adversaries use food as a weapon against opposing groups by destroying or poisoning crops, blocking relief supplies[118] and displacing people from their homes with the aim of depriving them of their livelihoods.[119] In other cases, vulnerable groups, such as women, children, detainees and prisoners of war, are subject to neglect or left to starve.[120]

Conventional and customary international humanitarian law regulate the use of food and water, which can be used as a weapon, and posits the obligation to provide aid for civilians. International humanitarian law is a set of rules which seek, for humanitarian reasons, to limit the effects of armed

---

[115] Committee on World Food Security, 'Framework for Action for Food Security and Nutrition in Protracted Crises' (13 October 2015) online: <www.fao.org/3/a-bc852e.pdf>.

[116] *Ibid.*

[117] FAO and WFP, *Monitoring Food Security in Countries with Conflict Situations: A Joint FAO/WFP Update for the United Nations Security Council* (July 2016) online: <www.fao.org/3/a-c0335e.pdf>.

[118] Maggie Michael, 'Food Supplies to Yemeni Families Blocked by Militias, Investigation Reveals' *Independent* (31 December 2018) online: <www.independent.co.uk/news/world/middle-east/yemen-famine-food-supplies-civil-war-block-a8705031.html>.

[119] Human Appeal, *Hunger as a Weapon of War: How Food Insecurity Has Been Exacerbated in Syria and Yemen* (1 April 2018) online: <https://reliefweb.int/sites/reliefweb.int/files/resources/advocacy-report-v013-final.pdf>.

[120] *Ibid*, 11.

conflict. Three of the main principles: distinction, proportionality and precaution are designed to protect persons not participating in hostilities.[121]

Although, none of the humanitarian law principles mention the 'right to food' as such, many of its provisions are intended to ensure that people cannot be denied access to food during armed conflict. It further obliges parties to an armed conflict to implement the relevant rules immediately, and not progressively as in human rights law. As such, international humanitarian law should be treated as an essential and specific legal framework acting in harmony with international human rights principles in times of armed conflict to protect peoples' livelihoods and their access to food.[122]

The four Geneva Conventions of 1949 and two Additional Protocols of 1977 set out the major rules of international humanitarian law.[123] Many provisions of international humanitarian law are accepted as customary law, binding on all states whether or not a State is a party to the Additional Protocols.[124] International humanitarian law provides three major areas of protection relevant to the right to food:

i *Prohibition of the use of famine and starvation of civilians as a method of warfare*: in many situations, parties to the armed conflict deliberately undermine the food security of civilians for political or military reasons by intentionally targeting markets and ports, looting or besieging communities with the aim of causing hardship and starvation; simply using food as a weapon of war.[125] Under international humanitarian law, it is prohibited 'to attack, destroy, remove or render useless, for that purpose, objects indispensable to the survival of the civilian population, such as agricultural areas for the production of foodstuffs, crops, livestock, drinking water installations and supplies and irrigation

---

121 International Committee of the Red Cross (ICRC), ICRC Advisory Service, 'What is International Humanitarian Law' (1 January 2015) online: <www.icrc.org/en/document/icrc-advisory-services-international-humanitarian-law>.

122 Jelana Pejic, 'The Right to Food in Situations of Armed Conflict: The Legal Framework' (2001) 83(844) *Revue Internationale de la Croix-Rouge* 1097.

123 *Geneva Convention for the Amelioration of the Condition of the Wounded and Sick in Armed Forces in the Field*, 12 August 1949, 75 UNTS 31 (Geneva I), *Geneva Convention for the Amelioration of the Condition of Wounded, Sick and Shipwrecked Members of Armed Forces at Sea*, 12 August 1949, 75 UNTS. 85 (Geneva II), *Geneva Convention Relative to the Treatment of Prisoners of War*, 12 August 1949, 75 UNTS 135 (Geneva III), *Geneva Convention Relative to the Protection of Civilian Persons in Times of War*, 12 August 1949, 75 UNTS 287 (Geneva IV), *Protocol Additions to the Geneva Conventions of 12 August 1949, and Relating to the Protection of Victims of International Armed Conflicts*, 8 June 1977, 1125 UNTS 3, *Protocol II Additional to the Geneva Conventions of 12 August 1949 and Relating to the Protection of Victims of Non-International Armed Conflicts*, 8 June 1977, 1125 UNTS 609, *Protocol III Additional to the Geneva Conventions of 12 August 1949, and Relating to the Adoption of an Additional Distinctive Emblem*, 8 December 2005.

124 ICRC, 'Customary International Humanitarian Law', online: <https://ihl-databases.icrc.org/customary-ihl/eng/docs/home>.

125 Syrian Arab Republic, Yemen, and South Sudan are examples of such deliberate undermining security. UN Special Rapporteur on the Right to Food, *Interim Report* (21 July 2017) UN Doc.A/72/188, online: <https://undocs.org/A/72/188> [27–30].

works'.[126] These prohibitions are generally considered to be rules of customary international law, applicable to all types of armed conflicts (internal or international) according to the ICRC study on customary international humanitarian law.[127] Moreover, as it will be discussed further, deliberate starvation of civilians is considered a war crime under international criminal law.[128]

ii *Prohibition of forced displacement*: displacement is a major factor contributing to hunger and starvation in times of armed conflict. Intentional displacement is unlawful and constitutes a war crime under the Rome Statute of the International Criminal Court in the context of both international and non-international armed conflicts.[129]

iii *Prohibition of denying or blocking humanitarian assistance*:[130] parties to an armed conflict have the primary responsibility to meet the needs of the population under their control, including food and water. 'Humanitarian assistance must be provided in accordance with the principles of humanity, neutrality and impartiality'.[131] If parties to a conflict cannot meet those needs, they must allow and facilitate efforts by impartial humanitarian agencies to undertake relief action, including by granting an unimpeded right of free passage of relief supplies to besieged zones, in particular for women, children and the elderly.[132] The free passage of food is vital when the population is suffering from excessive deprivations, as well as the control of distribution by impartial humanitarian organisations so as to ensure that the food is not diverted by one of the parties to the conflict or other groups.

Humanitarian food assistance, which can provide a critical lifeline of support, also often faces serious political, security and infrastructure-related impediments that obstruct the effective delivery of food aid. Parties to the conflict might deliberately block humanitarian aid or be unwilling to fulfil their responsibility under humanitarian law to ensure access by the civilian

126 See Art 54(1) of Additional Protocol I and article 14 of Additional Protocol II.

127 See Rule 53 on starvation as a method of warfare and Rule 54 on attacks against objects indispensable to the survival of the civilian population.

128 See Rome Statute, Art 8, para 2(b)(xxv). *Rome Statute of the International Criminal Court* (adopted 17 July 1998, entered into force on 1 July 2002) 2187 UNTS 90 (Rome Statute).

129 *Ibid*, Art 8, paras 2(a)(vii) and (b)(viii).

130 Humanitarian food aid in periods of war should be distinguished from food aid in period of peace (see UN Economic and Social Council (ECOSOC)), *The Right to Food: Report by the Special Rapporteur on the Right to Food, Mr. Jean Ziegler, Submitted in Accordance with Commission on Human Rights Resolution 2001/25* (10 January 2002), UN Doc.E/CN.4/2002/58, online: <https://undocs.org/E/CN.4/2002/58>.

131 UN, *UN General Assembly Resolution 46/182: Strengthening of the Coordination of Humanitarian Emergency Assistance of the United Nations* (19 December 2019) UN doc. A/RES/46/182, online: <www.un.org/documents/ga/res/46/a46r182.htm>.

132 There are also a series of provisions that relate to relief assistance for civilians in occupied territories under the Geneva Convention relative to the Protection of Civilian Persons in Time of War (Arts 55 and 59) and Additional Protocol I (Arts 68–71). Geneva Convention Relative to the Protection of Civilian Persons in Time of War (n 84).

population to basic services and goods, including food. The delivery of humanitarian assistance may also be seriously hampered by combat conditions.[133]

States can only refuse to deliver food on the grounds of 'military necessity'. Although military necessity is an acceptable reason for exceptional conditions, it can be invoked only to regulate humanitarian access, not to prohibit definitively the possibility for an impartial humanitarian organisation to operate in certain areas. States can restrict humanitarian assistance only temporarily within specific geographical limits. To refuse passage for emergency food supplies would constitute a flagrant violation of the right to food and the right to life, especially if civilians die of hunger as a result. Also, wilfully impeding relief supplies is listed as a war crime under Article 8, paragraph 2 (b) (xxv), of the Rome Statute.[134]

4.3. International criminal law: individual responsibility for deliberately causing famine as a tactic of warfare

Certain gross violations of international human rights and humanitarian law have been considered of such gravity by the international community that they have been regulated under international criminal law, imposing individual criminal responsibility. Deliberate acts to prevent access to food and water not only constitute violations of the right to food, which could be prosecuted not only nationally but also internationally, but also may constitute war crimes (Article 8 of the Rome Statute), crimes against humanity (Article 7 of the Rome Statute),[135] or even genocide (Genocide Convention Article 6),[136] and torture (the Convention Against Torture and Other Cruel, Inhuman or Degrading Treatment or Punishment),[137] which could give rise to individual responsibility under international criminal law.

Article 7(1) of the Rome Statute lists acts that constitute crimes against humanity as murder, extermination, enslavement, forcible transfer of population, torture, rape, persecution, enforced disappearance, apartheid and 'other inhumane acts of a similar character intentionally causing great suffering, or serious injury to body or to mental or physical health'. The last part of the article provides a rather flexible or open-ended definition that allows for the extension of the catalogue of crimes against humanity to

[133] For example, in April 2017 the forced relocation of 100 aid workers in South Sudan due to active hostilities hampered the delivery of assistance to 180,000 people. In north-east Nigeria, attacks by Boko Haram and military operations against the group continue to limit humanitarian access and an estimated 700,000 people remain extremely hard to reach. Access is further restricted by the presence of mines and improvised explosive devices. *Ibid.*

[134] Rome Statute (n 128).

[135] *Ibid.*

[136] Convention on the Prevention and Punishment of the Crime of Genocide (opened for signature 9 December 1948, entered into force 12 January 1951) 78 UNTS 277 (Genocide Convention).

[137] Convention against Torture and Other Cruel, Inhuman or Degrading Treatment or Punishment (adopted 10 December 1984, entered into force 26 June 1987) 1465 UNTS 85 (CAT).

include a new type of 'inhumane act' such as starvation and/or famine. Armed conflict is not a precondition for such inhumane acts, although the acts must occur in a serious situation in which starvation results from officially adopted policies and practices.[138]

A crime against humanity has two components: (i) The accused must deliberately perpetrate the acts necessary to accomplish the specific offence; (ii) The act must be committed as part of a 'widespread and systematic attack' directed against the civilian population.[139] Famine automatically satisfies the second requirement because by definition famine must be widespread and systematic.

The first requirement, intentionality, however is harder to prove. The deliberate use of starvation as a weapon constitutes a crime if there is sufficient evidence of an intentional or reckless effort to block certain groups from access to food under conditions of conflict or hardship. The crime of famine could result from acts of omission, but also from indirect action such as blocking humanitarian assistance, failing to uphold the relevant laws of war or failing to provide international relief systems with the necessary resources in the context of famine conditions.

To prove specific intent as the basis for criminal responsibility is difficult, as death from starvation is slow and often results from diverse contributory causes. Famine normally occurs in conjunction with other severe crimes and as such the judgments rendered often do not identify famine as an independent crime. However, it is not necessary to prove *specific* intent for crimes against humanity (unlike for the crime of genocide). General intent as a condition for deliberate famine includes knowledge and/or reckless disregard for the consequences.[140] Deliberate creation of famine and starvation is clearly intended to be prohibited in all types of conflicts, but it is classified as a war crime only in international armed conflicts under Article 8(2)(b)(xxv) of the Rome Statute. This oversight should be corrected, as it is especially problematic to prosecute someone accused of committing the crime of famine in non-international conflict.

Although it is widely accepted by the international community that intentionally caused famine and forced starvation are prohibited under international law, there has never been a call for an international criminal trial against government officials or non-State actors for creating, inflicting or prolonging famine, in part because of the legal and political complexities surrounding charges of criminality that require proof of intent and evidence of

---

[138] Sigrun Skogly, 'Crimes Against Humanity—Revisited: Is There a Role for Economic and Social Rights?' (2001) 5(1) *International Journal of Human Rights* 58.

[139] Article 7(1) Crimes Against Humanity.

[140] Diana Kearney, 'Food Deprivations as Crimes Against Humanity' (2013) 46 *International Law and Politics* 270.

the acts complained of.[141] According to M. Cherif Bassiouni, one of the reasons for this is that the precise meaning of crimes against humanity 'has not yet settled into its final form. Its nature, scope, application, and legal elements are still somewhat unsettled'.[142] This view relies on the *travaux preparatories* of the Rome Statute, which reveal that the majority refused to include 'modern violations' such as mass starvation, economic embargoes, and terrorism into the contents of Article 7 during the discussions of the Rome Conference.[143] One of the arguments for this exclusion was that mass starvation would fit under the umbrella of acts such as persecution, extermination, and other inhumane acts and that therefore there was no need to include famine or mass starvation in the text.[144]

It is important to acknowledge the gap between what the law prescribes and the feasibility of its implementation in order to understand the necessary steps to close it. At present, the sources of legal authority are scattered and fragmented. The coherent formulation of the content of the crime in an authoritative text would be an important contribution to the development of international law, considering the massive abuse of fundamental human rights and the lack of accountability procedures in the current international setting. The establishment of the International Criminal Court was an important step forward, but its potential remains essentially unrealised at present. It is theoretically possible to bring to justice those responsible for allowing their populations or those of their adversaries to starve to death, but the political will to do so is not clearly manifested or even consistently present.

5. Conclusion

In the long-term, comprehensive policies that deal with root causes of starvation are essential if the international community has the political will to avoid the periodic recurrence of famine. This is a far more realistic prospect than expecting famines to disappear as soon as the hot conflict is over. Human rights violations, war crimes, repression, severe weather-related disasters, and all sorts of inequality and extreme poverty are conditions that frequently generate famine. The attention and commitment of the international community must, as a matter of highest priority, be directed at eliminating these root causes of famine, and not just addressing the visible symptoms of the prior

[141] David Marcus, 'Famine Crimes in International Law' (2003) 97(2) *American Journal of International Law* 245.

[142] M Cherif Bassiouni, 'Revisiting the Architecture of Crimes Against Humanity: Almost a Century in the Making with Gaps and Ambiguities Remaining – The Need for a Specialized Convention' in Leila Nadya Sadat (ed), *Forging a Convention for Crimes Against Humanity,* (Cambridge University Press, 2013) 43.

[143] Kearney (n 140) 272.

[144] *Ibid.*

food catastrophe.[145] An effective preventive approach to famine is likely to save many more lives than the current reactive approach.

The root causes of food insecurity in the context of conflict, natural disasters, and post-disaster settings also need to be understood and addressed in conjunction with other global problems. Climate change has deep, long term impact on food insecurity that could eventually bring hot conflicts to countries that have no capacity to respond and could easily be trapped in vicious cycles of conflict, disaster and food insecurity. This interdependence has never been part of a climate change policy discussion. Short-sided international policies prompt lack of compensation and remedy, unaccountability and impunity.

Severe food insecurity can be averted or substantially reduced if the right investments in agriculture are made in post-disaster and post-conflict periods. This would require better-constructed humanitarian 'emergency' responses, as well as effective 'development' and capacity-building activities.[146] Even at the earliest stages of a response, when the emphasis is on providing urgent life-saving food assistance, it is crucial to strengthen the resilience of affected communities. It is essential to ensure that the right to food of both individuals and communities are met not only in short-term responses to emergency situations but also with due regard for long-term impacts. In order to achieve these goals, the common understanding among the donor communities of food aid as a voluntary act should be replaced by negotiating a legal framework in the form of a comprehensive, multilateral treaty of general application.

Food assistance, although having a vital role as part of the humanitarian system, suffers from serious financial constraints and lack of coordination. Solving chronic hunger in natural disaster or conflict zones, combined with other calamities requires various forms of assistance—deploying a range of humanitarian, economic, political and even military tactics. This would only be possible through the political and financial commitments and coordinated efforts of developed countries.

There is the need for a global convention that gives States and the international community clear legal mandates to prevent famine and protect peoples' right to adequate food. This protection cannot be reliably achieved on a voluntary basis. If the international community is serious about the imperative character of the right to food and the eradication of massive starvation and famine, steps must be taken to encourage the implementation of existing standards as well as to codify and elaborate new rules. A proposed binding agreement should be enacted to cover essential elements of conflict

---

[145] de Waal (n 13).

[146] UN Office for Disaster Risk Reduction, 'Terminology', online: <www.unisdr.org/we/inform/terminology>.

prevention, prohibitions associated with famine and starvation, and post-conflict rehabilitation that includes the agricultural sector. Secondly, measures should be taken to maximise local and regional sourcing of food for aid, including increasing developmental assistance for long-term recovery. Lastly, international legal standards that strongly reinforce the norm that deliberate action causing starvation is a war crime or a crime against humanity should be developed, and that in the most serious cases these should be referred to the International Criminal Court for investigation and prosecution. Formal recognition of famine as a crime will impede the tendency of governments 'to hide behind a curtain of natural disasters and state sovereignty to use hunger as a genocidal weapon'.[147]

Disclosure statement

No potential conflict of interest was reported by the author.

[147] Marcus (n 141).

Third world sovereignty, indigenous sovereignty, and food sovereignty: living with sovereignty despite the map

Michael Fakhri

ABSTRACT
Sovereignty remains a theoretically unclear and politically problematic concept. I find some promise, however, in a practice of sovereignty that operates in spite of lines on a map. My study draws from a mix of personal narrative, historical study, doctrinal analysis, and institutional mapping. I examine sovereignty with one foot in Beirut and the other in Bandung; from this postcolonial and transnational setting, I run into a political and conceptual dead-end. I therefore look to two cases that I argue exemplify a practice of sovereignty worth supporting and replicating. The Inuit technique of geographical reframing through international doctrine and institutions is innovative and potentially something others can try. The food sovereignty movement highlights that power stems from social organising and change will not come from theoretical elegance. What these struggles confirm is that any understanding of change in international law must address the question of solidarity as a central concern.

I. Introduction

Even though sovereignty is a key concept in international law, I have avoided it for most of my life. This is not because notions of sovereignty often obscure more than they reveal. Nor is it because sovereignty's practical meaning is always different depending on when and how it is deployed. While I think those points are theoretically correct, up until recently, I did not rely too firmly on concepts of sovereignty in my research because it never made sense to me in how I lived my daily life. I have also made it a matter of political conviction to view sovereignty with suspicion.

I begin in **Part II** with an account of sovereignty from this perspective of personal narrative and political commitment. By rolling sovereignty into my own story, I do not have to reconcile with nationalist narratives or resist state-centric perspectives. Sovereignty's meaning becomes enveloped in how I make sense of myself through recalling memories, recounting family lore, listening to other stories nearby, and reading history. In this way, I can choose when to describe sovereignty as something in the background or I can focus on it in the foreground, all while never allowing it to dictate my political and legal understanding. Regardless of how I position sovereignty in my account, what makes sovereignty a useful concept is it often signals a claim to power in a sociopolitical struggle. More specifically, it is a concept that has always arisen in the context of imperial projects, used by expansionists to claim authority over indigenous peoples and their territory (the notorious colonial encounter).[1]

The descriptive task under these terms is to understand how sovereignty is defined by the results of people's manoeuvring in their struggle against imperialism, and how sovereignty reconfigures political stakes in a particular way. The question is then not a matter of being 'for' or 'against' sovereignty, as was the case during globalisation debates of the past several decades. Rather it is a question of determining how people deploy claims to sovereignty in ways that serves or alters a political agenda.

Sovereignty, in all its persistent and mercurial forms, is often studied in historical terms. The consistent conclusion is that sovereignty is a conceptual paradox and is theoretically frustrating. People often draw from this account of the past, to argue that in the politics of the present sovereignty is irrelevant and that we live (or should live) in a post-sovereign world.[2] This approach treats sovereignty as a concept that should be measured against itself. I instead take sovereignty to be a political practice and understand the temporality and historiography of sovereignty to be determined by the history of particular struggles.[3]

My leery posture is best reflected in lessons from Third World Approaches to International Law (TWAIL). If sovereignty's presence and meaning always arises from encounters between coloniser and colonised, then the political question is, 'how successfully the Third World could deploy sovereignty for the purpose of revealing and remedying the past'.[4] So far, there has been work that reveals the past, but the record for remedy has been dire.[5] One

[1] Antony Anghie, *Imperialism, Sovereignty and the Making of International Law* (Cambridge University Press, 2005).

[2] Martti Koskenniemi, 'Conclusion: Vocabularies of Sovereignty – Powers of a Paradox' in Hent Kalmo and Quentin Skinner (eds), *Sovereignty in Fragments* (Cambridge University Press, 2010).

[3] For a different but promising approach that examines sovereignty as a global aesthetic practice situated in histories of political thought, see Tsevi Ben-Dor Benite, Stefanos Geroulanos and Nicole Jerr (eds), *The Scaffolding of Sovereignty: Global and Aesthetic Perspectives on the History of a Concept* (Columbia University Press, 2017).

[4] Anghie, *Imperialism, Sovereignty and the Making of International Law* (n 1) 199.

[5] See for eg Sundhya Pahuja, *Decolonising International Law: Development, Economic Growth and the Politics of Universality* (Cambridge University Press, 2011); Michael Fakhri, *Sugar and the Making of International Trade Law* (Cambridge University Press, 2014); Luis Eslava, *Local Space, Global Life: The Everyday Operation of International Law and Development* (Cambridge University Press, 2015); Umut Özsu, *Formalizing Displacement: International Law and Population Transfers* (Oxford University Press, 2015). Resistance and social change remain undertheorized in TWAIL. For some examinations on resistance see Balakrishnan Rajagopal, *International Law from Below: Development, Social Movements, and Third World Resistance* (Cambridge University Press, 2003); Ruth Buchanan, 'Writing Resistance Into International Law' (2008) 10 *International Community Law Review* 445; John Reynolds, *Empire, Emergency, and*

indictment has been that Third World jurists of the past sixty years focused too much of their energy on international institutions.[6] This proved to be a limited tactic because international institutions are always sites of contestation, negotiation, and compromise and as such they will always de-radicalise political claims. Another charge is that Third World jurists did not reconceptualise sovereignty sufficiently because they still made certain assumptions that narrowed possibilities for change—things like a strong commitment to economic development plans and the predilection to imagine and practice politics through a state-centric view.[7]

From this perspective, postcolonial sovereignty has been a dead-end. And yet, despite all these misgivings, people in TWAIL are not willing to leave sovereignty alone. To some it is because sovereignty remains an unfulfilled promise of liberation for Third World peoples.[8] But I think many TWAILers still wrangle with sovereignty because it continues to structure the legal and political imagination of people committed to imperial administration and colonial practice as well as people resisting these expansionist projects; it has been a tenacious concept with no sign of abatement.

In **Part II**, I therefore situate my personal narrative within the political history of the Bandung Conference of 1955, which I treat as an epitome of the Third World project. I look at sovereignty with one foot in Beirut and the other in Bandung situating myself in a postcolonial setting.[9] This is not a *bildungsroman*, which is a common genre in international law; there is no clear advancement or notion of progress.[10] Rather, the story is one of a sojourn where I go 'there and back again'[11]—the destination is a curious future and the notion of home is equivocal. This allows me to imagine spaces not as an exercise in mapping but rather as the experience of travelling along roads and through networks, moving across land, air, and water to arrive at discreet locations.[12] I dislike

---

International Law (Cambridge University Press, 2017). For an exceptional sustained study on the question see Robert Knox, 'Valuing Race? Stretched Marxism and the Logic of Imperialism' (2016) 4 *London Review of International Law* 81.

6 Rajagopal (n 5); Vasuki Nesiah, 'Placing International Law: White Spaces on a Map' (2003) 16 *Leiden Journal of International Law* 1; Pahuja (n 5).

7 Rajagopal (n 5); Nesiah (n 6); Pahuja (n 5).

8 Partha Chatterjee, 'The Legacy of Bandung' in Luis Eslava, Michael Fakhri and Vasuki Nesiah (eds), *Bandung, Global History, and International Law* (Cambridge University Press, 2017).

9 In this instance, it would be more accurate to say Lebanon instead of Beirut, but I could not avoid the pleasure of this particular alliteration. I feel, however, it is still accurate since in Lebanon, it is Beirut that has left the most lasting imprint on me. And with Beirut comes an ongoing relationship with the Mediterranean Sea, which you may notice pops up here and there in my account.

10 Rose Sydney Parfitt, 'Newer Is Truer: Time, Space, and Subjectivity at the Bandung Conference' in Luis Eslava, Michael Fakhri and Vasuki Nesiah (eds), *Bandung, Global History, and International Law* (Cambridge University Press, 2017). See also Thomas Skouteris, *The Notion of Progress in International Law Discourse* (TMC Asser Press, 2009).

11 JRR Tolkein, *The Hobbit: Or, There and Back Again* (George Allen & Unwin, 1937).

12 Lauren A Benton, *A Search for Sovereignty: Law and Geography in European Empires, 1400–1900* (Cambridge University Press, 2010) 16; Achille Mbembe, 'The Idea of a Borderless World' (*Africa is a Country*, 11 November 2018) <https://africasacountry.com/2018/11/the-idea-of-a-borderless-world> (accessed 14 December 2018).

mapping because it is usually a technique used to control territory by imagining space as measurable and firmly bounded.[13] Moreover, attempts to redraw maps as an anti-imperial tactic are usually met with violent implications and a high death count.[14]

In this article, I instead want to think about a practice of sovereignty that operates despite existing maps and boundaries. I give an impressionistic personal account because my primary intent is not to describe the landscape in a way that highlights certain geographic features (rivers, islands, hills, etc.) as markers of sovereignty or to focus on local particularities in a way that resists generalisation; my aim is to take my particular experience of movement and abstract it out into the larger category of 'migrant' in order to bring out a transnational understanding of sovereignty.[15]

The other purpose of **Part II** is to identify the political limits of Third World sovereignty thus far and to provide some context to how I situate myself in relation to other anti-imperial struggles. My broader methodological purpose is to provide an example of what a TWAIL scholar might do in order to engage with, while not appropriating, other movements. I am not speaking for anyone or claim to bring forward anyone's voice. I situate myself in a particular way so that I can learn from those particular struggles and propose insights to others in TWAIL and law more broadly. I am also introducing myself, offering an account of who I am and where I am from, to scholars and activists in those other struggles as an invitation to collaborate with me and my comrades.[16]

Because my narrative is driven by my personal account, when I reach the same theoretical dead-end of sovereignty that others have pointed to in the postcolonial experience I cannot stop my story. My life continues, and I

---

[13] Nesiah (n 6); Benton (n 12); Karin Mickelson, 'The Maps of International Law: Perceptions of Nature in the Classification of Territory' (2014) 27 *Leiden Journal of International Law* 621. For a good argument against re-drawing the map in the Levant see Aslı Bâli, 'Sykes-Picot and "Artificial" States' (2016) 110 *AJIL Unbound* 115.

[14] This is not to say that an attempt to redraw a map is a call to violence; plans to redraw maps, however, often lead to violence. It is not enough to treat the effects of those plans as collateral damage and not theorise the expected violence itself. For an example from within TWAIL of such a call to redraw a map while eliding the question of violence, see Makau wa Mutua, 'Why Redraw the Map of Africa: A Moral and Legal Inquiry' (1995) 16 *Michigan Journal of International Law* 1113, 1175: 'It would be irresponsible to assume that the direction proposed in this article could not lead Africa down a more treacherous path in which power-mongers and cynical ethnic chauvinists would senselessly tear society apart in pursuit of self-aggrandizement. That possibility, which would be a real setback to pan-Africanism, exists. But it is far more damning to sit and wait for disaster to strike, precipitating the crises that have been witnessed in Somalia, Liberia, and Rwanda.'

[15] The irony is not lost on me that Philip Jessup developed his notion of transnational law at time that coincided with and in effect disrupted rising claims of Third World sovereignty through international law, see Phillip Jessup, *Transnational Law* (Yale University Press, 1956); Anghie, *Imperialism, Sovereignty and the Making of International Law* (n 1) 223. Jessup develops the concept to complicate distinctions between public and private, domestic and international. I instead use transnational law in a narrower way to recognise and describe the legal tools that shape the direction and conditions of the movement of people and capital through borders.

[16] This article is the product of a series of talks where I set out to do just that.

still have to confront or negotiate sovereign claims. My political imperative behind studying sovereignty is existential and not a matter of governance as such.[17]

After describing the limits of postcolonial sovereignty, in **Parts III and IV** I examine two cases of sovereignty constructed in spite of the map. They may help answer the question as to whether sovereignty can remedy imperial power and relieve colonised peoples. I want to quickly note on how to read these sections before providing a summary: most TWAIL scholars focus on how close encounters of the colonial kind generate sovereign claims. In my two examples, I instead focus on how sovereignty, while generated from those encounters, is being defined in terms of transnational solidarity. *If* there is any hope for conceptualising sovereignty in a way that counters imperial forces on a global scale, it will come from an understanding that reflects the fellowship that people create to neutralise those forces that want to centralise power in the hands of the few.

In **Part III** I examine Inuit assertions of Arctic sovereignty and look to how innovative techniques in geographic reframing brought new meaning to sovereignty. In **Part IV** I study the food sovereignty movement and argue that it enacted a new form of sovereignty that was created by a powerful force of transnational solidarity despite a diffuse definition and different interests. I find that people in the movement are adeptly navigating the line between using a transnational social movement to change institutions and not limiting their political ambition by institutionalising the movement.

Calling these two accounts 'case studies' is a bit of a misnomer because I want these two different struggles to be understood as exemplars. I highlight the specificities of each struggle, but also think about what aspects may be more generalisable. A common critique of international law has been that it presents itself as a universally applicable set of concepts and practices, while it is in fact the abstraction of a very particular (and often European and North American) experience. My premise is that if we understand that all international law is based on some sort of particular context, then if anyone wants to still rely on international law to make any sort of claim this should include being able to argue why a certain particular context warrants universalisation.

Now to summarise–

In **Part III**, I look at Inuit sovereignty as a claim made to constitute a single people across multiple jurisdictions. It is an example of how people with different citizenships, across a wide range of territory develop political concepts in order to exercise institutional power and resist imperial power. It is

---

[17] I learned this from long-standing conversations with Ibrahim Gassama. See for example, Ibrahim J Gassama, 'Bandung 1955: The Deceit and the Conceit' in Luis Eslava, Michael Fakhri and Vasuki Nesiah (eds), *Bandung, Global History, and International Law* (Cambridge University Press, 2017).

a claim that makes room for different anti-colonial tactics that range from secessionism to co-governance. The limits of universalising such an approach is that this still hinges on an ethno-nationalist notion of a singular 'people'. It may be the case that this approach is only applicable to others, like the Kurdish people, whose political space spans multiple jurisdictions. Or it may open up the concept of 'people' and make it something that can withstand borders—something that might serve people such as the Palestinians. My intent is not to conduct a comparative analysis, resolve any of these tensions, or overcome the limitations. I use this case to put forward the question to TWAIL and others as to whether the underlying theoretical concepts that arise from Inuit sovereignty—and the technique of using doctrine to geographically reframe a political argument—could be deployed in other contexts in a way that transforms and debilitates imperial power. I thus write in an idiom that is closer to doctrinal argument than sociological investigation.

In **Part IV**, I track how the food sovereignty movement developed an ambiguous conception of sovereignty that has served them well. The food sovereignty movement has been one of the most effective transnational movements to influence international institutions and international law. Members of the movement are acutely aware of the political limits of legal tools and the difficulty with working against and within institutions. They are also vigilant to ensure that the movement itself is not institutionalised. This is a movement whose explicit ambition is to universalise its experiences and agenda, and we see its effects across a multitude of contexts and at different scales. Like Inuit approaches, sovereignty is deployed despite existing maps. But the concept of 'people' can only be used in very specific cultural and historical contexts. Food sovereignty, however, provides a space of negotiated fellowship not ethnic membership, which is why I think it is a more generalisable, global form. Somehow the movement holds together even though multiple (and sometimes contradictory) understandings of sovereignty operate within it, including Bandungian and indigenous notions. It has quickly rearticulated sovereignty in transnational manifold terms while maintaining an ambivalence to the state and empowering millions of people across the world. My style here is in the form of an institutional tactical handbook where I note the experiences of this movement in forming networks of transnational solidarity with different perspectives and interests while also directly engaging, influencing, and resisting international institutions. The food sovereignty movement includes peoples from different struggles and like all solidarity projects this alliance needs constant attention. The movement began with a stronger foothold in postcolonial struggles, but indigenous peoples are leading with their food sovereignty ideas both from within and outwith the formal movement.

I conclude in **Part V** with a reflection on how my story about these struggles may allow us to think about new anti-imperial techniques and not be left with only 're-drawing the map'. I point to where one might go to in order to develop new techniques that overcome the wicked choice between 'arbitrary colonial frontiers and the ineptitude of our postcolonial regimes [to govern]' and 'a future of violent change, presaged by the spread of separatisms'.[18] To Adewale Maja-Pearce, extrapolating from experiences in Cameroon and Nigeria, the only option for people in the Third World is 'to reimagine ourselves and our societies all over again'.[19] For now, we will have to settle on making tools that enable such a reimagining.

After situating myself as a postcolonial migrant in **Part II**, this article is constructed as a doctrinal and institutional analysis sandwiched between two subjective accounts. I begin in **Part III** by situating myself personally in relation to indigenous struggles against settler colonialism and imperial power. I then tell a story about the Inuit struggle. In order to not interrupt the descriptive narrative, I continue with my story about the food sovereignty movement in **Part IV**, and end that section with a comment on how I position myself professionally as an academic jurist from a Third World tradition in relation to the food sovereignty movement and its embedded academics.

II. Third world sovereignty—'who are you and where are you from?'

I am always very careful how I answer that question. It sometimes comes from someone who feels that they can ask such a presumptuous question at the outset of a conversation. More often, it is someone officially required to ask me because I am requesting permission to do something or go somewhere. Regardless, the question indicates to me that the interrogator has reason to believe that they hold a position that grants them power over me. No one less than Polyphemus, the demi-god and human-eating giant, confronts Odysseus with that question on one of the Cyclopean islands in the Mediterranean Sea.[20] Anyone answering that question, exposes themselves because whatever they say brings with it meanings, histories, and consequences beyond their control, many of which could be painful. If you give up that information, it also means people are more able to find you against your will. Odysseus answered Polyphemus with a clever lie and a stab to the eye in order to avoid death and continue his epic journey home. While escaping on his ship, Odysseus calls out taunting the giant bragging about his guile. In his arrogance he reveals his true name, which grants the now-blind

[18] Adewale Maja-Pearce, 'Prospects for Ambazonia' (2018) 40(20) *London Review of Books* 23 <www.lrb.co.uk/v40/n20/adewale-maja-pearce/prospects-for-ambazonia> (accessed 15 December 2018).

[19] Ibid.

[20] There has been a recent bout of translations of The Odyssey by Homer. For a helpful review see Colin Burrow, 'Light Through the Fog' (2018) 40(8) *London Review of Books* 3 <www.lrb.co.uk/v40/n08/colin-burrow/light-through-the-fog> (accessed 15 December 2018).

Polyphemus power over Ulysses. It is all Polyphemus needs to get his father, the god of the sea, to punish this man who turned out to be the king of Ithaca.[21]

People often respond to that question about identity with some reference to a nation, people, or state. Underlying that type of answer is some notion of sovereignty. At a very young age, when I had to answer that question, I understood it in terms that assumed territorial integrity and clear borders. But I also knew all borders had pores and that you could always make perforations. This was because I was also implicitly taught how to traverse those borders.

That is all to say, I have experienced sovereignty in transnational terms. I am a migrant, and my people have always been migrants. This is one reason I have had an aversion to the notion of sovereignty. Being a migrant has meant knowing where I was from but never quite sure when or even whether I would go back. Unlike nomads, I did not move with my people nor was it within a specific space. Unlike Odysseus, my will to return was wavering. My family left home to different destinations with an undetermined possibility of coming back. Moving was always a matter of necessity and I could tell you a history of global economic crises or Lebanese political violence through each of my moves.

There is a dizziness that comes with being a migrant and it was sometimes difficult to determine whether I was going away or coming back. Returning home for a migrant can also be disorienting in time since it sometimes happens generations later or not at all. This instability is further exacerbated by the fact that at any given moment after settling in a new place we may be tolerated as minorities, welcomed as guests, vilified as threats, or assimilated as citizens.

Here is how I experienced those swirls in space and time: I was told that my grandmother sang to me songs in Portuguese when she was putting me to sleep as a baby. When I was born, she left Lebanon to where we lived in Canada to raise me in my first year. My grandmother's Portuguese lullabies came from her mother, who was born in Brazil, who sang to her when she was a young girl growing up in in the foothills of Mount Lebanon. My grandmother did not speak Portuguese, but those songs connected us to each other and to those who loved us from afar and in the past. On my father's side, in our village on the peak of the northern mountains in Lebanon, we have a house that was built with nineteenth century money. My great-grandfather went to Venezuela for a few years and travelled the country selling sundries. His cousins and siblings stayed in Venezuela, whereas he took his money and came back to his village to build his house. Two generations later, my uncle would leave Lebanon and move 'back' to Venezuela and marry a cousin.

[21] Homer, *The Odyssey* (Emily R Wilson tr, London: W W Norton & Company, 2018) Book 9.

By the time I was six, my parents took us to live in Saudi Arabia during the Civil War in Lebanon. We later fled Riyadh right before Operation Desert Storm and went back to Beirut. The Green Line between East and West Beirut had just been formally erased. This was the year that Parliament passed the controversial law that granted amnesty for all political crimes perpetrated before 28 March 1991.[22] This was my most confusing return: I was coming back home even though I was born somewhere else and had never lived in Lebanon. Up until then, I experienced Beirut in terms of three-month holidays having only visited every summer. What confused things even more is the fact that the amnesty law marked the exact moment that the war was turned into a memory designed for people to forget.

To understand the implications of the amnesty law you should know that a core aspect of contemporary political life in Lebanon is the fact that many high-ranking politicians and ruling families have blood on their hands from the war. What stability there is in Lebanon today hinges on the fact that no one can hold those in power accountable for the violence of those years. Some efforts have been made to create spaces for people to narrate to themselves and to each other what the war meant. That is one reason why when people in Lebanon recount the war, if they ever do, they do so in terms of the fragments of what they remember and not within any sort of collective narrative frame of forgiveness, catharsis, justice, or history. This is still a place where there has been very little opportunity for people to hold any constitutive conversations about how to create a new future despite the recent experience of violence, much less any opportunity for reconciliation.[23] So when I arrived in Beirut in 1991, it was to establish my relationship with the place in new terms as my home, all while everyone was collectively shifting from the punctuated absurdity of war into the fragmented politics of memory.

This was also when I learned that my grandparents were active members of a political party and had been involved, like everyone else in the family, in a failed coup in 1961. They were fighting for an idea of a Greater Syria (*Bilad Al Sham* or *Suriya Al-Kubra*) that included Lebanon, Syria, Palestine, Jordan,

---

[22] General Amnesty Law No. 84/91 (26 August 1991).

[23] Launched under the #CounteringAmnesia hashtag in the fall of 2018, Lebanon Support and forumZFD (Forum Civil Peace Service) recently announced their project entitled 'Mapping of initiatives addressing the past in Lebanon'. They document over 156 initiatives in the country attempting to address its past between the end of the civil war in 1990 and 2017. See Lebanon Support and forumZFD, 'Mapping of Initiatives Addressing the Past in Lebanon' (*The Civil Society Knowledge Centre*, 2018) <https://civilsociety-centre.org/hist/initiatives-addressing-conflict> (accessed 14 December 2018). The final report concludes with the following: 'Reconciliation in Lebanon has faced many challenges such as a state imposed amnesia, unresolved human rights violations, and a lack of accountability of the perpetrators of these violations. Despite civil society's efforts to address the contested past in Lebanon, the limited education and awareness about past conflicts remains omnipresent.', see Mia Bou Khaled, *Contested History, Conflicting Narratives, and a Multitude of Initiatives: An Analysis of the Mapping of Initiatives Addressing Past Conflicts in Lebanon* (Civil Society Knowledge Centre; Lebanon Support, 2018) <https://civilsociety-centre.org/paper/contested-history-conflicting-narratives-and-multitude-initiatives-analysis-mapping> (accessed 14 December 2018).

Iraq, and Cyprus. This was Levantine postcolonial nationalism at its widest in scope. It was based on an ethno-historical account constructed for a vision of a postcolonial future. Now, that redrawn map is in essence the same one that the Syrian Ba'ath Party and ISIS used as they killed each other and everyone around them, all parties claiming to be against Western imperialism and the 1916 Sykes-Picot Agreement. The main difference was competing historical constructions.

While my understanding of sovereignty may be transnational, it is also postcolonial. This has only augmented my ambivalence. Let me quickly explain what I mean by a postcolonial sense of sovereignty by focusing on the 1955 Bandung Conference. On 18–24 April 1955, delegates from 29 states whose combined population made-up approximately two-thirds of the world attended the Asian-African Conference in Bandung, Indonesia. By this point, almost all countries in Asia had attained independence and African peoples were to follow suit soon after. The Spirit of Bandung described the pre-existing wave of emotion of confidence that swept across the world as an unprecedented number of peoples fought against vestiges of European imperialism. The Conference evidenced a belief that cultures, civilisations, and countries from all over the world, and not just Europe, had always played a historical role in the development of international law.

Arguably, the Bandung conference laid the political, economic, cultural, and legal foundations for our world today. At the core of the Final *Communiqué* was the claim that sovereignty amongst states was to be respected as a matter of mutual interest and territorial integrity. Sovereignty was built on the principle that states were to abstain from intervening or interfering in the internal affairs of another country.[24] By 1955, all (First, Second, and Third World) states acted as if their sovereignty was premised on a clear sense of domestic jurisdiction.[25]

In practice the line between international sovereignty and domestic jurisdiction changed depending on the political context.[26] Time has revealed that sovereignty did not prove to be the great emancipatory power that people expected. It did not have to be that way. The Spirit of Bandung describes the incredible feeling of confidence, power, and desire that swept across the world. But postcolonial leaders took the idea of sovereign power, and like Europeans, they crystallised it into the form of a unitary state.

The dreadful result was that the postcolonial state continued a lot of the oppressive practices of the former imperial overlords. Postcolonial states

[24] Final *Communiqué* of the Asian-African Conference of Bandung (24 April 1955), in *Asia-Africa Speaks from Bandung* (Djakarta: Ministry of Foreign Affairs Republic of Indonesia, 1955) 161.

[25] Sundhya Pahuja, 'Laws of Encounter: A Jurisdictional Account of International Law' (2013) 1 *London Review of International Law* 63.

[26] George M Abi-Saab, 'The Newly Independent States and the Scope of Domestic Jurisdiction' (1960) 54 *Proceedings of the American Society of International Law at Its Annual Meeting* 84.

often brutalise indigenous peoples sometimes to the same degree as settler states.[27] This way of concentrating power, organising it in bureaucratic hierarchy, of ruling over territory; the practice of disciplining people and excluding others; this preoccupation with economic development and market forces was and remains brutal not just in the Third World but as a universalised state practice in nearly all countries. It may be more accurate to describe our juridical global order today as Bandungian and not Westphalian.

That leaves those of us who are part of the Bandung tradition with very little to build on in international law. If I am not too careful in my scholarship, I might slip and end up supporting the likes of the murderous lot running governments or leading militant rebel groups.[28] I say this with Syria in mind since what happens in Syria has almost-immediate repercussions in Lebanon and vice versa. This is because the border between Lebanon and Syria has always been a matter of renegotiation. If you look at the early economic history of this border, you can see an important aspect of its postcolonial character and appreciate that since its inception this border has been in flux.[29]

What are now considered modern Arab states began as a result of the dissolution of the Ottoman Empire after World War I. The Arab regions that were all related to each other in complex ways through Ottoman power, were now a series of places carved up by Great Britain and France into a system of mandates and protectorates. The exceptions were Yemen and the territories that later became Saudi Arabia which achieved independence after World War I.

In the 1920s, separate custom unions and currencies arose in the post-Ottoman region. Syria (which at the time included Lebanon[30] and other territories) had its Syrian pound which was tied to the French franc and retained high tariff duties.[31] Palestine and Transjordan (as it then was) adopted the Palestinian pound which was tied to the British pound. The tariff rate was considerably lower than Syria's at the time.[32] Even after Transjordan attained

[27] Pooja Parmar, *Indigeneity and Legal Pluralism in India: Claims, Histories, Meanings* (Cambridge University Press, 2015); Luwam Dirar, 'Rethinking the Concept of Colonialism in Bandung and Its African Union Aftermath' in Luis Eslava, Michael Fakhri and Vasuki Nesiah (eds), *Bandung, Global History, and International Law* (Cambridge University Press, 2017).

[28] Others in international law need to be wary of inadvertently supporting imperial powers (admittedly, some relish their role as apologists).

[29] For a more contemporary, political historical account see Bassel Salloukh, 'Syria and Lebanon: A Brotherhood Transformed' (2005) *Middle East Report* 14. Of course, I could also describe the contingency of this border through family genealogy.

[30] The French formally carved out what is now Lebanon from the rest of Syria in 1926. Alfred G Musrey, *An Arab Common Market: A Study in Inter-Arab Trade Relations, 1920-67* (Praeger, 1969) 11. There are more recent economic studies and histories of the border and the region more broadly. But I point to this book because it was written from a perspective that is seeking postcolonial Arab economic integration at a time when there were significant political and military attempts to redraw the map of the region.

[31] The rate ranged from 15% to 30% with certain exceptions. This was later raised to 25–50% in 1926. Ibid. See also Charles Philip Issawi (ed), *The Fertile Crescent, 1800-1914: A Documentary Economic History* (Oxford University Press, 1988).

[32] Averaging around 12% with some exceptions. Musrey (n 30) 11.

independence from Great Britain in 1934, it maintained economic ties with Palestine. Iraq, which attained independence from Great Britain in 1922, adopted the Indian rupee with a tariff rate similar in range to Palestine and Transjordan. The Arabian Peninsula territories adopted the silver riyal in 1928; they imported very little and had a very low tariff rate.[33] France and Great Britain (the mandatory powers) and the League of Nations recognised the existence of economic ties between certain Arab territories and claimed to make provisions to continue these ties. What happened instead during the 1920s was that occupying and mandatory European masters structured Arab nations' economies in a way that ensured Europe was the economic hub and they were separate spokes.[34] Even though there were trade agreements and customs unions between the Arab nations during the 1920s and 1930s, by 1939 'the process of Arab economic disintegration was well advanced'.[35]

This was reversed during the time of World War II. In 1942 the Middle East Supply Centre was created as an Anglo-American agency intended to act as a regional planning agency within the international wartime framework (thereby also establishing the notion of the 'Middle East'). Even though intra-regional trade increased (although not significantly) during this time, what did result was a 'functional integration' amongst the Arab countries.[36] However, in the post-war 1950s—despite the creation of the Arab League in 1945—the Arab states were functioning as independent political and economic entities with respect to each other. In 1958, various political experiments, such as the United Arab Republic (combining Egypt and Syria) and the United Arab States (combining the UAR and Yemen) all ended quickly.[37]

This historical/geographical record combined with my personal history leads me to ask: is there anything then in international law's future that can create options for people that neither apologises for oppressive national governments nor concedes to messianic militant hyper-masculine gangs? This is not only the question in Syria and the region, but (as I mentioned above) one for Third World peoples all over the world.[38] Unfortunately, I have not, and nor have I seen, anyone come close to an answer. It is not just that the debate on the war in Syria has run into a dead-end,[39] but so has international law.

---

[33] Ibid.

[34] Ibid 11, 25.

[35] Ibid 28. The Maghreb countries were well integrated into the French, Spanish and Italian economies with very little trade with other Arab countries. Egypt, Iraq and Saudi Arabia created non-preferential trade policies that restricted inter-Arab trade. Yemen and Sudan were removed geographically, economically and politically from other Arab countries. Kuwait basically only had economic ties to Iraq. Transjordan, Syria and Lebanon held a tenuous free trade agreement.

[36] Ibid 31–35.

[37] Ibid 74–76.

[38] See Maja-Pearce (n 18).

[39] Bassam Haddad, 'The Debate Over Syria Has Reached a Dead End: Two Warring Narratives Now Dominate Discussions—And Neither is Sufficient' *The Nation* (New York, 18 October 2016) <www.thenation.

III. Indigenous sovereignty (looking to the Arctic)

A. Friendship, solidarity, and incommensurability

If imperialism is the continuous expansion of spatial power by a single authority, it is likely not something you can defeat. If you are cunning and lucky, imperialism is something you diminish or abate while it continues to adapt and transmutate. Therefore, to fight imperialism, the best tactic is to ensure that not only is your home safe from imperial power, but that so is your neighbour's. Because if her home gets enveloped, you are more vulnerable. That is why, my liberation is bound to my neighbour's and we have to work together to keep imperialism in all its pernicious and ever-changing forms at bay.[40]

Asking *who is my neighbour?* is not a geographical question but a political one based on interdependence and 'mutual interest' (to go back to the language of the Bandung Final *Communiqué*).[41] I take the statement from the Black-Palestinian Solidarity movement to heart: solidarity against imperialism and state-sanctioned violence is neither a guarantee nor a requirement —it is a choice.[42] This freedom to choose whom to live with, help, and befriend has in it the potential for liberation because in choosing our neighbour, for all the complicated almost-arbitrary reasons that we do, we create new worlds. Now, once we find each other, it is even harder to establish the terms and develop the practices through which we want to eat, share, work, and play together. The stakes are too high, however, not to seek each other out and be left to live alone or be defined by pre-existing relationships.[43]

Let me start, however, with Eve Tuck and K. Wayne Yang's call for an ethic of incommensurability.[44] To Tuck and Yang, too often indigenous struggles against settler colonialism is swept up within other struggles against imperialism or for social justice causes in the name of solidarity. The result is that the specificity of settler colonialism is lost, the indigenous fight for land is diluted amongst other causes, and differences are elided. Instead, they clarify that, '[s]olidarity is an uneasy, reserved, and unsettled matter' and

---

com/article/the-debate-over-syria-has-reached-a-dead-end/> (accessed 14 December 2018); Bassam Haddad, 'The Left, Imperialism, and Syria at KPFA' (*Jadaliyya*, 21 December 2016) <www.jadaliyya.com/Details/33866/Jadaliyya-Co-Editor-Bassam-Haddad-on-the-Left,-Imperialism,-and-Syria-at-KPFA> (accessed 14 December 2018).

40 I am paraphrasing from Aboriginal activist groups in Queensland in the 1970s. The quote is 'If you have come here to help me, you are wasting your time. But if you have come because your liberation is bound up with mine, then let us work together.' There is no official reference for this quote and has developed a genealogy of its own that starts with Aboriginal activist groups in Queensland in the 1970s.

41 See also David Cayley (ed.), *The Rivers North of the Future: The Testament of Ivan Illich as Told to David Cayley* (House of Anansi Press, 2005) 50–52.

42 Maja-Pearce (n 18).

43 Ayça Çubukçu, 'In Solidarity: Rethinking Political Friendship' (*Tanqueed*, 15 November 2016) <www.tanqeed.org/2016/11/in-solidarity-rethinking-political-friendship-ayca-cubukcu/> (accessed 14 December 2018).

44 Eve Tuck and K Wayne Yang, 'Decolonization Is Not a Metaphor' (2012) 1 *Decolonization: Indigeneity, Education & Society* 1.

that '[o]pportunities for solidarity lie in what is incommensurable rather than what is common across these efforts'.[45] This approach is a constant reminder that relationships of solidarity are delicate tactical alliances, yet they provide parties with strength and power.

As a migrant living in different parts of North America, on Turtle Island, I entered into and occupied indigenous land because of the privileges granted to me by colonial governments. As I write this, I live in Eugene, Oregon located in the Willamette Valley. This is the area of the Kalapuya tribes, and more specifically this is the land of people such as the Chifin, Winefelly, Pee-u (Mohawk), and Chelamela tribes. Today this is the home of the Confederated Tribes of Grand Ronde Community of Oregon, a confederation of over twenty-seven tribes and bands from western Oregon, southern Washington, and northern California. The confederation brings together the tribes that had been forcibly displaced by the US Federal Government from their homelands to the Grand Ronde reservation in 1855–1856.[46]

Until indigenous peoples can determine who can come in or out of their territory and on what conditions, my presence here is not only as a postcolonial migrant but also as a settler in a colonial system. That in and of itself is not a place of irreconcilability but it is the place of contingency. I accept the discomfort of the fact that to fight for decolonisation in the settler colony where I live, means that I have be to be prepared for a future where I will be subject to indigenous law, in whatever form and however defined. That authority may deny me entry or ask me to leave. Or indigenous hospitality will provide me with the conditions for which I can stay. As a migrant, I am always ready for that moment, so I do not consider it something to avoid.

What I can offer from a TWAIL perspective (or Bandungian tradition) to others struggling for liberation and equality is an idiom that understands international law as a way to both enhance and resist imperial ambition. From where we stand, international law is by definition an imperial conceit.[47] Put in other terms, TWAIL generates knowledge about how international law and institutions support different projects and practices of occupation and administration.[48]

---

[45] Ibid 28.

[46] David Lewis, 'Native Community History of Eugene Area' (*NDNHistory Research: Indigenous, Public & Critical Essays*, 11 April 2016) <https://ndnhistoryresearch.com/2016/04/11/native-community-history-of-eugene-area/> (accessed 14 December 2018).

[47] Nesiah (n 6); Anghie, *Imperialism, Sovereignty and the Making of International Law* (n 1); Pahuja (n 5); BS Chimni, 'Capitalism, Imperialism, and International Law in the Twenty-First Century' (2012) 14 Oregon Review of International Law 17; Christopher Gevers, 'International Criminal Law and Individualism: An African Perspective' in Christine EJ Schwöbel (ed), *Critical Approaches to International Criminal Law: An Introduction* (Routledge, 2014). My thanks to Sundhya Pahuja since I find her use of the word 'idiom' a helpful description of TWAIL.

[48] See eg Usha Natarajan, 'Creating and Recreating Iraq: Legacies of the Mandate System in Contemporary Understandings of Third World Sovereignty' (2011) 24 *Leiden Journal of International Law* 799; Ntina Tzouvala, 'Food for the Global Market: The Neoliberal Reconstruction of Agriculture in Occupied Iraq

TWAIL also provides a historical record of what not to do. One reason that many people experience the Third World project as a tragedy is because its demise was foreseeable and therefore theoretically avoidable. Fanon, a patron saint of anti-colonial struggles all over the world, wrote some of his most famous tracts at a time when the indigenous struggle in Algeria he fought for was shifting into a postcolonial project. He warned that soon after victory, the oppressed can easily become oppressors and people will 'find out that the iniquitous fact of exploitation can wear a black face, or an Arab one' in their own country.[49] History has shown that the people of the Third World already lost when postcolonial leaders all turned to state-building as the principal goal for liberation.

Thankfully, the historical relationship between anti-colonial indigenous struggles and postcolonial ones are not linear and indigenous struggles will not inevitably become postcolonial. Sometimes, the distinction between indigenous and postcolonial is historically arbitrary.[50] Today, anti-colonial and postcolonial struggles are operating in tandem, each with their own notions of time and space. Indigenous peoples have always been very active in international law, and their victories and defeats in international law ebb and flow as they do for everybody.[51] Indigeneity to some degree is defined by people struggling every day for their land, air, and water in real time with high existential stakes, the trauma more immediate. Postcoloniality and TWAIL operates more in the everyday of historical time, looking to the continuity and evolution of institutional projects and practices, with violence wrapped up more around access to state apparatuses.

B. Inuit sovereignty

TWAIL has much to learn from indigenous struggles.[52] Looking to indigenous experiences with international law's inherent imperial dynamics, I must

(2003–2004) and the Role of International Law' (2017) 17 *Global Jurist* 11; Kerry Rittich, 'Occupied Iraq: Imperial Convergences?' (2018) 31 *Leiden Journal of International Law* 479.

49 Frantz Fanon, *The Wretched of the Earth* (Richard Philcox tr, Grove Press, 2004) 94.

50 For eg the 1916 Sykes-Picot Agreement (combined with the 1917 Balfour Declaration) created a new international border between people in Lebanon and Palestine; this later made the Palestinian liberation struggle an indigenous action against settler colonialism, and the Lebanese project a postcolonial fight over the nature of the state. See Antony T Anghie, 'Introduction to Symposium on the Many Lives and Legacies of Sykes-Picot' (2016) 110 *AJIL Unbound* 105; Bâli (n 13); Victor Kattan, 'Palestine and the Secret Treaties' (2016) 110 *AJIL Unbound* 109; Umut Özsu, 'Sykes-Picot: The Treaty That Carved up the Middle East' (*OUPblog*, 9 May 2016) <https://blog-oup-com.libproxy.uoregon.edu/2016/05/sykes-picot-treaty-middle-east-international-law/> (accessed 19 December 2018).

51 S James Anaya, *Indigenous Peoples in International Law* (Oxford University Press, 2004); Lillian Aponte Miranda, 'Indigenous Peoples as International Lawmakers' (2014) 32 *University of Pennsylvania Journal of International Law* 61.

52 Gerardo Munarriz, 'Rhetoric and Reality: The World Bank Development Policies, Mining Corporations, and Indigenous Communities in Latin America' (2008) 10 *International Community Law Review* 431; Amar Bhatia, 'The South of the North: Building on Critical Approaches to International Law with Lessons from the Fourth World' (2012) 14 *Oregon Review of International Law* 131; Fernanda Cristina

first reconsider what terms I start with when I think about nations. In settler colonies, indigenous people's sovereignty is often negotiated through domestic or what one might call colonial laws. But if we assume these laws are the product of sovereign negotiation and contestation (again, the notorious colonial encounter), then we must also recognise them as inter-national.

This is why when I wanted to understand how Inuit communities were fighting the EU seal regime in the World Trade Organization (WTO) and EU courts, I had to also study Inuit struggles in Alaska through US federal and state law.[53] Seal hunting is central to Inuit self-understanding and is a practice that expresses sovereign power across the multiple borders that constitute the Arctic. At the time I thought I was comparing seal hunting laws in Alaska to the EU seal regime. I realise now, however, that my interpretive technique was transnational and not comparative. I did not compare the laws of different regimes to discern patterns of commonality and difference; rather I looked to the Inuit struggle as a singular act that traversed multiple legal regimes.[54]

To understand Inuit sovereignty, one good place to start is with the Inuit Circumpolar Conference (ICC). The ICC is a transnational organisation that represents approximately 155,000 Inuit. It comprises Inuit/Yupik peoples living in Alaska (United States), Canada, Greenland, and Chukotka (Russia). It was established in 1977 in Utqiaġvik (formerly known as Barrow), Alaska during a time when indigenous peoples throughout the Arctic were responding to resource development in the North American Arctic and Inuit in Greenland were pressing for greater autonomy (obtaining home rule in 1979).[55]

Twenty years later, when the Arctic Council was established the ICC was already a well-organised and a powerful Arctic authority framing a circumpolar world. The Arctic Council's original purpose was primarily to focus on

---

De Oliveira Franco, 'Oportunidades e desafios das TWAIL no contexto latino-americano a partir de perspectivas dos povos indígenas ao direito internacional [TWAIL's Opportunities and Challenges in the Latin American Context from Indigenous Peoples' Perspectives to International Law]' (2015) 12 *Brazilian Journal of International Law* 227 [with thanks to Erika Wozniak for translating from the Portuguese]. See also Sujith Xavier, 'Loving, Working, and Living on Stolen Land: People of Colour, Settler Colonialism & White Supremacy' (*reconciliationsyllabus*, 8 December 2018) (accessed 14 December 2018).

53 Michael Fakhri, 'Gauging US and EU Seal Regimes in the Arctic Against Inuit Sovereignty' in Nengye Liu, Elizabeth A Kirk and Tore Henriksen (eds), *The European Union and the Arctic* (Brill Nijhoff, 2017).

54 Not to say that comparative legal technique does not offer useful analytical tools for international law or indigenous struggles. Today, one can talk about comparative approaches to international law. See Boris N Mamlyuk and Ugo Mattei, 'Comparative International Law' (2011) 36 *Brooklyn Journal of International Law*; Robert J Miller, 'The International Law of Colonialism: A Comparative Analysis' (2011) 15 *Lewis & Clark Law Review* 847. I am also inspired by Robert A. Williams, Jr.'s course at the University of Arizona entitled 'Comparative Legal Systems & Their Role in Nation Building' Robert A Williams, Jr., 'Comparative Legal Systems & Their Role in Nation Building' (*University of Arizona Indigenous Governance Program*) <http://igp.arizona.edu/comparative-legal-systems-their-role-nation-building> (accessed 17 December 2018).

55 Jessica Shadian, 'Remaking Arctic Governance: The Construction of an Arctic Inuit Polity' (2006) 42 *Polar Record* 249; Gary N Wilson and Heather A Smith, 'The Inuit Circumpolar Council in an Era of Global and Local Change' (2011) 66 *International Journal* 909.

environmental protection and sustainable development issues, but it has become the principal forum for negotiating and constituting Arctic sovereignty and policy. It has eight Member Countries: Canada, Denmark (including Greenland and the Faroe Islands), Finland, Iceland, Norway, Russia, Sweden, and the United States. Six Arctic indigenous communities have Permanent Participant status: the ICC, Aleut International Association, Arctic Athabaskan Council, Gwich'in Council International, Russian Association of Indigenous Peoples of the North, and Saami Council. They are all supported by the Indigenous Peoples Secretariat.

While the Permanent Participants do not have voting power, they have the same procedural power as national governments, an equal 'seat at the negotiating table'. Moreover, Member States must consult Permanent Participants before the Arctic Council can do anything. This status was hard-won by indigenous leaders, making the Arctic Council a unique site of global governance.[56]

As the effects of climate of change continue to unfold and temperatures in the Arctic rise, the Arctic is increasingly becoming a 'global' issue. National governments all over the world are manoeuvring to gain access to emerging shipping routes and untapped sources of minerals, oil, and gas. One way non-Arctic governments buttress their position is by obtaining Observer Status in the Arctic Council. Observers have the right to attend Arctic Council meetings and observe council workings. They can only more actively participate at the discretion of Member States or Permanent Participants. To date, Observers include 13 non-Arctic States,[57] 13 intergovernmental and inter-parliamentary organisations,[58] and 13 non-governmental organisations (NGOs).[59]

Indigenous peoples still maintain privileged power and standing over all these governments and organisations as Permanent Participants, even as council membership grows. This leads to a very unique situation in international law and politics where in the Arctic Council, for example, the

[56] Leif Halonen, 'Full Interview' (*Indigenous Peoples Story Map project at GRID-Arendal*, 2017) <www.grida.no/resources/4879> (accessed 14 December 2018). The indigenous delegates were influential players in determining the constitution and Terms of Reference of Arctic Council.

[57] France, Germany, the Netherlands, Poland, Spain, United Kingdom, People's Republic of China, Italy, Japan, South Korea, Singapore, Switzerland, and India.

[58] International Council for the Exploration of the Sea, International Federation of Red Cross & Red Crescent Societies, International Union for the Conservation of Nature, Nordic Council of Ministers, Nordic Environment Finance Corporation, North Atlantic Marine Mammal Commission, OSPAR Commission, Standing Committee of the Parliamentarians of the Arctic Region, United Nations Economic Commission for Europe, United Nations Development Program, United Nations Environment Program, World Meteorological Organization, and the West Nordic Council.

[59] Advisory Committee on Protection of the Seas, Arctic Institute of North America, Association of World Reindeer Herders, Circumpolar Conservation Union, International Arctic Science Committee, International Arctic Social Sciences Association, International Union for Circumpolar Health, International Work Group for Indigenous Affairs, National Geographic Society, Northern Forum, Oceana, University of the Arctic, and World Wide Fund for Nature-Global Arctic Program.

Russian Association of Indigenous Peoples of the North has greater political standing than Germany or the People's Republic of China. There remains a disparity, however, because Permanent Participants have less resources to devote to Arctic Council politics than many of the Observers—but that is changing with the establishment of the Álgu Fund.

Even though indigenous peoples fought hard for the powers and privileges of Permanent Party status at the creation of the Arctic Council, this is a position they have had to preserve and defend. In 2007, Artur Chilingarov, as part of a Russian-led polar expedition, planted a titanium-supported Russian flag on the seabed four kilometres beneath the North Pole, declaring 'The Arctic has always been Russian'.[60] Not only was the act reminiscent of imperial explorations of the past, but the editorial and scholarly commentary that followed also mirrored the past. There was nervous talk about the political fallout by the Russian divers, a worry about a potential 'scramble for the Arctic' if governments were to compete to secure Arctic territory and riches.[61] Since such language was used ignorantly, this story of scramble made little reference to the indigenous communities that lived there.

National governments did rush to the north, but it was to a diplomatic meeting in Ilulissat, Greenland. The five Arctic Ocean coastal states—Canada, Denmark, Norway, Russia and USA—met to 'explain to the rest of the world that there was no scramble for resources going on in the Arctic, but rather an orderly development'.[62] The national governments produced the Ilulissat Declaration where they stated, 'By virtue of their sovereignty, sovereign rights and jurisdiction in large areas of the Arctic Ocean the five coastal states are in a unique position to address [the] possibilities and challenges [of climate change]'.[63]

Indigenous communities were mentioned but not invited to the summit. National governments did not have to invite indigenous leaders because this meeting was held outside the auspices of the Arctic Council. Instead, this declaration in effect asserted state authority over Arctic space, ecology, and its indigenous communities. It enveloped indigenous 'livelihood' into

---

[60] 'Frozen Conflict: Denmark Claims the North Pole' *The Economist* (London, 17 December 2014) <www.economist.com/international/2014/12/17/frozen-conflict> (accessed 14 December 2018).

[61] 'Scramble for the Arctic' *Financial Times* (London, 19 August 2007) <www.ft.com/content/65b9692c-4e6f-11dc-85e7-0000779fd2ac> (accessed 14 December 2018).

[62] Timo Koivurova, 'Redefining Sovereignty and Self-Determination through a Declaration of Sovereignty: The Inuit Way of Defining the Parameters for Future Arctic Governance' in Asbjørn Eide, Jakob Th Möller and Ineta Ziemele (eds), *Making Peoples Heard: Essays on Human Rights in Honour of Gudmundur Alfredsson* (Martinus Nijhoff Publishers, 2011) 494.

[63] Ilulissat Declaration adopted at the Arctic Ocean Conference (28 May 2008) <https://arcticportal.org/images/stories/pdf/Ilulissat-declaration.pdf> (accessed 14 December 2018). See also Jon Rahbek-Clemmensen and Gry Thomasen, *Learning from the Ilulissat Initiative: State Power, Institutional Legitimacy, and Governance in the Arctic Ocean 2007-18* (University of Copenhagen Centre for Military Studies, 2018) <https://cms.polsci.ku.dk/publikationer/learning-from-the-ilulissat-iniative/download/CMS_Rapport_2018__1_-_Learning_from_the_Ilulissat_initiative.pdf> (accessed 14 December 2018).

each state's domestic sphere thereby reasserting the states' role as territorial stewards.[64]

Inuit people were insulted and angered by the Ilulissat Declaration. They responded by producing what would prove to be an affirmation of sovereignty that used international legal doctrine to geographically reframe a political debate—*A Circumpolar Inuit Declaration on Sovereignty in the Arctic* (the 'Inuit Declaration').[65] The Inuit Declaration, in Part 1, took on the fact that the Ilulissat Declaration only referenced one type of law, which was the law of the sea. It challenged this narrow approach by first asserting their authority and jurisdiction with detailed terms.[66] The terms were respectively geographical, temporal, and political:

1.1. Inuit live in the Arctic

1.2. Inuit have been living in the Arctic from time immemorial

1.3. Inuit are a people

By asserting themselves as a people, the Inuit were claiming their position as a collective of rights-holders and not stakeholders, continuing the trend of recognising indigenous rights in the Arctic.[67]

Then the Inuit Declaration made several assertions, each of which respectively relied on international, regional, national, and local law. I list the headings which can be read as claims of sovereignty; I also provide a description of the authority used to support the assertion:

1.4. Inuit are an indigenous people

—referencing international legal treaties and instruments such as the 2007 UN Declaration on the Rights of Indigenous Peoples

1.5. Inuit are an indigenous people of the Arctic

—referencing their status as Permanent Participants of the Arctic Council

1.6. Inuit are citizens of Arctic states

—referencing national constitutions, laws, policies, and programmes

---

[64] Koivurova (n 62) 498. This is a classic colonial technique, see Usha Natarajan and Kishan Khoday, 'Locating Nature: Making and Unmaking International Law' (2014) 27 *Leiden Journal of International Law* 573; Mickelson (n 13).

[65] Inuit Circumpolar Council, A Circumpolar Inuit Declaration on Sovereignty in the Arctic (April 2009) <www.inuitcircumpolar.com/sovereignty-in-the-arctic.html> (accessed 14 December 2018).

[66] I only excerpt the headings and leave out the extensive arguments of the Inuit Declaration.

[67] Gail Fondahl, Viktoriya Filippova and Liza Mack, 'Indigenous Peoples in the New Arctic' in Birgitta Evengård, Joan Nymand Larsen and Øyvind Paasche (eds), *The New Arctic* (Springer International Publishing, 2015); Jessica M Shadian, 'Reimagining Political Space: The Limits of Arctic Indigenous Self-Determination in International Governance?' in Kathrin Keil and Sebastian Knecht (eds), *Governing Arctic Change* (Palgrave Macmillan UK, 2017) 54.

1.7. Inuit are indigenous citizens of Arctic states

—referencing national constitutions, laws, policies, and programmes

1.8. Inuit are indigenous citizens of each of the major political subunits of Arctic states (states, provinces, territories and regions)

—referencing local law

In this way, the Inuit Declaration embeds sovereignty within a multi-scalar mesh of authority, but without any necessary hierarchy amongst the different legal scales. This is not federal system in which one national authority trumps. Nor is it a clear delineation between international and domestic. This embeds national and local law into a complex geography of power in which there are overlapping sources of authority. This in effect counters the Ilulissat Declaration's reliance on national law as the sole defining authority *over* indigenous people and space. This allows the Inuit people to weave national and local law into their sovereign power while also asserting, 'These rights and responsibilities do not diminish the rights and responsibilities of Inuit as a people under international law' (paras. 1.6, 1.7, and 1.8).

The Inuit Declaration is not a demand to secede, which is what national governments fear the most when it comes to indigenous sovereignty claims.[68] Rather, as seen in Part 1, it is an intervention specific to the Arctic and the political conditions of the time. It presents the Inuit as a singular people with a unitary claim.

The Inuit not only used their declaration to respond to the Ilussiat Declaration but also to strengthen their position in ongoing struggles against, and negotiations with, colonial powers. Due to the fact that the Inuit people are spread across several states, the Inuit Declaration includes references to specific land claims and hunting rights within the legal regimes of the United States, Canada, Denmark/Greenland, and Russia (paras. 1.2, 1.3, 2.1, 2.2). What lies in the background are the various strategies different communities pursue within the colonial regimes of those states. For example, in Alaska, Inuit and other indigenous people pursue sovereignty as a demand for equal standing in negotiations with the governments of Alaska and the United States within the bounds of so-called Indian Law. Whereas Inuit in Greenland were and continue to be inspired by the Spirit of Bandung;[69] they obtained home rule in 1979, continue to expand their autonomy, and are having an active debate over whether or how they want to pursue full independence.[70]

[68] United Nations Declaration on the Rights of Indigenous Peoples, UNGA Res 61/295 (13 September 2007), Article 46.1.

[69] Inuk Silis Høegh, *Sumé: The Sound of a Revolution* (DR Sales, 2014).

[70] Hannes Gerhardt, 'The Inuit and Sovereignty: The Case of the Inuit Circumpolar Conference and Greenland' (2011) 14 *Politik* 6.

In these terms, the Inuit Declaration can be understood as a declaration of intra-Inuit solidarity as much as a stand against colonial power.

Even though Part 2 of the Declaration is entitled 'The Evolving Nature of Sovereignty in the Arctic', the opening sentence, unlike many of the other provisions, is in written in more universal terms:

> 'Sovereignty' is a term that has often been used to refer to the absolute and independent authority of a community or nation both internally and externally. Sovereignty is a contested concept, however, and does not have a fixed meaning. Old ideas of sovereignty are breaking down as different governance models, such as the European Union, evolve. Sovereignties overlap and are frequently divided within federations in creative ways to recognize the right of peoples.

To some, the Inuit Declaration may be a novel conception of sovereignty.[71] But the Inuit Declaration makes an empirical claim that sovereignty is a dynamic idea and frames itself as reflecting an existing reality of 'different governance models' (para. 2.1).

Old or new, the Declaration's universality lies in how it codifies an experience of sovereignty that traverses several boundaries. Most formal declarations of sovereignty demand the securing of some border or clarification of a line on a map.[72] This declaration is innovative because it challenges the assumption that sovereignty is something that is always determinatively settled. The Inuit people draw from the context of their 'long history of struggle to gain recognition and respect' (para. 2.1), to highlight the fact that sovereignty is a concept that people deploy in different ways when they argue over who gets to create the rules, practices, and institutions that govern territory.

I will conclude with a brief abstraction of the Inuit Declaration. To some, sovereignty is about the authority to rule over people and things within a particular territorial jurisdiction, that is established through military exercises, government outposts, flag planting, or regular scientific expeditions. This understanding does not capture the multiple ways that sovereignty is expressed and defined in practice. Sovereignty is pluralist and relational, involves the regular negotiation of authority and jurisdiction, and constitutes a complex relationship to land. Learning from the Inuit, we can take sovereignty as a historically contingent concept, but in which the understanding of time is inseparable from a physical, cultural, and spiritual experience of space.[73]

---

[71] Fiammetta Borgia and Paolo Vargiu, 'The Inuit Declaration on Sovereignty in the Arctic: Between the Right to Self-Determination and a New Concept of Sovereignty?' (2012) 4 *Yearbook of Polar Law* 189.

[72] See for eg Michael Byers, *International Law and the Arctic* (Cambridge University Press, 2013) 10–16, 235; David L VanderZwaag and Jonathan R Edge, 'Canada–Russia Relations in the Arctic: Conflictual Rhetoric, Cooperative Realities' in Suzanne Lalonde and Ted L McDorman (eds), *International Law and Politics of the Arctic Ocean* (Brill, 2015).

[73] For example some have argued that one way to understand the Arctic is through the relationship between people and seals, Nikolas Sellheim, 'The Right Not to Be Indigenous: Seal Utilization in Newfoundland' (2014) *Arctic Yearbook* 546; Fakhri (n 53).

IV. Food sovereignty

A. 'A movement of movements'

While TWAIL provides analytical tools to understand international law as an imperial project, its ambition to develop the tools to contest, resist, and redefine international law to assist those people fighting imperial power remains untested. It is still unclear whether TWAIL can serve people who want to build a new future. This is not because of any inherent limitations of TWAIL, but because of the uncertain role that law should play, or indeed what law will even mean, in the future.

Some in TWAIL are looking at the food sovereignty movement as an exemplary case of how one group has navigated those tensions around law in a way that has led to specific political gains. The focus so far has been treating the movement as a political success or inspiration.[74] My focus is more on how the movement has organised itself around a novel understanding of sovereignty in order to hold multiple interests together in solidarity. I also note how the movement has used legal tools but kept legalistic politics at bay.

A key element of the food sovereignty movement has been La Vía Campesina, one of the most dynamic and influential transnational peasant movements in its own right. La Vía Campesina comprises peasants, small and medium size farmers, landless people, rural women and youth, indigenous people, migrants and agricultural workers from around the world. Its members include 182 organisations spanning 81 countries and by their own count represent over 200 million people.[75]

It is through the International Planning Committee for Food Sovereignty (IPC), an autonomous organisation, that the food sovereignty movement primarily interacts with international institutions. The IPC 'facilitates dialogue and debate' and creates a space for discussion that is autonomous from 'political parties, institutions, governments and [the] private sector'.[76] Its members include transnational social movements (such as La Vía Campesina, the World Forum of Fishers People, and the World Alliance of Mobile Indigenous Peoples); regional organisations (such as: ROPPA, PROPAC, and Movimento Agro Ecologico Latino Americano); and NGOs that provide support (such as FIAN and Friends of the Earth International).[77] So while

---

[74] See eg Carmen Gonzalez, 'Climate Change, Food Security, and Agrobiodiversity: Toward a Just, Resilient, and Sustainable Food System' (2011) 22 *Fordham Environmental Law Review* 493; James Thuo Gathii, 'Food Sovereignty for Poor Countries in the Global Trading System' (2011) 57 *Loyola Law Review* 509; BS Chimni, 'Anti-Imperialism: Then and Now' in Luis Eslava, Michael Fakhri and Vasuki Nesiah (eds), *Bandung, Global History, and International Law* (Cambridge University Press, 2017).

[75] 'Who Are We?' (*La Vía Campesina*) <https://viacampesina.org/en/who-are-we/regions/> (accessed 14 December 2018).

[76] 'About Us' (*International Planning Committee for Food Sovereignty*) <www.foodsovereignty.org/about-us/> (accessed 14 December 2018).

[77] 'Structure and Organization' (*International Planning Committee for Food Sovereignty*) <www.foodsovereignty.org/about-us/structure-and-organization/> (accessed 14 December 2018).

La Vía Campesina took to the streets to protest against the WTO, the IPC provided support to its members who wanted to work with the Food and Agriculture Organization (FAO) to develop new programmes and policies.

In the 1990s, small-holder farmers and other small-scale food producers around the world were fed up with international economic institutions, disappointed with their national governments, and cynical when it came to development discourse. For fifty years, most national governments across the Third World were preoccupied with development. Regardless of their particular understanding of development, very few governments and advisors were committed to easing the life its food producers in a way that allowed them to continue their way of life. The emphasis was on industrialisation. Generally, the plan was to industrialise agriculture in order to reduce labour costs and then funnel that surplus labour to cities to work in or to serve the manufacturing sector.

During this time food producers in different countries organised themselves and protested against their governments in order to resist this plan. Then, small-holder farmers, other small-scale food producers, and indigenous peoples around the world, especially in South America and Mexico, began to organise themselves into transnational movements committed to opposing international economic institutions like NAFTA and the World Bank. By May 1993, the movement became global when La Vía Campesina was formed in Mons, Belgium.[78] Seven months later, this new movement marched in Geneva against the newly created WTO.[79]

It was in 1996, when La Vía Campesina attended the NGO Forum of the World Food Summit, that the concept of 'food sovereignty' was publicly announced. Much as how the Inuit used sovereignty to consolidate their own interests in international law and politics, La Vía Campesina successfully established 'unity through diversity' by devoting its first years (1993–1999) to internal consolidation amongst its members in order to work through their differences.[80] Also, like the Inuit Declaration, the food movement treats sovereignty as an ever-changing concept. Unlike the Inuit Declaration, the different articulations of food sovereignty more clearly display the defining tensions and paradoxes of the movement.[81]

---

78 La Vía Campesina, Mons Declaration (16 May 1993) <https://viacampesina.org/en/mons-declaration> (accessed 14 December 2018).

79 Annette Aurélie Desmarais, 'The Vía Campesina: Consolidating an International Peasant and Farm Movement' (2002) 29 *Journal of Peasant Studies* 91, 93.

80 Hannah Wittman, 'Food Sovereignty: A New Rights Framework for Food and Nature?' (2011) 2 *Environment and Society: Advances in Research* 87, 96–97; Annette Aurélie Desmarais, Marta G Rivera-Ferre and Beatriz Gasco, 'Building Alliances for Food Sovereignty: La Vía Campesina, NGOs, and Social Movements' in Douglas H Constance, Marie-Christine Renard and Marta G Rivera-Ferre (eds), *Research in Rural Sociology and Development*, vol 21 (Emerald Group Publishing Limited 2014) 92.

81 Raj Patel, 'What Does Food Sovereignty Look Like?' (2009) 36 *Journal of Peasant Studies* 663.

There are significant class tensions within La Vía Campesina amongst medium to rich farmers, subsistence farmers, and landless workers.[82] In everyday politics, pastoralists and land-owners of all classes often dispute over land.[83] In fact, La Vía Campesina is dominated by farmers' voices, and others—such as pastoralists, fisherfolk, landless agricultural workers, migrant workers, and forest dwellers—are less prominent.[84]

Gender equality is a central tenant to La Vía Campesina and influenced its internal governance structures. At first, all elected coordinators were men but due to feminist struggles within the movement, by 2000 the governance structures were amended to ensure that women and men were equally represented.[85] Nevertheless, much work remains to be done to use food sovereignty to transform food practices in households, farms, and fields in terms more equitable to women.[86] Indigenous communities have had their own histories and politics when it comes to the importance of food in struggles for sovereignty, have a different relationship with trade, and sometimes have often come into conflict with settler farmers.[87] There is also a wide-range of ideological tendencies that are independent from class identity and include: radical agrarian populists; different strands of Marxists, including Maoists; anarchists; feminists; and radical environmentalists.[88]

Despite these differences, members of La Vía Campesina used food sovereignty to consolidate their transnational peasant movement in complex and dynamic ways.[89] Starting in 1999, they also used the concept to expand their strategic alliances to NGOs and other movements.[90] The process has not been easy or linear, but it has proven to be key to the movement's institutional interventions. In 2002, in preparation for the World Food Summit:

---

[82] For a summary on these tensions see Marc Edelman and Saturnino M Borras, *Political Dynamics of Transnational Agrarian Movements* (Fernwood Publishing, 2016) 37–60.

[83] Maryam Rahmanian, 'Food sovereignty – A critical dialogue' (*TNI*, 21 February 2014) <www.tni.org/en/multimedia/maryam-rahmanian-food-sovereignty-critical-dialogue> (accessed 14 December 2018).

[84] Edelman and Borras (n 82) 45.

[85] Esther Vivas, 'La Via Campesina: Food Sovereignty and the Global Feminist Struggle' (*Pambazuka News*, 31 October 2012) <www.pambazuka.org/gender-minorities/la-campesina-food-sovereignty-and-global-feminist-struggle> (accessed 14 December 2018).

[86] Maggie Ellinger-Locke, 'Food Sovereignty Is a Gendered Issue' (2010) 18 *Buffalo Environmental Law Journal* 157; Rajeev C Patel, 'Food Sovereignty: Power, Gender, and the Right to Food' (2012) 9 *PLoS Medicine*; Bina Agarwal, 'Food Sovereignty, Food Security and Democratic Choice: Critical Contradictions, Difficult Conciliations' (2014) 41 *Journal of Peasant Studies* 1247; Clara Mi Young Park, Ben White and Julia, 'We Are Not All the Same: Taking Gender Seriously in Food Sovereignty Discourse' (2015) 36 *Third World Quarterly* 584.

[87] Sam Grey and Raj Patel, 'Food Sovereignty as Decolonization: Some Contributions from Indigenous Movements to Food System and Development Politics' (2015) 32 *Agriculture and Human Values*; Dordrecht 431; Kyle Whyte, 'Food Sovereignty, Justice and Indigenous Peoples: An Essay on Settler Colonialism and Collective Continuance' in Anne Barnhill, Mark Budolfson and Tyler Doggett (eds), *The Oxford Handbook of Food Ethics* (Oxford University Press, 2017).

[88] Edelman and Borras (n 82) 54.

[89] Annie Shattuck, Christina M Schiavoni and Zoe VanGelder, 'Translating the Politics of Food Sovereignty: Digging into Contradictions, Uncovering New Dimensions' (2015) 12 *Globalizations* 421.

[90] Desmarais, Rivera-Ferre and Gasco (n 80).

five years later, La Vía Campesina joined with others to create the IPC; this was the point at which one could talk about food sovereignty as a concept and movement that was something more than La Vía Campesina (but with the transnational peasant movement at its core).

The IPC has been a 'network of networks, movement of movements' on a grand scale.[91] It does not act as a singular institutional actor and is instead a decentralised network that coordinates members' actions in relationship to governments and international institutions. Since 2003, it has had a formal relationship with the FAO in four priority areas: the right to food, agro-ecological approaches to food production, local access to and control of natural resources, and agricultural trade and food sovereignty.[92]

The IPC and FAO agreed to 'establish common priority themes for a collaborative work in the fight against hunger and food insecurity'.[93] This signalled that the food sovereignty movement has some access to influence the language of decision-making around and within the FAO. Of course, there is always the danger that the FAO will use the enhanced legitimacy granted from working with influential social movements to define and implement the right to food and food sovereignty in ways that do not necessarily benefit the movement (ie 'co-optation').

Like many movements of this kind, and like TWAIL,[94] the IPC holds within it a tension between reformist and radical tendencies. Many in La Vía Campesina were wary of working within the UN system and reforming the FAO in particular; they worried that this would demand a significant amount of resources that could otherwise be committed to national or regional organisations or to more radical tactics, all without a clear sense of the benefits. While at the same time, many of the movement leaders also recognised that they could not cede the FAO to multinational agribusiness.[95] The IPC further complicated this dynamic since it included a fair number of reformist movements and NGOs who already were comfortable navigating the halls of international institutions.

Nevertheless, the IPC was the vehicle through which La Vía Campesina successfully achieved its slogan of 'globalizing hope and globalizing the struggle'.[96] In light of food sovereignty being taken up by an increasing number of groups, governments, and organisations, La Vía Campesina and

---

[91] Edelman and Borras (n 82) 68–70.

[92] Nora McKeon, *The United Nations and Civil Society: Legitimating Global Governance--Whose Voice?* (Zed Books, 2009) 101–03.

[93] Letter from Jose Graziano da Silva (Director-General of the FAO) to Members of the Facilitating Committee of IPC (23 May 2014) <www.foodsovereignty.org/the-ipc-and-fao-establish-common-priority-themes-for-a-collaborative-work-in-the-fight-against-hunger-and-food-insecurity/> (accessed 14 December 2018).

[94] Luis Eslava and Sundhya Pahuja, 'Between Resistance and Reform: TWAIL and the Universality of International Law' (2011) 3 *Trade, Law and Development* 103.

[95] McKeon (n 92) 104.

[96] Desmarais, Rivera-Ferre and Gasco (n 80) 101–07.

others turned to the IPC to ensure that the meaning and goals of food sovereignty were always a product of dialogue and debate, and was deeply understood by members of the movement. Along these lines, in 2007 the IPC Secretariat coordinated the International Nyéléni Forum for Food Sovereignty in Mali. The result was the most comprehensive definition of food sovereignty to date, the Nyéléni Declaration.[97]

The source of food sovereignty's authority has changed over the years. In 1996 in Rome, the movement defined food sovereignty as, 'the right of each nation to maintain and develop its own capacity to produce its basic foods respecting cultural and productive diversity'. The declaration focused on national constitutions and national territory.[98] This focus on national sovereignty was a continuation of Bandung as seen in older doctrines such as Permanent Sovereignty over Natural Resources and the right to development, in effect linking authority to the state's national territory.[99] This was different to how many people, especially indigenous people like the Inuit, understood sovereignty as a cultural, political, or ethnic concept with an unclear relationship with the state.[100]

Later, in 2002, with the advent of the IPC, the movement moved away from the singular 'nation' and defined food sovereignty in terms of 'peoples, communities, and countries', in effect pluralising food sovereignty's authority.[101] By 2007, the movement buried the state more into the background and simply focused on 'peoples' in the Nyéléni Declaration: 'Food sovereignty is the right of peoples to healthy and culturally appropriate food produced through ecologically sound and sustainable methods, and their right to define their own food and agriculture systems'.[102]

Some have criticised this all as incoherent and confusing.[103] Instead, as Patel has argued, the movement has proven that such a flexible organising concept is 'blowing apart the notion that the state has a paramount authority, by pointing to the multivalent hierarchies of power and control that exist within the world food system'. But while food sovereignty displaces the singular sovereignty of the state, it is does not put forward other particular notions of sovereignty.[104]

---

97 Declaration of Nyéléni, adopted at the Forum for Food Sovereignty (27 February 2007) <https://nyeleni.org/spip.php?article290> (accessed 14 December 2018).

98 La Vía Campesina, The Right to Produce and Access to Land. Food Sovereignty: A Future Without Hunger (11–17 November 1996) <www.acordinternational.org/silo/files/decfoodsov1996.pdf> (accessed 14 December 2018).

99 Julio Faundez, 'Between Bandung and Doha: International Economic Law and Developing Countries' in Luis Eslava, Michael Fakhri and Vasuki Nesiah (eds), *Bandung, Global History, and International Law* (Cambridge University Press, 2017).

100 Otto Hospes, 'Food Sovereignty: The Debate, the Deadlock, and a Suggested Detour' (2014) 31 *Agriculture and Human Values* 119, 122.

101 Ibid.

102 Declaration of Nyéléni (n 97).

103 Eg Marc Edelman, 'Food Sovereignty: Forgotten Genealogies and Future Regulatory Challenges' (2014) 41 *Journal of Peasant Studies* 959; Hospes (n 100).

104 Patel, 'What Does Food Sovereignty Look Like?' (n 81) 668.

Such an open concept allows for different elements of the movement to use food sovereignty and deploy it within their particular juridical contexts at whatever scale. For example, food sovereignty has been written into constitutions governing states, used in local law to challenge federal law, and deployed to change internal governance structures of international institutions without state endorsement.[105]

La Vía Campesina and its allies deploy food sovereignty to delegitimise food policies that feed people but have no regard for concentrations of political power. Their goal is to generate laws and policies that instead empower the large number of decentralised small-scale food producers. Many governments, international institutions, and experts frame hunger as a problem of distribution with a focus on access and commerce, whereas food sovereignty asks the question: who controls the systems of production and consumption?[106]

In these terms, the movement is trying to think of authority and territory in a way that grants small-scale and vulnerable food producers more control. But this is not a mapping exercise. The movement knows that they want a future where communities are defined by how they make and eat food; where people have the power to define themselves and therefore their food practices; a place where power and resources are distributed more equitably on a global scale. The appropriate verbal metaphor is not map-making but trailblazing. The path leading to their destination will be created through radical equality, dialogue, and direct participation of all members. The closer they get to a world of multiscalar and interconnected sovereignties the more they are able to look back and appreciate the path they marked.[107]

In less metaphorical terms, the food sovereignty movement has made some political gains at the global scale which provide the rest of us with a sense of how international institutions operate. The Rome-based institutions (FAO, IFAD, WFP) radically reformed the UN Committee for World Security (CFS) through the collective efforts of the G77 government leaders, the food sovereignty movement, and key international civil servants from within institutions. They pulled the CFS out of irrelevance and obscurity and established it as the most influential intergovernmental policy space on food security to come immediately out of the global food crisis that first hit in 2007.[108]

---

[105] Nadia CS Lambek and others (eds), *Rethinking Food Systems: Structural Challenges, New Strategies and the Law* (Springer, 2014).

[106] Raj Patel, 'Food Sovereignty' (2009) 36 *Journal of Peasant Studies* 663; Hannah Kay Wittman, Annette Aurelie Desmarais and Nettie Wiebe, 'The Origins & Potential of Food Sovereignty' in Hannah Wittman, Annette Aurelie Desmarais and Nettie Wiebe (eds), *Food Sovereignty: Reconnecting Food, Nature and Community* (Food First Books, 2010).

[107] Christina M Schiavoni, 'Competing Sovereignties, Contested Processes: Insights from the Venezuelan Food Sovereignty Experiment' (2015) 12 *Globalizations* 466.

[108] McKeon (n 92); Jessica Duncan, *Global Food Security Governance: Civil Society Engagement in the Reformed Committee on World Food Security* (Routledge, 2015); Josh Brem-Wilson, 'Towards Food

Recent studies describe the CFS as a place that hosts a 'discursive turf war' which allows for political give-and-take and not ideological posturing.[109] The consensus is that the CFS is, so far, a unique space that allows people directly affected by the issues in question to have direct influence in global policy coordination. It is inclusive in the sense that it is the result of trying to *recalibrate* power in more equitable terms, and not simply a matter of token civil society participation.

What also makes the new CFS unique is that the food sovereignty movement managed to carve out an autonomous space for themselves through the Civil Society Mechanism (CSM). The CSM is an open organisation with 'participating organisations' rather than formal 'members'. Any organisation that 'belongs to civil society and works on food security and nutrition can join and participate'.[110]

Recent studies outline the functions of the CSM and detail the internal formal and practical matrix of power and decision-making.[111] Two of the most unique features, evidence of the food sovereignty movement's influence, is that the CSM participants organise themselves. Moreover, social movements are granted privileged representation over NGOs.[112] Thus, much like indigenous Permanent Participants in the Arctic Council, the CSM has been the place where delegates who do not represent state governments convene and directly engage with the international institutional decision-making.

The CFS's main purpose is to act as a place to develop global policy and cohesion across international institutions and national governments. It derives its legitimacy in its ability to be accepted by all people, wealthy, poor or otherwise, whose lives are acutely and directly affected by global food markets.

Since 2010, the private sector (represented by the International Agri-Food Network) has been more actively involved in the CFS and is lobbying hard to have a number of seats at least equal to that of civil society organisations.[113]

Sovereignty: Interrogating Peasant Voice in the United Nations Committee on World Food Security' (2015) 42 *Journal of Peasant Studies* 73.

109 Duncan (n 108) 62.

110 'What is the CSM?' (*Civil Society Mechanism for the UN Committee on World Food Security*) <www.csm4cfs.org/the-csm/> (accessed 14 December 2018).

111 Duncan (n 108) 130–52; Ingeborg Gaarde, *Peasants Negotiating a Global Policy Space: La Vía Campesina in the Committee on World Food Security* (Routledge, 2017).

112 Civil Society Mechanism for the UN Committee on World Food Security, Terms of Reference for CSO members of the CFS Advisory Group (May 2017) <www.csm4cfs.org/wp-content/uploads/2016/03/Eng_Terms-of-Reference-for-Advisory-Group-Members-amended-May-2017.pdf> (accessed 14 December 2018).

113 CFS Evaluation Meeting, Implementation of the CFS Evaluation – Recommendation 4 (5 February 2018) Doc. No. CFSEvaluation/2018/02/05/04 <www.fao.org/fileadmin/templates/cfs/Docs1718/Evaluation/05Feb/CFS_Evaluation_2018_02_05_04_Outcomes%E2%80%8C.FINAL.pdf> (accessed 14 December 2018); CFS Bureau and Advisory Group Meeting, CFS Advisory Group 2018–2019 Composition Information Note (6 February 2017) Doc. No. CFS/Bur Ag/2017/02/06/05 <www.ipcinfo.org/fileadmin/user_upload/cfs/doclibrary/CFS_Bur_AG_2017_02_06_05_Advisory_Group_2018_2019_Info_note.

The private sector's interest reflects the growing influence and authority of the CFS. This increase in private sector involvement also puts the food sovereignty movement is in a delicate position: members of the movement wants to ensure that the CFS remains the principal site for global food security policy-making because it does not have the resources to influence governments working across a number of international institutions. The movement also wants to maintain the legitimacy of the CFS because the FAO, which houses the CFS, remains committed to civil society organisations and the food sovereignty movement. But if civil society organisations do not make the right compromises, the private sector or philanthropic organisations (mainly the Bill and Melinda Gates foundation) will withdraw from the institution thereby destabilising its legitimacy. If civil society organisations cede too much power, they lose what gains they made. As one La Vía Campesina member stated, '[at the CFS] we get to know both our enemies and ourselves better from the engagement'.[114]

Meanwhile, government leaders are trying to navigate amongst the different stakeholders. Ever since the anti-globalisation protests of the 1990s and food riots of the 2000s, they are acutely attuned to the fact that civil society organisations, especially the food sovereignty movement, can easily activate their network and confront politicians through mass demonstrations in home streets.[115]

If one is measuring degrees of ongoing influence within the CFS, then La Vía Campesina is correct in their claim that their work so far at the CFS has been a victory.[116] Through the CFS, the movement has significantly influenced global governance structures and policy. The result is that the CFS is a unique space that advances the right to food as a legal doctrine.[117] This means that the CFS reinforces the argument that the issue of ensuring people have adequate food, access to food, and control over their own food treated as a political necessity and not as a matter of charity or a method of exerting cruel pressure. This is an argument that remains important in light of ongoing geopolitics today in places like Gaza and Yemen.

pdf> (accessed 14 December 2018); CFS, Evaluation of Committee on World Food Security: Final Report (14 April 20) <www.fao.org/fileadmin/templates/cfs/Docs1617/Evaluation/CFS_Evaluation_Final_Report__14_April_2017.pdf> (accessed 14 December 2018).

[114] Quoted in Gaarde (n 111) 81.

[115] Brem-Wilson (n 108) 81; McKeon (n 92) 51–52.

[116] La Vía Campesina, *The Committee on World Food Security (CFS): A New Space for the Food Policies of the World, Opportunities and Limitations* (September 2012) La Vía Campesina Notebook No. 4 <https://viacampesina.org/en/the-committee-on-world-food-security-cfs-a-new-space-for-the-food-policies-of-the-world-opportunities-and-limitations/> (accessed 14 December 2018). See also Joe Wills, *Contesting World Order?: Socioeconomic Rights and Global Justice Movements* (Cambridge University Press, 2017) 94–150.

[117] Nadia Lambek, 'The Right to Food: Reflecting on the Past and Future Possibilities—Synthesis Paper' (2015) 2 *Canadian Food Studies / La Revue canadienne des études sur l'alimentation* 68.

But policy wins to any degree do not necessarily turn into redistribution of resources and reconfigurations of power, as required by the food sovereignty movement's broader agenda. The CFS is strictly a normative space with no authority over financial resources; the CFS is not able to provide funds or personnel towards implementing any of the global policies. This is left to institutions like the FAO, IFAD, WFP and national governments.

As Ibrahim Coulibaly, from Mali and a leader of a farmers' movement in West Africa summed up in 2011 at a CFS policy roundtable on food price volatility:

> Instead of responding to the causes of our poverty and of price volatility, we have seen whole catalogues of projects and programmes financed in the name of the agricultural sector, billions of dollars are mobilized every year, but the truth is that more than half of the peasant families in the majority of our countries do not have access to money to buy a plough, a couple of oxen, a cart, or a donkey.[118]

Even if projects were implemented under CFS policies, this alone does not ensure that food producers have access to more resources.

B. 'What do you want?'

The question I discussed earlier, *who are and where are you from?*, is often immediately followed with the other political question of desire and demand. In order to work through that question of *what do you want?*, I had to write and think about Inuit people and the food sovereignty movement in a style that does not speak for them. Like many in TWAIL, I want to decolonise international law leaving it open whether this would debilitate or resuscitate international legal practice. In fact, many in TWAIL are thinking through the relationship between their theoretical and practical work (or praxis, if you prefer) in international law.[119] Part of the reason I usually write in a theoretical and historical register is so that I am not misunderstood as writing on behalf of anyone. To me, writing from a Third World perspective is to stylise my experiences in a way that relates with others wrestling with similar questions of imperialism.[120]

---

118 Quoted in Jessica Duncan and David Barling, 'Renewal Through Participation in Global Food Security Governance: Implementing the International Food Security and Nutrition Civil Society Mechanism to the Committee on World Food Security' (2012) 19 *International Journal of the Sociology of Agriculture and Food* 143, 157.

119 This was the theme of the TWAIL conference in Cairo in 2015. Since then there have been several special journal issues on this question, see for example Sujith Xavier, Amar Bhatia, John Reynolds and Usha Natarajan (eds), *Conspiring in Cairo & Canada: Placing TWAIL Scholarship and Praxis* (2016) 33(3) *Windsor Yearbook of Access to Justice*; James Thuo Gathii, Henry J. Richardson and Karen Knop (eds.), 'Theorizing TWAIL Activism' (2016) 110 *AJIL Unbound*; Usha Natarajan, John Reynolds, Amar Bhatia and Sujith Xavier (eds), *On Praxis and the Intellectual* (2016) 37(11) *Third World Quarterly*.

120 TWAIL is an open movement that allows anyone to self-identify. That means everyone position themselves in their own way when writing from a Third World perspective.

For this article I have had to work out my ethical position in relation to writing about a movement that I am sympathetic to but not a part of. The stakes are especially high since the food sovereignty movement has spent a lot of political resources ensuring that no one speaks on their behalf. The food sovereignty movement comprises people who have the most to lose if they do not effectively ensure that national governments and international institutions establish a food regime that best serves members of the movement; the current food regime is not just a threat to the economic livelihood of people in the food sovereignty movement, but also to their sense of who they are and where they are from. In contrast, as a scholar I have more options available to me regarding what I decide to focus on and how to research.

The food sovereignty movement worked to protect the autonomy of their voice from the very beginning. At the 1996 World Food Summit in Rome, when La Vía Campesina participated in its first international conference they attended the official NGO forum.[121] At this forum, Southern organisations confronted Northern NGOs for acting as gatekeepers to international organisations. More specifically, many Northern (urban) NGOs assumed peasant groups were not 'capable and articulate' enough to represent their own interests.[122] Also at the forum, groups like La Vía Campesina wanted to sharpen the distinction between people's organisations/social movements established by and representing particular groups versus NGOs who do not represent the population they serve or are accountable to them.

Starting in 1999, La Vía Campesina expanded their strategic alliances to academics, NGOs, and other movements through the IPC.[123] IPC processes ensure that peasants drive the dialogue around the meaning of food sovereignty and the political agenda. The food sovereignty movement has successfully reproduced this practice within institutional processes; as discussed above, you see this in relation to how social movements ensured that they would have more power than NGOs within the CFS through the CSM.

The academics that have been the most active in examining and spreading the idea of food sovereignty have been participant-observers and activist-academics. They are sometimes associated with local, regional, or global NGOs that support the IPC.[124] Many also come from the field of critical agrarian studies, and publish their work on food sovereignty mostly in the *Journal of Peasant Studies*. The jurists involved tend to have a direct relationship with the office of the Special Rapporteur on the Right to Food.

[121] Nora McKeon, 'Who Speaks for Peasants? Civil Society, Social Movements and the Global Governance of Food and Agriculture' (2009) 1 *Interface* 48.

[122] Desmarais (n 79) 103.

[123] Desmarais, Rivera-Ferre and Gasco (n 80).

[124] Global NGOs include FIAN, Friends of the Earth International, Centro Internazionale Crocevia, and the International Collective in Support of Fishworkers. See 'About Us' (*International Planning Committee for Food Sovereignty*) <www.foodsovereignty.org/about-us/> (accessed 14 December 2018).

Academics that embed themselves in such a way, drawing on sociological and anthropological methodologies, have to create a direct relationship with the movement in order to gain access to privileged knowledge.[125] This means that not only do they have to abide by standard ethical rules that come with qualitative research, but they also have to maintain individual members' trust so that they do not lose access to the movement. At the same time, the academic/scholar benefits from this privileged information since it becomes a significant part of their research; they use it to meet certain professional standards and buttress their own professional standing. Embedded academics often gain entry by positioning themselves as an ally to the movement, but also maintain some critical distance to ensure scholarly independence. They therefore need to secure their own political integrity and not publish their findings in a way that makes them an informant. If such an academic is working in good faith, there is no clear reconciliation between these different demands and each person finds their own way of navigating the fact that they are held accountable by the movement, their profession, and themselves.

In this article I am not drawing from any privileged position as a scholar in the food sovereignty movement. I take the position of the international jurist, writing with the food sovereignty movement and about international law. I do have similar competing demands as the embedded academic, but the movement that holds me accountable is TWAIL. My principal worry then is ensuring that I do not find myself becoming a native Third World informant in the field of international law.

From this perspective, the normative value of the food sovereignty struggles, as for all international jurists learning from social movements, will not be found in determining whether they succeed or fail. The jurist's task is to closely follow people's understanding of law collectively expressed as they traverse transnational institutions. People in these struggles are often clever and nimble. As they navigate the existing institutional landscape they are constantly changing their legal and political tactics. I take it that only through those high-stakes experiences will we be able to appreciate the possibilities and limits of contemporary law.[126]

I make this stark contrast between embedded academic and academic jurist in order to highlight the different ethical positions. Of course, academics occupy different positions depending on the piece of writing and attend to the appropriate ethical demands. Each position also lends itself to a particular style: the embedded scholar is well suited to focus on the tension between

[125] In this article I out leave the aspect of some people's work that depends on international institutional patronage for their research. See for eg Deval Desai and Mareike Schomerus, '"There Was A Third Man ... ": Tales from a Global Policy Consultation on Indicators for the Sustainable Development Goals' 49 *Development and Change* 89, 92. I discuss this in 'The International Political Economy of the Right to Food' in Nehal Bhuta (ed), *Human Rights and Global Governance* (Oxford University Press, 2019).

[126] Amy J Cohen, 'The Law and Political Economy of Contemporary Food: Some Reflections on the Local and the Small' (2015) 78 *Law and Contemporary Problems* 101.

social movements and institutions; the jurist is adept at parsing the multiple stakes of the doctrinal debates and describing the inter-institutional landscape in historical terms (in this case, the food regime). Since both people and ideas matter, such a distinction is also only a heuristic to understand where a piece of work lies in between these two points.[127]

From my position, I meet the food sovereignty movement in two ways. First, I take the fact that they articulate their interests and demands in the language of international law and in the idiom of TWAIL. This allows me to look to things like the Nyéléni Declaration as a global communal articulation of sovereignty that warrants consideration and study as a core dynamic in international legal practice today. To ignore such a declaration and fall back on state-centric perspectives would be a disservice to the movement. Second, this article was only made possible because this journal and the editors of this special issue brought together a certain group of people. This created a unique and exhilarating space of interface between the embedded academic and the academic jurist (among us and within us). I imagined this article to be situated within the dynamics of that specific space with its dialogues, disagreements, friendships, and political commitments. My work, as you can see in the footnotes, depends on the work of embedded academics. I, therefore, also hold myself accountable to them.

V. Conclusion

The Spirit of Bandung was a name to a phenomenon that preceded the Asian-African Conference held in Bandung on 1955. The conference was an attempt by world leaders to harness and shape the wide-spread feeling of liberation and hope that swept across the world and to define sovereignty as a matter of mutual dependence. To be sure, the sentiment was not limited to the peoples of Africa and Asia, for example inspiring Inuit people in Greenland and Black people in the United States.[128] Part of its inspiration was from the liberation movements of Latin America in the early nineteenth century.[129] The Spirit of Bandung is the name of

---

[127] An example of work that exquisitely does both—while also placing indigenous perspectives at its core —is Parmar (n 27).

[128] Malcolm X, 'Message to the Grass Roots. November 10, 1963, Detroit' in George Breitman (ed), *Malcolm X Speaks: Selected Speeches and Statements* (Grove Press, 1965) 3; Mohammed Alnaiem, 'The African Roots of MLK's Vision' (*JSTOR Daily*, 14 February 2018) <https://daily.jstor.org/the-african-roots-of-mlks-vision/> (accessed 14 December 2018).

[129] The histories of national liberation and postcolonial state-building in Latin America, of course, has its own set of dynamics. See Liliana Obregón, 'Between Civilisation and Barbarism: Creole Interventions in International Law' (2006) 27 *Third World Quarterly* 815; Jorge L Esquirol, 'Alejandro Álvarez's Latin American Law: A Question of Identity' (2006) 19 *Leiden Journal of International Law* 931; Arnulf Becker Lorca, *Mestizo International Law: A Global Intellectual History 1842-1933* (Cambridge University Press, 2014); Fabia Fernandes Carvalho Veçoso, 'Bandung in the Shadow: The Brazilian Experience' in Luis Eslava, Michael Fakhri and Vasuki Nesiah (eds), *Bandung, Global History, and International Law* (Cambridge University Press, 2017).

something that was a cultural and aesthetic phenomenon as much as it was political.[130]

That spirit has been harnessed, disciplined, and crystallised into state practice.[131] Although in the past I was suspicious of sovereignty, I am now more agnostic on the question of whether sovereignty can be constructed and deployed in a way that fundamentally transforms and neutralises imperial authority today. Indigenous struggles and the food sovereignty movements' campaigns may help us undo or at least loosen existing political forms and release that spirit again. They have taught us how sovereignty is a way to claim lawful authority in order to both consolidate solidarity and engage with rivals. This practice of sovereignty has proven to be transnational—or to be more accurate transjurisdictional—across multiple forms and scales of territory.

I was only able to learn from these other movements by situating myself as a postcolonial migrant. The stakes of elevating a migrant perspective is becoming more acute every day. Current understandings of sovereignty treat the movement of people as the exception, and blocking people at a border with armed force or physical walls as the rule. This has produced deadly results. For example, waterways such as the Mediterranean Sea are being turned into a 'collective graveyards' amassing the corpses of migrants who had left their homes at a moment of desperation.[132] Universalising a migrant perspective reflects, as a historical matter and urgent issue, an understanding of sovereignty that starts with the transnational movement of people as the norm.

That method of reframing the exception as the rule is a classic technique. In fact, all the techniques in this article—provincialising Europe, universalising the particular, foregrounding my positionality—are prevalent in international legal thought today. I used them here in novel ways: in some regard I reframe migration as the rule, but then when I imagine that identity as a guest in indigenous land, I reconfigure the migrant as an exception.

I provincialise the Global North by placing it in the periphery of my analysis. In a reflexive move, I also decentralise Bandung and put it in

130 Vik Kanwar, 'Not a Place, but a Project: Bandung, TWAIL, and the Aesthetics of Thirdness' in Luis Eslava, Michael Fakhri and Vasuki Nesiah (eds), *Bandung, Global History, and International Law* (Cambridge University Press, 2017).

131 Antony Anghie, 'Bandung and the Origins of Third World Sovereignty' in Luis Eslava, Michael Fakhri and Vasuki Nesiah (eds), *Bandung, Global History, and International Law* (Cambridge University Press, 2017). For the Arab world this started in the late nineteenth century, see Saree Makdisi, '"Post-colonial" Literature in a Neocolonial World: Modern Arabic Culture and the End of Modernity' (1995) 22 *boundary 2* 85.

132 Samera Esmeir, 'Bandung: Reflections on the Sea, the World, and Colonialism' in Luis Eslava, Michael Fakhri and Vasuki Nesiah (eds), *Bandung, Global History, and International Law* (Cambridge University Press, 2017) 93.

the semi-periphery, leaving the Arctic and food sovereignty movement as the centre. In doing so, I am arguing that it may be helpful to displace the Final *Communiqué* of Bandung as one cornerstone of postcolonial sovereignty, and replace it with something that is directly inspired by the Inuit Declaration and Nyéléni Declaration. In temporal terms, I want to live in world where the Peace of Westphalia is prehistoric, the Bandung Final *Communiqué* is the past, and the Inuit and Nyéléni declarations are the future.

In articulating my positionality, it is not in relation to my subject of study. My subjectivity is presented in the spirit of solidarity and is in relation to potential allies. I started this article explaining how dangerous it is when you have to answer the question, 'Who are you and where are you from?' I nevertheless proceeded to do so but not as an answer to an authority figure, but as an offering to people whom I want to invite into my political life. It is intended to provide a descriptive entry point for others who may want to meet my comrades and me.

When I universalise a particular, I redirect this technique's energy so that it is not a critique of international legal doctrine. I instead use it as an argument to international jurists that we should imagine the world in the multitude of ways that people in these struggles do, as articulated in the Inuit and Nyéléni declarations.

As imperial practices change, so must the techniques to counter them. I have used these classic techniques in oblique ways in an effort to think of them anew in contemporary contexts. At this moment of time, it may be that these techniques have lost their critical edge even when used in unorthodox ways. In the least, they are an alternative to mapping and might provide enough of an analytical sharpness that can cut through the current institutional landscape. The Inuit technique of geographical reframing through international doctrine and institutions is innovative, sophisticated, and potentially something others can try. The food sovereignty movement highlights that power stems from social organising and change will not come from theoretical elegance. This is a lesson that is still not deeply encoded in international legal thought. What these struggles confirm is that any understanding of change in international law must address the question of solidarity as a central practical and theoretical concern.

Change in international law, however, still does not guarantee a better future for anyone. What the Third World experience teaches everyone is that international law is by definition generated by expanding or resisting imperialism. At its best, international law can only create the spaces that make way for new technologies acutely aware of imperialism, but not defined by it.

Acknowledgements

I am very grateful to Emily Webster for her editorial guidance and great patience.

Disclosure statement

No potential conflict of interest was reported by the author.

The effects of oil pollution on the marine environment in the Gulf of Guinea—the Bonga Oil Field example

Ifesinachi Okafor-Yarwood

ABSTRACT

Fish makes a significant contribution to the food security of millions of people in the Gulf of Guinea, accounting for up to 80 per cent of the animal protein, and sometimes the only source of animal protein consumed in coastal communities across the region, including those in the Niger Delta area of Nigeria. However, this contribution is increasingly undermined by unsustainable practices that are harmful to the marine environment such as pollution, illegal, unreported and unregulated (IUU) fishing, and by climate change. This paper focuses on the role that pollution from oil spillages plays in damaging the marine environment, thereby exacerbating food insecurity in the region. Using the Bonga Oil Field spillage example, the paper exposes, from a policy perspective, the manner in which the shortcomings of existing environmental regulations and their implementation in Nigeria weaken efforts for a sustainable marine environment and, by extension, threaten the food security of coastal communities.

1. Introduction

Fisheries contribute to enhancing food security either by acting directly as a source of essential nutrients or as a source of income for coastal communities who mostly depend on the resource for subsistence.[1] They serve as a source, and sometimes the only source of animal protein for many living in coastal communities in West and Central Africa—which make up the Gulf of Guinea defined here, in the broad sense, as the coastal states stretching from Senegal to Angola.[2] Fisheries also play a significant role in food security

[1] Serge M Garcia, 'World Inventory of Fisheries. Contribution of Fisheries to Food Security. Issues Fact Sheets' (Rome, 2005). All websites accessed on 16 December 2018.

[2] See Ifesinachi Okafor-Yarwood, 'The Guinea-Bissau–Senegal Maritime Boundary Dispute' (2015) 61 *Marine Policy* 284, online: https://doi.org/10.1016/j.marpol.2015.08.008, 285; Ifesinachi Okafor-Yarwood, 'Illegal, Unreported and Unregulated Fishing, and the Complexities of the Sustainable

by augmenting food supply and consumption in times of scarcity and by generating income for the purchase of food.[3] For 40 per cent of the West African population who live in the coastal areas, the fisheries sector plays a significant role in their food and economic security, employing an estimated nine million people in the region alone.[4] However, these contributions are existentially threatened by the impact of climate change, pollution and unsustainable fishing practices that undermine the marine environment.[5]

The sustainability of the marine environment and the resources that lie beneath it have been undermined by the global rise in sea levels, which has resulted in a significant increase in the ocean's uptake of CO_2; the release of toxic wastes into the ocean; and, further to this, unsustainable practices such as illegal, unreported and unregulated (IUU) fishing.[6] These issues make the potential for food insecurity a high risk for coastal communities across the Gulf of Guinea. Specifically, climate change has been implicated as undermining the marine environment and leading to a depletion in fisheries resources.[7] According to the World Bank, by 2050 climate change will contribute to the reduction of fisheries resources by up to 53 per cent in Nigeria, 56 per cent in the Ivory Coast and 60 per cent in Ghana.[8] Also implicated in exacerbating the decline of marine resources is the impact of overfishing and criminal activities such as IUU fishing.[9] So prevalent is the threat in the region that it amounts to an estimated 65 per cent of the legal

Development Goals (SDGs) for Countries in the Gulf of Guinea' (2019) 99 *Marine Policy* 414, online: <https://doi.org/10.1016/j.marpol.2017.09.016>.

3 Serge M Garcia and Andrew A Rosenberg, 'Food Security and Marine Capture Fisheries: Characteristics, Trends, Drivers and Future Perspectives' (2010) 365, (1554) *Philosophical Transactions of the Royal Society* 2869.

4 Okafor-Yarwood (n 2).

5 Robert E Katikiro and Edison D Macusi, 'Impacts of Climate Change on West African Fisheries and Its Implications on Food Production' (2012) 15(2) *Journal of Environmental Science and Management* 83; UNEP, 'Environmental Assessment of Ogoniland' (2011), online: https://doi.org/10.3370/lca.2.73; Lawrence Etim, Dyhia Belhabib, and Daniel Pauly, 'An Overview of the Nigerian Marine Fisheries and a Re-Evaluation of Its Catch Data for the Years 1950 to 2010' in Dyhia Belhabib and Daniel Pauly (eds), *Fisheries Catch Reconstructions: West Africa, Part II. Fisheries Centre Research Reports Vol.23(3)* (Vancouver: Fisheries Centre, University of British Columbia, 2015), 66–76.

6 I Okafor-Yarwood, 'Nigeria's Depleting Fish Stocks May Pose a Threat to Regional Security' (2018), The Conversation, online: https://theconversation.com/nigerias-depleting-fish-stocks-may-pose-a-threat-to-regional-security-105168.

7 Vickie WY Lam et al., 'Climate Change Impacts on Fisheries in West Africa: Implications for Economic, Food and Nutritional Security' (2012) 43 *African Journal of Marine Science* 103; Edward H Allison et al., 'Vulnerability of National Economies to the Impacts of Climate Change on Fisheries' (2009) 10(2) *Fish and Fisheries* 173, online: https://doi.org/10.1111/j.1467-2979.2008.00310.x.

8 Magda Lovei, 'Climate Impacts on African Fisheries: The Imperative to Understand and Act' (2017) The World Bank Blog, online: http://blogs.worldbank.org/nasikiliza/climate-impacts-on-african-fisheries-the-imperative-to-understand-and-act.

9 Alkaly Doumbouya et al., 'Assessing the Effectiveness of Monitoring Control and Surveillance of Illegal Fishing: The Case of West Africa' (2017) 4 *Frontiers in Marine Science*, online: https://doi.org/10.3389/fmars.2017.00050; Lawrence Etim, Dyhia Belhabib, and Daniel Pauly, 'An Overview of the Nigerian Marine Fisheries and a Re-Evaluation of Its Catch Data for the Years 1950 to 2010' in Dyhia Belhabib and Daniel Pauly (eds), *Fisheries Catch Reconstructions: West Africa, Part II. Fisheries Centre Research Reports Vol.23(3)* (Vancouver: Fisheries Centre, University of British Columbia, 2015), 66–76.

catch, with Nigeria losing about $29 million per annum to illegal shrimping alone.[10] Likewise, a great deal has been written about the impact of pollution by multinational oil companies and their role in damaging the marine environment in the Niger Delta area and by extension the rest of the Gulf of Guinea.[11]

It has been argued that the role of pollution in adversely affecting the ocean's resources is limited when compared to the impact of overfishing. Espousing this view, Till notes that the crisis in fish supply is largely due to unsustainable fishing—overfishing and IUU fishing—and not pollution.[12] Whereas this paper recognises that overfishing and IUU fishing contribute to the decline in fisheries resources, it will focus on the role of pollution resulting from oil spillages by multinational oil companies operating in Nigeria. It does so by using the Bonga Oil Field spillage of 2011 as a case study. Emphasis on the Bonga Oil Field incident is crucial because little has been written regarding its effect on fisheries and the many people living in the affected communities who depend on fish for subsistence. The Niger Delta is usually described as ecologically diverse, its mangroves serving as a breeding ground for different species of fish in the Gulf of Guinea.[13] This makes it a useful case study for understanding the long-term food security implications of the decline in fisheries resulting from pollution.

This paper employs qualitative research methods, such as primary interviews with the Coordinating Chairman of the Akwa-Ibom State, who is also the Acting Chairman of the Niger Delta Artisan Fishers Association of Nigeria (ARFAN) and the President of the Bonny Island Fishers Association, Bonny Local Government Area in Rivers State, as well as focus group discussions with fisher folks from the Island. In response to the empirical research, this paper argues that multinational oil companies continue to undermine the environment in which they operate not least as the existing regulations on petroleum exploration, and the obligations that they impose upon these multinationals in relation to the ecosystems under threat, are not robustly

---

[10] Okafor-Yarwood (n 2).

[11] Kevin Nengia, 'Pollution:Bonny Communities, Group Lament Illegal Bunkering' (2013) *The Tide*, online: http://www.thetidenewsonline.com/2013/12/04/pollutionbonny-communities-group-lament-illegal-bunkering/; Patience Ivie Ihejirika, 'Niger Delta Oil Pollution Has Badly Affected Agriculture, Fishing' (2016) *Leadership*, online: http://leadership.ng/news/534056/niger-delta-oil-pollution-badly-affected-agriculture-fishing; Emma Amaize, 'Pollution Forces N-Delta Fishermen, Farmers to Abandon Occupation' (2016) Vanguard Nigeria, online: https://www.vanguardngr.com/2016/09/pollution-forces-n-delta-fishermen-farmers-abandon-occupation/; Adati A Kafada, 'Environmental Impacts of Oil Exploration and Exploitation in the Niger Delta of Nigeria' (2012) 12(3) *Global Journal of Science Frontier Research Environment & Earth Science* 18.

[12] Geoffrey Till, Sea Power - a Guide for the Twenty Fisrt Century, 3rd ed. (London & New York: Routledge, 2013) 285.

[13] Olanike Kudirat Adeyemo, Oniovosa Eloho Ubiogoro, and Olufemi Bolarinwa, 'Oil Exploitation, Fisheries Resources and Sustainable Livelihood in the Niger Delta, Nigeria' (2009) 24(1) *Nature & Faune* 56.

implemented.[14] Section two sets the scene, using the Bonga Oil Field example to emphasise the food security implications of oil spillages on coastal communities in the Niger Delta region. This is followed by a review of selected environmental legislations and/or guidelines and the role of agencies in Nigeria such as the Federal Environmental Protection Agency (FEPA), the National Oil Spill Detection and Response Agency (NOSDRA), the National Environmental Standards and Regulation Enforcement Agency (NESREA) and Environmental Guidelines and Standards for the Petroleum Industry in Nigeria (EGASPIN). Although there are others,[15] investigating the aforementioned provides sufficient concrete examples of the failures of existing regulations and agencies charged with the responsibility of ensuring a sustainable environment in Nigeria. The paper concludes with a brief discussion on the imperative of enacting amendments to further strengthen existing regulations and either establishing a new independent agency or enable an existing one to oversee a robust response to incidences of oil spillages.

2. Pollution and food insecurity—The Bonga Oil Field spillage example

Fisheries contribute to the food security of communities in the Niger Delta, by serving as sources of income for many of the people living in the region. In some communities such as those in Bonny Local Government Area in Rivers State, around 70 per cent of the population depends on fish for their livelihood.[16] For many women living in the region, fish also provides an opportunity for them to earn a living as fisherwomen or fishmongers.[17] However, the continued contribution of fish as a central food security resource is threatened by pollution in the form of oil spillages from the multinational oil companies operating in the area.

The food security implications of reduced catch have a devastating impact on the fisher folks who depend on fish for subsistence. According to Vreÿ, one cause of this is oil pollution which aggravates the threat to the marine environment, and thus undermines its contribution as a source of

[14] The interviews and focus groups were conducted between December 2015 and June 2017 as part of the author's PhD thesis data collection.

[15] See Eghosa Osa Ekhator, 'Environmental Protection in the Oil and Gas Industry in Nigeria: The Roles of Governmental Agencies' (2013) 5 *International Energy Law Review* 196; C Cragg, J Hurst-Croft, and I Samiama, 'Pollution Control in the Global Oil Industry in Relation to Reform in Nigeria' (2011), online: http://www.stakeholderdemocracy.org/wp-content/uploads/2016/06/Environmental-Regulation-and-Pollution.pdf.

[16] Dick Wittenberg, 'Oil, Gas and Mining: The Bonny Island LNG Project: In Bonny It Never Becomes Night Anymore' (2004) ECA Watch, online: http://www.eca-watch.org/problems/oil_gas_mining/bonnyisland/BonnyIsland130704.html.

[17] Tendai Marima, 'There's an Invisible Cost to Nigeria's Oil Spill Disasters' (2016), Quartz Media, online: https://qz.com/859201/theres-an-invisible-cost-to-nigerias-oil-spill-disasters/; Ibim Adaba Tonye and Amiye Francis, 'Women and Post Harvest Fish Production in the Niger Delta Area' (2014) 7(3) *Journal of Agriculture and Veterinary Science* 78.

food.[18] The Niger Delta region is one area that, over the years, has experienced severe pollution resulting from oil spillages. Specifically, since the exploitation of oil started in 1958, an estimated 13 million barrels of oil have been spilled in more than 10,000 incidents in the region.[19] The multinational oil companies that operate in the area are of the view that most of these spillages are due to sabotage and/or vandalisation of the pipelines.[20] Whilst the role of sabotage in the many incidences of oil spillages in the Niger Delta cannot be denied, the reality, however, is that some of the pipelines used by the oil companies are dilapidated, with a considerable amount of the oil spillages due to the corrosion of aging facilities.[21] The resulting effects of such pollution not only undermine the coastal environment, but they also increase human suffering especially for the communities affected. This is because those that rely on fisheries for subsistence are sometimes not able to engage in the trade for months as they are forced to wait for the clean-up exercises to be completed. The suffering is made worse because, in some cases, they are never compensated for their loss.[22]

In an interview with Rev. Samuel Ayadi, the Coordinating Chairman of the Akwa-Ibom State and the Acting Chairman of the Niger Delta Branch ARFAN, he noted that the bad management and lack of respect for the environment by oil companies have robbed his members of the ability to provide for their families. According to him, the oil leakages which result in the pollution of the coastal environment are due to lack of management, as some of these pollutions are caused by rusty pipelines that are no longer fit for purpose. He also noted that the current system is ineffective in holding oil companies to account, which makes them less concerned about caring for the environment in which they work, compared to how the same oil companies operate in the developed countries—especially their countries of origin in the global North— where they are held accountable for their

[18] Francois Vreÿ, 'Good Order at Sea off West Africa' in Towards Good Order at Sea: African Experiences, ed. Thomas Mandrup and Francois Vreÿ (South Africa: Sun Press, 2015), 183–206.

[19] Hans Langeveld and Simon Delany, 'The Impact of Oil Exploration, Extraction and Transport on Mangrove Vegetation and Carbon Stocks in Nigeria' (2014), online: https://milieudefensie.nl/publicaties/rapporten/oil-industry-impact-nigeria.

[20] Barisere Rachel Könnet, 'Inadequate Monitoring and Enforcement in the Nigerian Oil Industry: The Case of Shell and Ogoniland' (2014) 47(1) *Cornell International Law Journal* 181; Tom Bawden, 'Shell 'Uses Sabotage Claims to Avoid Blame for Nigeria Oil Spills', (2013) Independent, online: https://www.independent.co.uk/news/business/news/shell-uses-sabotage-claims-to-avoid-blame-for-nigeria-oil-spills-8664202.html.

[21] Könnet (n 20) 181.

[22] See Chioma Onuegbu, 'Oil Spill: Mobil Hasn't Paid Any A'Ibom Community Compensation in 46 Years – Chief Nduese Essien' (2017) Vanguard Nigeria, online: https://www.vanguardngr.com/2017/08/oil-spill-mobil-hasnt-paid-aibom-community-compensation-46-years-chief-nduese-essien/; P Steyn, 'Oil, Ethnic Minority Groups and Environmental Struggles against Multinational Oil Companies and the Federal Government in the Nigerian Niger Delta State since the 1990s' in Lise Sedrez and Marco Armiero (ed) *A History of Environmentalism: Local Struggles, Global Histories*, (London.New Delhi.New York.Sydney: Bloomsbury, 2014), 57–82.

actions.[23] The lack of respect for the marine environment, he adds, is evident also in the way oil companies engage in haphazard clean-up exercises, or no clean up at all, which causes lasting harm to the marine environment.[24] Espousing this view, Ndimele, Saba, Ojo, Ndimele, Anetekhai and Erondu argue that the degradation caused by oil spillages is worsened by the fact that the oil companies are often reluctant to clean up their spillages and, even when they do, the methods used tend to cause/result in more harm to the marine environment.[25]

The Bonga Oil Field Spillage by the Shell Nigeria Exploration and Production Company (SNEPCO) on the 20th December 2011 exemplifies his claims. The spill, which was caused by equipment failure, resulted in the discharge of an estimated 40,000 barrels of crude oil into the Atlantic Ocean—with more than 168, 000 people from 350 communities in the Niger Delta area affected.[26] As well as the immediate damage caused to the marine environment—the pollution of the mangrove where 60 per cent of the fish in the Gulf of Guinea breed[27]—by the spillage, which covered 185 kilometres along the Nigeria coast, disrupted the source of livelihood of an estimated 28,000 fishermen operating in the region.[28]

Beyond the immediate environmental damage caused by the spillage, Rev. Ayadi noted that it resulted in the suspension of fishing activities for his members for nine months to allow for the clean-up exercise. This period was extremely difficult for many of the fisher folks and their families as they did not have an alternative source of livelihood, nor were they compensated for their loss.[29] Rev. Ayadi also noted that the Bonga fish, which the facility is named after and which were commonly caught in the area, are now difficult to catch, due to the Bonga oil spill and the subsequent environmentally unfriendly clean-up exercise that followed. According to him:

> There is hunger in the fishing communities, there is no fuel subsidy from the government, our effort to survive is threatened by pollution. Fishing is the only thing we know. The Bonga fish that is common in our region throughout

[23] Interview with Rev. Ayadi, Coordinating Chairman Akwa-Ibom State and the Acting Chairman Niger Delta Branch of ARFAN. Telephone interview, June 28th (2017).

[24] *Ibid.*

[25] Prince E Ndimele et al., 'Remediation of Crude Oil Spillage' in PE Ndimele (ed) *The Political Ecology of Oil and Gas Activities in the Nigerian Aquatic Ecosystem*, (United Kingdom: Elsevier Academic Press, 2018), 367–86.

[26] Arodiegwu Eziukwu, 'Bonga Oil Spill Affected 168,000 People in 350 Communities — Monarch' (2015) Premium Times, online: https://www.premiumtimesng.com/regional/south-south-regional/180674-bonga-oil-spill-affected-168000-people-in-350-communities-monarch.html.

[27] André Standing, 'Corruption and Industrial Fishing in Africa' (2008) 7 *U4 Brief*, online: https://www.cmi.no/publications/file/3188-corruption-andindustrial-fishing-in-africa.pdf.

[28] Arodiegwu Eziukwu, 'Bonga Oil Spill Affected 168,000 People in 350 Communities — Monarch' (2015) Premium Times, online: https://www.premiumtimesng.com/regional/south-south-regional/180674-bonga-oil-spill-affected-168000-people-in-350-communities-monarch.html.

[29] Interview with Rev. Ayadi, Coordinating Chairman Akwa-Ibom State and the Acting Chairman Niger Delta Branch of ARFAN. Telephone interview, June 28th, 2017.

> the year is now impossible to catch due to the oil spillage. Rather than execute an effective clean-up, the company used chemicals to sink the oil, which leads to further damage to the surviving species. As I speak to you, we don't even see Bonga fish to catch as much as we used to, which is why some fishermen are turning to crayfish.[30]

Whether or not his claim can be substantiated, what is evident is that pollution from the operations of multinational oil companies has a devastating impact on the food security of the people whose source of livelihood is predominantly from the sea.[31] The outcome is not only the immediate pollution of the marine environment, but, for the families affected, the spillage results in the lack of income leading to poverty, hunger, ill health and the ceasing of education for their children.[32] This is damaging to the achievement of the United Nations Sustainable Development Goals (SDGs) such as SDG 14 which seeks to ensure the sustainable use of the sea, marine and ocean resources, whose attainment is already threatened by IUU fishing by commercial/foreign vessels.[33]

In a region with limited employment opportunities, one cannot ignore the potential impact food insecurity might have on the overall security of the region as those affected seek an alternative source of livelihood.[34] There is nowhere that this is more accurate than in the Niger Delta region, as the actions of multinational oil companies have contributed to environmental degradation and untold hardship in the affected communities, especially for women.[35] Some of these women tend to diversify their livelihood activities by engaging in trading business, especially when their husbands or partners have left in search of alternative income following the pollution of their

---

[30] *Ibid.*

[31] I Okafor-Yarwood, 'Nigeria's Depleting Fish Stocks May Pose a Threat to Regional Security' (2018), The Conversation, online: https://theconversation.com/nigerias-depleting-fish-stocks-may-pose-a-threat-to-regional-security-105168; Julius Osahon, 'Oil Exploration Threatening 6.5 Million Fishing Population in Niger Delta' (2018) The Guardian Nigeria, online: https://guardian.ng/news/oil-exploration-threatening-6-5-million-fishing-population-in-niger-delta-2/.

[32] See Arodiegwu Eziukwu, 'Bonga Oil Spill Affected 168,000 People in 350 Communities — Monarch' (2015) Premium Times, online: https://www.premiumtimesng.com/regional/south-south-regional/180674-bonga-oil-spill-affected-168000-people-in-350-communities-monarch.html.; Owen Akenzua, 'Oil Spill Victims Sue Shell in UK over Alleged $3.6b Compensation' (2017)The Guardian Nigeria, online: https://guardian.ng/news/oil-spill-victims-sue-shell-in-uk-over-alleged-3-6b-compensation/; Adeyemo, Ubiogoro, and Bolarinwa (n 13) 56.

[33] Also affected: SDG 1 seeks to see an end to poverty, SDG 2, seeks to have a world without hunger, SDG 3, seeks to ensure good health, SDG 4, seeks to promote education and SDG 8 seeks to promote economic growth. See Okafor-Yarwood (n 2).

[34] Freedom C Onuoha, 'Piracy and Maritime Security in the Gulf of Guinea : Nigeria as a Microcosm' (2012) Aljazeera Centre for Studies 1, online: http://studies.aljazeera.net/ResourceGallery/media/Documents/2012/6/12/201261294647291734Piracy%20and%20Maritime%20Security%20in%20the%20Gulf%20of%20Guinea.pdf; Michael Baghebo, Ubi Peter Samuel, and N Nwagbara Eucharia, 'Environmental Damage Caused by the Activities of Multiinational Oil Giants in the Niger Delta Region of Nigeria' (2012) 5(6) *Journal of Humanities and Social Science* 9.

[35] Prince E Ndimele et al., 'Remediation of Crude Oil Spillage' in PE Ndimele (ed) *The Political Ecology of Oil and Gas Activities in the Nigerian Aquatic Ecosystem*, (United Kingdom: Elsevier Academic Press, 2018), 367–86.

farmlands and fishing grounds.[36] For others, alternative source of livelihood includes 'taking advantage of the cash inducement of oil workers and others in the oil economy'[37] by engaging in prostitution. Suffice to say that the membership of the once active militant groups in the Niger Delta is comprised of former farmers and fishermen who have lost their sources of income to pollution attributed to oil companies.[38]

The increased potential for transborder conflict, as fisher folks travel beyond their usual fishing grounds in search for fish, is also worth mentioning. During the interview with Rev. Ayadi, he noted that it is common practice for the Cameroonian '*gendarme*' (police) to intimidate fisher folks from Nigeria by extorting money from them or confiscating their fishing equipment.[39] It came as a shock, nevertheless, when, in July 2017, it was reported that the same police killed 97 Nigerian fisher folks following a dispute over an alleged levy.[40] Although this claim is contested by the Cameroonian government, the Nigerian government have accused Cameroon of breaching an agreement to protect its citizens.[41]

Given the migratory/transboundary nature of fish and the fact that an estimated 60 per cent of the fisheries species in the Gulf of Guinea breed in the mangrove of Niger Delta,[42] the continued pollution of the marine environment in the Niger Delta is likely to undermine the fish food security of coastal communities in other countries in the Gulf of Guinea.[43] This will also have financial implications for countries in the region, especially where some of the species are already on the overexploited list, as depleting stock

---

[36] Emem B Inyang and Ekaete E Udong, 'Livelihood Insecurity and Diversification among Women in an Environmentally-Challenged Niger Delta Region, Nigeria' (2013) 1(1) *The International Journal of Humanities & Social Studies* 35.

[37] Edlyne Ezenongaya Anugwom and Kenechukwu N Anugwom, 'The Other Side of Civil Society Story: Women, Oil and the Niger Delta Environmental Struggle in Nigeria' (2009) 74(4) *GeoJournal* 333, online: https://doi.org/10.1007/s10708-008-9239-4, 342.

[38] Victor Ojakorotu and Lysias Dodd Gilbert, *Checkmating the Resurgence of Oil Violence in the Niger Delta of Nigeria*, (2010) 6 *Journal of Energy Security*, online: http://www.iags.org/Niger_Delta_book.pdf; Tarila Marclint Ebiede, 'Beyond Rebellion: Uncaptured Dimensions of Violent Conflicts and the Implications for Peacebuilding in Nigeria's Niger Delta' (2017) 10(1) *African Security* 25, online: https://doi.org/10.1080/19392206.2016.1270140; Freedom Onuoha, 'Poverty, Pipeline Vandalisation/Explosion and Human Security: Integrating Disaster Management into Poverty Reduction in Nigeria' (2010) 16(2) *African Security Review* 94.

[39] Interview with Rev. Ayadi, Coordinating Chairman Akwa-Ibom State and the Acting Chairman Niger Delta Branch of ARFAN. Telephone interview, 28 June (2017).

[40] I Okafor-Yarwood, 'Nigeria's Depleting Fish Stocks May Pose a Threat to Regional Security' (2018), The Conversation, online: https://theconversation.com/nigerias-depleting-fish-stocks-may-pose-a-threat-to-regional-security-105168.

[41] Emman Ovuakporie, 'Reps Probe Alleged Killing of 97 Nigerians by Cameroonian Gendarmes' (2017), Vanguard Nigeria, online: https://www.vanguardngr.com/2017/07/reps-probe-alleged-killing-97-nigerians-cameroonian-gendarmes/

[42] André Standing, 'Corruption and Industrial Fishing in Africa' *U4 Brief*, (2008) 7, online: https://www.cmi.no/publications/file/3188-corruption-andindustrial-fishing-in-africa.pdf.

[43] See Beth Polidoro et al., 'Red List of Marine Bony Fishes of the Eastern Central Atlantic' (2016) International Union for Conservation of Nature 1; Tony J Pitcher and William WL Cheung, 'Fisheries: Hope or Despair?' (2013) 74(2) *Marine Pollution Bulletin* 506, online: https://doi.org/10.1016/j.marpolbul.2013.05.045, 510 and 514.

means less resources to attract investors from distant water fishing nations.[44]

Finally, whilst it is important to highlight the role of multinational oil companies in undermining the marine environment and thus threatening the long-term food security of coastal communities, it is impossible to ignore the role bad governance has played in contributing to the neglect of the marine environment. This is especially evident when one takes into account that these same oil companies tend to operate in a different manner and uphold existing environmental regulations in their home countries and/or when operating in developed countries.[45] To this end, the ensuing section looks at existing environmental regulations in Nigeria and their limitations.

3. Environmental regulations and their shortcomings

The Niger Delta region has strategic value to Nigeria due to the abundance of energy resources within its boundaries. The crude oil derived from the region accounts for 95 per cent of Nigeria's foreign exchange earnings, and 80 per cent of the total revenue accruable to the Federal account.[46] The gross domestic product (GDP) contribution from oil in 2017 was 8.68 per cent, rising to 9.61 per cent in the first quarter of 2018 which generates the bulk of the government's revenue.[47] Also, abundant in the region are the once arable land, forests, rivers and mangroves teeming with fisheries and aquaculture resources.[48] However, the former richness of the region is no longer reflected in the day to day reality of the people living in it, many of whom

---

44 Alfonso Daniels et al., 'Western Africa's Missing Fish; the Impacts of Illegal, Unreported and Unregulated Fishing and under-Reporting Catches by Foreign Fleets' (2016), Overseas Development Institute, online https://www.odi.org/sites/odi.org.uk/files/resource-documents/10665.pdf; Lawrence Etim, Dyhia Belhabib, and Daniel Pauly, 'An Overview of the Nigerian Marine Fisheries and a Re-Evaluation of Its Catch Data for the Years 1950 to 2010' in Dyhia Belhabib and Daniel Pauly (eds), *Fisheries Catch Reconstructions: West Africa, Part II. Fisheries Centre Research Reports Vol.23(3)* (Vancouver: Fisheries Centre, University of British Columbia, 2015), 66–76.

45 See Emma Amaize, 'Pollution Forces N-Delta Fishermen, Farmers to Abandon Occupation' (2016) Vanguard Nigeria, online: https://www.vanguardngr.com/2016/09/pollution-forces-n-delta-fishermen-farmers-abandon-occupation/; John Vidal, 'Nigeria's Agony Dwarfs the Gulf Oil Spill. The US and Europe Ignore It' (2010) The Guardian, online: https://www.theguardian.com/world/2010/may/30/oil-spills-nigeria-niger-delta-shell ; Peter Roderick, 'Gas Flaring in Nigeria: A Human Rights, Environmental and Economic Monstrocity' (2005) Climate Justice Programme, https://doi.org/http://dx.doi.org/10.1016/j.pan.2012.11.029.

46 Donald O Omagu, 'Oil Multinationals: Environmental Genocide and Socioeconomic Development in Nigeria's Niger Delta' in Toyin Falola and Adam Paddock (eds), *Environment and Economics in Nigeria* (New York & London: Routledge, 2012), 107–24; E K Agbaeze, S N Udeh, and I O Onwuka, 'Resolving Nigeria's Dependency on Oil – The Derivation Model' (2015) 7(1) *Journal of African Studies and Development* 1, online: https://doi.org/10.5897/JASD2014.0303.

47 NBS, 'Nigerian Gross Domestic Product Report Q4 & Full Year 2017' (2018), National Bureau of Statistics online: https://nigerianstat.gov.ng/elibrary?queries[search]=GDP; NBS, 'Nigeria Gross Domestic Product Report Q1 2018' (2018), National Bureau of Statistics, online: https://nigerianstat.gov.ng/elibrary?queries[search]=GDP; Solape Renner, 'Nigeria First-Quarter GDP Growth Slows Even as Oil Output Rises' (2018) Bloomberg, online: https://www.bloomberg.com/news/articles/2018-05-21/nigerian-economy-expands-in-first-quarter-as-oil-output-rises.

48 Samuel Inyang, 'South-South: The Anatomy of a People, Resources' (2009) NBF, online:http://www.nigerianbestforum.com/generaltopics/south-south-the-anatomy-of-a-people-resources/.

are either fisher folks or farmers. This is ultimately due to poor governance,[49] which has resulted in environmental degradation—pollution of the farmlands and water sources—and by the multinational oil companies operating in the region, thereby undermining the sources of livelihood of families and communities.[50]

The multinational oil companies operating in Nigeria have to take responsibility for their laxity, evident in decades of poor maintenance and underinvestment, which have resulted in the corrosion of ageing facilities and the subsequent equipment failure and oil spillages.[51] Similarly, the Nigerian state may be criticised for not having a robust system for regulating the activities of these companies and holding them responsible for their actions. The first oil exploration in the Niger Delta occurred in 1956; however, it was not until 1992 (36 years later) that the first ever environment impact assessment was undertaken.[52] The first ever statute aimed exclusively at addressing environmental issues was enacted in 1988 under Decree 58 of the same year—the Federal Environmental Protection Agency Act. The amended ACT No. 59 of 1992 saw the establishment of FEPA—now the Ministry of Environment—which is responsible for instituting natural environmental standards.[53] However, since it was established, FEPA has not implemented any legal sanctions or compelled any of the multinational oil companies operating in the country to pay compensation or restore the polluted environment to an acceptable level. Hence it is deemed to be ineffective.[54] The lack of and/or weak enforcement of FEPA resulted in low compliance by the oil companies and

[49] Emmanuel M Akpabio and Nseabasi S Akpan, 'Governance and Oil Politics in Nigeria's Niger Delta: The Question of Distributive Equity' (2010) 30(2) *Journal of Human Ecology* 111, online: https://doi.org/10.1080/09709274.2010.11906280.

[50] Beloveth O Nwankwo, 'The Politics of Conflict over Oil in the Niger Delta Region of Nigeria: A Review of the Corporate Social Responsibility Strategies of the Oil Companies' (2015) 3(4) *American Journal of Educational Research* 383, online: https://doi.org/10.12691/education-3-4-1; Amnesty International, 'Nigeria: Petroleum, Pollution and Poverty in the Niger Delta' (2009), online: http://search.ebscohost.com/login.aspx?direct=true&db=a9h&AN=15491079&site=ehost-live; Joseph C Ebegbulem, Dickson Ekpe, and Theophilus Oyime Adejumo, 'Oil Exploration and Poverty in the Niger Delta Region of Nigeria: A Critical Analysis' (2013) 4(3) *International Journal of Business and Social Science* 4, no. 279.

[51] OO Emoyan, IA Akpoborie, and EE Akporhonor, 'The Oil and Gas Industry and the Niger Delta: Implications for the Environment' (2008) 12(3) *Journal of Applied Environmental Management* 29, online: 1183-1184a29-37, https://doi.org/10.1007/BF00730279; Amnesty International, 'Negligence in the Niger Delta: Decoding SHELL and ENI's Poor Record on Oil Spills' (2018), online: https://www.amnesty.ch/de/themen/wirtschaft-und-menschenrechte/fallbeispiele/nigeria/dok/2018/nigeria-fahrlaessigkeit-von-shell-eni/negligence-in-the-niger-delta.pdf; CH Achebe, UC Nneke, and OE Anisiji, 'Analysis of Oil Pipeline Failures in the Oil and Gas Industries in the Niger Delta Area of Nigeria' (2012) 2 *Proceeding of International MultiConference of Engineers and Computer Scientiest* 1274, online: https://doi.org/10.3982/ECTA6706.

[52] Donald O Omagu, 'Oil Multinationals: Environmental Genocide and Socioeconomic Development in Nigeria's Niger Delta' in Toyin Falola and Adam Paddock (eds), *Environment and Economics in Nigeria* (New York & London: Routledge, 2012), 107–24, 107 & 112.

[53] SI Omofonmwan and GI Osa-Edoh, 'The Challenges of Environmental Problems in Nigeria' (2008) 23(1) Journal of Human Ecology 53, online: https://doi.org/10.1080/09709274.2008.11906054, 56.

[54] Omagu (n 52) 107–24, 112; Aniefiok E Ite et al., 'Petroleum Exploration and Production: Past and Present Environmental Issues in the Nigeria's Niger Delta' (2013) 1(4) *American Journal of Environmental Protection* 78, online: https://doi.org/10.12691/env-1-4-2.

subsequently lead to its repeal and replacement by the National Environmental Standards and Regulation Enforcement Agency Establishment Act in 2007.[55]

Beyond FEPA, other regulators have been introduced, but they too have not yet brought about any significant changes. NOSDRA was established in 2006 for the purpose of implementing the National Oil Spill Contingency Plan (NOSCP).[56] The institution of the contingency plan and the agency that followed are in compliance with the International Convention on Oil Pollution Preparedness, Response and Cooperation (OPRC 90),[57] to which Nigeria is a signatory. Specifically, Article 1 (1) of OPRC stipulates that member states should take appropriate measures to prepare for and respond to an oil pollution incident.[58] However, as with the limitations of other existing regulations, executing their role and enforcing the provisions of NOSCP have been difficult due to what the Director-General of NOSDRA describes as 'inadequate funds, manpower, equipment and a weak legal framework ... '.[59] These inadequacies have hindered their ability to execute their mandate effectively.

The National Environmental Standards and Regulation Enforcement Agency Establishment Act 2007—replacing the Federal Environmental Protection Act—is responsible for environmental protection, biodiversity conservation, and sustainable exploitation of natural resources in the country.[60] In addressing the subject of spillages and/or the deposit of harmful materials in the environment, section 27(1) notes:

> The discharge in such harmful quantities of any hazardous substance into the air or upon the land and the waters of Nigeria or at the adjoining shorelines is prohibited, except where such discharge is permitted or authorised under any law in force in Nigeria.[61]

---

[55] Muhammed Tawfiq Ladan, 'Review of NESREA Act 2007 and Regulations 2009-2011: A New Dawn in Environmental Compliance and Enforcement in Nigeria' (2012) 8(1) *Law, Environment and Development Journal* 118, 119.

[56] Peter C Nwilo and Olusegun T Badejo, 'Impacts and Management of Oil Spill Pollution along the Nigerian Coastal Areas' (2005) 36 *Administering Marine Spaces: International Issues, the International Federation of Surveyors* (FIG), online: https://www.fig.net/resources/publications/figpub/pub36/chapters/chapter_8.pdf.

[57] ILO, 'International Convention on Oil Pollution Preparedness , Response and Co-Operation, 1990' (1990), online: https://www.ilo.org/dyn/natlex/docs/ELECTRONIC/93349/109093/F578688552/International Convention on Oil Pollution Prepare.pdf.

[58] IMO, 'International Convention on Oil Pollution Preparedness, Response and Cooperation, 1990, (with Annex and Procès- Verbal of Rectification). Concluded at London on 30 No Vember 1990' (Entered into force 13 May 1995, accession by Nigeria, 25 May 1993) (1995) United Nations - Treaty Series, online: https://treaties.un.org/doc/publication/unts/volume 1891/volume-1891-i-32194-english.pdf.

[59] Egufe Yafugborhi, 'No TitleaNigeria Lags behind in Response to Oil Spill —NOSDRA' (2018) Vanguard Nigeria, online: https://www.vanguardngr.com/2018/04/nigeria-lags-behind-response-oil-spill-nosdra/.

[60] NESREA, 'National Environmental Standards and Regulations Enforcement Agency (Establishment) Act, 2007' (2007), online: http://extwprlegs1.fao.org/docs/pdf/nig120569.pdf; Muhammed Tawfiq Ladan, 'Review of NESREA Act 2007 and Regulations 2009-2011: A New Dawn in Environmental Compliance and Enforcement in Nigeria' (2012) 8(1) *Law, Environment and Development Journal* 118, 120.

[61] NESREA, 'National Environmental Standards and Regulations Enforcement Agency (Establishment) Act, 2007' (2007), online: http://extwprlegs1.fao.org/docs/pdf/nig120569.pdf.

However, the prohibition of the discharge of hazardous substances in 'harmful quantities' by the NESREA Act, according to Oshionebo, undermines the Act itself. According to him, by prohibiting the discharge of hazardous wastes in 'harmful quantities', the Act infers that 'unharmful quantities' of such substances can be discharged.[62] Whilst there is an established limit on the discharge of effluents in Nigeria,[63] Oshienobo and Cui argue that NESREA does not have the capability to enforce this provision because the agency does not have the expertise and equipment to do so.[64] Ekhator has compared the similarities between NOSDRA and NESREA and arrived at the conclusion that in an attempt to prevent a conflict of interest between the two agencies, the investigation of oil spills was removed from the ambit of NESREA.[65] As a result, NOSDRA is 'statutorily required to prevent, control and respond to oil spill incidences in Nigeria'.[66] NESREA however, despite 'its innovative provisions of mobile courts in environmental cases, has been criticised on the ground that it is narrowly focused in comparison with the now defunct FEPA Act'.[67] Evidentially, the problem does not lie with the lack of legislation as there are many, but, rather, the lack of capacity to enforce them. Specifically, there are different underlying causes as to why existing regulations and efforts to implement them have failed, including, but not limited to a perceived lack of political will, corruption, ineffective implementation of regulations where they exist, the lack of enforcement when regulations are violated, the lack of institutional capacity of regulatory agencies and overambitious legislation or guidelines.[68]

---

[62] Evaristus Oshionebo, Regulating Transnational Corporations in Domestic and International Regimes: An African Case Study (Toronto: University of Toronto Press, 2009), 57.

[63] Nigeria, 'National Environmental Protection (Effluent Limitation) Regulations' (1991) Federal Environmental Protection Agency, online: http://extwprlegs1.fao.org/docs/pdf/nig120290.pdf.

[64] Evaristus Oshionebo, Regulating Transnational Corporations in Domestic and International Regimes: An African Case Study (Toronto: University of Toronto Press, 2009), 57; Roberto Cui, Oil Multinationals in Nigeria: Human Rights, Sustainable Development and the Law (Hamburg: Anchor Academic Publishing, 2015), 50-51.

[65] Eghosa Osa Ekhator, 'Environmental Protection in the Oil and Gas Industry in Nigeria: The Roles of Governmental Agencies' (2013) 5 *International Energy Law Review* 196, 199.

[66] *Ibid.*

[67] DK Derri and SE Abila, 'A Critical Examination of the National Enviromental Standards and Regulation Enforcement Agency (Establishment) Act 2007' in Festus Emiri and Gowon Deinduomo (eds), Law and Petroleum Industry in Nigeria: Current Challenges : Essays in Honour of Justice Kate Abiri (Lagos: Malthouse Press Limited, 2009) 1–10, 10.

[68] Stakeholder Democracy, 'Rumuekpe a Study in Disempowerment, Conflict, and Peacebuilding' (2015) Human Impact of Conflict Rumuekpe, online: http://www.stakeholderdemocracy.org/wp-content/uploads/2016/06/22.9.15-Rumuekpe-Human-Impact-of-Conflict.pdf; Abiodun Odusote, 'Nigeria: The Matrix Between Fragility of Livelihoods and Conflict' (2016) 10(2) *Journal of Global Initiatives: Policy, Pedagogy, Perspective 9*; UNEP, 'Environmental Assessment of Ogoniland' (Kenya, 2011), online: https://doi.org/10.3370/lca.2.73; Oludayo G Amokaye, 'Environmental Pollution and Challenges of Environmental Governance in Nigeria' (2012) 10(1) *British Journal of Arts and Social Sciences* 26; Hakeem Ijaiya and O T Joseph, 'Rethinking Environmental Law Enforcement in Nigeria' (2014) 5 *Beijing Law Review* 306, online: https://doi.org/10.4236/blr.2014.54029; Lisa Stevens, 'The Illusion of Sustainable Development: How Nigeria's Environmental Laws Are Failing the Niger Delta' (2011) 36 *The Vermont Law Review* 388.

The failure to implement existing regulations in their entirety can also be put down to a conflict of interest, as the Federal Government is responsible for instituting and implementing the environmental regulations, yet they also own some of the oil companies being regulated.[69] According to Cragg, Hurst-Croft and Samiama, 'if the regulators, or indeed the ministry, rely on the oil sector for revenue in any way … ',[70] there might be instances where they (in the Nigerian case, those charged with the responsibility of putting into effect the many environmental laws or guidelines) may be reluctant to enforce the stipulations of the regulations because enforcement will mean a reduction in their income.[71] For instance, effecting the implementation of the environmental regulation in its entirety may require the suspension of oil production, to allow for the clean-up of contaminated lands and water sources.[72] However, since the Federal government rely on the oil sector for a huge part of their revenue, it is not surprising that the agencies responsible for enforcing these regulations appear to be inadequately alert to the many violations of the regulations and sometimes are seen to turn a blind eye. Espousing this argument, Ezike notes that the 'penalty for gas flaring remains a paltry sum of N10.00 (£0.0215) … for every cubic [foot] of gas flared',[73] which makes one wonder whether there were any real intentions to put an end to gas flaring in an industry which accounts for an estimated 85 per cent of the gas produced in Nigeria.[74]

The preceding argument is true for Nigeria, where the regulating authority is also aligned with the Ministry of Energy (Petroleum Resources). The possibility for a conflict of interest is evinced by the fact that it is within the remit of the Nigerian Department of Petroleum Resources (DPR) to supervise and regulate the oil and gas sector, as well as enforce environmental laws. Moreover, the DPR is formally part of the Ministry of Petroleum Resources (MPR) and the Nigerian National Petroleum Corporation (NNPC) and thus, is closely aligned with the Ministry of Energy, which is responsible for developing the country's energy resources, of which the oil and gas industry is an integral part.[75] It follows that, the DPR, cannot independently enforce regulations

[69] Könnet (n 20) 195.

[70] C Cragg, J Hurst-Croft, and I Samiama, 'Pollution Control in the Global Oil Industry in Relation to Reform in Nigeria' (2011), online: http://www.stakeholderdemocracy.org/wp-content/uploads/2016/06/Environmental-Regulation-and-Pollution.pdf., 15.

[71] *Ibid* 6.

[72] *Ibid.*

[73] Chukwuemeka Chuks Ezike, 'Environmental Crime Liability of the Nigerian Government in Its Oil Pollution Menace' (2018) 2(2) *Environmental Risk Assessment and Remediation* 1, online: https://doi.org/10.4066/2529-8046.100035, 2.

[74] *Ibid.*

[75] Könnet (n 20) 181.

regarding oil pollution due to these said conflicts of interest.[76] Encapsulating this position, the World Bank notes,

> this situation has resulted in the Government inadequately regulating oil pollution while, at the same time, being party to [the cause of] much of the oil-related environmental problems of the Niger Delta.[77]

There is also the issue of corruption, especially by the elites in the communities hosting the oil companies (Kings and village heads), which underscores the limitations of the spillage compensation policy when it is implemented. This practice, according to Adeyemo, is termed the 'benefit captor syndrome'. These are elites that supposedly represent and or receive compensation on behalf of their communities; however, this compensation is rarely in fact received by the communities.[78] During a focused group discussion with fisher folks in Bonny Island, those present shared their experience of misappropriation of compensation money by the traditional ruling elites. According to them:

> [C]ommunity Chiefs especially, the King is [sic] as bad as the government. They spend the money given to the communities as compensation for pollution or as gifts from the oil companies on expensive cars and sending their children abroad. While the people were hungry and struggling to make ends meet, the King had a party some years ago to celebrate his first billion.[79]

Similar narratives abound across most communities in the Niger Delta, as traditional leaders often fail to redistribute funds to the relevant people, which has resulted in resentment and frustration, especially amongst the youth.[80]

The implementation of the existing regulations/guidelines are also hampered by a triad of problems—ineffective implementation of regulations where they exist, the lack of enforcement when those regulations are violated and the lack of institutional capacity of regulatory agencies. The latter issue, which strongly contributes to the second, has resulted in poor monitoring

---

[76] Mark C Thurber, Ifeyinwa M Emelife, and Patrick R P Heller, 'NNPC and Nigeria's Oil Patronage Eco-System' in David G Victor, David R Hults, and Mark C Thurber (eds), *Oil and Governance: State-Owned Enterprises and the World Energy Supply* (New York: Cambridge University Press, 2011), 701–52; Philip Ejoor Agbonifo, 'Risk Management and Regulatory Failure in the Oil and Gas Industry in Nigeria: Reflections on the Impact of Environmental Degradation in the Niger Delta Region' (2016) 9(4) *Journal of Sustainable Development* 1, online: https://doi.org/10.5539/jsd.v9n4p1.

[77] The World Bank, 'Defining an Environmental Development Strategy for the Niger Delta' (1995) 2 *World Bank* 1, online: http://documents.worldbank.org/curated/en/506921468098056629/pdf/multi-page.pdf, 45.

[78] Ademola Morakinyo Adeyemo, 'Environmental Policy Failure in Nigeria and the Tragedy of Underdevelopment of Niger Delta Region' (2008) 63 *University of PortHarcourt Inaugural Lecture Series* 1-105 2008, online: https://www.uniport.edu.ng/files/Inaugural%20Lectures/63rd%20Inaugural%20Lecture%20-%202008%20Prof_%20A_%20M_%20Adeyemo.pdf, 57.

[79] This was the views of the Fisher folks from one of the fishing settlements in Bonny, during a focus group discussion in December (2015).

[80] Stakeholder Democracy, 'Rumuekpe a Study in Disempowerment, Conflict, and Peacebuilding' (2015) Human Impact of Conflict Rumuekpe, online: http://www.stakeholderdemocracy.org/wp-content/uploads/2016/06/22.9.15-Rumuekpe-Human-Impact-of-Conflict.pdf.

and complete reliance on the oil companies for data, thus allowing them to follow their own assessment.[81] As a result, regulating agencies cannot corroborate the data provided by the oil companies, as they do not have the resources to do so. More precisely, NOSDRA is statutorily responsible for detecting and responding to oil spillages in Nigeria; however, a 2013 report by Amnesty International noted that oil companies' personnel usually spearhead the investigations for such spillages, not NOSDRA. The agency is thus seen to be dependent on the company involved in an oil spill incident, as the oil company provides the transport to the site of the spillages as well as technical expertise and data, all of which agencies such as NOSDRA and the DPR do not have.[82] This also gives the oil companies the freedom to decide when the investigation starts. The historical failure to establish an independent regulator that is well equipped to enforce the regulations and guidelines, despite the efforts of previous governments to do so, is, according to Thurber, Emelife and Heller 'part of a lurching reform that does nothing to sustainably alter the functioning of the petroleum sector'.[83]

Finally, environmental regulations or guidelines have not always led to any meaningful outcome for communities in the Niger Delta because they are overambitious and unrealistic, and thus falter very easily.[84] This has made some of the stipulations of EGASPIN, which is within the auspices of the DPR, impossible to implement.[85] Specifically, EGASPIN requires that, in cases of oil spills, actions must be taken within 24 hours of the spillage, which is impractical given that, in many instances, the oil companies might not be aware of such spillages until much later, which often is outside the 24 hour time limit.[86] Even when the oil companies are able to meet the 24 hour deadline as stipulated, as previously stated NOSDRA, which is the

[81] UNEP, 'Environmental Assessment of Ogoniland' (Kenya, 2011), online: https://doi.org/10.3370/lca.2.73; Könnet (n 20) 181; OC Eneh and VC Agbazue, 'Protection of Nigeria's Environment: A Critical Policy Review' (2011) 4(5) *Journal of Environmental Science and Technology* 490.

[82] Amnesty International, 'Bad Information: Oil Spill Investigations in the Niger Delta' (2013), online: www.amnesty.org/en/library/asset/AFR44/.../afr440282013en.pdf.

[83] Thurber, Emelife, and Heller (n 76) 701–52, 716.

[84] Lisa Stevens, 'The Illusion of Sustainable Development: How Nigeria's Environmental Laws Are Failing the Niger Delta' (2011) 36 *The Vermont Law Review* 388; C Cragg, J Hurst-Croft, and I Samiama, 'Pollution Control in the Global Oil Industry in Relation to Reform in Nigeria' (2011), online: http://www.stakeholderdemocracy.org/wp-content/uploads/2016/06/Environmental-Regulation-and-Pollution.pdf.; Kingsley Edu, 'A Review of the Existing Legal Regime on Exploitation of Oil and the Protection of the Environment in Nigeria' (2011) 37(2) *Commonwealth Law Bulletin* 307, online: https://doi.org/10.1080/03050718.2011.572637; Amokaye, 'Environmental Pollution and Challenges of Environmental Governance in Nigeria'.

[85] As a regulatory tool the DPR issued the EGASPIN in 1991, this was later reviewed in 2002. See DPR, 'Environmental Guidelines and Standards for the Petroleum Industry in Nigeria (EGASPIN), Issued by the Department of Petroleum Resources Lagos 1991' (2002) Revised Edition, online: http://www.ngfcp.gov.ng/media/1066/dprs-egaspin-2002-revised-edition.pdf.

[86] Ayobami Olaniyan, 'The Law and Multi-Agency Response to Oil Spill Incidents in Nigeria' (2015) *Interspil Amsterdam, online:* http://www.interspill.org/previous-events/2015/WhitePapers/Interspill2015ConferenceProceedings/25%20MARCH%202015/Multi-Agency%20Response%20-%20Experiences/Law-and-Multi-Agency-Response-to-Oil-Spill-incidents-in-Nigeria.pdf.

enforcement agency, does not have the capacity to enforce the regulations as they rely on the oil companies for transportation to spillage sites and data. The failures in the enforcement agencies are evident from the fact that six years since the Bonga Oil Field Spillage, communities and even the government have not been compensated, with SNEPCO refusing to pay a US$3.6 billion fine despite a court ruling in June 2018[87] for it to do so.[88] Amongst other things, the Bonga Oil Field example not only shows the lack of respect by SNEPCO for the communities that have welcomed them, but also highlights the incapacity of the enforcement agencies to fully implement the responsibilities associated with their institutions. The Bonga Oil Field example is typical of how spillages are addressed in the Niger Delta. In Bonny Island for instance, which is home to the company Nigerian Liquefied Natural Gas (NLNG), in cases of oil spillages fisher folks have been known to be unable to fish in the affected area for up to six months to allow for the clean-up of the spillages. According to the President of the Bonny Fishers Association:

> Spillages spoil our nets, so we tend not to fish in a particular area for up to six months until such spillages are cleared, with little to no compensation for the accrued loss in earning.[89]

This has resulted in some of the affected fisher folks fishing further afield or looking for an alternative source of income to adapt to the impact of depleting fisheries.

4. Conclusion

This paper has explored the role of pollution as one of the key factors that undermine the sustainable use of the marine environment, especially in the Niger Delta region. It has argued that pollution in the form of spillages by the multinational oil companies operating in the region has played a significant role in undermining the marine environment leading to the depletion of fisheries resources. This has had severe consequences on the food security of the coastal communities across the Niger Delta, as their main source of livelihood has been diminished. In reviewing the responsibility of the Nigerian government to ensure that the perpetrating companies are held accountable for their actions, the paper has found that, whereas the existing regulations sometimes do not go far enough, the main problem is that the enforcement agencies do not have the capacity to fulfil their mandate which perpetuates

---

87 Shell Nigeria Exploration and Production Company Limited v National Oil Spill Detection and Response Agency (Federal High Court, 24 May 2018), GU Ugwuoma, 'Litigation Update: Court No. 1' (2018) Advocaat Law Practice, online:http://www.advocaat-law.com/assets/resources/341e36a14b167a82e12df3ff9e6c4e3b.pdf.

88 Chineme Okafor, 'NOSDRA to Shell: Obey Court Order, Pay $3.6bn Fine over Bonga Oil Spill' (2018) ThisDay Live, online: https://www.thisdaylive.com/index.php/2018/07/05/nosdra-to-shell-obey-court-order-pay-3-6bn-fine-over-bonga-oil-spill/.

89 Interview with Mr. Bristol, held in Bonny Island, December (2015).

the downward spiral of environmental degradation affecting coastal communities.

To this end, this paper notes that it is impossible for a country like Nigeria to reverse the impact of years of neglect of their marine environment unless the government takes firm action in holding the oil companies accountable for their pollution. The first step required is a comprehensive strengthening of some of the legal frameworks and/or guidelines on the environment—such as EGASPIN, by addressing some of the loopholes that have already been identified such as the unrealistic timeline for reporting and acting on oil spills. Coupled with that, for the legal frameworks to be effective, there is a need to ensure adequate support for the enforcement agencies in the form of investment in equipment and manpower that would allow them to carry out their duties to implement both existing and enhanced regulations with less dependence on the oil companies. There is also an urgent need to ensure that affected communities are duly compensated, and clean-up exercises are carried out to the same level that is found in developed countries. Furthermore, effective implementation of the existing environmental regulations can only happen through enhancing the powers of regulating agencies and/or making them independent of the Ministry of Energy to allow for unbiased representation and implementation of said regulations. The review of the existing guidelines and regulations should also be swiftly followed by investment in infrastructure to be funded with fines generated from the infringement of laws.

Finally, the government must work to ensure that personnel are trained to be able to do their jobs effectively, as well as provide a better channel for the general public to get involved. These measures will make way for a stronger agency that will be committed to rooting out corrupt practices and fulfilling its primary responsibility, which is a commitment to a sustainable Nigerian environment. Failure to regulate and empower these institutions would see an increase in the negative cycle of the response to the perceived injustices in the Niger Delta, as the people affected by oil spillages continue to seek alternative sources of livelihood, including engaging in activities that threaten the security of the Nigerian state itself. Taking this much-needed action would go a long way in ensuring the sustainability of the marine resources, not only in Nigeria, but across the Gulf of Guinea.

Acknowledgements

The author would like to thank Mr Peter Sharpe and Mr Anthony Davenport for copyediting the initial drafts of this paper. The author also wants to thank her PhD supervisors, Dr Eka Ikpe and Prof. Funmi Olonisakin for their continued guidance. A special thank you also to Rev. Ayadi and fisher folks in Bonny Local Government area in Rivers State, Nigeria, for contributing to the data for this paper, and to the organisers of the Transnational Food Law Symposium for providing the platform for the subject to be discussed. Above all, the author is thankful to Almighty God.

Disclosure statement

No potential conflict of interest was reported by the author.

ORCID

Ifesinachi Okafor-Yarwood http://orcid.org/0000-0003-4952-9979

Compromised collaborations: food, fuel, and power in transnational food security governance

Matthew Canfield

ABSTRACT

This essay analyses how the relation between food and fuel shapes the practice of collaborative food governance. Dominant explanations for the persistence of global hunger often point to the influence of political-economic inequalities on the production, distribution, and governance of global food. The causes of the 2007–2008 global food crisis, however, suggest the need to examine the entanglements between food and other forms of ecological extraction. I draw on the concept of 'energopolitics' to demonstrate how changing material processes of energy extraction condition the calculative logics through which transnational food governance is constituted. An energopolitical analysis, I argue, illuminates how collaborative food governance supresses the conflict between food and fuel that it was developed to mediate. In an era of climate change, such an approach reveals the links between food and broader struggles over carbon-fuelled inequalities.

The 2007–2008 global food crisis was a powerful reminder of the critical role that food production and provisioning play in constituting transnational normative orders. Just as ending global hunger, or what is now called 'food security', played an important role in the formation of the post-World War II international order, recent food crises have served as contentious conflicts that have challenged hegemonic regulatory regimes. The 2007–2008 global food crisis was one such moment of transformation. The regulatory failure pushed 100 million more people into hunger and caused food riots in over thirty countries.[1] As states, transnational social movements, corporations, and international institutions struggled for control, a new paradigm of collaborative transnational food security governance emerged. Today, the practice of collaborative food governance offers a critical site through which to analyse changing forms of power amidst a shifting political economic and ecological context.

[1] Food and Agriculture Organization of the United Nations, & World Food Program, *The State of Food Insecurity in the World 2009*, (FAO 2009), online: <http://www.fao.org/3/a-i0876e.pdf>; Raj Patel and Philip McMichael, 'A Political Economy of the Food Riot' (2009) 32 *Review (Fernand Braudel Center)* 9–35.

Most accounts of food security politics point to political-economic asymmetries as the driving factor shaping the production, distribution, and governance of global food. These asymmetries were particularly manifest in the negotiation of the Agreement on Agriculture and other global trade agreements, which have perpetuated hunger among small-scale producers and rural peoples in the developing world.[2] The inclusion of civil society and other actors into new arenas and global decision-making processes thus offered hope of democratizing global food governance. Yet though multi-stakeholder and collaborative arenas of global food governance have been designed to offer a more level playing field, inequalities persist. Analysts of global food security governance are thus becoming increasingly disillusioned with collaborative and multi-stakeholder paradigms of governance.[3] Such failures to produce more equitable outcomes even through collaborative models suggests the need to look beyond 'capitalocentric' political economic accounts of power within transnational governance processes.

Indeed, the causes of the 2007–2008 global food crisis, point to a set of ecological entanglements overlooked by political economic accounts. While several factors converged to cause the crises, concern over *energy* was a key factor; rising oil prices and concurrent increased biofuel demand were major causes of the global food crisis.[4] As crops whose starches, sugars, oils, and cellulose can be harvested to produce carbon energy, biofuels have been pursued with an increasing zeal by powerful states seeking to wean themselves from fossil fuels while maintaining their national energy security. As states replaced food crops with fuel crops, however, they limited global food stocks, causing food prices to skyrocket.[5] The crisis thus revealed the significance of the 'food-fuel nexus'—a mutually dependent relationship that had also been at the centre of the 1973–1974 global food crisis. The causal role of

---

[2] Carmen G Gonzalez, 'Institutionalizing Inequality: The WTO Agreement on Agriculture, Food Security, and Developing Countries' (2002) 27 Columbia Journal of Environmental Law 433; Jennifer Clapp, 'World Hunger And The Global Economy: Strong Linkages, Weak Action' (2014) 67 Journal of International Affairs 1.

[3] Nora McKeon, 'Are Equity and Sustainability a Likely Outcome When Foxes and Chickens Share the Same Coop? Critiquing the Concept of Multistakeholder Governance of Food Security' (2017) 14:3 *Globalizations* 379.

[4] Those concerned with the interactions between food and fuel often prefer the term 'agrofuels,' over 'biofuels.' The term 'biofuels' is promoted by powerful states, transnational agri-business corporations, and other associated interest groups in an effort to frame the production of fuel crops as a sustainable alternative to fossil-fuels. Those who use the term 'agrofuels' seek to emphasize the political drivers of land use change and the resulting impact on economic inequality and food insecurity. As Deitz and others note, "the term agrofuels alludes to agro-industrial agriculture and its inherent commodification of nature and to the modernization and industrialization of rural areas with all impact on social relations and ecological conditions." See Kristina Dietz and others, The Political Ecology of Biofuels (Routledge, 2014) 3. While I prefer the term 'agrofuels', I use the term 'biofuels' throughout this article for consistency, since it served as the dominant framing of the negotiation within the Committee on World Food Security, which I analyse later in this article.

[5] Mark W Rosegrant. (International Food Policy Research Institute), *Biofuels and Grain Prices: Impacts and Policy Responses* (2008), online: <http://ebrary.ifpri.org/utils/getfile/collection/p15738coll2/id/10350/filename/10351.pdf>.

the food-fuel nexus in both crises therefore suggest that while political economic inequalities certainly play a key role in transnational food governance, understanding the contemporary operation and exercise of power requires attending to the energetic foundations of power.

This brief article reassesses how competition over energy shapes transnational food security governance. Building on recent studies that have located energy, rather than capital, at the core of global relations of power, this article proposes that the recognition of the food-fuel nexus necessitates a new conceptual framework to assess the power exercised both *within* global food governance and *across* transnational legal processes. In analysing the production and practice of transnational food security governance, I draw on the concept of 'energopower'—the power generated and exercised 'over and through energy.'[6] In applying this framework to analyse transnational food security governance, I suggest that the development and practice of collaborative governance serves to maintain carbon-fuelled inequalities as food and fuel increasingly compete over land. By assuming that this conflict can be resolved through consensus, without recognising energy-driven power asymmetries, multi-stakeholder processes supress the conflict they have been deployed to mediate. In an era when climate change threatens humanity's survival, an energopolitical lens thus connects conflicts over food and agriculture with broader struggles over ecological extraction.

Part I offers a short history of the rise of transnational food security governance, emphasising the often-overlooked role of the food-fuel nexus. I describe how the biofuel-caused food crisis of 2007–2008 led to a transformation of the UN Committee on World Food Security (CFS) from an intergovernmental institution to a collaborative, multi-stakeholder arena. In Part II, I draw on ethnographic fieldwork within the CFS to analyse the negotiation of the Recommendations on Biofuels and Food Security. I describe how unequal power relations throughout the process profoundly shaped the outcomes of the negotiations. While most accounts suggest that such a failure of collaboration is the product of inadequately designed processes to account for asymmetries of bargaining power (which are themselves considered a reflection of inequalities of capital), in Part III, I offer an alternative account, focusing on the role of energopower. In this section, I develop a thumbnail sketch of the way that the food-fuel nexus has historically shaped shifting ideologies of transnational regulation. I suggest that collaborative governance has arisen in response to the failure of previous calculative logics of energy within transnational legal arrangements, but like previous regulatory ideologies seeks to depoliticise the food-fuel nexus in order to maintain dominant distributions of power. Ultimately, through this energopolitical analysis of global food

[6] Dominic Boyer, 'Energopower: An Introduction' (2014) 87:2 *Anthropological Quarterly* 309, 323.

governance, this article contributes to this Symposium by situating the study of transnational food governance within broader struggles over ecological extraction in an age of climate change.

I. The rise of transnational food security governance

Contemporary transnational food security governance has its roots in the world food crisis of 1972–1974. The crisis' immediate cause was a large global grain trade, a *détente*, between the Soviet Union and the United States (US) after the Soviet Union faced a massive crop failure. The trade created a sudden shortage on global grain markets that caused cereal prices to skyrocket.[7] Yet underlying the crisis was an oil shock that caused the US, then the world's main guarantor of global food security, significant anxiety. Since the development of 'scientific farming' in the late nineteenth and early twentieth centuries, industrial food production had become dependent on cheap and easy access to fuel for agricultural inputs such as fertiliser and pesticides as well as for transport.[8] The US also actively promoted these fossil-fuel dependent forms of agro-industrial production in Latin America and South Asia through the Green Revolution. The crisis illuminated the mutual dependence of states on food and fuel and immediately produced a political struggle over global food regulation. Standing before the UN General Assembly in 1974, US President Gerald Ford made the link between food and energy clear, when he declared:

> The food and oil crises demonstrate the extent of our interdependence … Energy is required to produce food and food to produce energy—and both to provide a decent life for everyone. A global strategy for food and energy is urgently required.[9]

In the aftermath of the crisis, participants in the 1974 World Food Summit agreed to form the World Food Council (WFC) to coordinate the UN's response to the global food crisis as well as a standing FAO Committee on World Food Security. Soon after the crisis, however, to cope with both increasing global competition and the ongoing threat of energy insecurity, the US embraced a more market-oriented approach to relieve its agricultural surpluses. It sought to limit the WFC's mandate and, along with other OECD countries, to dismantle the UN Food and Agriculture Organization's (FAO) authorities, reorganising them to allow for greater control and oversight by donor countries.[10] Rather than building an international architecture to monitor global food stocks and manage global food markets, the US and

---

[7] Harriet Friedmann, 'The Political Economy of Food: A Global Crisis' (1993) *New Left Review* 29.

[8] Deborah Fitzgerald, *Every Farm a Factory: The Industrial Ideal in American Agriculture* (Yale University Press, 2010).

[9] *The New York Times*, Transcript of President Ford's Address to Session of U.N. General Assembly (1974), online: <https://www.nytimes.com/1974/09/19/archives/transcript-of-president-fords-address-to-session-of-un-general.html>.

other grain exporting countries became increasingly focused on trade. International finance institutions and the Global Agreement on Tarriffs and Trade became the primary arenas driving global food governance. By 1995, the Washington Consensus emerged as the dominant economic ideology and the Agreement on Agriculture was signed, unevenly opening up formerly protected agricultural markets.

The penetration of neoliberalism in global food and agriculture may have helped to manage the contradictions of the US-dominated global 'food regime' of the post-World War II period, but it did not address concerns about energy security.[11] In the 1970s, the mutually dependent relationship between food and fuel grew increasingly contradictory. In response to efforts by the Organization of Petroleum Exporting Countries' (OPEC) to take greater control over their natural resources, powerful oil dependent states began to turn to biofuels as a fuel additive and source of transport fuel. As concerns about foreign energy dependence, 'peak oil', and fossil fuel-caused climate change grew increasingly salient, the US, Canada, the European Union, Brazil and other countries began to implement biofuel mandates and subsidies to stimulate a market for renewable fuels.[12] By the early 2000s, the global biofuel market had rapidly expanded and US imports tripled.[13] Ethanol output grew from 16.9 to 72.0 billion litres and biodiesel output grew from 0.8 to 14.7 billion litres.[14] In 2008 alone, 16% of the world's soy crop, 18% of the world's sugar cane, and 11% of the world's corn harvest went into biofuel production.[15] Consequently, food and fuel crops were in direct competition for land.

In the aftermath of the biofuel-caused food crisis 2007–2008, multiple actors and institutions began to vie for authority over food and agricultural governance. In the meantime, a powerful set of transnational agrarian

---

[10] Nora McKeon, *Food Security Governance: Empowering Communities, Regulating Corporations* (Routledge, 2015) 16.

[11] Harriet Friedmann and Philip McMichael describe 'food regimes' as 'rule-governed structure[s] of production and consumption of food on a world scale.' They identify three food regimes: the colonial food regime dominated by the United Kingdom (1870–1930s), a 'mercantile industrial' food regime dominated by the United States (1940s–1970s), and a third regime starting in the 1970s that has sometimes been called the 'corporate food regime' or the 'corporate-environmental regime.' The food regime framework reveals how internal contradictions and struggles for control within each regime has facilitated shifting arrangements of global agricultural power. See Philip McMichael, 'A Food Regime Genealogy' (2009) 36:1 *The Journal of Peasant Studies* 139; Harriet Friedmann, 'From Colonialism to Green Capitalism: Social Movements and Emergence of Food Regimes' (2015) 11 *New Directions in the Sociology of Global Development* 227.

[12] For an empirical analysis of biofuel mandates see: Timothy Wise and Emily Cole, 'Global Development and Environment Institute, Mandating Food Insecurity: The Global Impacts of Rising Biofuel Mandates and Targets' (2015), GDAE Working Paper No. 15-01.

[13] See Gustavo de LT Oliveira, Ben McKay and Christina Plank, 'How Biofuel Policies Backfire: Misguided Goals, Inefficient Mechanisms, and Political-Ecological Blind Spots' (2017) 108 *Energy Policy* 765.

[14] Giovanni Sorda, Martin Banse and Claudia Kemfert, 'An Overview of Biofuel Policies across the World' (2010) 38 *Energy Policy* 6977, 6977.

[15] Robert Bailis and Jennifer Baka, 'Constructing Sustainable Biofuels: Governance of the Emerging Biofuel Economy' (2011) 101:4 *Annals of the Association of American Geographers* 827, 830.

movements had formed to oppose neoliberalism in agriculture. These movements, along with a cadre of international NGOs, began to demand inclusion into decision-making processes. They argued that the FAO and the CFS, the institution in which they had had the greatest access, were the most appropriate arenas for global food governance. With the FAO's authority waning, it initiated a reform process that would lead the CFS to become the *most* inclusive global food security policy space, in an attempt to subsume competing initiatives.[16]

Although participants of the CFS approached the reform process with very different visions of 'inclusivity', multi-stakeholder partnerships offered a popular template for governance. Multi-stakeholder initiatives emerged in the 1990s in response to both neoliberal challenges to the hierarchical 'command and control' paradigm of regulation as well as demands for participation from below, particularly in the domain of environmental politics.[17] Grounded in a pragmatic and collaborative approach to problem-solving, multi-stakeholder initiatives are based on the primary assumption that 'more participation and deliberation by affected groups will generate more effective collective problem-solving.'[18] Proponents of collaborative governance suggest that non-hierarchical, deliberative, and consensus-based processes can produce 'win-win' solutions for global conflicts.

In the context of struggles between food and fuel, collaborative forms of governance suggested a compromise could be reached between competing demands and social values. Hence, in response to the biofuel-caused food crisis, the CFS adopted a complex hybrid structure that draws together intergovernmental decision-making, multi-actor negotiation, and expert guidance. At the same time, different institutional arrangements of collaborative governance proliferated to manage a variety of crop-specific conflicts over biofuels, including the Roundtable on Responsible Palm Oil, Bonsucro (formerly the Better Sugarcane Initiative), the Roundtable on Responsible Soy, and the Roundtable on Sustainable Biomaterials. By drawing on the symbols of participation, inclusion, and consensus, the emerging multi-stakeholder paradigm seemed to offer the promise of greater global democracy.[19]

---

[16] See Christoffersen, Leif E. and others, *Food and Agricultural Organization, FAO: The Challenge of Renewal: Report of the Independent External Evaluation of the Food and Agriculture Organization of the United Nations (FAO)*, (2007), online: <http://www.fao.org/unfao/bodies/IEE-Working-Draft-Report/K0489E.pdf>.

[17] The language of 'stakeholders' however itself emerged from management strategy. See R Edward Freeman, *Strategic Management: A Stakeholder Approach* (Cambridge University Press, 2010).

[18] Karin Bäckstrand, 'Multi-Stakeholder Partnerships for Sustainable Development: Rethinking Legitimacy, Accountability and Effectiveness' (2006) 16 *European Environment* 290, 295.

[19] As McKeon notes, 'It is in this democratic 'public sphere' that the tendencies represented by the reformed CFS can be situated and—hopefully—reinforced by extending their authority over the economic world.' McKeon (n 10) 202.

II. The practice of collaborative food governance

Biofuels were one of the key issues that the CFS sought to address in its reform. However, they proved deeply controversial.[20] In 2011, when the CFS negotiated a set of recommendations to address food price volatility, civil society walked out because the US and other biofuel producers refused to recognise the impact of biofuels on rising food prices. Two years later, at the fortieth session of the CFS in 2013, the Committee met to develop a set of Policy Recommendations on Biofuels and Food Security (Recommendations), which I observed as part of a multi-year ethnographic project on the CFS.

In the preparatory meetings of the Civil Society Mechanism—the autonomous platform for the coordination of peoples' organisations, social movements, and international NGOs—activists expected the negotiations to be tense. However, because the CFS' mandate is focused on the elimination of hunger and the progressive realisation of the right to food, they hoped to develop a strong statement that prioritised food security *over* energy extraction and markets. Some participants described the negotiations over the Recommendations as a 'test' for the CFS—an evaluation of the possibility of multi-stakeholder, collaborative processes to engage in the reasoned, non-hierarchical negotiation in the context of contentious issues related to food security.

The process for developing guidelines and recommendations in the CFS is multi-faceted. All documents, however, are negotiated in face-to-face meetings through 'Friends of the Chair' sessions during the annual, weeklong meetings of the CFS.[21] At CFS 40, the Chair of the CFS (Chair) selected a delegate from Bangladesh to serve as the rapporteur or facilitator of the negotiations, which were supposed to be completed over three days' time. Conflict erupted almost as soon as the negotiations began. For twenty minutes, civil society and powerful biofuel producing states debated just the adjective that should define the link between energy and food security. Closely linked? Maybe linked? Should it be 'energy security and food

---

[20] Biofuels are also controversial because they are not energy efficient. In fact, it is highly debated whether biofuels are more sustainable than other fuel sources. Research suggests that there may somewhere between a net zero and twenty percent net gain in energy efficiency from biofuels. Biofuels promoters suggest that 'second' and 'third-generation' biofuels can promote a more sustainable future, they depend on technologies that do not yet exist at commercial scales. Moreover, biofuels are a subsidised industry that is increasingly consolidated and unevenly distributed. Fred Magdoff, 'The Political Economy and Ecology of Biofuels' (2008) 60 *Monthly Review* 34; The High Level Panel of Experts on Food Security and Nutrition, Biofuels and Food Security: A report by the High Level Panel of Experts on Food Security and Nutrition of the Committee on World Food Security, (2013), UN Committee on World Food Security, online: <http://www.fao.org/fileadmin/user_upload/hlpe/hlpe_documents/HLPE_Reports/HLPE-Report-5_Biofuels_and_food_security.pdf>, 93.

[21] CFS 40 took place in from 7–11 October 2013. For an overview of the process as well as the history of civil society engagement, see: John L Comaroff and Simon Roberts, *Rules and Processes* (University of Chicago Press 1986).

security'? Energy policy? The debate over the word that should define the link between food security and energy security lay at the very core of the conflict. It became immediately clear that major biofuel producing nations—Canada, the US, Brazil, and Australia—were steadfast in promoting their own biofuel industries. While they agreed to recognise the *potential* harmful consequences, they also sought to ensure that the text encouraged biofuels as a potential form of renewable energy and economic development. Activists sought to continually remind participants of the CFS' mandate and that any recommendations should be grounded in the prior commitments of stakeholders to protect food security.

Halfway through the first page, negotiations started to break down over a sentence that underscored 'that food security and the progressive realisation of the right to adequate food in the context of national food security should be priority concerns for all the relevant stakeholders in biofuel development.'[22] Civil society wished to include the names of already agreed upon human rights frameworks and guidelines that would inform this priority. In response to civil society member's push to include the right to food, the Canadian delegate stated, 'the right to food is not an agreed and established right in the same way as an international declaration.' Though the comment was surprising since the right to food lies at the very core of the CFS' mandate, it reflected the intensity of the dispute.

As time when on, the rapporteur of the negotiations increasingly began to recognise that biofuel promoting states would not compromise. He started to chasten developing countries and civil society when they continued to question the benefits of biofuels. When one African country sought to exert the same 'veto power' that powerful northern countries had been exercising throughout the negotiations, the rapporteur said that he thought that the country 'should be convinced.'[23] At another point he told civil society groups to come up with a more 'compromising attitude.' Consensus became a discourse that was coercively applied to less powerful countries and civil society.

Although space does not allow a thick ethnographic description of the negotiation, members of civil society were disappointed with the final product. They read a strongly worded statement in the Plenary, explaining that the negotiations 'failed to reflect the views of countries whose right to food is affected by biofuels policies' and argued that, 'the text overwhelmingly reflect[ed] the opinion of countries defending the interests of their own biofuels industry.' The Chair of the CFS responded by asking what he should do with this statement. 'How can we move forward without consensus?' he asked.

22 Zero draft version of the Policy Roundtable on Biofuels and Food Security. UN Committee on World Food Security. Copy on file with author. 8–10 October 2013.

23 All quotes are drawn from the author's fieldnotes of observations of the negotiations of the Recommendations on Biofuels and Food Security at CFS 40 in Rome, Italy.

According to the formal rules of the CFS, only states need to vote on final standards. Yet the CFS often operates as if all stakeholders are part of the consensus. Civil society's rejection of the biofuels thus unsettled this conceit. In response, a long-time civil society participant stated that it was civil society's right to withdraw from the consensus, but that they would continue to participate in the CFS processes. The Chair looked relieved and responded that he was happy that civil society was not going to try to 'block' the process and allow it to move forward.

In analysing this negotiation, one might point to the informal rules by which powerful actors exercised power. Indeed, anthropologists have long deployed ethnographic analyses of legal processes to excavate the implicit rules and forms of power that structure legal processes.[24] Certainly, both scholars and participants of deliberative processes have laboured to emphasise how such process inequalities shape unequal outcomes.[25] Multiple other analyses of multi-stakeholder negotiations in the CFS and other arenas of transnational biofuel governance also have found that their participatory procedures often fail to be as authentically 'inclusive' and non-hierarchical as they claim.[26] Such analyses thus prescribe a 'thickening' of deliberative processes to render them more democratic.[27] Yet by focusing on political-economic power as the primary driver of political interests, such analyses may overlook the ecological entanglements that constitute power relations. Given the proliferation of collaborative mechanisms to manage conflicts between food and fuel, a new understanding of power within transnational food security governance is needed. In the final section, therefore, I introduce the concepts of 'energopolitics' and 'energopower' and suggest their utility for

---

[24] See, for example: Comaroff and Roberts, *Rules and Processes* (University of Chicago Press 1986).

[25] Taehyon Choi and Peter J Robertson, 'Deliberation and Decision in Collaborative Governance: A Simulation of Approaches to Mitigate Power Imbalance' (2014) 24 *Journal of Public Administration Research and Theory* 495; Jill M Purdy, 'The Role of Power in Collaborative Governance' in Richard D Margerum and Cathy J Robinson (eds), *The Challenges of Collaboration in Environmental Governance: Barriers and Responses* (Edward Elgar Publishing, 2016).

[26] For a recent view of the CFS, see: Nora McKeon, 'Are Equity and Sustainability a Likely Outcome When Foxes and Chickens Share the Same Coop? Critiquing the Concept of Multistakeholder Governance of Food Security' (2017) 14:3 *Globalizations* 379. For critical appraisals of biofuel governance, see: Theresa Selfa, Carmen Bain and Renata Moreno, 'Depoliticizing Land and Water "Grabs" in Colombia: The Limits of Bonsucro Certification for Enhancing Sustainable Biofuel Practices' (2014) 31 *Agriculture and Human Values* 455; Michiel Köhne, 'Multi-Stakeholder Initiative Governance as Assemblage: Roundtable on Sustainable Palm Oil as a Political Resource in Land Conflicts Related to Oil Palm Plantations' (2014) 31 *Agriculture and Human Values* 469; Greetje Schouten, Pieter Leroy and Pieter Glasbergen, 'On the Deliberative Capacity of Private Multi-Stakeholder Governance: The Roundtables on Responsible Soy and Sustainable Palm Oil' (2012) 83 *Ecological Economics* 42; Emmanuelle Cheyns, 'Multi-Stakeholder Initiatives for Sustainable Agriculture: Limits of the "Inclusiveness" Paradigm' in Stefano Ponte, Jakob Vestergaard and Peter Gibbon (eds), *Governing Through Standards: Origins, Drivers and Limitations* (Palgrave Macmillan, 2011). More broadly, for a more general critique of multi-stakeholder processes, see: Harris Gleckman, Transnational Institute, *Multi-Stakeholderism: A Corporate Push for a New Form of Global Governance* (2016), online: <https://www.tni.org/en/publication/multi-stakeholderism-a-corporate-push-for-a-new-form-of-global-governance>.

[27] For a description of 'thick' and 'thin' proceduralism see: Julia Black, 'Proceduralizing Regulation: Part II' (2001) 21:1 *Oxford Journal of Legal Studies* 33.

understanding transformations in transnational food security governance and transnational law, more broadly.

III. Energopolitics and the food-fuel nexus

In an era when humans are facing the ecological constraints of climate change, critical scholars have begun to re-evaluate dominant accounts of power and capitalist development by highlighting the under-acknowledged role of nature in enabling processes of accumulation.[28] This move is part of a broader shift within the social sciences and humanities to recognise the ecological foundations of inequality in the age of the 'Anthropocene'—the geological epoch recently named to recognise that human activity is the primary driver of environmental transformation. Energy is at the core of these analyses. As the capacity to work, energy is crucial for labour and the production of value. Yet humans cannot produce energy on their own. As Alfred Crosby puts it, we are all 'children of the sun' that rely on plants or technologies to convert solar energy into usable carbon energy.[29] Competition for carbon energy has thus served as the basis for capital accumulation and larger global political economies. Seen through an energy-focused lens, Tim di Muzio summarises that 'the global political economy is at base a solar economy whereby humans have come to monetise energy and natural resources in hierarchical domestic and international relationships.'[30] Scholars from multiple disciplines are thus beginning to reassess the constitutive role of energy in politics, law, and the economy.[31]

Recent studies have primarily focused on fossil fuels, but agriculture has been central throughout the *longue duree* of energy extraction and consumption. Before fossil fuels, biomass served as the primary form of fuel that powered human civilisation. In these mostly agrarian societies, control over agricultural surpluses created the material foundation for different relationships of power.[32] The development of technologies that could take advantage

[28] Dipesh Chakrabarty, 'The Climate of History: Four Theses' (2009) 35 *Critical Inquiry* 197. Jason Moore describes this as a 'world ecological' approach that integrates the political economic lens of world systems theory with political ecological analyses of planetary extraction. Jason W Moore, *Capitalism in the Web of Life: Ecology and the Accumulation of Capital* (Verso, 2015).

[29] Alfred W Crosby, *Children of the Sun: A History of Humanity's Unappeasable Appetite for Energy* (W W Norton & Company, 2007).

[30] Tim Di Muzio, 'Energy, Capital as Power and World Order' in *The Palgrave Handbook of Critical International Political Economy* (Springer, 2016) 267.

[31] Tim Di Muzio, *Carbon Capitalism: Energy, Social Reproduction and World Order* (Rowman & Littlefield International, 2015); Andreas Malm, *Fossil Capital: The Rise of Steam Power and the Roots of Global Warming* (Verso Books, 2016); Hannah Appel, Arthur Mason and Michael Watts, *Subterranean Estates: Life Worlds of Oil and Gas* (Cornell University Press, 2015); Laura Nader, *The Energy Reader* (John Wiley & Sons, 2010).

[32] Michael W Young, *Fighting With Food: Leadership, Values and Social Control in a Massim Society* (Cambridge University Press, 2009). See also: Jane Fajans, 'The Transformative Value of Food: A Review Essay' (1988) 3 *Food and Foodways* 143.

of the 'buried sunshine' of carbon-dense fossil fuels transformed Western European agrarian societies and spurred colonial schemes to secure food for industrialising states, causing massive transformations in the geography of global food production.[33] The industrialisation of agriculture through fossil fuel-based inputs and fuel-run machinery in the Global North deepened the relationship between food and fuel. It was not until after the 1972–1973 global food and fuel crises, however, that powerful states recognised the economic and political vulnerability caused by the 'food-fuel nexus'.[34]

The function of agriculture as a source of human energy and, increasingly, as transport fuel suggests that disputes over global food are substantively changing how powerful states assess the relation between food and fuel. Though political-economic accounts of power—whether in agrarian studies or those deployed in collaborative governance scholarship—emphasise the competition for capital accumulation, they often overlook the way that the material processes of extraction shape the calculative logics upon which regulation is constructed.[35] In effort to remedy this, Dominic Boyer developed the concepts of 'energopolitics' and 'energopower'. In developing these concepts, Boyer draws on the Foucauldian notion of biopolitics, which emphasises 'the specific strategies and contestations over problematizations of collective human vitality, morbidity and mortality,'[36] but he challenges the human-centric understandings of power and knowledge inherent in the Foucault's analysis.[37] He defines energopolitics as 'a genealogy of modern power that rethinks political power through the twin analytics of electricity and fuel.'[38] Such an intervention seeks to 'make energy a crucial part of the story of the formation of the modern subject and the constitution of the contemporary state.'[39]

Studies of energopolitics emphasise how socio-technical arrangements of energy extraction, production, processing, and consumption constitute contingent assemblages of political authority and expertise.[40] In doing so, they reveal how energy has shaped national and global regulatory ideologies. For example, Timothy Mitchell has analysed how oil shaped the calculative

[33] Crosby (n 29).

[34] Robert Bailey, 'The "Food Versus Fuel" Nexus' in Andreas Goldthau (ed), *The Handbook of Global Energy Policy* (John Wiley & Sons Ltd, 2013).

[35] In agrarian studies, see, for example: Henry Bernstein, *Class Dynamics of Agrarian Change* (Kumarian Press 2010); For collaborative governances scholarship see: Choi and Robertson (n 26); Purdy (n 26).

[36] Paul Rabinow and Nikolas Rose, 'Biopower Today' (2006) 1 *BioSocieties* 195, 197.

[37] Boyer (n 6).

[38] Boyer, 'Energopower: An Introduction' (n 6) 325. See also Dominic Boyer, 'Energopolitics and the Anthropology of Energy' (2011) 52 *Anthropology News* 5, 5.

[39] Imre Szeman, 'Conclusion: On Energopolitics' (2014) 87 *Anthropological Quarterly* 453, 459.

[40] See, for example: Douglas Rogers, 'The Materiality of the Corporation: Oil, Gas, and Corporate Social Technologies in the Remaking of a Russian Region' (2012) 39 *American Ethnologist* 284; Catherine Alexander and Joshua O Reno, 'From Biopower to Energopolitics in England's Modern Waste Technology' (2014) 87 *Anthropological Quarterly* 335; Jennifer Richter, 'Energopolitics and Nuclear Waste: Containing the Threat of Radioactivity' (2017) 30 *Energy Research & Social Science* 61.

logics of the post-war Keynesian welfare state. As he explains, the availability of seemingly endless amounts of oil enabled post-war economic theorists such as Keynes to bracket natural resources and flows of energy, which had previously thought to have been finite and instead build a modern science of economics based on money and prices.[41] Mitchell argues that these calculative logics enabled the 'economy' to emerge as an independent sphere of expert knowledge and management, thereby facilitating the rise of the US regulatory state. While the materiality of oil—its abundance, location, and ease of transport—helped shape the forms of knowledge that allowed for administrative control, food also played a key role.[42] Fossil fuel-based inputs provided the agricultural surpluses that were used by the US as a tool of peace (and warfare).

Together, the food-fuel nexus of the mid-twentieth century helped to form what Wolfgang Friedman called the 'international law of cooperation'.[43] The post-war order was envisioned as a global economy regulated by institutions modelled in the image of the Keynesian welfare state—premised on national economic development, import-substitution industrialisation, and agricultural protection.[44] The formation of transnational food and agricultural institutions thus helped to inscribe the Keynesian-Fordist development project into the post-war international order.

Yet as early as the 1950s, struggles to maintain control over oil foreshadowed a normative set of transformations that would become more dominant in later decades. During this period, Philip Jessup observed what he described as 'transnational law,' a new form of legality that combined public and private law and incorporated both states and non-states.[45] Jessup's use of examples from agreements and arbitrations between nation-states and multi-national oil corporations to analyse this new legal form is often overlooked. In the bid to secure their oil resources British and American states elevated multinational oil corporations' status into an almost quasi-state, embracing an 'international law of contract' in which states and corporations were aligned as

[41] Timothy Mitchell, *Carbon Democracy: Political Power in the Age of Oil* (Verso Books, 2011); Christophe Bonneuil and Jean-Baptiste Fressoz, *The Shock of the Anthropocene: The Earth, History and Us* (Reprint edition, Verso, 2017).

[42] Mitchell notes the important role of agriculture, explaining, 'We think of industrialization (and the democracy that followed) as an urban phenomenon based on fossil fuels, but it depended on an agrarian and colonial transformation based on organic forms of energy'. Mitchell (n 41) 16.

[43] Wolfgang Friedmann, *The Changing Structure of International Law* (Columbia University Press, 1964).

[44] As Anne-Marie Slaughter explains, in its early formation, Roosevelt hoped to design the Food and Agriculture Organization (FAO) in the model of a US regulatory agency. She writes, 'In 1943, Roosevelt envisioned the conferences of the Food and Agriculture Organization as prototypes for a series of permanent international agencies in social and economic fields'. Anne-Marie Burley-Slaughter, 'Regulating the World: Multilateralism, International Law, and the Projection of the New Deal Regulatory State' in Robert Howse (ed), *The World Trading System: Critical Perspectives on the World Economy* (Routledge, 1998); See also, Amy LS Staples and Amy L Sayward, *The Birth of Development: How the World Bank, Food and Agriculture Organization, and World Health Organization Changed the World, 1945–1965* (Kent State University Press, 2006).

[45] Philip Jessup, *Transnational Law* (Yale University Press, 1956).

equal private actors.[46] When the world faced oil and food crises in the 1970s, the 'transnational situations' observed by Jessup became increasingly commonplace as concern over oil propelled the ascendance of neoliberalism. Indeed, the oil shocks were used by neoliberal economists as evidence for what they argued was the failure of Keynesian regulation.[47] Both Keynesianism and neoliberalism were thus shaped by energopolitics; Just as Keynesian ideology was enabled by the calculative logics of abundant energy, neoliberal theory attempted to externalise the increasingly recognised scarcity of energy through the price system. Beginning in the late 1970s and 1980s, this led to a more market-oriented, and corporate consolidated system of global food production and provisioning.

By the 2000s, the food-fuel nexus facilitated yet another set of normative transformations. The increasing demand for biofuels and the pressures this put on agricultural land, especially through land grabs, caused a global food crisis that revealed a fundamental conflict between food and fuel.[48] To mediate this conflict, collaborative and multi-stakeholder models emerged as a new common-sense for transnational food and environmental governance.[49] By including civil society and social movements, this participatory paradigm created the possibility of democratising the governance of global food. In fact, collaborative multi-stakeholder models of governance have become most widespread in fields related to energy: food, agriculture, and mining.[50] Yet collaboration, is not restricted to environmental conflicts. In response to the failure of neoliberal forms of coordination, Annelise Riles suggests that collaboration has become increasingly a 'template for social and political life, as well as market activity.'[51]

While scholars have described the organisational diffusion of multi-stakeholder models as an expression of the politics of sustainability,[52] they can also

---

[46] Antony Anghie, *Imperialism, Sovereignty and the Making of International Law* (Cambridge University Press, 2007) 229–34.

[47] The development of the field of resource economics, played an important role in defeating Keynesian economics by developing new market mechanisms including an oil futures market on the New York Mercantile Exchange and carbon markets that could serve to coordinate the petro-economy. See Timothy Mitchell, 'The Resources of Economics' (2010) 3:2 *Journal of Cultural Economy* 189. In addition, Sandy Smith-Nonini traces the ways in which the oil crisis and the petrodollars that were generated from it enabled neoliberalism to emerge. Sandy Smith-Nonini, 'The Role of Corporate Oil and Energy Debt in Creating the Neoliberal Era' (2016) 3 *Economic Anthropology* 57.

[48] Philip McMichael, 'Biofuels in the Food Regime' (2010) 37:4 *The Journal of Peasant Studies* 609; Marc Edelman, Carlos Oya and Saturnino M Borras JR, 'Global Land Grabs: Historical Processes, Theoretical and Methodological Implications and Current Trajectories' (2013) 34:9 *Third World Quarterly* 1517.

[49] Neil Gunningham, 'The New Collaborative Environmental Governance: The Localization of Regulation' (2009) 36:1 *Journal of Law and Society* 145.

[50] MSI Integrity and Duke Human Rights Center at the Kenan Institute for Ethics, The New Regulators? Assessing the Landscape of Multi-Stakeholder Initiative (2017), online: <https://msi-database.org/data/The%20New%20Regulators%20-%20MSI%20Database%20Report.pdf>.

[51] Annelise Riles, 'From Comparison to Collaboration: Experiments with a New Scholarly and Political Reform' (2015) 78 *Law and Contemporary Problems* 147, 153.

[52] Klaus Dingwerth and Philipp Pattberg, 'World Politics and Organizational Fields: The Case of Transnational Sustainability Governance' (2009) 15:4 *European Journal of International Relations* 707.

be understood as a product of energopolitics. For the multi-stakeholderisation of the food-fuel nexus represents an effort to re-internalise planetary limits back into socio-economic forms of regulation that were once excised in Keynesian and neoliberal regulatory forms of regulation. However, through the multi-stakeholder model, food and fuel are constructed as a set of equivalents that assumes a consensus can be reached between these two goods. By re-internalising the environmental limits through the bargaining model of multi-stakeholder governance, the contradiction between food and fuel is diffused and the relation between them is reconstructed as complementary.

An energopolitical account of collaborative governance thus reveals how material processes of energy extraction and consumption shape how contestation related to the food-fuel nexus is constituted. In this context, energopower operates through both construction of its subjects and as a process of dispute management. First, multi-stakeholder governance constructs 'stakeholders' as formally equal parties to a conflict. Rather than recognising the historically-shaped hierarchies and differentiated responsibilities that have resulted from uneven energy consumption and emissions, collaborative arrangements seek to transcend inequalities between stakeholders through 'authentic' and 'inclusive' dialogue. However, the biofuel negotiation described above unsettles this conceit. This was clear from the rapporteur's efforts to coerce less powerful countries and civil society actors into being 'more compromising.' Yet only certain actors needed to adopt a more compromising attitude, illuminating the implicit hierarchies of power underlying the multi-stakeholder process.

Second, multi-stakeholder processes reconstitute deeply political conflicts over energy-fuelled inequalities as technocratic problems that can be solved through consensus-based solutions. Throughout the negotiations, the rapporteur constantly echoed the refrain that 'we need to get to consensus' in attempt to diffuse antagonism between stakeholders. This techno-managerial approach to mediating conflict has thus been described as 'post-political.'[53] The post-political frame emphasises the contradiction that while climate change, fossil fuels, and food security each have become highly politicised and contentious issues, energy-fuelled conflicts of profound distributional concern are being managed through processes that depoliticise them. Such an analysis suggests that collaborative forms of governance serve to repress the political ecological contradictions of capital, just as was accomplished through previous regulatory ideologies.

As multi-stakeholder forms of governance continue to proliferate, an energopolitical lens thus connects seemingly disparate sites of contestation to

[53] Erik Swyngedouw, 'Apocalypse Forever? Post-Political Populism and the Specter of Climate Change' (2010) 27:2–3 *Theory, Culture & Society* 213, 225; see also: J Duncan, 'Governing in a Postpolitical Era: Civil Society Participation for Improved Food Security Governance' in David Barling (ed), *Advances in Food Security and Sustainability*, vol 1 (Elsevier, 2016).

larger struggles over carbon extraction, emissions, and consumption. Indeed, today, multi-stakeholder processes are increasingly proffered as a best practice for managing ecological conflicts; both the Sustainable Development Goals and the CFS are promoting multi-stakeholder partnerships.[54] While political-economic approaches suggest that collaborative processes may reproduce existing power relations, an energopolitical lens reveals how they are both constituted by and constitutive of the broader political ecologies responsible for climate change. For as climate change poses an increasing threat to global food security, an energopolitical lens connecting larger struggles over carbon-fuelled climate change is critical.

IV. Conclusions: food, fuel, and the political ecology of transnational law

Transnational food security governance is an increasingly important site of study for transnational legal scholars. Struggles over food and agricultural regulation in the national context have long been constitutive socio-legal processes through which new understandings of public and private are constructed. As these conflicts are projected into transnational arenas, they become formative in reshaping relations between state, society, and markets. Yet the rise of biofuels at a time of increasing concern over fossil fuel-produced climate change also serves as a reminder of the enduring role of the food-fuel nexus and provides an impetus to rethink dominant accounts of power within the law and politics of global food security. Following recent political ecological analyses of global capitalism, I have argued that understanding the food-fuel nexus within larger global processes of energy extraction, processing, and distribution illuminates the ecological foundation of contemporary power asymmetries. Drawing on such an approach reveals how the proliferation of new multi-stakeholder forms to manage the mutually dependent but contradictory relationship between food and fuel reflects a larger process of energopolitical transformation.

New forms of multi-stakeholder governance are premised on the assumption that participation and non-hierarchical collaboration can produce new compromises between competing social, economic, and environmental values. Indeed, the development of this normative form in response to both neoliberal welfare state withdrawal as well as new concerns over the global public good of the environment, is a product of larger energopolitical and political-economic transformations. Yet as both my observations of the biofuel negotiation in the CFS as well as numerous studies of biofuel 'Roundtables'

---

[54] See SDG #17 (17.16 and 17.17) See: http://www.un.org/ga/search/view_doc.asp?symbol=A/RES/70/1&Lang=E. In addition, the High Level Panel of Experts of the CFS recently undertook a study of 'Multi-Stakeholder Partnerships to Finance and Improve Food Security and Nutrition in the Framework of the 2030 Agenda'. See: http://www.fao.org/3/CA0156EN/CA0156en.pdf.

suggest,[55] these arenas often serve as processes through which powerful biofuel producing states and multinational corporations seek to legitimise their economic and energy interests. By framing concerns over food security and energy security as equivalent values, these processes depoliticise the tension between food and fuel thereby concealing the ways in which access to and control over energy serve as the foundation of modern political power. Analysing transnational food security governance from the vantage of energopolitics thus suggests that collaborative processes are often themselves *compromised*.

Ultimately, as collaboration becomes the *sine-qua-non* for sustainability in an age of climate change, an energopolitical analysis is essential. For as we enter the new geological epoch known as the Anthropocene, new analytical tools are needed to integrate nature back into our accounts of how power operates. Towards this end, energopolitics offers a new conceptual tool for this analytical programme, for which transnational legal scholars are now beginning to advocate.[56] By connecting disparate sites of conflict, an energopolitical approach illuminates the shifting operation of global power and moves us towards a greater understanding of the political ecology of transnational law.

Acknowledgements

I would like to thank Marie-Claire Foblets, Priscilla Claeys, Amy Cohen, Julia Dehm, James J.A. Blair, Leon Castellanos-Jankiewicz, and Marta Morvillo for comments on various versions of this paper.

Disclosure statement

No potential conflict of interest was reported by the author.

Funding

Research funding for this paper was generously provided by a National Science Foundation Directorate for Social, Behavioral, and Economic Sciences, Law and Social Science Program, Doctoral Dissertation Research Improvement Grant (SES# 1323743).

---

[55] See (n 26) for example Cheyns (2011).

[56] See Julia Dehm, 'Post Paris Reflections: Fossil Fuels, Human Rights and the Need to Excavate New Ideas for Climate Justice' (2017) 8 *Journal of Human Rights and the Environment* 280; Christine Parker and Fiona Haines, 'An Ecological Approach to Regulatory Studies?' 45:1 *Journal of Law and Society* 136; Luis Eslava, Usha Natarajan and Rose Parfitt, '(Post)Revolutionary Interlinkages: Labour, Environment and Accumulation' (2013) 4:1 *Transnational Legal Theory* 108; Usha Natarajan and Kishan Khoday, 'Locating Nature: Making and Unmaking International Law' (2014) 27:3 *Leiden Journal of International Law* 573.

International law and feeding the world in times of climate change

Anne Saab

ABSTRACT
Growing consensus that climate change exacerbates hunger has led to enhanced efforts to find new ways to feed the world. The prevailing approach to feeding the world in times of climate change is informed by neoliberal tenets, in line with the dominant contemporary global food regime. At the same time, there is resistance against neoliberal solutions to hunger, led primarily by food sovereignty movements. This short paper explores the role that international law plays in constructing a neoliberal narrative of hunger and a food sovereignty narrative of hunger in the context of climate change. The main conclusion is that the dominant neoliberal narrative promotes certain fundamental assumptions about hunger and climate change, and the food sovereignty narrative fails to challenge these assumptions. The language of international law limits the options food sovereignty advocates have to challenge the dominant neoliberal narrative and its underlying assumptions.

Hunger, climate change, and international law

'History', as historian James Vernon tells us, 'cannot escape hunger'.[1] Hunger is by no means a new phenomenon, but the reality of climate change has prompted a renewed sense of urgency of global hunger as a problem. Whilst agricultural practices contribute significantly to greenhouse gas emissions that cause climate change, the agricultural sector is also one of the most vulnerable to the impacts of climate change. Agriculture is highly dependent on climate, and changes in climate—including higher average temperatures, increased soil salinity, and more droughts—affect the types of food crops that can grow, how much food can be grown, and where food can be grown. The fifth and latest assessment report by the Intergovernmental Panel on Climate Change (IPCC) contains a chapter on food security and food production systems, which emphasises the adverse impacts of climate

[1] James Vernon, *Hunger: A Modern History* (The Belknap Press of Harvard University Press, 2007) 1.

change on food production.[2] The 2017 UN report on the State of Food Security and Nutrition in the World presents climate change as one of the main reasons, in addition to conflict, for rising global hunger.[3] Recently published research in *The Lancet* predicts that the effects of climate change on the availability and quality of food will cause more than half a million deaths worldwide by 2050.[4] UN Special Rapporteur on the Right to Food, Hilal Elver, has stated that climate change 'poses severe and distinct threats to food security',[5] and the World Food Programme underscores that the impacts of climate change 'increas[e] the risk of hunger'.[6]

The starting point of this research is the premise that climate change has an adverse impact on agriculture, therefore exacerbating global hunger. This premise raises the question: how do we feed the world in times of climate change? Many actors involved in tackling the issue of global hunger in the face of climate change employ international law and the language of international law in an attempt to provide answers to this question. The solution to any problem depends on how the problem is understood in the first place. Frances Mooré Lappe and Joseph Collins plainly note that 'how we understand hunger determines what we think are its solutions'.[7] In line with this ostensibly obvious statement and rather than studying international law as part of the solution, this exploration examines the role of international law in framing the problem of hunger in the face of climate change.

I study the role of international law through the example of so-called climate-ready seeds. Climate-ready seeds are seeds that are genetically engineered for resistance to certain climatic conditions, including drought, and are advanced as a possible means to adapt to the adverse impacts of climate change on food production and hunger.[8] The heated debates over the value

---

[2] John R Porter et al, 'Food Security and Food Production Systems' in *Climate Change 2014: Impacts, Adaptation, and Vulnerability. Part A: Global and Sectoral Aspects. Contribution of Working Group II to the Fifth Assessment Report of the Intergovernmental Panel on Climate Change* (Cambridge University Press, 2013) Chapter 7. See also: Ove Hoegh-Guldberg et al, 'Impacts of 1.5°C Global Warming on Natural and Human Systems' in Valerie Masson-Delmotte et al (eds), *Global Warming of 1.5°C. An IPCC Special Report on the Impacts of Global Warming of 1.5°C above Pre-Industrial Levels and Related Global Greenhouse Gas Emission Pathways, in the Context of Strengthening the Global Response to the Threat of Climate Change, Sustainable Development, and Efforts to Eradicate Poverty* (In press, 2018), which includes numerous references to food and agriculture.

[3] 'The State of Food Security and Nutrition in the World 2017: Building Resilience for Peace and Food Security' (FAO, IFAD, UNICEF, WFP and WHO, 2017).

[4] Marco Springmann et al, 'Global and Regional Health Effects of Future Food Production under Climate Change: A Modelling Study' (2016) 387(10031) *The Lancet* 1937. See also: Damian Carrington, 'More than Half a Million Could Die as Climate Change Impacts Diet – Report', *The Guardian*, 3 March 2016.

[5] Office of the High Commissioner for Human Rights, 'Climate Change Poses Major Threat to Food Security, UN Expert Warns', 3 November 2015, online: www.ohchr.org/EN/NewsEvents/Pages/DisplayNews.aspx?LangID=E&NewsID=16702.

[6] World Food Programme, 'How Climate Change Affects Hunger', online: www.wfp.org/climate-change. Emphasis added.

[7] Frances Moore Lappé and Joseph Collins, *World Hunger: Twelve Myths* (Earthscan, 2nd ed 1998) 4.

[8] One example is Monsanto's DroughtGard® maize, which was allowed for commercialisation in the US in late 2011. See 'DroughtGard® Hybrids', online: www.genuity.com/corn/Pages/DroughtGard-Hybrids.aspx.

of climate-ready seeds illustrate two narratives of hunger in the face of climate change. The neoliberal narrative is consistent with the dominant neoliberal food regime. Central features include an emphasis on food production, technological solutions, privatisation, and strong corporate influence.[9] The promotion of climate-ready seeds as means to feed the world reflects the neoliberal food regime. The food sovereignty narrative, in contrast, is consistent with food sovereignty movements that seek to oppose and reject the neoliberal food regime. Its main features include an emphasis on access to and distribution of food, local production, and strong opposition to the privatisation and corporatisation of the food system. Philip McMichael describes food sovereignty as 'a culminating protective movement against the deceit of "feeding the world" by undermining farming with the false economy of value relations of the food regime'.[10] The rejection of climate-ready seeds, and particularly the criticism of the corporate domination of these seeds is in line with the food sovereignty narrative.

The two narratives of hunger reveal controversies over climate-ready seeds and also reflect broader contemporary debates about how to govern the global food system.[11] Each narrative presents seemingly different understandings of what kind of problem hunger is, and contradictory solutions to feeding the world. The neoliberal narrative promotes increasing food production through agricultural biotechnologies with private sector seed corporations taking a leading role. This is evident in the growing number of patent applications on purportedly 'climate-resilient' crops, as well as the fact that the overwhelming majority of these patent applications are done by a handful of large private seed corporations.[12] The food sovereignty narrative promotes greater access to and distribution of available food, and above all resists the corporate-dominated technological solutions advocated by the neoliberal narrative. This is evident in fierce calls for 'No patents on seeds!' and protests against seed corporations such as Monsanto.[13] Voices in the food sovereignty

[9] David Harvey, *A Brief History of Neoliberalism* (Oxford University Press, 2007) 2. See also: Philip McMichael, 'Global Development and the Corporate Food Regime' in Frederick H Buttel and Philip McMichael (eds), *New Directions in the Sociology of Global Development* (Elsevier, 2005) 273.

[10] Philip McMichael, 'Historicizing Food Sovereignty: A Food Regime Perspective' (paper presented at 'Food Sovereignty: A Critical Dialogue Conference', Yale University, New Haven, CT, 14–15 September 2013), 1.

[11] For some recent discussions about food regimes, see: 'Bernstein-McMichael-Friedmann Dialogue on Food Regime' (2016) 43(3) *Journal of Peasant Studies.*

[12] See, for instance: Shardul Agrawala et al, 'Adaptation and Innovation: An Analysis of Crop Biotechnology Patent Data' (2012) OECD Environment Working Papers No. 40, 33–34, which shows that four out of the five most active patenting organisations are private sector corporations. See also: ETC Group, 'Patenting the "Climate Genes" ... and Capturing the Climate Agenda' (2008); ETC Group, 'Capturing "Climate Genes": Gene Giants Stockpile Patents on "Climate-Ready" Crops in Bid to Become "Biomassters"' (2010). These ETC Group reports show the rapidly growing number of patent applications on climate-resilient traits in agricultural seeds and crops by a small group of corporations.

[13] See, for instance: The International Coalition of 'No Patents on Seeds', 'Stop Patents on Plants and Animals!', no-patents-on-seeds.org/; No Patents on Seeds, 'Monsanto Soon to Receive 30 European Patents on Food Plants: Coalition of No Patents on Seeds! Publishes Appeal to European Governments',

narrative—most notably civil society organisations and NGOs such as ETC Group and La Via Campesina, as well as many food regime theorists—contend that neoliberal policies worsen both climate change and hunger, and they seek to provide better solutions to feeding the world.[14]

My main finding is that while the two narratives appear contradictory, they are based on the same underlying fundamental assumptions about hunger and climate change. These underlying assumptions support the neoliberal status quo. International law invoked by neoliberal actors promotes these assumptions, and international law invoked by food sovereignty actors fails to effectively challenge these assumptions. Keeping the same fundamental assumptions about hunger and climate change in place prevents us from formulating radically different narratives of hunger and providing new ways of feeding the world that deviate from the dominant neoliberal approach. Assuming that the neoliberal approach is falling short of effectively tackling global hunger, the underlying assumptions must be more explicitly questioned in order to find better ways to feed the world. International law and the actors employing the language of international law play a part in keeping these assumptions in place, and therefore can also play a role in challenging them.

In the following sections the article will explore the role of international law in constructing these two narratives of hunger and reinforcing the underlying assumptions. It should be noted that even though the term 'international' law is used in this writing, much of the analysis falls in the domain of what can be called 'transnational' law. While international law strictly understood covers only the relationship between States, transnational law deals with the relationship between different domestic legal systems without necessarily attempting to create one overarching legal system. There is much discussion about the definition, the value and function of transnational law.[15] It is not my intention here to get into this debates, but suffice it to say that transnational law for the purpose of this examination underscores the relevance of a range of actors—state and non-state, international and domestic, public and private, individual and collective—and different levels of regulation in global food governance.

21 May 2015, https://no-patents-on-seeds.org/en/information/news/monsanto-soon-receive-30-european-patents-food-plants.

[14] For instance, La Via Campesina has written in a report: 'Monsanto and other agribusiness corporations … claim that GM crops are a solution to hunger … and the effects of climate change including drought and flooding—even though trials have repeatedly failed. Analysis has shown that there is no evidence that GM crops produce greater yields than conventional crops, and there are no "miracle" crops available that tolerate drought, flooding or salt … What has happened though, rather than solving hunger, is that the corporate grip on agriculture has tightened as we head towards one billion people going hungry globally.' La Via Campesina, Friends of the Earth International, Combat Monsanto, 'Combatting Monsanto Grassroots: Resistance to the Corporate Power of Agribusiness in the Era of the "Green Economy" and a Changing Climate', March 2012, 4. https://viacampesina.org/en/wp-content/uploads/sites/2/2012/04/Monsanto-Publication-EN-Final-Version.pdf.

[15] See, for instance: Roger Cotterrell, 'What is Transnational Law?' (2012) 37(2) *Law & Social Inquiry*.

Studying the global food system from a legal perspective requires not only attention to laws that apply between States, but also more importantly, the complex relationships between all levels of national and international law that transcend the idea of national borders.

Climate-ready seeds and international law in narratives of hunger

There is a broad consensus that climate change negatively impacts global agricultural production,[16] and consequently that climate change is exacerbating global hunger.[17] One of the solutions devised to tackle climate change-induced hunger is '[e]ngineering seeds to make them cope better with altered climates',[18] known colloquially as climate-ready seeds. The research and development of so-called climate-ready seeds is dominated by a small number of large private sector seed corporations, including Monsanto, Syngenta, BASF, DuPont Pioneer, and Bayer.[19] The idea behind climate-ready seeds is that these seeds can produce crops in spite of adverse climate conditions. Much of the research efforts have focused particularly on drought-resistant seeds, to ensure adequate food production in the face of droughts worsened by climate change. Climate-ready seeds are presented by some as valuable means to feed the world in times of climate change.[20]

As much as climate-ready seeds are hailed by some as valuable for agriculture due to their supposed ability to adapt to the impacts of climate change, they are also fiercely criticised by others. Criticisms of climate-ready seeds focus on various features. One criticism is that these seeds have—at least to date—not been successful in actually producing higher crop yields.[21] The

---

16 Porter et al, (n 23); Deepak K Ray et al, 'Climate Variation Explains a Third of Global Crop Yield Variability', (2015) 6 *Nature Communications*.

17 Martin Parry et al, *Climate Change and Hunger: Responding to the Challenge* (World Food Programme, 2009) 14; Gerard C Nelson et al, *Food Security, Farming, and Climate Change to 2050: Scenarios, Results, Policy Options* (International Food Policy Research Institute, 2010) 1; Ben Block, 'Climate Change Will Worsen Hunger, Study Says', WorldWatch Institute, www.worldwatch.org/node/6271; Food and Agriculture Organization, International Fund for Agricultural Development and World Food Programme, 'The State of Food Insecurity in the World 2015. Meeting the 2015 International Hunger Targets: Taking Stock of Uneven Progress' (FAO, 2015) Box 5 on p. 40.

18 Stephen H Schneider and Jessica Lane, 'Dangers and Thresholds in Climate Change and the Implications for Justice', in W Neil Adger et al (eds), *Fairness in Adaptation to Climate Change* (MIT Press, 2006) 46.

19 See, for instance: Agrawala et al (n 12) 33–34, which shows that four out of the five most active patenting organisations are private sector corporations.

20 For a comprehensive overview of how climate-ready seeds are promoted by seed corporations, see: Matthew Rimmer, 'Climate-Ready Crops: Intellectual Property, Climate Change and Agriculture' in Matthew Rimmer and Alison McLennan (eds), *Intellectual Property and Emerging Technologies: The New Biology* (Edward Elgar, 2012) especially at 'Part II Patent Law and Agricultural Biotechnology', 333–47.

21 See, for instance: Doug Gurian-Sherman, *Failure to Yield: Evaluating the Performance of Genetically Engineered Crops* (Union of Concerned Scientists, 2009). See also: Natasha Gilbert, 'Cross-Bred Crops Get Fit Faster: Genetic Engineering Lags Behind Conventional Breeding in Efforts to Create Drought-Resistant Maize' (2014) 513 *Nature* 292.

most explicit criticism of climate-ready seeds, voiced by various food sovereignty movements, is directed at the corporate control of them. Critics contend that seed corporations' benefit from taking patent rights of commercially viable climate-ready crops while denying most of the world's farmers access to them. ETC Group, a civil society organisation, has referred to seed corporations as 'Gene Giants' and 'climate change profiteers' who present false solutions for hunger and climate change.[22]

Contentions over whether climate-ready seeds will provide a means to feed the world in times of climate change are illustrations of the broader struggles between the neoliberal food regime and food sovereignty movements; between the neoliberal narrative of hunger and the food sovereignty narrative of hunger. But how is international law implicated in these narratives?[23] This exploration studies three areas of international law in relation to narratives of hunger, namely climate change law, intellectual property law, and human rights law.

International climate change law supports the dominant neoliberal narrative and opens the way for climate-ready seeds as a valuable adaptation strategy by emphasising agricultural productivity as the primary problem and presenting technologies and private sector engagement as important parts of the solution. The scientific data on climate change collected in the IPCC assessment reports is an important basis for informing international climate change law. The chapter on food security and food production systems in the latest assessment report puts a great deal of emphasis on crop yield losses in the face of climate change. This is evident, for instance, in the figures and tables throughout the chapter that highlight the projected impacts of climate change on crop yields.[24] While the authors of the report do emphasise the complexity of the relationship between climate change and food (in)security, the production aspect prevails over other considerations.[25] The emphasis on food production is also apparent in the Paris Agreement, with the Preamble stipulating that States Parties '*recogni*[*ze*] the

[22] ETC Group, 'News Release: Gene Giants Grab "Climate Genes": Amid Global Food Crisis, Biotech Companies Are Exposed as Climate Change Profiteers', 13 May 2008, available at www.etcgroup.org/content/news-release-gene-giants-grab-climate-genes.

[23] For a more detailed analysis of the relevance of international law to food regime theory, see: Anne Saab, 'An International Law Approach to Food Regime Theory' (2018) 31(2) *Leiden Journal of International Law* 251.

[24] Porter et al (n 2) Figure 7.2: 'Summary of estimates of the impact of recent climate trends on yields for four major crops'; Figure 7.5: 'Summary of projected changes in crop yields, due to climate change over the 21st century'; Figure 7.7: 'Boxplot summary of studies that quantify impact of climate and CO2 changes on crop yields, including historical and projected impacts, mean and variability of yields, and for all available crops in temperate and tropical regions'; Box 7.1: 'Projected Impacts for Crops and Livestock in Global Regions and Sub-Regions under Future Scenarios'.

[25] Porter et al (n 2). The authors write on p.490: 'The impacts of climate change on food systems are expected to be widespread, complex, geographically and temporally variable, and profoundly influenced by socioeconomic conditions … Changes in food system drivers give rise to changes in food security outcomes (medium evidence, high agreement), but often researchers consider only the impacts on the food production element of food security.'

fundamental priority of safeguarding food security and ending hunger, and the *particular vulnerabilities of food production systems* to the adverse impacts of climate change'.[26]

In addition to focusing on crop yield losses and food production, international climate change law actively promotes technological solutions to climate change impacts. The texts of the UN Framework Convention on Climate Change (UNFCCC), the Kyoto Protocol, and the Paris Agreement include many references to technologies, opening the way for technological solutions to climate change.[27] Special reports by the UNFCCC and the IPCC,[28] as well as international adaptation initiatives, promote agricultural technologies more explicitly. The National Adaptation Programmes of Action (NAPAs) are part of a work programme for the least developed countries, established at the 2001 meeting of the Conference of the Parties to the UNFCCC. Many of the submitted NAPAs contain references to technologies, including technologies for agriculture.[29] A browse through the Nationally Determined Contributions (NDCs) submitted by States' Parties to the Paris Agreement also include frequent references to technologies.[30]

International climate change law, moreover, encourages private sector engagement. One article in the Kyoto Protocol stipulates that Parties shall cooperate in the 'creation of an *enabling environment for the private sector*, to promote and enhance the transfer of, and access to, environmentally sound technologies'.[31] The Paris Agreement requires States Parties to incentivise and enhance not only public sector but also private sector engagement in mitigating greenhouse gas emissions and implementing the NDCs.[32] Adaptation initiatives under the UNFCCC also invite private sector engagement. A good example of this is the Private Sector Initiative (PSI) which '[a]ims to catalyze the involvement of the private sector in the wider adaptation community'.[33] Agricultural biotechnology corporations—including Bayer, BASF,

---

[26] *Paris Agreement*, adopted at 21st session of the Conference of the Parties, 12 December 2015, FCCC/CP/2015/L.9/Rev.1. Second emphasis added.

[27] On the basis of a cursory count, the term 'technology' is mentioned 21 times in the text of the UNFCCC, 18 times in the text of the Kyoto Protocol, and 23 times in the text of the Paris Agreement.

[28] See, for instance: Intergovernmental Panel on Climate Change, 'Methodological and Technological Issues in Technology Transfer – Special Report of Working Group III of the Intergovernmental Panel on Climate Change' in Bert Metz et al (eds), *IPCC Reports* (IPCC, 2000); Richard JT Klein et al, 'Application of Environmentally Sound Technologies for Adaptation to Climate Change' (10 May 2006) FCCC Technical Papers, FCCC/TP/2006/2.

[29] UNFCCC, 'NAPAs Received by the Secretariat', online: unfccc.int/adaptation/workstreams/national_adaptation_programmes_of_action/items/4585.php.

[30] The UNFCCC, 'INDCS and Technology: A Synthesis of Technology Issues Contained in Intended Nationally Determined Contributions', 27 April 2016, online: unfccc.int/ttclear/misc_/StaticFiles/gnwoerk_static/HOME_infobox_2/a61f9f4b94704dd78f06b2bc7cd0b547/f7bbe982812a469db476fd4917714813.pdf.

[31] *Kyoto Protocol to the United Nations Framework Convention on Climate Change*, 11 December 1997, 37 ILM 22 (Entered into force 16 February 2005), Article 10(c). Emphasis added.

[32] *Paris Agreement* (n 25), Articles 6.4(b) and 6.8(b).

[33] UNFCCC, 'Adaptation Private Sector Initiative (PSI)', online: unfccc.int/adaptation/workstreams/nairobi_work_programme/items/4623txt.php.

Syngenta, and Monsanto—have submitted projects on genetically engineered crops to achieve higher yields despite adverse climate conditions, or climate-ready seeds, under this initiative.[34]

Most of the discord surrounding climate-ready seeds concentrates on the corporate domination of this adaptation strategy, which is manifest in the growing number of patent applications for these seeds filed by corporations.[35] Intellectual property rights are tools of privatisation and in that sense are closely related to the neoliberal food regime. A prime justification for intellectual property rights is that they provide necessary incentives for technological innovations.[36] The Agreement on Trade-Related Aspects of Intellectual Property Rights (TRIPS), an annex to the agreement instituting the World Trade Organization, in Article 27.3(b) effectively requires all States Parties to apply patent rights or another form of intellectual property protection to plants.[37] In the neoliberal narrative of hunger, the patent applications for climate-ready seeds are framed, and so legitimised, as necessary incentives for seed corporations to invest in the research and development of these arguably valuable technologies that may contribute to feeding the world. Intellectual property law most evidently supports the neoliberal narrative of hunger.

The legal governance of plant genetic resources, including seeds, is an area of significant contention. Debates over whether plant genetic resources should be considered private property or part of the common heritage of mankind have been coined the 'Seed Wars'.[38] Those who reject climate-ready seeds and food sovereignty movements more broadly are critical of intellectual property rights, especially strong corporate patent rights for seeds. This is evident in the opposition against the patent rights applied to climate-ready seeds by a handful of large seed corporations.[39] Intellectual property law is most directly associated with the neoliberal narrative, but the food sovereignty narrative also draws on law to oppose corporate patents. The food sovereignty narrative invokes the terms such as farmers' rights[40] and sovereign rights over

[34] See, for the complete database so far: UNFCCC, 'Private Sector Initiative – Database of Actions on Adaptation', online: unfccc.int/adaptation/workstreams/nairobi_work_programme/items/6547.php.

[35] See, for instance: Agrawala et al (n 18).

[36] Robert P Merges, *Justifying Intellectual Property* (Harvard University Press, 2011), 300; William Fisher, 'Theories of Intellectual Property', in Stephen R Munzer (ed), *New Essays in the Legal and Political Theory of Property* (Cambridge University Press, 2001) 169.

[37] *Agreement on Trade-Related Aspects of Intellectual Property Rights*, Annex 1C Marrakesh Agreement Establishing the World Trade Organization, 15 April 1994, 1869 UNT. 299, 33 ILM 1197 (Entered into force 1 January 1995) [TRIPS Agreement]. The relevant part of Article 27.3(b) reads as follows: 'Members shall provide for the protection of plant varieties either by patents or by an effective *sui generis* system or by any combination thereof.'

[38] Jack Kloppenburg Jr. and Daniel Lee Kleinman, 'Seed Wars: Common Heritage, Private Property, and Political Strategy' (1987) 95 *Socialist Review* 7; Keith Aoki, *Seed Wars: Controversies and Cases on Plant Genetic Resources and Intellectual Property* (Carolina Academic Press, 2008).

[39] See, for instance: ETC Group (2008) and ETC Group (2010) (n 12).

[40] As coined in Article 9 of the *International Treaty on Plant Genetic Resources for Food and Agriculture*, Food and Agriculture Organization (Entered into force 29 June 2004) [Plant Treaty].

natural resources[41] in an attempt to resist the growing number of corporate patent rights when it comes to seeds. Farmers' rights and sovereign rights over natural resources are concepts that are put forth in an effort to garner more recognition for the contribution of farmers in biodiversity conservation and assert the rights of developing states over the natural resources found within their territories. Promoting farmers' rights and sovereign rights over natural resources is, however, not quite the same as advancing the idea of seeds as the common heritage of mankind. While the latter does not connote any form of ownership, the term 'rights' does suggest some kind of proprietary definition. The question is then not whether intellectual property rights should be applied to seeds and plants, but rather *who* should own *which* rights.

The neoliberal narrative of hunger views food as a commodity; the food sovereignty narrative, on the contrary, views food as a right. Food sovereignty movements draw heavily on human rights law, and particularly on the right to food.[42] Human rights law and language are invoked as a means to direct attention to people who are suffering from hunger and food insecurity and their needs, rather than focusing primarily on seed technologies and corporations as in the neoliberal narrative.[43] In addition to farmers' rights and sovereign rights over natural resources, the right to food is used as a means to oppose strong corporate patent rights. Former UN Special Rapporteur on the Right to Food, Olivier De Schutter, stated in a report on seed policies that the right to food could be used

> to limit the negative impacts of the recent trend towards patent claims made following the adaptation of specific gene traits that could confer one or more forms of stress tolerance linked to climate change (including salinity, drought or flood, heat or cold).[44]

While the food sovereignty narrative draws on human rights law most directly and explicitly, actors promoting the neoliberal narrative also appeal to human

[41] As included in the Preamble, Article 3 (Principles) and Article 15 (Access to Genetic Resources) of the *Convention on Biological Diversity*, 5 June 1992, ATS 32, 1760 UNTS 79, 31 ILM 818 (Entered into force 29 December 1993) [CBD].

[42] See, for instance: Priscilla Claeys, 'Vía Campesina's Struggle for the Right to Food Sovereignty: From Above or from Below?' in Nadia CS Lambek, Priscilla Claeys, Adrienna Wong and Lea Brilmayer (eds), *Rethinking Food Systems: Structural Challenges, New Strategies and the Law* (Springer, 2014); Raj Patel, 'What Does Food Sovereignty Look Like?' (2009) 36(3) *Journal of Peasant Studies* 663. Although food sovereignty movements draw on the right to food, the 'food sovereignty' paradigm and the 'right to food' paradigm are distinct. The scope of this paper does not allow for any in-depth analysis of either paradigm.

[43] See, for instance: Elisabeth Caesens and Maritere Padilla Rodriguez, 'Climate Change and the Right to Food: A Comprehensive Study', in Heinrich Boll Foundation (ed), *Heinrich Boll Stiftung Publication Series on Ecology*, Volume 8 (Columbia Law School – Human Rights Institute, 2009). This comprehensive report demonstrates efforts to focus on those people most vulnerable to the impacts of climate change on food security and finding ways to address their specific needs through a human rights-based approach to climate change.

[44] Olivier De Schutter, 'The Right to Food: Seed Policies and the Right to Food: Enhancing Agrobiodiversity and Encouraging Innovation' (2009) *United Nations General Assembly* 12.

rights law. The duty-bearers of international law, including human rights law, are States. Formally, the private sector have no obligations under human rights law. Nevertheless, there is increasing recognition that the private sector also has a role to play in upholding human rights. This is evidenced by, for example, the UN Guiding Principles on Business and Human Rights, commonly known as the Ruggie Principles, outlining the responsibility of the State to protect human rights and concurrently the responsibility of corporations to respect human rights.[45] Most corporations, including seed corporations developing climate-ready seeds, publicly proclaim their commitments to human rights.

The definition of the right to food is extremely open-ended and includes 'neoliberal' objectives such as a focus on production and technologies. Article 11.2(a) of the International Covenant on Economic, Social, and Cultural Rights (ICESCR) spells out that States are required to take the following measures to contribute to realising the right to food: '[t]o improve methods of production, conservation and distribution of food by making full use of technical and scientific knowledge.'[46] While conservation and distribution of food are more readily linked with food sovereignty, improving methods of production using technical and scientific knowledge can be easily connected to the neoliberal food regime.

A pyramid of assumptions

The neoliberal narrative and the food sovereignty narrative present seemingly contradictory accounts of hunger and different answers to the question of how to feed the world in times of climate change. As demonstrated through the example of climate-ready seeds, the neoliberal narrative that promotes these seeds presents hunger primarily as a problem of production, and advocates for technological solutions and private sector investments to increase production. The food sovereignty narrative, on the contrary, opposes this view of hunger and method of feeding the world, focusing instead on access to and distribution of food, and rejecting corporate domination of climate-ready seeds. The previous section outlined the role of climate change law, intellectual property law, and human rights law in the two narratives of hunger by exploring the particular case of climate-ready seeds.

Despite the apparent contradictions and the distinct ways in which both narratives draw on law, both narratives are grounded on a common set of fundamental assumptions about hunger and climate change. This exploration identifies five assumptions. The assumptions are arranged in a pyramid,

[45] United Nations Office of the High Commissioner for Human Rights, 'Guiding Principles on Business and Human Rights: Implementing the United Nations "Protect, Respect and Remedy" Framework' (2011).

[46] United Nations General Assembly Resolution 2200A, International Covenant on Economic, Social and Cultural Rights (3 January 1976).

with the first assumption at the base of the pyramid and each subsequent assumption one step higher in the pyramid. Each assumption is dependent on the (implicit) acceptance of the foregoing assumption(s). The significance of the pyramid structure is that, despite serious contentions about each distinct assumption, the acceptance of each subsequent assumption renders the previous ones more ingrained and more difficult to challenge.

The five assumptions are as follows:

1) Climate change causes hunger;
2) Food production must increase to feed the world in times of climate change;
3) Agricultural biotechnologies are necessary to increase food production;
4) Private sector investments are necessary to develop agricultural biotechnologies;
5) Intellectual property rights on seeds are necessary to incentivise these investments.

These assumptions together reflect central features of the dominant neoliberal food regime and the neoliberal narrative of hunger. Climate change law reinforces most clearly the first four assumptions in the pyramid, with its emphasis on the impacts of climate change on agricultural crop yields, the need to increase production, and attention to technological innovations and private sector engagement. Intellectual property law, especially as contained in Article 27.3(b) of the TRIPS Agreement, presents intellectual property rights as necessary investments for innovations, including climate-ready seeds, in accordance with the fifth assumption in the pyramid.

The fact that the neoliberal narrative builds on these assumptions is not surprising. The more notable conclusion of this exploration is that the food sovereignty narrative of hunger, and specifically the way in which international law is implicated in constructing this narrative, fails to provide strong challenges to the pyramid of assumptions. Each of the assumptions is highly contested in itself, and these contestations do feature in food sovereignty movements that oppose the neoliberal food regime. There is recognition that the relationship between climate change and hunger is complex, as the reports of the IPCC indicate.[47] There are moreover continued debates about the causes of hunger and whether tackling hunger should be a matter of more production or better access and distribution.[48] The role of

[47] See n 24.

[48] These views between production and access as primary means to tackle hunger are best articulated as Malthusian perspectives (too many people, too little food) and Senian perspectives (hunger is about some people not having enough to eat). Thomas Robert Malthus, *An Essay on the Principle of Population* (J. Johnson, 1st edn 1798), Chapter I. The book is available online at www.esp.org/books/malthus/population/malthus.pdf, © Electronic Scholarly Publishing Project, 1998; Amartya Kumar Sen, *Poverty and Famines: An Essay on Entitlement and Deprivation* (Clarendon Press; Oxford University Press, 1981).

the private sector and the value of technologies in addressing hunger remain disputed in general, and in particular in discussions on feeding the world in times of climate change.[49] There is a great amount of debate regarding the value and function of intellectual property rights, particularly focusing on whether intellectual property rights are necessary to incentivise innovation and to whose benefit.[50] However, when looking at how hunger in the context of climate change is presented and how the question of feeding the world is answered, these five fundamental assumptions receive little air time and are often not explicitly questioned or challenged.

Civil society organisations and other voices critical of climate-ready seeds direct most of their criticism at what they perceive to be a corporate monopoly over seeds, as evidenced through the growing number of patent applications submitted by a handful of large corporations.[51] Objections to a corporate monopoly in the global seed and food markets extend beyond the specific example of climate-ready seeds and are also central to the food sovereignty discourse more generally. This criticism of corporate monopoly and the growing number of patent applications by a few corporations is situated in the tip of the pyramid, above the fifth assumption. While this is without a doubt a valid criticism of climate-ready seeds and the neoliberal food regime more broadly, placing so much emphasis on this point leaves little space to consider the underlying assumptions situated lower in the pyramid.

Farmers' rights, sovereign rights over natural resources, and the right to food, are called upon in efforts to resist the corporate domination through the application of patent rights. Craig Borowiak has astutely noted that:

> Given the way that, in the latter half century, 'rights' have effectively become the only normative game in town, with property rights in the preeminent position, the successful mobilization of breeders' rights by large pharmaceutical and agriculture interests has left opponents with few avenues of resistance aside from positing rights claims of their own.[52]

---

[49] Although private sector corporations dominate in the research and development of climate-ready seeds, it is not the private sector's principal goal to feed the world. As Henry Shue astutely wrote: '[i]f there were lots of profit to be made in solving the world's hunger problem, market forces would presumably have sent people rushing in to solve it long ago'. Henry Shue, 'Solidarity among Strangers and the Right to Food' in William Aiken and Hugh LaFollette (eds), *World Hunger and Morality* (Prentice Hall, 1996) 128. Discussions about the value of technologies in agriculture have been intense since the time of the Green Revolution in the 1970s. See: International Food Policy Research Institute, *Green Revolution: Cure or Blessing* (International Food Policy Research Institute, 2002).

[50] See Fisher and Merges (n 35). See also: James Boyle, *The Public Domain: Enclosing the Commons of the Mind* (Yale University Press, 2008).

[51] ETC Group, *Patenting the "Climate Genes" ... and Capturing the Climate Agenda* (ETC Group, 2008), Table 1 on p.4: 'Who Controls "Climate-Ready" Genes and Traits?'. See also: ETC Group, *Capturing "Climate Genes": Gene Giants Stockpile Patents on "Climate-Ready" Crops in Bid to Become "Biomassters"* (ETC Group, 2010). Figure 1 on p.6: 'Public vs. Private Climate-Ready Patent Families', which shows that over 90% of patent applications are done by the private sector. See also Agrawala et al (n 18) and ETC Group (n 21).

[52] Craig Borowiak, 'Farmers' Rights: Intellectual Property Regimes and the Struggle over Seeds' (2004) 32 (4) *Politics & Society* 511, 522.

Although farmers' rights and sovereign rights are not formally considered to be intellectual property rights, these concepts do not expressly deny that some form of 'rights' incentivise necessary innovations. Human rights law, and especially the right to food, in the way it is framed does not deny the value of the private sector and agricultural biotechnologies.

My objective of this analysis is not to provide answers to each of the assumptions in the pyramid. It is not to say unequivocally what the precise impact of climate change is on hunger, whether more food needs to be produced, and what the value and function of agricultural biotechnologies, the private sector, and intellectual property rights are. The main purpose is to demonstrate that the two seemingly contradictory narratives of hunger are both grounded on this common set of fundamental assumptions, and subsequently to affirm that these assumptions must be questioned if we are to find better, alternative answers to feeding the world in times of climate change. International law as it is framed and invoked plays a role in keeping these assumptions in place and obscuring explicit and necessary challenges to each of the assumptions.

Questioning assumptions and finding better ways of feeding the world

In the introduction to this piece, I cited Frances Moore Lappé and Joseph Collins in writing that '[h]ow we understand hunger determines what we think are its solutions'.[53] As simple and as obvious as this statement may be, in discussions about how to go about addressing climate change-induced hunger there is plenty of attention for the possible solutions but very little attention for understanding the problem. Different fields of international law are frequently invoked as means of tackling hunger in the face of climate change, as this exploration has demonstrated through the example of climate-ready seeds. The neoliberal narrative of hunger promotes climate-ready seeds as viable adaptation strategies, while the food sovereignty narrative rejects climate-ready seeds and the dominant neoliberal narrative. What I have sought to show in this exploration is that despite seemingly contradictory narratives, the way that international law is used in both narratives contributes to sustaining shared underlying assumptions about hunger. Without questioning these assumptions and prevailing understandings of hunger, solutions that are radically different from the persistently dominant neoliberal ones will be difficult to imagine, let alone enforce.

This exploration was not about how international law can contribute to solving hunger in times of climate change, but rather about how international law contributes to shaping understandings—or narratives—of hunger. My

53 Moore Lappé and Collins (n 7) 4.

primary intention in this research was not to support one narrative over another; it was not, in other words, to promote climate-ready seeds and endorse the neoliberal narrative or to reject climate-ready seeds and lend support to the food sovereignty narrative. My principal objective was to lay bare the fundamental assumptions about hunger and climate change that underlie both the neoliberal narrative and the food sovereignty narrative, and the role that international law plays in leaving these assumptions largely unquestioned. Only by questioning these underlying assumptions can we hope to construct different narratives and more effective ways to feed the world, whether based on the concept of food sovereignty or otherwise.

Beyond hunger, climate change, and climate-ready seeds, my broader purpose is to highlight the narrative power of law. The focus here was specifically on international law, but it is not difficult to see how the global food system is shaped by complex layers of transnational law, made up of not only sovereign State actors but also private actors, non-governmental players, domestic, regional, and local contexts and laws. The aim of this exploration is to uncover the narrative power of law and ultimately encourage more questions to be asked and more assumptions to be challenged, whatever the answers to those questions or the outcomes of those challenges might turn out to be.[54] I hope to encourage readers to think critically about our own roles, as agents of (inter/trans-national) law, in constructing narratives. Only when questions are asked and assumptions are challenged will we be able to conceive of alternative narratives and—much needed—better solutions to the world's problems.

Acknowledgement

With many thanks to the organisers and participants of the Transnational Legal Theory Symposium 2018 on Transnational Food Security. This short paper is a synopsis of a forthcoming book with Cambridge University Press entitled *Narratives of Hunger in International Law: Feeding the World in Times of Climate Change.*

Disclosure statement

No potential conflict of interest was reported by the author.

[54] See: Andrea Bianchi, 'On Asking Questions' in Andrea Bianchi (ed), *Theory and Philosophy in International Law* (Edward Elgar, 2017).

GMO risks, food security, climate change and the entrenchment of neo-liberal legal narratives

Giulia Claudia Leonelli

ABSTRACT

This article explores the artificial nature of the neo-liberal legal narratives on GMOs, complementing Anne Saab's analysis of the Public International Law ('PIL') climate change adaptation regime with a deconstruction of the hegemonic transnational legal discourse on the risks, costs and benefits of agricultural biotechnologies. The enquiry into the dominant regulatory approach to the governance of GMO risks sheds light on its specific political and socio-economic implications, lending support to the argument that GMOs are identified as a strategy to tackle food insecurity and facilitate climate change adaptation simply because their development, patenting and trade serve the profit-making goals of transnational market actors. Against this backdrop, the PIL discourse on climate resilient GMOs and the hegemonic transnational legal narrative on GMO safety and food security turn out to be two sides of the same coin.

What are the connections between climate change, the development of international climate change adaptation strategies, Genetically Modified Organism (GMO) patenting and trade and the entrenchment of a GMO-led food security paradigm? What lies at the heart of the legal narratives on GMO risks, GMOs and food security and GMOs and climate change? This article endeavours to sketch out an answer to these questions. The analysis unfolds against the twofold backdrop of Public International Law (hereafter, 'PIL') responses and transnational legal paradigms, complementing Saab's analysis of the PIL regulatory framework on climate change adaptation[1] with an enquiry into the hegemonic transnational legal narrative on the risks, costs and benefits of agricultural biotechnologies.[2]

---

[1] Anne Saab, 'Climate-Resilient Crops and International Climate Change Adaptation Law' (2016) 29(2) *Leiden Journal of International Law* 503. See also Anne Saab, 'International Law and Feeding The World In Times of Climate Change' (forthcoming 2019) *Transnational Legal Theory*.

[2] Giulia Claudia Leonelli, *The Transnational Law and Governance of GMOs* (on file with author).

Section 1, drawing on Saab's work on climate-resilient GM crops, starts off with a PIL overview of GMO-led strategies to facilitate climate change adaptation and tackle food insecurity; it specifically emphasises the connection between the—alleged—need to increase agricultural production through GMOs and the need to safeguard and strengthen the intellectual property rights of biotech companies. Section 2, on the other hand, explores the dominant transnational legal narrative on GMO risk regulation, deconstructing its political and socio-economic implications and its direct connections to the elimination of non-tariff barriers to trade, transnational regulatory convergence and further trade liberalisation.[3]

Section 3 concludes by casting some light on the social embeddedness and artificial construction of all neo-liberal legal narratives on GMOs. Are GM crops 'safe' for public health, the environment and biodiversity? Are they going to feed the world and tackle food insecurity? And are they a viable strategy to achieve climate change adaptation?

PIL frameworks: climate change adaptation, climate-resilient GM crops, food security and the TRIPs agreement

Climate-resilient GM crops, genetically engineered[4] to achieve environmental resistance to drought or flooding, are just one of the latest metamorphosis of agricultural biotechnologies.[5] Whilst GMO supporters argue that this specific application of bio-engineering techniques will play a key role to increase global agricultural production in the face of climate change, there is almost nothing new in this discourse on the presumed benefits of GMOs. Indeed, throughout the years, agricultural biotechnologies have in turn been alleged

[3] For an in-depth deconstruction of the foundations and implications of the hegemonic legal narrative on GMO risks, see Leonelli (n 2). For a broader overview on transnational risk regulation, see Giulia Claudia Leonelli, 'A Closer Look at Transnational Risk Regulation: Transnational Law As A Methodology and Critical Theory' (on file with author).

[4] Under the Cartagena Protocol on Biosafety, articles 1 and 4, 'modern biotechnology' is defined as encompassing the application of in vitro nucleic acid techniques, including recombinant DNA and direct injection of nucleic acid, as well as the fusion of cells beyond the taxonomic family, overcoming physiological barriers and traditional breeding selection. See Convention on Biological Diversity, *The Cartagena Protocol on Biosafety*, online: <https://bch.cbd.int/protocol> (last accessed 12/02/2018). For a different definition of GMOs, as laid out under EU law, see Directive 2001/18/EC of the European Parliament and of the Council of 12 March 2001 on the Deliberate Release into the Environment of Genetically Modified Organisms and Repealing Council Directive 90/220/EEC OJ [2001] L106/1, Annex I A.

[5] The genetic modification of crops is aimed at achieving herbicide tolerance, to better control weeds; insect resistance; environmental resistance to drought or flooding; and disease resistance. In a few cases, crops have been genetically engineered to alter their nutritional qualities or to target consumer related-features. For more information, see Genetic Literary Project, *Featured Articles*, online: <http://geneticliteracyproject.org> (last accessed 12/02/2018). At the time of writing, the only climate-resilient GM crop variety approved in the US is Monsanto's 'droughtgard' (MON 87460) drought resistant corn; see Genuity, *DroughtGard Hybrids*, online: <http://www.genuity.com/corn/Pages/DroughtGard-Hybrids.aspx> (last accessed 12/02/2018).

to result in a reduction in the use of herbicides and insecticides—in so far as GM crops are engineered to achieve herbicide tolerance and insect resistance;[6] to increase agricultural productivity, cuttings costs for both farmers and consumers; to pave the way for the development of nutritionally enhanced and vitamin-fortified crops;[7] and to serve the purpose of feeding an expanding global population, tackling starvation and food insecurity in developing and less developed countries.[8] Most famously, upon a refusal by Mozambique, Zambia and Zimbabwe to accept a US donation of GM foods, the former US President G.W. Bush contended that the EU precautionary approach to GMO risks had obstructed the global fight for food security, urging the EU to end its opposition to GMOs 'for the sake of a continent threatened by famine'.[9] Indeed, the linkage between climate change adaptation strategies and trade in climate-resilient GM crops is nothing but the latest—and somehow natural—evolution of the hegemonic legal discourse on GMOs.

Saab's accurate analysis has documented how the legal narrative on the value of climate-resilient GM crops to adapt to the effects of climate change and increase global agricultural production has by now entrenched in all PIL frameworks for the governance of climate change adaptation.[10] Her enquiry into the 'international climate change adaptation law regime'[11] has focused on the main PIL regulatory instruments, ie, the 1992 United Nations Framework Convention on Climate Change ('UNFCCC')[12], the 1997 Kyoto Protocol and the 2015 Paris Agreement,[13] the UNFCCC technical

---

[6] Herbicide resistant crops are estimated to be about 53% of GM crops; it is worth noting that the same biotech corporations which hold patent rights for herbicide resistant GM crops are also, in most cases, the producers of the specific herbicide products GMOs are resistant to. A plurality of environmental organisations have provided evidence that herbicide resistant crops, far from reducing the employment of herbicides, have in fact caused a remarkable intensification in their use, as weeds gradually develop increased resistance. See GMWatch, *Superweeds: It's game over for GM herbicide-tolerant crops* (2016), online: <http://www.gmwatch.org/news/latest-news/17338-superweeds-it-s-game-over-for-gm-herbicide-tolerant-crops>; and Stop the Crop, *Toxic Crops*, online: <http://stopthecrop.org/toxic-crops> (last accessed 12/02/2018). For more information about the decline in use of 'Roundup' and the turn to 'Dicamba', due to the increased herbicide resistance of so-called 'Super-Weeds', and for an overview of the significant problems posed by the use of 'Dicamba' and '2, 4-D' – with all ensuing state measures in the USA, see GMWatch, *Koch, Spiked, and Mark Lynas: Uncomfortable befellows?* (2018), online: <http://www.gmwatch.org> (last accessed 12/02/2018). For an overview of the glyphosate – i.e. 'Roundup' – controversy and the 'Monsanto Papers' issue, see Tina Bella, Thomson Reuters, *Monsanto ordered to pay $289 million in world's first Roundup cancer trial* (2018), online: <https://www.reuters.com/article/us-monsanto-cancer-lawsuit/monsanto-ordered-to-pay-289-million-in-worlds-first-roundup-cancer-trial-idUSKBN1KV2HB> (last accessed 10/08/2018).

[7] *Inter alia*, see GMWatch, *GM Myths*, online: <http://www.gmwatch.org/en/articles/gm-myths> (last accessed 12/02/2018).

[8] *Ibid.*

[9] For a reference to this speech, see Mark Pollack and Gregory Shaffer, *When Cooperation Fails. The International Law and Politics of Genetically Modified Foods* (Oxford University Press, 2009) at 116.

[10] Saab, 'Climate-Resilient Crops and International Climate Change Adaptation Law', and Saab, 'International Law and Feeding The World In Times of Climate Change' (n 1).

[11] Saab, 'Climate-Resilient Crops and International Climate Change Adaptation Law' (n 1), 505–508.

[12] 1992 United Nations Framework Convention on Climate Change (UNFCCC), 1771 U.N.T.S. 107 (1992).

[13] 1997 Kyoto Protocol to the United Nations Framework Convention on Climate Change, 37 I.L.M. 22 (1997). 'and 2015 Paris Agreement, FCCC/CP/2015/L.9/Rev.1 (2015)'.

papers, the assessment reports of the Intergovernmental Panel on Climate Change (IPCC) and all relevant international adaptation standards and initiatives.[14]

To begin with, her analysis has testified that 'the accent in discourse about climate change impacts on agriculture is on declining crop yields';[15] this has directly concurred to frame the challenges of climate change adaptation in the agricultural sector in terms of a set of strategies to increase food production.[16] Further than that, the overarching goal of tackling the effects of climate change by increasing global food production is explicitly connected to market-led strategies. Whilst Article 10(c) of the Kyoto Protocol already stated that all parties shall cooperate in the creation of an enabling environment for the private sector, promoting the development of new and environmentally 'sound' technologies,[17] the focus and emphasis on the role of private sector actors in devising climate change adaptation strategies for the agricultural sector has dramatically increased throughout the years. This is where climate-resilient GM crops come into play.

As Saab's detailed analysis has shown, references to climate-resilient GMOs are ubiquitous in international climate change adaptation law frameworks. Paragraphs 55, 58, 206, 216 and 221 of the 2006 UNFCCC technical paper explicitly mention drought-resistant seeds and/or gene technologies as viable and desirable options to contribute to climate change adaptation.[18] The 2000 IPCC Special Report on 'Methodological and Technological Issues in Technology Transfer' extensively deals with the matter of 'Genetic Improvements Critical to Climate Adaptation',[19] lamenting the decline in public funding for agricultural biotechnologies and defining the transnational controversies over the uncertain risks posed by GMOs as a significant concern for the implementation of climate change adaptation strategies.[20] The IPCC fourth assessment report expressly refers to climate-resilient GMOs, with a specific focus on drought, disease, pest and salt-tolerant varieties; equally,

[14] Inter alia, see United Nations Framework Convention on Climate Change, Decision I/CP.16: The Cancun Agreements: Outcome of the Work of The Ad Hoc Working Group on Long-Term Cooperative Action, Section II Enhanced Action on Adaptation (2011). See also the IPCC reports, available at <https://www.ipcc.ch/> (last accessed 25/12/2018). For more information on National Adaptation Programmes of Action (NAPAs) see <https://unfccc.int/topics/resilience/workstreams/national-adaptation-programmes-of-action/introduction> (last accessed 25/12/2018).

[15] Saab, 'Climate-Resilient Crops and International Climate Change Adaptation Law' (n 1), 508.

[16] *Ibid.* As noted at 508, Article 2 of the UNFCCC, in the face of the challenges posed by climate change, lists the 'adequate availability of food' as one of its objectives. See also Saab, 'International Law and Feeding The World In Times of Climate Change' (n 1).

[17] Saab, 'Climate-Resilient Crops and International Climate Change Adaptation Law' (n 1), 524.

[18] *Ibid*, 523. See R.J.T. Klein et al. 'Application of Environmentally Sound Technologies for Adaptation to Climate Change, FCCC/TP/2006/2', *FCCC Technical Papers* (2006).

[19] Saab, 'Climate-Resilient Crops and International Climate Change Adaptation Law' (n 1) 522, where Saab expressly refers to Section 11.3.3. of the Special Report. IPCC, 'Methodological and Technological Issues in Technology Transfer – Special Report of Working Group III of the IPCC', in B. Metz et al. (eds) *IPCC Reports* (2000).

[20] Saab, 'Climate-Resilient Crops and International Climate Change Adaptation Law' (n 1) 522.

the IPCC fifth report remarks that GM crops are a possible adaptation option to enhance yields in the face of climate change.[21] Finally, a plurality of international adaptation initiatives—such as the Cancun Adaptation Framework and the National Adaptation Programmes of Action—have advocated the further development and commercial upscaling of climate-resilient GMOs.[22]

On these grounds, Saab has rightfully concluded that the field of international climate change law is actively promoting the development and use of climate-resilient GM crops, creating an enabling environment for market actors to devise and implement climate change adaptation strategies.[23] Further than that, the dominant legal discourse in PIL has established a direct connection between the need to *increase agricultural production* through *climate-resilient GMOs*, in order to *adapt to climate change* and tackle *food insecurity*, and the need to safeguard and strengthen the *intellectual property rights* of biotech corporations, which develop and patent climate-resilient GM crops.[24] These safeguards rely on the Agreement on Trade-Related Aspects of Intellectual Property (TRIPs).[25]

It is beyond any reasonable doubt that the TRIPs Agreement serves the purpose of protecting the profit-making prospects of transnational corporations and market actors;[26] indeed, the privatisation and commodification of public goods—in this case, seeds—has been the object of heated scholarly and societal debate.[27] However, and besides this specific aspect, the broader

---

[21] *Ibid*, 520. See M.L. Parry et al. (eds), *Climate Change 2007: Impacts, Adaptation and Vulnerability*, Contribution of Working Group II To The Fourth Assessment Report of the IPCC (2007).

[22] Saab, 'Climate-Resilient Crops and International Climate Change Adaptation Law' (n 1) 520–521. See supra (n 14). For a mention to the Paris Agreement, see Saab, 'International Law and Feeding The World In Times of Climate Change' (n 1).

[23] Saab, 'Climate-Resilient Crops and International Climate Change Adaptation Law' (n 1) 527–528. Also see ActionAid International, *Clever Name, Losing Game?* (2014) online: <http://www.actionaid.org/sites/files/actionaid/csag_clevernamelosinggame_0.pdf> (last accessed 12/06/2018) [*ActionAid*]. The notion of 'Climate Smart Agriculture', encompassing the development and use of climate-resilient GM crops, was originally developed by the Food and Agriculture Organisation ('FAO') and the World Bank; as the ActionAid report highlights at 2, 'a number of industrialised countries (the US in particular), along with a number of agribusiness corporations, are now the most enthusiastic promoters of the concept'. Sections of the scientific community also support the development of climate-resilient GM crops; for more information see infra (n 28).

[24] Saab, 'Climate-Resilient Crops and International Climate Change Adaptation Law' (n 1) 527, drawing on Section 11.3.4. of the UNFCCC Report—which explicitly refers to the lack of intellectual property rights as an obstacle to private sector investment in climate-resilient seeds. See also Saab, 'International Law and Feeding The World In Times of Climate Change' (n 1).

[25] And, specifically, on Article 27.3(b) therein. For the full text of the Agreement, see World Trade Organization, *Annex 1C Agreement on Trade-Related Aspects of Intellectual Property Rights*, online: <https://www.wto.org/english/docs_e/legal_e/27-trips.pdf> (last accessed 12/02/2018). For further information, see also Anne Saab, 'Climate-Ready Seeds and Patent Rights: A Question of Climate (In)Justice?' (2015) 15(2) *Global Jurist* 219.

[26] The point which is debatable and open to challenge is, rather, whether furthering trade liberalisation and transnational market access will *also* serve the broader public interest through wealth maximisation, positive spill-overs and – ultimately – transnational wealth redistribution: see infra, section 2.

[27] See *inter alia* Holger Hestermeyer, *Human Rights and the WTO: The Case of Patents and Access to Medicines* (Oxford University Press, 2007); and Holger Hestermeyer, 'Reality or Aspiration? Solidarity in International Environmental and World Trade Law' in Holger Hestermeyer (ed.), *Coexistence, Cooperation and Solidarity: Liber Amicorum Rüdiger Wolfrum* (Martinus Nijhoff, 2012) 45.

PIL linkage between the development and entrenchment of climate-resilient GMOs, the challenges posed by climate change and the food security debate triggers an array of different and more complex questions. Is the PIL climate change framework contributing to devising a strategy for the achievement of *climate change adaptation* and *food security*, or is it rather—or primarily—serving the *market interests* of transnational biotech corporations, just like the TRIPs Agreement does? Is the recurrent PIL narrative on the crucial role of climate-resilient GMOs merely ancillary to free trade in GM crops?

On the one hand, it is worth highlighting that the effectiveness of climate-resilient GM crops is yet to be established. Not only is there no clear proof that using these GM seeds will result in an increase of crop yields, but also—and importantly—the same objectives may be achieved through the application of conventional breeding techniques.[28] On the other hand, the assumption that food insecurity will be tackled by a GMO-led strategy has been fiercely challenged by a plurality of NGOs and food sovereignty activists.[29]

At the heart of the dispute lies a divergent framing of the issues at stake in the debate. The dominant narrative, as reflected in the position of inter-governmental organisations[30] and PIL discourses, relies on the premise that GMOs will help improve agricultural productivity and increase food production, thus achieving food security. From a diametrically opposed perspective, NGOs and food sovereignty advocates point to issues of food distribution and food access, which an overall increase in food production cannot possibly tackle. Food insecurity has—in fact—always existed; the main obstacles to food security and access to food are thus identified in the long-standing

[28] For the view that further scientific and technological developments in agricultural biotechnologies are likely to facilitate climate change adaptation and increase yields, see National Academies of Sciences, Engineering and Medicines, *Genetically Engineered Crops: Experiences and Prospects* (The National Academies Press, 2016). For the opposite view, see Doug Gurian-Sherman, Union of Concerned Scientists, *'High and Dry: Why Genetic Engineering Is Not Solving Agriculture's Drought Problem in A Thirsty World'* (2012), online: <https://www.ucsusa.org/sites/default/files/legacy/assets/documents/food_and_agriculture/high-and-dry-report.pdf> (last accessed 12/06/2018). For an overview of the broad range of *non-GM* success stories, with a specific reference to drought tolerance, flood tolerance, salt tolerance, high yield and tolerance to specific soil and weather conditions, see GMWatch, *Non-GM successes: introduction*, online: <http://www.gmwatch.org/en/articles/non-gm-successes> (last accessed 12/02/2018); equally, for a defence of agroecological approaches to climate change adaptation, see *ActionAid* (n 23) 5–8. This lends support to the argument that conventional breeding could be just as effective – or even more effective – than genetic engineering for the purpose of developing climate-resilient crops.

[29] Among the various active networks, see La Via Campesina, online: <https://viacampesina.org/en/>; and People's Coalition on Food Sovereignty, online: <www.foodsov.org/> (last accessed 12/02/2018).

[30] The position of inter-governmental organisations – and particularly the Food and Agriculture Organisation ('FAO') – on GMOs has always been rather conciliating and diplomatic; despite acknowledging that agricultural biotechnologies have not delivered on many of their promises, the Food and Agriculture Organisation ('FAO') and World Health Organisation ('WHO') still regard GM products as an important vehicle for food security across developing and least developed countries. See *inter alia* FAO, *Biotechnologies for Agricultural Development. Proceedings of the FAO International Conference on Agricultural Biotechnologies in Developing Countries: Options and Opportunities in Crops, Forestry, Livestock, Fisheries and Agro-Industry to Face the Challenges of Food Insecurity and Climate Change* (FAO, 2011); and FAO, *FAO International Symposium on the Role of Agricultural Biotechnologies in Sustainable Food Systems and Nutrition* (FAO, 2016).

exploitation of developing and less developed countries and in the socio-economic conditions of marginalised small-scale farmers—rather than in the production methods themselves.[31] As rightfully noted, whilst '500 million small farms in developing countries already support the [food needs of] almost two billion people, nearly one third of humanity'[32] through conventional or organic agriculture, 300–500 corporations and companies in the agri-business sector control 70% of the resources in the global food system.[33] In this light, the foundations of the debate are deeply rooted in the eternal dilemma of (neo)-liberalism: will aggregate wealth *maximisation* eventually pave the way for wealth *redistribution*? Will trade in GMOs in fact result in positive spill-overs, and will it help fight food insecurity? GMO advocates and food sovereignty activists could not disagree more in this specific respect.

Against this background, it is ultimately unclear whether climate-resilient GMOs could be a viable and desirable strategy for climate change adaptation and food security. Equally, it is legitimate to question whether the PIL discourse on GMOs, climate change and food security is nothing more than an artificial legal narrative, serving the profit-making purposes of transnational market actors. The next section analyses the heated transnational debate on the uncertain risks posed by GMOs; by looking at the GMO conundrum through the lens of transnational risk regulation, it will shed further light on the social embeddedness and artificial construction of the PIL narrative on GMOs, climate change adaptation and food security.

One step further: GMO risks and the—complementary—legal narrative on sound science and cost-benefit analysis

Neo-liberal legal narratives on GMOs have unfolded well beyond PIL, well beyond the inter-governmental dimension and well beyond the fields of climate change and food security. This is clear from a deconstruction of the hegemonic transnational narrative on the regulation of GMO risks,[34] and from an analysis of its political and socio-economic implications.[35]

---

[31] For more information see Terry Marsden, Kevin Morgan and Johnathan Murdoch (eds.) *Worlds of Food. Place, Power and Provenance in the Food Chain* (Oxford University Press, 2006); Jennifer Clapp and Doris Fuchs, *Corporate Power in Global Agrifood Governance* (MIT Press, 2009); Terry Marsden and Adrien Morley (eds.) *Sustainable Food Systems. Building A New Paradigm* (Routledge, 2014).

[32] Oxfam International, Grow: Frequently asked questions, online: <https://www.oxfam.org/en/campaigns/grow-frequently-asked-questions> (last accessed 12/02/2018).

[33] *Ibid.*

[34] Where the terminology of 'transnational' is structurally distinguished from the traditional inter-governmental perspective underpinning PIL; indeed, the transnational category casts light on the restructuring of societal activities and regulation *beyond* the nation state and *beyond* state-to-state interactions. For an introduction, see Peer Zumbansen, 'Transnational Legal Pluralism' (2010) 10(2) *Transnational Legal Theory* 141; and Terence Halliday and Gregory Shaffer, 'Transnational Legal Orders' in Terence Halliday and Gregory Shaffer (eds.) *Transnational Legal Orders* (Cambridge University Press, 2015) 3.

[35] For an in-depth deconstruction of the social embeddedness and political and socio-economic implications of transnational GMO regulation, see Leonelli (n 2).

Further than that, and as anticipated at the end of the first section, casting light on the foundations of the dominant transnational narrative on GMO risks lends support to the argument that the discourse on GMOs, climate change adaptation and food security primarily serves the interests of transnational market actors. From this perspective, the emphasis of the PIL climate change regime on climate-resilient GM crops and the hegemonic transnational discourse on the risks, costs and benefits of agricultural biotechnologies turn out to be two sides of the same coin. GMOs are held to play a key role to achieve climate change adaptation and food security simply *because* GMO development, patenting and trade responds to the profit-making goals of market actors; symmetrically, sound science and Cost–Benefit Analysis (CBA) have come to dominate the landscape of transnational risk regulation and transnational GMO regulation *because* they are ancillary to transnational regulatory convergence, the elimination of non-tariff barriers to trade and—consequently—transnational market access and further trade liberalisation.[36] Both GMO narratives are artificially constructed and embedded in a neoliberal paradigm of transnational governance; further than that, and importantly, these two narratives turn out to be complementary and mutually reinforcing.

The dominant transnational discourse on 'evidence-based'[37] risk regulation relies on a sound science approach to risk assessment and on the application of CBA heuristics to risk management.[38] A sound science approach to technical risk assessment postulates a direct focus on what science has proven and quantified, rather than on the relevant margins of scientific uncertainty and the importance attached to the specific values at stake. CBA, on the other hand, mandates that uncertain risks shall only be regulated if—and in so far as—risk regulation is liable to maximise the expected aggregate utility of society, in terms of economic wealth. Under CBA, the economic-pecuniary costs that risk regulation would shift onto market actors are thus quantified and weighed against any potential public health and environmental benefits: as a result, risk regulation will only be enacted if it is held to be cost–benefit effective.[39]

The hegemonic transnational legal narrative on GMO risks is a perfect exemplification of this approach. To begin with, GMO supporters have consistently argued that there is no direct and unequivocal scientific evidence that GMOs may pose any risks to public health, the environment and biodiversity.[40] Secondly, they point to the economic costs that a precautionary

---

[36] *Ibid.*

[37] For the terminology of 'evidence-based' risk regulation see Alberto Alemanno, 'Risk Versus Hazard and the Two Souls of EU Risk Regulation: A Reply to Ragnar Lofstedt' (2011) 2(2) *European Journal of Risk Regulation* 169.

[38] For a detailed overview, see Leonelli (n 2) and (n 3).

[39] Again, for a detailed overview, see Leonelli (n 2) and (n 3).

[40] In this perspective, see for instance National Academies of Sciences, Engineering and Medicines (n 28).

approach to the governance of GMO risks would shift onto market actors, preventing further technological developments and obstructing transnational trade.[41] Finally, they argue that GMOs are liable to yield benefits to producers and consumers, increasing agricultural production at the global level and thus contributing to fight food insecurity in developing or less developed countries.[42] On these grounds, the economic costs of a stringent approach to GMO risks are held to outweigh any public health and environmental benefits ensuing from precautionary GMO regulation. A sound science and cost–benefit effective approach to GMO regulation is held to maximise aggregate societal wealth, thus resulting in positive spill-overs and transnational wealth redistribution. Precautionary approaches, on the other hand, have been famously defined as an 'infantile disease' of risk regulation,[43] or as 'laws of fears'.[44]

On the other side of the barricade a diametrically opposed discourse on precautionary risk governance, (originally) developed in the EU,[45] has since expanded at the transnational level. A 'socially acceptable risk' approach to risk regulation[46] calls for a 'prudential'[47] technical risk assessment, whereby due consideration shall be given to what science cannot prove and establish in the face of scientific uncertainty. Symmetrically, risk management involves the weighing and balancing of all interests at stake and a political—rather than economic—determination of the threshold of socially acceptable risk. In other words, a 'socially acceptable risk' approach to risk governance is meant to address whether a risk is acceptable and worth running in the light of scientific uncertainty, the values at stake, the intended level of protection,[48] the pervasiveness of any potential hazards and a range of other legitimate factors

[41] See inter alia Cass Sunstein, *Laws of Fear. Beyond the Precautionary Principle* (Cambridge University Press, 2005), and Pollack and Shaffer (n 9).

[42] In this perspective, see inter alia Pollack and Shaffer (n 9).

[43] Giandomenico Majone, 'Foundations of Risk Regulation: Science, Decision-Making, Policy Learning and Institutional Reform' (2010) 1(1) *European Journal of Risk Regulation* 5 at 16.

[44] Sunstein (n 41).

[45] For an analysis of the gradual – albeit discontinuous – decline of this discourse under EU risk regulation, see Leonelli (n 2) and Giulia Claudia Leonelli, 'The Glyphosate Saga and The Fading Democratic Legitimacy of European Union Risk Regulation' (2018) 25(5) *Maastricht Journal of European and Comparative Law* 582.

[46] For a theorisation and exhaustive definition of 'socially acceptable risk' approaches to risk governance, see Leonelli (n 2) and Leonelli (n 45).

[47] For the distinction between 'prudential' risk assessment and 'precautionary' risk management see Commission of the European Communities, *Communication from the Commission on the Precautionary Principle*, COM (2000) 1 Final, at 12 (Section 5).

[48] See *COM(2000)* (n 47) at 12 (Section 5) and 16 (Section 6.2.). When in the face of scientific uncertainty, and upon a technical risk assessment, there are reasonable grounds to believe that a potential risk may *be inconsistent with the chosen level of health and environmental protection*, risk managers shall take a decision as to whether to act, and how to act. See also Recitals 8 and 21 and Article 5 of Regulation (EC) No 178/2002 of the European Parliament and of the Council of 28 January 2002 Laying Down the General Principles and Requirements of Food Law, Establishing the European Food Safety Authority and Laying Down Procedures in Matters of Food Safety [2002] OJ L31 (the General Food Law, 'GFL') whereby, in the face of scientific uncertainty, the precautionary principle provides a mechanism for determining risk management measures to ensure the *high level of health protection chosen*.

('OLFs')[49]—encompassing enhanced consumer protection, environmental sustainability, socio-economic fairness and distributional stakes.

The counter-hegemonic transnational legal narrative on GMOs and GMO risk regulation is permeated by this approach. First of all, GMO opposers have constantly pointed to persisting scientific uncertainty over the long-term, indirect and unforeseeable impact of GMOs on public health, the environment and biodiversity.[50] Secondly, they have consistently argued that the uncertain risks posed by GMOs are not socially acceptable and not worth running in the light of the intended level of public health and environmental protection and the specific OLFs at stake. The latter do not only include the public perception of GMO risks, environmental sustainability and the importance attached to alternative (conventional and organic) models of agriculture, but also a range of distributional implications, which CBA heuristics unavoidably disregard.

As already mentioned, CBA underpins a calculation of the marginal economic costs and benefits of risk regulation, thus identifying the regulatory option which is expected to maximise *aggregate* societal wealth; nonetheless, the CBA toolbox is completely silent on *distributional* issues. Which constituency will bear the costs of risk regulation, and which constituency will benefit from them? CBA cannot provide any answer to these questions, in so far as its goal is merely to identify an aggregate value: under this methodological approach, redistribution effects and positive spill-overs[51] are in fact nothing more than a working assumption. This lends support to the argument that the dominant evidence-based paradigm of risk regulation shifts *economic costs* away from market actors, allocating *diffuse externalities* to a range of different constituencies;[52] in other words, evidence-based approaches are—methodologically —liable to allocate economic benefits to market actors, while shifting diffuse —consumer protection, environmental and socio-economic—costs onto broader constituencies. Further than that, and crucially, this

---

[49] Notably, in this perspective, see Recital (19) and Articles 5, 6(2), 6(3) and 7(2) of the GFL (n 48). Article 6 (3) maintains that 'risk management shall take into account the results of risk assessment [...], other factors legitimate to the matter under consideration, and the precautionary principle where the conditions laid down in article 7(1) are relevant [...]'. A similar clause can be found in Recital (32) of Regulation (EC) No. 1829/2003 of the European Parliament and of the Council of 22 September 2003 on Genetically Modified Foods OJ [2003] L268/1, stating that 'it is recognised that [...] scientific risk assessment alone cannot provide all the information on which a risk management decision should be based, and that other legitimate factors [OLFs] relevant to the matter under consideration may be taken into account'.

[50] On the uncertain risks that GMOs may pose to public health, see for example European Network of Scientists for Social and Environmental Responsibility, *Home*, online: <http://www.ensser.org/> (last accessed 12/02/2018). See also GMWatch, *Cultivation of GM maize in the EU must be suspended – legal dossier* (2016), online: <http://www.gmwatch.org/news/latest-news/17356-cultivation-of-gm-maize-in-the-eu-must-be-suspended-legal-dossier>; and Mute Schimpf, Euractiv, *New GM crops once again fail the safety test* (2016), online: <https://www.euractiv.com/section/agriculture-food/opinion/new-gm-crops-once-again-fail-the-safety-test/> focusing on the risks to the environment and to biodiversity flowing from the Syngenta's Bt11 and Pioneer's 1507 GM maize varieties.

[51] Just like the original and most famous Adam Smith's definition of the 'invisible hand'.

[52] For a further development of this point, see Leonelli (n 2) and Leonelli (n 3).

factor lies at the core of the argument that GMOs will *not* tackle food insecurity, in so far as the latter has always been caused by issues of food *distribution* and *access* to food.

A plurality of transnational NGOs have argued that the development, patenting and commercialisation of GMOs have only benefited transnational corporations, serving their profit-making interests while perpetuating distributional conflicts and inequalities across developed, developing and less developed countries. NGOs claim that several transnational constituencies are bearing the costs and running the diffuse risks associated to agricultural biotechnologies, while a limited group of market actors are capitalising on their economic benefits.[53] From this perspective, NGO actors and food sovereignty activists have in fact directly challenged the 'myth' that the benefits of GMOs will spill over onto consumers and farmers in developing and less developed countries; and indeed, it is important to highlight that all transnational regulatory standards enacted by NGO actors categorically prohibit the cultivation or use of any GM varieties by farmers.[54]

Against this overall backdrop, and to conclude this brief overview, the counter-hegemonic transnational legal narrative on GMOs paves the way for a diametrically opposed approach to the governance of agricultural biotechnologies. Indeed, the uncertain public health and environmental risks and the socio-economic costs of GMOs are held to considerably outweigh any potential benefits that agricultural biotechnologies may ever yield.

What conclusions are we to draw from this analysis? To begin with, it is worth remarking that both transnational legal narratives—the discourse on evidence-based risk regulation as well as 'socially acceptable risk' approaches—are *socially embedded* and *socially constructed*. Although the denigrators of the precautionary principle are used to contrasting an 'objective', 'neutral' and 'universal' evidence-based approach to 'politicised' precautionary approaches, there is nothing 'sound' in sound science;[55] equally, CBA

[53] The position of Slow Food and its constituent networks, for instance, could not be any clearer: a statement from the organisation lists and explains the many reasons why Slow Food is directly opposed to GMOs. These range from safety reasons, with a specific focus on human and animal health, to environmental reasons, such as the many risks to biodiversity and the contamination of crops and soils, and socio-economic reasons, to begin with corporate control, the myth of GMO development as the way forward to achieve food security, and the threat that GMOs directly pose to small-scale farmers and traditional food cultures; see SlowFood, *Why we are against GMOs*, online: <https://www.slowfood.com/what-we-do/themes/gmos/why-we-are-against-gmos/> (last accessed 12/02/2018). For an analysis of the regulation of GMOs by transnational no-profit actors, see Leonelli (n 3).

[54] The regulatory standards enacted by the most important transnational NGOs—i.e. IFOAM Organics International, Fair Trade International, Pro Terra Foundation, Slow Food—and certified under ad hoc accreditations systems set out a clear and unequivocal prohibition of GMO cultivation.

[55] See *inter alia* Vern Walker, 'The Myth of Science as a Neutral Arbiter for Triggering Precautions' (2003) 26 (2) *Boston College International and Comparative Law Review* 197; Sheila Jasanoff, *Designs on Nature. Science and Democracy in Europe and the United States* (Princeton University Press, 2005); Maria Lee, *EU Regulation of GMOs* (Edward Elgar, 2008); Michelle Everson and Ellen Vos (eds.), *Uncertain Risks Regulated* (Routledge, 2009); Maria Weimer and Anniek de Ruijter (eds.) *Regulating Risks in the European Union. The Co-Production of Expert and Executive Power* (Hart Publishing, 2017); and Leonelli (n 2) and (n 45).

heuristics rely on an inherently value-laden determination and quantification of the notions of 'cost' and 'benefit'.[56] In fact, the divergence between the two approaches boils down to the *procedural* application of quantitative methodologies and heuristics versus qualitative criteria,[57] which in turn results from the different framing of a range of *substantive*—political and socio-economic —stakes.[58] Divergent approaches to risk regulation ultimately reflect different 'designs on nature'[59] and 'socio-technical imaginaries':[60] nonetheless, the determination that a risk is acceptable and worth running is always and unescapably socially embedded.

Building on this consideration, it is worth looking back at the foundations of the hegemonic legal narrative on GMOs. If both the evidence-based and the 'socially acceptable risk' paradigms are socially embedded and socially constructed, why is the hegemonic legal narrative on GMO risks unequivocally rooted in the evidence-based approach? It is legitimate to suggest that the evidence-based approach has come to dominate the landscape of transnational GMO risk regulation simply *because* it is ancillary to transnational regulatory convergence, the elimination of non-tariff barriers to trade and—consequently—transnational market access.[61]

From this perspective, and as anticipated since the opening of this section, the analysis of the hegemonic transnational narrative on GMO risk regulation sheds light on the artificial nature of the PIL discourse on climate-resilient GM crops. GMOs are held to play a key role in climate change adaptation and food security debates *because* their development, patenting and trade responds to the profit-making goals of market actors, just like evidence-based approaches to GMO risk regulation have entrenched *because* they facilitate and underpin transnational regulatory convergence and trade liberalisation. The two narratives, indeed, turn out to be two sides of the same coin.

Crumbling mythologies and new methods: the case for cross-disciplinary analysis

As the analysis so far has endeavoured to show, both the PIL discourse on climate-resilient GMOs and the hegemonic transnational narrative on GMO risk regulation are artificially constructed. GMOs will not be a panacea for climate change and food insecurity. Equally, there is nothing

56 See Leonelli (n 2).

57 *Ibid.*

58 *Ibid.*

59 Jasanoff (n 55).

60 Sheila Jasanoff and Sang-Hyun Kim (eds.) *Dreamscapes of Modernity. Socio-Technical Imaginaries and the Fabrication of Power* (Chicago University Press, 2015).

61 For an in-depth analysis of how the – allegedly 'neutral', 'objective' and 'universal'—technocratic model of evidence-based risk regulation has in fact been merely instrumental to the achievement of transnational regulatory convergence and further trade liberalisation, see Leonelli (n 2). For a shorter version of the argument, see Leonelli (n 3) and (n 45).

neutral, objective and universal about the contention that GMOs are safe and that the uncertain risks that they pose are worth running, and should be run. Both hegemonic legal narratives are embedded in a neo-liberal approach to the governance of the challenges and externalities of globalisation.

One final question ensues from this consideration. To what extent are market actors part of the problem, and to what extent are they part of its solution? Whilst it would be far-fetched to argue that climate change and food insecurity have only or directly been caused by transnational market actors, it is beyond any doubt that globalisation as we know it —or, a 'neo-liberal' paradigm of globalisation—has exacerbated them. Although market actors are actively engaged under PIL frameworks to devise and implement climate change adaptation strategies, they do often stand as an obstacle in the way to climate change mitigation; the very framing of climate change discourses in terms of market-led adaptation, rather than mitigation,[62] is thus arguably the reflection of a neo-liberal approach. This is even easier to highlight in the context of food insecurity: although GMOs are alleged to feed the world, an unprecedented number of patents and trade rights for seeds, herbicides and insecticides are in fact concentrated in the hands of three transnational macro-corporations.[63] Again, to what extent are market actors part of the problem, and to what extent are they part of its solution? From this perspective, the legal narratives on GMO risk regulation, climate change and food insecurity are diverting the focus away from the problems caused or exacerbated by a neo-liberal model of globalisation: the contribution that market-led strategies may give to solve these complex problems, however, is at best limited.

Different transnational strategies and solutions are being obscured, neglected or discarded as a result of the entrenchment of artificial—neo-liberal—transnational legal narratives. Legal analysis is thus called upon to give its contribution, deconstructing law's social embeddedness and casting light on the political and socio-economic implications of different regulatory approaches. This will be all the more important, as globalisation progresses;

[62] For an express acknowledgment that the focus in PIL discourses has gradually shifted from issues of 'climate change mitigation' to strategies for 'climate change adaptation' see Saab, 'Climate-Resilient Crops and International Climate Change Adaptation Law' (n 1) 505–506. This shift has become particularly clear, Saab argues, with the publication of the 2001 assessment report of the IPCC.

[63] Bayer and Monsanto have now merged into one macro-corporation; on the 7th of June 2018 Bayer AG reported it had completed its purchase of Monsanto Co., estimating the costs of the deal at around 63 billion dollars including debt. The company name will remain 'Bayer'; the 'Monsanto' brand, on the other hand, will no longer exist. Dow Agrosciences and DuPont's merger into the DowDuPont corporation was completed in mid-September 2017: see Corporate Dow, *Dowdupont Merger Successfully Completed* (2017), online: <https://www.dow.com/en-us/news/press-releases/dowdupont-merger-successfully-completed> (last accessed 12/02/2018). Finally, Syngenta was also purchased by ChemChina in May 2017: for more information, see Syngenta Global, *Syngenta to sell remedy assets in the EEA in relation to the ChemChina acquisition* (2017), online: <https://www.syngenta.com/media/media-releases/yr-2017/23-10-2017a> (last accessed 12/02/2018).

and indeed, this is the challenge that methodological transnationalism[64] is striving to face.

ORCID

Giulia Claudia Leonelli http://orcid.org/0000-0001-9567-3280

Acknowledgements

I am grateful for the kind comments and suggestions provided by the anonymous reviewer of Transnational Legal Theory

Disclosure statement

No potential conflict of interest was reported by the author.

[64] See Zumbansen (n 34); Peer Zumbansen, 'Neither Public Nor Private, National Nor International: Transnational Corporate Governance from a Legal Pluralist Perspective' (2011) 38(1) *Journal of Law and Society*, 50; Peer Zumbansen, 'Lochner Disembedded: The Anxieties of Law in a Global Context' (2013) 20(1) *Indiana Journal of Global Legal Studies* 29; Peer Zumbansen, 'Theorising as Activity: Transnational Legal Theory in Context', in Christopher McRudeen, Upendra Baxi and Abdul Paliwala (eds.) *Law's Ethical, Global and Theoretical Contexts. Essays in Honour of William Twining* (Cambridge University Press, 2015) 280; Leonelli (n 2) and (n 3).

Financialisation of the transnational food chain: from threat to leverage point?

Tomaso Ferrando

Law and Development Research Center and Center of Development Policy, University of Antwerp

ABSTRACT

The 2008–2009 spike in food prices brought to the forefront the link between the transnational food system and the mechanisms of finance. However, the interconnections between food and finance go far beyond trading in futures and buying indexes and is redefining the chain from farm to fork. Having identified the main implications of a financialised food system, the article identifies two categories of legal and quasi-legal reaction that differ in objectives and processes: the approach of those who prefer engaging from within the financial paradigm and that of those who call for more stringent regulations. With the use of examples, it then reflects on the potential and limits demonstrated by each approach in engaging with the financialisation of food and suggests that complexity and interconnections of finance may become allies against unsustainable practices. The tactical use of EU Directive 95/2015 on non-financial disclosure is analysed with particular care.

I. Introduction

The 2008–2009 commodity bubble, the food shortages and the riots that ensued in several countries around the world brought to the forefront the link between the transnational food system and the mechanisms of finance: the impact that speculation can have on the availability of food became visible.[1] However, the connection between the food system and financial capital is deeper than trading in futures and food-related indexes: global finance has stretched to the roots and fundamentals of the food chain and is penetrating its daily practices. In the last decade, news from the financial

[1] Jennifer Clapp, 'Financialization, Distance and Global Food Politics' (2014) 41(5) *Journal of Peasant Studies* 797; SOMO, *Building a coalition against food speculation* (2011), online: <www.somo.nl/building-a-coalition-against-food-speculation>; Oliver De Schutter, 'Observations on the current food price situation', Background note (January 2011); Oliver De Schutter, 'Food Commodities Speculation and Food Price Crises: Regulation to reduce the risks of price volatility', United Nations, Briefing Note 02 (2011); Luigi Russi, *Hungry Capital: The Financialization of Food* (Zero Book, 2011); Steve Wiggins and Sharada Keats, *Grain Stocking and Price Spikes* (Overseas Development Institute, 2011); David Burch and Geoffrey Lawrence, 'Towards a Third Food Regime: Behind the Transformation' (2009) 26 (4) *Agricultural and Human Values* 267.

world and academic studies suggest that private equity funds, pension funds, insurance groups and commercial banks have targeted the agri-food system as a safe harbour in which to allocate their shareholders' money and extract high returns.[2] Through equity, debt or other legal tools, financiers have been increasing their role in defining what is produced, eaten, distributed and consumed. The consequences of such a massive flow of money that is invested in the food system in order to reward pensioners, billionaires and rent-seeking shareholders (in the order of tens of billions of dollars per year) cannot be ignored.

The fact that the food system has been financialised should not come as a surprise. Rather than an exception, the link between Wall Street and food is the manifestation of a process of transformation and expansion of capitalism that has been discussed by several authors adopting different perspectives and looking at other sectors of the economy.[3] Although not unexpected, the redefinition of the agri-food system to satisfy the aspirations and objectives of financial actors raises specific questions and poses ad hoc challenges. In a world were almost two billion people are food insecure (not having access to enough adequate food or eating too much and of poor quality),[4] a third of the food for human consumption is thrown away,[5] 36% of global crops are fed to livestock,[6] food systems in 2012 contributed 19–29% of global anthropogenic greenhouse gas (GHG) emissions,[7] and financial investors hold around 80% of all the shares available on stock markets,[8] we must take the presence and actions of finance seriously. Decisions made by few

---

[2] See, e.g., BlackRock, *BlackRock World Agricultural Fund* (2018), online: <www.blackrock.com/hk/en/products/229904/blackrock-world-agriculture-fund-a2-usd>; Ecofin Agency, 'Phatisa Food Fund 2 first closes at us$ 121.5 million' (*Ecofin Agency*, 3 October 2018), online: <www.ecofinagency.com/finance/0310-39030-phatisa-food-fund-2-first-closes-at-us-121-5-million>and Tatiana Freitas, 'Harvard Blew $1 Billion in Bet on Tomatoes, Sugar, and Eucalyptus' (Bloomberg, 1 March 2018), online: <www.bloomberg.com/news/articles/2018-03-01/harvard-blew-1-billion-in-bet-on-tomatoes-sugar-and-eucalyptus>. Among the academic publications that have reflected on the link beterrn food and finance, see, e.g., Jennifer Clapp and Ryan Isakson. *Speculative Harvest. Financialization, Food and Agriculture* (Fernwood Publishing, 2018); Jennifer Clapp and Ryan Isakson, 'Risky Returns: The Implications of Financialization in the Food System' (2018) 49(2) *Development and Change* 437.

[3] Gerald Epstein, *Financialization and the World Economy* (Edward Elgar, 2005); Ben Fine, 'Financialization from a Marxist perspective' (2014) 42(4) *International Journal of Political Economy* 47; Philip Arestis, Aurélie Charles and Giuseppe Fontana. 'Financialization, the Great Recession and the stratification of the US labor market' (2013) 19(3) *Feminist Economics* 152.

[4] Food and Agriculture Organization, *The State of Food Security and Nutrition* (Food and Agriculture Organization, 2018).

[5] Nicola Lucifero, 'Food Loss and Waste in the EU Law between Sustainability of Well-Being and the Implications on Food System and on Environment' (2016) 8 *Agriculture and Agricultural Science Procedia* 282; Tomaso Ferrando and Julie Mansuy, 'European Action Against Food Loss and Waste: Co-Regulation and Collisions on the Way to the Sustainable Development Goals' (2018) 15 *Yearbook of European Law* 1.

[6] Emily S Cassidy, Paul C West, James S Gerber and Jonathan A Foley, 'Redefining Agricultural Yields: from Tonnes to People Nourished Per Hectare' (2013) *Environmental Research Letters* 1.

[7] Sonja J Vermeulen, Bruce M Campbell and John SI Ingram, 'Climate Change and Food Systems' (2012) 37 *Annual Review of Environment and Resources*, 195.

[8] Charles McGrath, 80% of Equity Market Cap Held by Institutions (Pensions & Investments, 25 April 2017), online: <www.pionline.com/article/20170425/INTERACTIVE/170429926/80-of-equity-market-cap-held-by-institutions>.

key financial players are increasingly transforming land into a financial asset and making it harder for small-scale farmers to stay on the land, supporting the expansion of large scale conventional monoculture, relying on the consolidation of long distance trading, providing liquidity to livestock producers to satisfy the protein demand of emerging countries and 'covering with gold' companies that patent and sell genetically modified seeds because of the desire for higher yields.[9] In one sentence, finance is actively engaged in globalising a transnational food chain that produces high economic return independently from people's needs and the ecological limits of the planet.

This transition has not gone unnoticed and different approaches have been adopted both within and without social movements. Yet, reactions and engagement may be limited by the complexity of the matter, the lack of clarity and the intensification of the imbalance of power between those who profit from the system and those who suffer from its externalities.[10] On the one hand, there is the conflictual position, based on the assumption that the increasing financialisation of the food chain and the distance between decision making and conducts produce a multiplicity of negative effects and hinder resistance.[11] Even when institutional investors and large financial players are involved, this position claims, responsible forms of ownership and good governance would not be transformative,[12] mainly because of the obsession with shareholders' value and because of the way in which growth has to be constantly achieved. Geographically separated from the low paid producer workforce, the starving populations and the unbreathable air contaminated by pesticides, financial investors are only looking at quarterly performances, so that financial report and profitability become the sole possible language of communication between principals and agents.[13]

A more optimistic position endorses the ideas of stewardship and sustainable finance, whose proponents believe that an efficient system of accounting

---

[9] Madeleine Fairbarn, "Like Gold with Yield': Evolving Intersections between Farmland and Finance' (2014) 5(41) *Journal of Peasant Studies* 777.

[10] Clapp and Isakson (n 2).

[11] Clapp (n 1) 797; Anna Chadwick, *Law and the Political Economy of Hunger* (Oxford University Press, 2019); Russi (n 1). On distancing and the food system, see, e.g., Harriet Friedmann, 'Distance and Durability: the Shaky Foundation of the World Food System' (1992) 13(2) *The World Quarterly* 371. On distancing and the limits of enforcing responsibility in the global economy, see, e.g., Thomas Princen, 'The Shading and Distancing of Commerce: When Internalization is not Enough' (1997) 20(3) *Ecological Economics* 235. On resistance against financialization, see, e.g., Andrea M Collins, 'Financialization, Resistance and the Question of Women's Land Rights' (2018) *International Feminist Journal of Politics* 1; Per Forsberg, Anna-Karin Stockenstrand, 'Resistance to Financialization: Insights About Collective Resistance Through Distancing and Persistence from Two Ethnographic Studies' (2014) 3(2) *Journal of Organizational Ethnography* 169.

[12] Lorraine Talbot, 'Why Shareholders Shouldn't Vote: A Marxist-progressive Critique of Shareholder Empowerment' (2013) 76(5) *The Modern Law Review* 791; Charlotte Villiers, 'Has the financial crisis revealed that responsible ownership is a myth?' in Ian MacNeil and Justin O'Brien (eds), *The Future of Financial Regulation* (Hart, 2010).

[13] Eugene Fama, 'Agency Problems and the Theory of the Firm' (1980) 88 *Journal of Political Economy* 288; Frank Easterbrook and Daniel Fischel, 'The Corporate Contract' (1989) 89 *Columbia Law Review* 1416.

and transparency, coupled with the internalisation of the environmental and social impact of economic activities, provides an opportunity to improve the economy and reduce externalities.[14] Although finance is seen as distant and removed from the real life of the agri-food system, any change in the conduct of large investors would generate a positive domino effect that would reach the four corners of the planet because of the intangible connections that equity, debt and derivatives create between financial hubs and the territoriality of the investments that they realised. When the financial sector intervenes in the production, transformation and distribution of food, it could be said that their investments operate as 'legal chokeholds',[15] i.e. leverage points for legal interventions aimed at challenging misconducts across the food chains and increasing liability.[16]

In the context of opposing paradigms, this contribution reflects on the potential and limits of leveraging finance as a 'legal chokehold' to improve the social and environmental quality of the global food system. After an introduction on the financialisation of food and the notion of chokeholds, this paper uses concrete examples to discuss the potential and limits of organising around 'leverage points' that are both external (mandatory rules, limits to commodity trading, etc.) and internal (Principle for Responsible Investments, shareholder activism, etc.) to the financial sector. Halfway between external and internal, the European Union (EU) Directive 95/2014 on non-financial reporting is discussed in Section IV as a mixed mechanism of engagement with finance. With optimism, the European meta-regulation may help mapping, exposing and (possibly) challenging the actions of those who really benefit from the financialisation of the transnational food regime. Yet, the conclusions reflect on the inherent limits of a strategy that engages with financialisation without addressing the systemic and inherent problems that arise when the food chain is structured around the premises and objectives of finance.

II. Financialisation of the transnational food chain: speculation, indexes and more

Financialisation has been described as 'the increasing role of financial motives, financial markets, financial actors and financial institutions in the operation of the domestic and international economies.'[17] This mainly assumes the

[14] Frank Curtis, Ida Levine and James Browning, 'The Institutional Investor's Role in 'Responsible Ownership'', in Ian MacNeil and Justin O'Brien (eds), *The Future of Financial Regulation* (Hart, 2010); David Monciardini, 'The 'Coalition of the Unlikely' Driving the EU Regulatory Process of Non-Financial Reporting' (2016) 36(1) *Social and Environmental Accountability Journal* 76.

[15] Tomaso Ferrando, 'Land Rights at the time of Global Production: Leveraging Multi-Spatiality and 'Legal Chokeholds'' (2017) 2(2) *Business and Human Rights Journal* 275.

[16] Deborah Cowen, *The Deadly Life of Logistics* (University of Minnesota Press, 2014); David Harvey, *The Enigma of Capital and the Crises of Capitalism* (Profile Books, 2010).

[17] Epstein (n 3) 3.

form of dividends, interests on debt or remuneration of financial instruments like derivatives and indexes. The macro and micro components of our socio-economic system are thus increasingly defined by the pressure that financial actors exercise to generate returns on an increasing amount of investments. Decisions made in a few offices by men in suits are redefining the economic system and, at the same time, redesigning individual lives. Let's take two examples: as we are all aware, the 2008 global financial meltdown was deeply determined by the combination of collateralisation, securitisation and the creation of money through debt (itself a financial product). At the other extreme of the spectrum, the pensions of millions of workers all over the world depends on the financial strategy of investors who are entrusted with their savings and whose job is to invest workers' savings today so to guarantee their pensions in the future. Through finance, global and local intensify their interconnection.

From the point of view of the food system, the first evidence of financialisation reaching the broader public was with the 2008–2010 food crisis, when a combination of derivatives, grain stocking and climate events led to price spikes, hunger and riots.[18] However, financial capital is increasingly involved in the definition of what food is produced, where, how and for whom. It is transforming food production and consumption according to investors' desire for a stable return on their investment rather than by the wider needs of people and ecological limits.[19] According to Burch and Lawrence, in 2009 the food regime was already heading towards a situation where:

> a number of financial institutions and instruments that have the capacity to re-organise various stages of the agri-food supply chain, and to alter the terms and conditions under which other actors in the chain can operate. In the case of the private equity company, for example, we see a fraction of capital which views the agri-food company—whether it is a third-party auditor, an input supplier, a farm operator, a food manufacturer or a retailer—as a bundle of resources which provide opportunities for a quick profit, which may or may not involve a restructuring, but which will eventually return the enterprise to the share market and then move on to another bundle of resources.[20]

That transnational food production is on the radar of financial investors is not a mystery. Financial advisors, pension funds managers and brokers from the four corners of the planet are open and transparent in highlighting the economic potential of investing in food. This is often justified by the food needs of a growing population, the shift in diets towards a Western model

---

[18] Russi (n 1); Steve Wiggins and Sharad Keats, *Grain Stocking and Price Spikes* (Overseas Development Institute, 2011).

[19] Burch and Lawrence (n 1) 267; Philip McMichael, 'A Food Regime Genealogy' (2009) 36(1) *The Journal of Peasant Studies* 139; Harriet Friedmann, 'Commentary: Food Regime Analysis and Agrarian Questions: Widening the Conversation' (2016) 43(3) *The Journal of Peasant Studies* 671; Jennifer Clapp and Ryan Isakson, *Speculative Harvest. Financialization, Food and Agriculture* (Fernwood Publishing, 2018).

[20] Burch and Lawrence (n 1) 275.

of consumption, the scarcity of resources, the possibility to extract resources controlling logistics, and the possibility of return represented by controlling one of the essential elements of life. Not investing in food would be a lost opportunity.[21] A narrative that is shared with multi-lateral agricultural projects like the G8 New Alliance on Food and Nutrition Security and the Agenda 2030, in particular of Sustainable Development Goal 2 on Zero Hunger and Goal 17 on Partnership for the Goals.[22]

Throughout the world, financial capital is distributed along the food chain so that corporations are acquired, merged, invested and reorganised according to principles of effectiveness, efficiency and financial return. Although more liquidity may lead to a strengthening of the sector, what is happening is a radical transformation. We only need to spend six minutes watching a short video telling the story of Richard David and Desmond Cheung, co-managers of the BlackRock Global Fund-World Agricultural Fund, to have a sense of the scale of the issue already back in 2011.[23] In the video, the two financers share their experience on the ground, meeting with corporations and people working for them, with the aim to convince the viewer (a possible investors in the Fund) that investing in land, traders, seeds companies and retailers is safe and profitable. Not only they are sharing their consideration on the current food system, but they are making projections about the future of food and what the food system is that they envisage, i.e., they believe that money could be generated in the future.

The financialisation of the food system means, therefore, to allocate resources according to Richard and Desmond's vision (or any other financer's vision), to invest them where analysts believe the highest profits can be generated. From farm to fork, the food chain is witnessing acquisitions, mergers, vertical and horizontal concentration, investments in commodity indexes, purchases of lands, an increasing use of debt as a mechanism to support agricultural activities and an intense competition for futures and other financial instruments that can reduce the risk of the investment. Two financial actors (Vanguard and BlackRock) were the main investors in four seeds and chemical companies that recently gave birth to two of the three largest mergers in the sectors of seeds and agricultural inputs (Monsanto and Bayern, Dupont and DowChemical). Similar scenarios characterise

---

21 Lutz Goedde, Maya Horii, and Sunil Sanghvi, 'Pursuing the Global Opportunity in Food and Agribusiness' (McKinsey & Company, July 2015) www.mckinsey.com/industries/chemicals/our-insights/pursuing-the-global-opportunity-in-food-and-agribusiness (accessed 17 December 2018); Financial Tribune, 'Advantages of Investment in Food Industry' (Financial Tribune, 18 March 2015)https://financialtribune.com/articles/economy-domestic-economy/13557/advantages-of-investment-in-food-industry accessed 17 December 2018; Caroline Bergdolt and Anuradha Mittal, 'Betting on World Agriculture: US Private Equity Managers Eye Agricultural Returns' (2012) The Oakland Institute.

22 United Nations, *Transforming Our World: The 2030 Agenda for Sustainable Development* (UN Publishing, 2015).

23 BlackRock, *BlackRock Global Fund – World Agricultural Fund* (2011), online: <www.youtube.com/watch?v=AMYPPalcoac>.

global supermarket chains, logistic companies, farmland, food processors and retailers.

Decisions made in a few hubs by a few investors are creating networks and threads that connect geographies and people through common investors that see in that business a potential for financial return. BlackRock, for example, keeps together farmers, trades and consumers across different sectors and different parts of the world. Similarly, in December 2018 the Norwegian Pension Fund had investments in more than 9,000 companies in 72 countries. A sense of the widespread nature of finance and the 'hub' role of few actors is evident.[24] Financial connections and financialisation go beyond the material interactions of the transnational food chains and are obliquely operating across commodities and sectors. If finance is the main driver behind the transformation of the global food system, it is increasingly the target of dissent and resistance.

Throughout the world, the desire to react against the implications and consequences of financialisation has favoured the emergence of a series of local and global reactions: sometimes they overlap but they seldom coordinate. As discussed in the next sections, some interventions try to subordinate finance to the superior authority of the state and bring the state-market relationship closer to the former,[25] while others operate within a context of coexistence between the localism of the environmental and human rights violations (material or potential) and the global expansion of financial capital that cuts across borders and reaches multiple geographies. For the supporters of the latter approach, the idea is that in the context where financial players own the equity or debt of thousands of companies around the world, it is more effective to challenge the source of funding rather than engaging with the companies operating on the ground. Like a revised version of the trickle-down economy, the expectation is that a change at the top of the financial pyramid may trickle down to the ground. This difference of approach between opposition and coordination is what I define as the 'without or within', which I discuss in the next Section.

III. Reacting without or within the system?

The recent history of resistance against the financialisation of the food system is characterised by a series of attempts to expand the objectives of legal activism and directly target financial actors rather than (or together with) the companies that receive funds from them. As discussed in Section III.a below, some actors have tried to leverage public law and the existence of

[24] Norges Bank Investment Management, 'Government Pension Fund Global – The Fund' (2018), online: <www.nbim.no/en/the-fund/>.

[25] Karl Polanyi, *The Great Transformation: The Political and Economic Origins of Our Time* (Beacon Press, 2001).

top-down legal constraints and sanctions. Among the tools that belong to this category, there are regulatory changes, new interpretations of the legal framework and the strategic use of litigation to obtain new judicial implementation of the existing discipline. On the other hand, Section III.b focuses on interventions that are embedded in the vocabulary and vision of finance, like the adoption of investments standards that are presented as comparative advantage, the recognition of the financial relevance of non-financial risk and the divestment from stranded assets. In this latter case, the financialisation of the food system is not necessarily 'the enemy' but a possible ally in the improvement of the global food chain. While the former category challenges the financial system from the outside, the latter gathers experiences that are fully embedded in the premises and mechanisms of the financialised economy and aims to twist its own assumptions.

III.a. Reacting from outside: bringing finance under public control

Around the first decade of the 2000s, the value of Canadian farmland had been steadily increasing by 14.5%.[26] In response, the national government of Saskatchewan proposed legislative reform forbidding the purchase of agricultural land by pension funds: independently from their nationality, financial actors should not have been allowed to access land and bring up the prices.[27] Around the same time, the Canadian Province of British Columbia was, reportedly, considering the introduction of extra taxation for those investors purchasing agricultural land for speculative and non-agricultural purposes.[28] In both cases, a regulatory intervention justified by the need to protect the agricultural nature of land and its accessibility, would impact existing and future investment strategies and reveal the possibility for public actors to contribute to the allocation of the resources that are responsible for the production of food. In this context, a law territorially framed and limited by the jurisdictional boundaries of the Province would have achieved the desired outcome: the sole objective was to regulate what happens under the authority of the government and prevent the subordination of land to the global interests of finance.

Another example is represented by the legal measures adopted (or proposed) by local and national authorities in the attempt to reduce the negative consequences of speculation on food. On the wave of the 2008–2010 food price peak, proposals were advanced in the USA, Switzerland and the EU to limit the possibility of trading in commodity derivatives, and agricultural

[26] *Ibid.*

[27] Jacqueline Nelson, 'Saskatchewan Stops Pension Funds from Buying Farmland as Prices Rise' *The Globe and Mail* (13 April 2015).

[28] Mark Hume and Kathy Tomlison, 'B.C. Considers Tax Changes for Farmland Speculators' *The Globe and Mail* (20 November 2016).

derivatives more specifically. In all these cases—which obtained different levels of support and success—members of civil society, farmers associations, NGOs and some regulators united around the desire to stabilise the commodity market and introduce regulatory reforms that would 'include strict, legally binding and ex ante "position limits", i.e., clear measures that would restrict the number and/or the value of commodity derivatives contracts ("positions") held by financial player.'[29]

Of the three experiences mentioned above, one of the most interesting was launched in Switzerland at the beginning of 2016. A referendum was held under the name 'No speculation of foodstuffs' with the intention of curbing dramatic price rises on foodstuffs by restricting financial institutions from speculating on food and agricultural commodities.[30]Although it was defeated with 60% of the vote, the initiative highlighted the connection between Switzerland and the global food chain, but also the possibility of directly involving citizens in the West in decision affecting the transnational actions of financiers and the lives of people all over the world. Despite the land-locked nature of the country that positions it far from most physical trading routes, Switzerland represents the world's most important trading hub with as much as one-third of the global transit trade in vital commodities such as oil, metals and agricultural goods that is realised by Swiss companies,[31] most of which engage in hedging, speculative trading and OTC investments.[32] Instead of assuming a protective and introverted approach to finance, as in the case of land acquisitions, the Swiss referendum would have been an expansionist and extroverted attempt to leverage the economic and legal 'weight' that a jurisdiction plays in the global food chain.

The EU offers another interesting example of the possibility for regulators to redefine the relationship between financial actors, derivatives and commodities such as food. Since the 3rd January 2018, position limits on financial derivatives have become a reality in the EU.[33] According to the Markets in Financial Instruments Directive, national competent authorities are now required to establish and enforce a maximum amount of commodity derivatives that a person can hold at all times with the aim of preventing market abuse and market distorting positions. Above all, the aim of the Directive is to avoid the convergence between prices of derivatives and the spot

[29] SOMO, 'Building a Coalition Against Food *Speculation* (2011), online: <www.somo.nl/building-a-coalition-against-food-speculation/>.

[30] Anand Chandrasekhar, 'Game Over for Food Speculation Initiative' *Swissinfo* (28 February 2016).

[31] STSA, Commodity Trading in Switzerland (STSA, 2016), online: <https://stsa.swiss/knowledge/switzerland>.

[32] PWC, The Hand that Rocks the Cradle -Regulation and the Future of Commodities Trading in Switzerland (2015), online: <https://news.pwc.ch/wp-content/uploads/2015/11/commodity-trading-event_ge_25.11.2015.pdf>.

[33] Directive 2014/65/EU of the European Parliament and the Council of 15 May 2014 on markets in financial instruments and amending Directive 2002/92/EC and Directive 2011/61/EU (MiFID II).

prices for the underlying commodity,[34] a conjuncture that was considered by some authors as one of the main drivers of the 2008 peak in food prices.[35] Of the nine commodities that are covered by the directive, three are food: London cocoa, Robusta coffee and white sugar.

It is too early to assess the impact of the Directive on speculative practices that often prejudice small-scale farmers. In the future, it will be of particular interest to enter into the details of national implementation and assess the material impact that they have had on investors, farmers and all the other actors operating along the three chains. Despite the partiality of the Directive's scope (derivatives are issued in connection with several more food commodities) and the fact that it does not ban speculation on food commodities (i.e., the purchase of derivatives independently from the interest in the underlying commodity), the EU Directive and the other interventions like the Swiss referendum have the merit of proposing strategic thinking about trading regulation as the link between the materiality of food shortages and the global nature of finance. If the peak in prices that negatively affected millions of people all over the world was also the result of the speculative practices taking place in few stock exchanges under specific rules, these proposals may help delinking the food system from speculative interests.[36]

A third external reaction against the financialisation of the food system may come—unexpectedly—from competition law and the regulators' interest in looking closely at the fact that few financial players hold relevant amounts of shares in undertakings that are competing for the same market. This situation, which is technically known as 'horizontal ownership',[37] has been neglected in the scholarship and only recently has obtained some attention from academics and practitioners,[38] probably due, in part, to the recent acquisition of Monsanto by Bayer. In that case, BlackRock and Vanguard, two of the largest financial actors in the world, were major shareholders in both companies and thus significantly increased their power in the seeds and chemical sector after the deal was cleared.[39] In order to take finance seriously,[40] it would be the task of national competition authorities (and of the European Commission in the case of mergers and acquisitions of EU relevance) to

---

34 BaFin, *Position Limits for Commodity Derivatives* (2018), online: <www.bafin.de/EN/Aufsicht/BoersenMaerkte/PositionslimitsWarenderivate/positionslimits_warenderivate_node_en.html>.

35 Russi (n 1).

36 *Ibid.*

37 Einer Elhauge, 'Horizontal Shareholding' (2016) 109 *Harvard Law Review* 1267.

38 Eric Posner, Fiona Scott Mortong and E Glen Weyl, 'A Proposal to Limit the Anti-Competitive Power of Institutional Investors' (Forthcoming) *Antitrust Law Journal*; Ioannis Lianos, 'The Bayer Monsanto/Merger: A Critical Appraisal' (2018), Report submitted to the German Parliament (Bundestag), 32.

39 Reuters, *Major Syngenta Shareholders Would Back Monsanto Bid Around $50 bln* (2015), online: <www.reuters.com/article/syngenta-ma-investors/major-syngenta-shareholders-would-back-monsanto-bid-around-50-blnidusl5n0xz3v720150508>.

40 iPES-Food, *Letter to the European Commission on the Bayer-Monsanto Merger* (2017), online: <www.ipes-food.org/images/CoreDocs/IPES-Food_Bayer-Monsanto-merger6.10.2017.pdf>.

shift their attention from the concentration in the market to the concentration at the financial level and assess its implications in terms of competition, effectiveness and distortion of the economy.[41] However, it seems that financial concentration and the common ownership across the food chain are far from being taken seriously (or even considered at all). In the Bayer/Monsanto case, to use the same example, the European Commission required Bayer to divest parts of its business and identified BASF as the purchaser. Although an analysis was proposed on the anti-competitive impact of this structural reconfiguration, the Commission completely overlooked the fact that BlackRock and Vanguard—leading shareholders in the two merging companies —are also leading shareholders of BASF.[42]

As these examples reveal, there are multiple ways in which public authorities (regional, national and local) can limit the operations of financial actors and the financialisation of the food system. They can single out institutional investors when it comes to having access to land, impose new rules for publicly traded financial instruments and adopt an approach to competition law that is more attentive to the role of finance in defining the economy. In all these cases, territories and jurisdictions are connected by the financial ties of the global chain of food production, so that changes operating within them can have a consequence on the content and procedure of the financialised food system. Legal bottlenecks, chokeholds, barriers and leverage points do exist or can be created—even when we talk about finance.[43] The tendency is, however, to engage finance from within.

III.b. Reacting from within: the food chain through financial lenses

Actions that challenge finance from within can be categorised according to the mechanism and the objectives. With regards to the former, we can identify two macro-groups: interventions that leverage the ethical and reputational component of financial investors and those that mobilise the environment and society as non-financial considerations that funds' managers have the duty to consider when they act in the best interest of their funds'

[41] Jose Azar, Martin C Schmalz and Isabel Tecu, 'Anticompetitive Effects of Common Ownership' (2018) 73 (4) *Journal of Finance* 1; Einer Elhauge, 'The Increasing Evidence that Horizontal Shareholding is Distorting Our Economy' (29 June 2017), Harvard Law School Forum on Corporate Governance and Financial Regulation, online: <https://corpgov.law.harvard.edu/2017/06/29/the-increasing-evidence-that-horizontal-shareholding-is-distorting-our-economy/>; Einer Elhauge, OECD, 'Tackling Horizontal Shareholding: An Update and Extension to the Sherman Act and EU Competition Law-Note by Einer Elhauge (6 December 2017), online: <https://one.oecd.org/document/DAF/COMP/WD(2017)95/en/pdf>; Eric A Posner, Fiona Scotto Morton and E Glen Weyl, 'A Proposal to Limit the Anti-Competitive Power of Institutional Investors' (2017) *Antitrust Law Journal* (forthcoming).

[42] Clapp and Isakson (n 2).

[43] Cowen (n 16); Harvey (n 16); Tomaso Ferrando, 'Land Rights at the Time of Global Production: Leveraging Multi-Spatiality and 'Legal Chokeholds'' (2017) 2(2) *Business and Human Rights Journal* 275.

members.[44] Through the years and across different sectors, civil society, NGOs, regulators and investors have been ideating and implementing strategies and interventions that can be located in a chart that has objectives and leverage points as its two axes. As discussed below, some cases were characterised by third parties' decision to impact one specific investment, while in other circumstances they challenged any investment realised by a particular financial actor. Independently from the geography of these actions, they all have in common the intention to engage with finance from within to generate material improvements in the real economy. Four are presented below to provide some food for thought about the combination between objectives and leverage points and to contextualise the EU Directive that is discussed in section IV: the Principles for Responsible Investments; two cases concerning concentrated animal factories operations (CAFOs); the use of debt relationships as a leverage for change; and divestment from unsustainable operations in the name of the fiduciary duty towards members.

One of the oldest initiatives concerning international investors was the creation of the United Nations Principles for Responsible Investments (PRI), a network of (now) more than 2,000 financial actors which rotates around six voluntary recommendations elaborated by a group of financial experts. These recommendations express the importance of bringing environmental and social governance (ESG) considerations into existing approaches to investments in order to make them less risky and therefore more resilient.[45] Members of the PRI report on these six recommendations and the way in which they are performing them. The PRI have been appreciated because of their systematisation and translation into ESG terminology of several circumstances that are faced by companies all over the world. However, they have been criticised for their open and non-binding nature, which is only partially counterbalanced by the fact that annual reporting is a condition to remain part of the scheme.[46]

Concerning transnational food chains, the PRI network has contributed, among other things, to the education of the financial sector on the relevance of ESG and has produced specific guidelines and recommendations that aim at nudging investors to consider the way in which climate change, poor conditions of labour and the excessive use of water may generate negative returns. For example, PRI and the WWF recently published an Investor guide on water risks in the agricultural supply chain which recognises agriculture as

[44] Christine Berry, 'Fiduciary Duty and Responsible Investment: An Overview', in Karen Wendt (ed), *Responsible Investment Banking* (Springer, 2015).

[45] Rolf D Häßler and Till Hendrik Jung. 'In Principle Good: The Principles for Responsible Investment', in Karen Wendt (ed) *Responsible Investment Banking* (Springer, 2015).

[46] PRI, *Reporting for Signatories* (2018), online: <www.unpri.org/signatories/reporting-for-signatories>.

the world's largest user of water[47] and presents it as a risk for investors that must be understood, mitigated and integrated into their financial analysis.[48] Similarly, the network published an online resource entitled 'Engage the Chain: An Investor Guide to Agricultural Supply Chain Risk' that provides investors with information about the social and environmental impacts driving material business risks for eight key commodities: beef, corn, dairy, fibre-based packaging, palm oil, soybeans, sugarcane and wheat[49] and launched a collaborative programme on deforestation that recognises the financial risk of cattle raising.[50]

In terms of leverage points, the PRI clearly stresses that responsible investment is not a matter of ethics but of fiduciary duty.[51] The adoption of the principles and of its ESG guidelines should thus be of interest to all financial actors, including those unconcerned by ethical or moral considerations, because it has to do with the good financial performance of the investments and the satisfaction of the managers' mandate. 'To ignore ESG factors is to ignore risks and opportunities that have a material effect on the returns delivered to clients and beneficiaries,' it is stated on the PRI website.[52] This is an affirmation that clearly illustrates the priority of financial motivations behind the establishment of the principles. If financial performance is the leverage, stable returns on investments is the objective reached through voluntary adoption; however, there is no requirement that investors rule out investments or divest from companies that do not reach a specific ESG threshold.

Differently from the divestment strategy discussed in the forth example below, and because the focus of PRI is the financial opportunity represented by ESG-performing investments and of the flexibility in the implementation,

---

47 OECD, *Water Risk Hotspots for Agriculture* (OECD Publishing, 2017).

48 PRI and WWF, *Growing Water Risk Resilience: An Investor Guide on Agricultural Supply Chain* (2018), online: <www.unpri.org/download?ac=4195>.

49 Ceres, *Engage the Chain* (2018), online: <https://engagethechain.org/>.

50 Principles for Responsible Investments, *PRI and Ceres Open Collaborative Engagement on Deforestation to Global Investors* (2017), online: <www.unpri.org/news-and-press/pri-and-ceres-open-collaborative-engagement-on-deforestation-to-global-investors/350.article>.

51 The notion of 'fiduciary duty' itself has been the object of controversies and legal challenges. The traditional vision, for example, considers that '[t]rustees have a legal duty to not only invest, but to actively seek the best possible financial return … even if it is contrary to the personal, moral, political or social views of the trustees or beneficiaries.' This would mean that any ESG consideration would be taken into consideration only if financially superior to the non-ESG option, despite the ethical and moral desire of beneficiaries. See, e.g., Principle for Responsible Investments, *Fiduciary Duty* (2015), online: <www.unpri.org/fiduciary-duty/fiduciary-duty-in-the-21st-century/244.article>; Principle for Responsible Investments, Fiduciary Duty in the 21st Century (2018), online: <www.unpri.org/fiduciary-duty/fiduciary-duty-in-the-21st-century/244.article>; ClientEarth, *Shell Pension Fund Member Warns of Legal Action* (2018), online: <www.clientearth.org/shell-pension-fund-member-warns-of-legal-action/>; Sarah Barker, Mark Baker-Jones, Emilie Barton and Emma Fagan, 'Climate Change and the Fiduciary Duties of Pension Fund Trustees- Lessons from the Australian Law' (2016) 6(3) *Journal of Sustainable Finance and Investment*; Christine Berry and Charles Scanlan, 'The Voice of the Beneficiary', in James P Hawley et al. (eds), *Handbook of Institutional Investment and Fiduciary Duty* (Cambridge University Press, 2014).

52 Principle for Responsible Investments, *What is Responsible Investment?* online: <www.unpri.org/pri/what-is-responsible-investment>.

the scheme supports engagement with the investee with the aim of improving their conduct rather than advocating divestment. Yet, the primacy of financial performance and the voluntary nature of the scheme determines the need to make a business case for the adoption of ESGs[53] and means that little is done by investors and companies until the materiality of the ESG is proven and evident. For example, in Brazil several institutional investors, banks and insurers have signed up to the PRI and the Principles for Sustainable Insurance (PSI). Nevertheless, in 2015 the country still supported cattle ranching, agriculture, fishing, and food and beverage companies with a high ESG risk profile, perfectly illustrating this limitation.[54]

A second example concerns factory farming. There, investors' eagerness to capitalise on the ongoing increase of world meat consumption is integrated in two initiatives, the Farm Animal Investment Risk and Return (FAIRR) and the Business Benchmark on Farm Animal Welfare (BBFAW), which look at Concentrated Animal Factory Operations (CAFOs) from the perspective of risk and financial return. As evident from the presentation of BlackRock's World Agricultural Fund discussed at the beginning of this paper,[55] financiers are betting that while the world will continue consuming animal protein, and are therefore channelling their funds to companies that adopt this same vision. Without entering into the details of the two initiatives, they are of interest because they attempt to translate animal welfare into something more than matters of ethics, rights and compassion: animal welfare is translated into financial terms to redirect investment strategies.

BBFAW is a benchmark that ranks how the world's leading food companies are managing and reporting their farm animal welfare practices. By ranking companies, they aim to attract investors and consumers to those performing best and to sanction those at the bottom by indirectly making access to capital more expensive, thereby triggering positive reactions. FAIRR is a project launched by a private equity manager that reinterprets animal protein production (livestock and fisheries) through 28 ESG criteria and the Coller FAIR Protein Producer Index. For FAIRR, animal protein production is a matter of reputation, human health, regulatory compliance, climate change, deforestation,[56] local community support and, ultimately, longer-

---

[53] Gunnar Friede, Timo Busch & Alexander Bassen, 'ESG and Financial Performance: Aggregated Evidence from More Than 2000 Empirical Studies' (2025) 5(4) *Journal of Sustainable Finance & Investment* 210.

[54] Danielle Carreira, Aaron Re'em and Miriam Tarin, Trucost, *Natural Capital Risk Exposure of the Financial Sector in Brazil* (2015), online: <http://cebds.org/wp-content/uploads/2015/07/GIZ-Natural-Capital-Risk-Exposure.pdf>.

[55] BlackRock (n 2).

[56] FAIRR is one of the promoters, along with six transnational food companies, of the Cerrado Manifesto, a pledge to work with local companies in Brazil to reduce the conversion of forest into soy production. The wording and aims of the Cerrado Manifesto trigger several considerations that can only be sketched here. The Manifesto is a chain-based approach to deforestation that also involves financial actors; it is a recognition of the link between meat production and deforestation, although through the medium of soy; it states that local companies are under pressure to convert land and therefore a 'coalition of the

term returns.[57] The bottom-line is that better production means higher returns and lower financial risk and that investors should put their money where the combination of these two elements is most effective.

In FAIRR's words:

> [m]ore humane farming practices tend to be more productive too. For example using 'controlled atmosphere killing' as a method of slaughter for chickens is described as both more compassionate and more cost-effective. Similarly, pasture-based grazing for cows means less stress and therefore more lactation cycles over their lifetime.[58]

In FAIRR's approach to the food chain, livestock and fish are proteins with a financial value and a risk. The vocabulary and the investment strategies are not defined by ethical or moral considerations, although reputation is considered. In this vision, CAFOs are like 'new coal'; stranded assets with no future value that should be abandoned by means of improvement or divestment.[59] Meat consumption and slaughtering are not problematised *per se*, but rather seen as a reliable source of income because of the changing dietary patterns in emerging countries.

A third kind of engagement with finance and the food chain is exemplified by WWF and Greenpeace's separate campaigns against Banco Santander[60] and HSBC.[61] There, the two international NGOs decided to leverage debt as a means to stop ongoing deforestation and the killing of orangutans connected with palm-oil production. In those cases, the two NGOs mapped, identified and targeted specific loans that Santander Bank and HSBC had provided to palm-oil companies and leveraged the reputation of the two banks to prevent the renewal of the financial support. Rather than concerning the overall portfolio of the banks or suggesting that the banks engage with the

---

willing' should be established to steer local actors towards more sustainable practices; it affirms that the legal standards of the Brazilian Forest Code are insufficient to prevent deforestation and therefore the higher private standard suggested by the coalition should be implemented. Finance and companies on the ground are thus coordinating to change production patterns, a process that would be of interest both for competition lawyers and for academics interested in private regulation and private legal transplant. On private legal transplant, see Tomaso Ferrando, 'Private Legal Transplant: Multinational Enterprises as Proxies of Legal Homogenization' (2015) 4(1) *Transnational Legal Theory* 20. The Cerrado Manifesto is available online. FAIRR, *Cerrado Manifesto* (2018), online: https://cerradostatement.fairr.org/.

[57] FAIRR, *Considering Farm Animal Welfare in Investment Decision-Making-Case Studies and Guidance* (2015), online: <www.fairr.org/wp-content/uploads/FAIRR-Case-Studies-and-Guidance-June-2015.pdf>.

[58] *Ibid*, 3.

[59] The 2015 FAIRR Report contains one reference to divestment, that of Boston Common Asset Management from a company that appeared in breach from the organic requirements despite advertising its milk as organic. See FAIRR, *ibid*, 11.

[60] Richard George, Green Peace, 'Result: Santander Stops Financing Forest Destroyer APRIL' (26 February 2015), online: <www.greenpeace.org.uk/result-santander-stops-financing-forest-destroyer-april-20150226/>.

[61] Anna Rahmawati, Green Peace, 'HSBC Promises to Cut Ties with Forest-Trashing Palm Oil Companies' (21 February 2017), online: <www.greenpeace.org.uk/hsbc-promises-cut-ties-forest-trashing-palm-oil-companies-20170221>.

two company, WWF and Greenpeace pushed for a visible financial sanction that—they intended—would make it more expensive for the company to obtain funds. Similarly, FIAN international recently denounced the human rights violations connected with the actions of an agribusiness companies operating on contested land in the Matopiba region of Brazil.[62] Unlike other cases of anti-land grabbing resistance, the objective was not to identify the companies that were directly responsible for the enclosures, but to connect the operations on the ground with the global financial system and pressure the Swedish National Pension Scheme—which had invested in the operations—to divest.[63]

Because companies raise funds through equity and debt, we could thus imagine potential actions targeting not only shareholders but also bonds' subscribers and loans providers that are directly supporting companies that market genetically modified organisms (GMOs), use slave and child labour, are responsible for the appropriation of water and biodiversity, or contribute to non-communicable diseases because of the poor nutritional content of the food that is produced. Unlike a pure financial approach, the actions mentioned here were not constructed around the financial unsustainability of the investment and the viability of the divestment, but on the reputational implications of non-divesting and on the power of naming and shaming.

A fourth possible intervention is represented by the call for divestment, which can be promoted on moral ground and/or on the basis of the legal consideration that investors have a fiduciary duty towards their members to move money away from risky or unsustainable operations that may affect the financial viability of the portfolios. In this latter case, activists, lawyers and civil society are not (only) exercising reputational pressure but have been working hard to build a financial case for divestment which is couched in the vocabulary and 'Return on the Investment' (ROI) perspective that financial actors are familiar with. At the core of these interventions is the transformation of ESG consideration into material financial risks and the capacity of the proponents to demonstrate that the fiduciary duty—and not the moral nature of the investor—requires certain sectors and companies to be ruled out as potential investments.

---

[62] FIAN, *Land Grabbing and Human Rights: The Role of EU Actors Abroad* (2017), online: <www.fian.org/fileadmin/media/publications_2017/Announcements_Calls_Flyer/WEB_Eng.pdf>.

[63] In a 2011 study of five investment funds falling under the Swedish national pension fund, Hamilton and Eriksson present a set of influence factors that were used by civil society actors to convince the funds' managers to take ESG into considerations and redefine their investment strategies. See, Ian Hamilton & Jessica Eriksson, 'Influence Strategies in Shareholder Engagement: A Case Study of All Swedish National Pension Funds' (2011) 1(1) *Journal of Sustainable Finance and Investment* 44. For a similar research on the Dutch fund, see Frank AJ Wagemans, CSA (Kris) van Koppen & Arthur PJ Mol, 'Engagement on ESG Issues by Dutch Pension Funds: Is it Reaching its Full Potential?' (2018) 8(4) *Journal of Sustainable Finance & Investment* 301.

One of the more interesting aspects of the ongoing campaign to divest from fossil fuel—that could be transplanted into a potential campaign concerning the transnational food system—has been the identification of specific investors as preferred targets of the campaigns. The hope is that an operation realised by visible and financially relevant players could trigger a domino effect of competitors, whether because they mimic their investment strategies, do not want to lose clients concerned with the environment or society, or because they are worried of being the ones ending up with the worthless assets in their portfolios. When the Norwegian Pension Fund (the largest in the world which invests in more than 9,000 companies in 72 countries) proposed to drop any investment in fossil fuel in December 2018,[64] it communicated to the rest of the financial sector that it doubted the safety and reliability of this specific sector and forced investors all over the world to take the financial risk associated with climate change seriously.[65] Interestingly, and as a proof of the complexity of engaging with finance in a coordinated way, the concentration of ownership that creates concern from the point of view of competition law, is often seen as a strong opportunity behind an effective divestment campaign.

What is often dismissed, is that any of the four tactics described above have required NGOs, civil society and the broader public interest in divestment to financialise their own vision of the world and their strategies. Bound by the need to produce technical arguments that resonate with the expertise and vocabulary of the financial sector, they may have abandoned or limited the use of other forms of resistance.[66] When ethics or morals are replaced (or rephrased) by accounting for sustainable finance, fiduciary duty, ESG and the 'materiality of non-financial issues',[67] engagement embraces a very technical vocabulary and is forced to process, assess and organise financial data as investors do. This is what is happening with the EU Directive 95/2014 on sustainable finance and the ongoing operations of the EU High-Level Panel on Sustainable Finance concerning taxonomy and benchmarks. At their core,

[64] Norges Bank Investment Management (n 24).

[65] Adam Vaughan, 'World's Biggest Sovereign Wealth Fund Proposes Ditching Oil and Gas Holdings' *The Guardian* (London, 16 November 2017), online: <www.theguardian.com/business/2017/nov/16/oil-and-gas-shares-dip-as-norways-central-bank-advises-oslo-to-divest>.

[66] Divestment and ESG are a very technical sector dominated by the vocabulary, taxonomy and perspective of finance. NGOs engaging in this area, e.g., the World Wildlife Fund (WWF) have been adapting their narrative and strengthening their financial expertise. Such process, which may facilitate the dialogue with financial actors and investors, may be seen as a form of elitism of environmental and social engagement and may pose problems in terms of communicability with the broader public and subordination to the premises and paradigm of the financial sector.

[67] The concept of 'materiality' of non-financial risks is central to the construction of the EU Directive 95/2014 on disclosure of non-financial considerations. The underlying assumption is that non-financial aspects of a company's activities (protection of the environment and respect of human rights, labour conditions, corruption, etc.), have or may have a financial—material—impact on the value of the shares or of the overall enterprise, thus affecting the performance of investors' portfolios. This means—among that non-material issues, i.e., risks that are borne by communities and the planet without any impact on the company's financial performance, may be invisible.

these two processes have the idea of promoting transparency, disclosure, financial accounting of non-financial issues and the identification of a common taxonomy that can reduce asymmetry of information. In order to make finance sustainable, it is often stated at the EU level, the cost of ESG accounting must be reduced by adopting a common language and by creating a common ESG level playing field where financiers can operate and allocate resources towards environmentally (and socially) sustainable projects. In the context of this paper, the EU Directive can be interpreted as a new space of interaction between financial capital, legislators and civil society. Thus, the next section engages with the main elements of the Directive as a possible (but inherently limited) leverage point in the struggle to address the main flaws of the transnational food regime.

IV. Sustainable finance and the EU Directive 95/2014

In 2014, six years after Lehman Brothers filed for bankruptcy, the EU issued Directive 95/2014[68] with the aim to support and facilitate the provision of finance to investments taking into account ESG considerations.[69] From a technical point of view, the Directive amends the accounting directive 2013/34/EU[70] to introduce new accounting requirements for 'large undertakings which are public-interest entities exceeding on their balance sheet dates the criterion of the average number of 500 employees during the financial year' (Article 1).[71] This equally applies to companies that are national of a Member State (incorporated in the EU), those that operate in the EU and whose EU operations reach that quantitative threshold, and parent companies of corporate groups that satisfy the same requirements (Article 3).[72]

68 Directive 2014/95/EU of the European Parliament and of the Council of 22 October 2014 amending Directive 2013/34/EU as regards disclosure of non-financial and diversity information by certain large undertakings and groups.

69 European Commission, *High-Level Expert Group on Sustainable Finance: Financing a Sustainable Economy* (European Commission, 2018).

70 Directive 2013/34/EU of the European Parliament and of the Council of 26 June 2013 on the annual financial statements, consolidated financial statements and related reports of certain types of undertakings, amending Directive 2006/43/EC of the European Parliament and of the Council and repealing Council Directives 78/660/EEC and 83/349/EEC.

71 Directive 95/2014, Article 1:

> large undertakings which are public-interest entities and to those public-interest entities which are parent undertakings of a large group, in each case having an average number of employees in excess of 500, in the case of a group on a consolidated basis. This should not prevent Member States from requiring disclosure of non-financial information from undertakings and groups other than undertakings which are subject to this Directive.

72 Directive 95/2014, Article 3:

> Public-interest entities which are parent undertakings of a large group exceeding on its balance sheet dates, on a consolidated basis, the criterion of the average number of 500 employees during the financial year shall include in the consolidated management report a consolidated non-financial statement containing information to the extent necessary for an understanding of the group's development, performance, position and impact of its activity, relating to, as a

According to the 2017 EU Commission's implementation Guidelines, the Directive covers approximately 6,000 large companies and groups across the EU, including listed companies, banks, insurance companies and other companies designated by national authorities as public-interest entities.[73] In the global competition for foreign and national investments, the Directive starts from the assumption that

> [g]reater transparency is expected to make companies (1) more resilient and perform better, both in financial and non-financial terms. Over time this will lead to more robust growth and employment and increased trust among stakeholders, including investors and consumers. Transparent business management is also consistent with longer-term investment.[74]

Environmental protection, social responsibility, treatment of employees, respect for human rights, anti-corruption and bribery and the diversity on company boards (in terms of age, gender, educational and professional background) are the areas that should benefit of the Directive as the outcome of the work realized by unions, NGOs and the financial sector as members of a 'coalition of the unlikely.'[75]

In contrast to the fully privatised approach of the PRI or the regulatory approach utilised in the case of large-scale land acquisitions, the rationale behind the Directive is that it is possible to improve global capitalism through the interaction of states, market and civils society. The regulatory power, in this case both European and national, identifies and implements new disclosure requirements; investors select where to invest according to the information on their material ESG impacts; civil society can name and shame companies that disclose that their practices have negative effects (or risk them) or that do not disclose material conditions that should have been disclosed. Viewing the Directive from the perspective of the labyrinth of the financialised and transnational food chain, there are three main reasons to suggest it may act as a helpful tool to limit or redress current environmental and social degradation.

Firstly, the Directive would apply to financial actors themselves. This is evident from the 2017 Commission Guidelines, that identifies banking and insurance as two sectors whose members have to report.[76] Secondly, Member States have the option to extend this duty to other actors: as recently highlighted in a report by CSR Europe and the Global Reporting Initiative,

---

minimum, environmental, social and employee matters, respect for human rights, anti-corruption and bribery matters.

[73] European Commission, *Commission Guidelines on Non-Financial Reporting* (European Commission, 2017) 2.

[74] *Ibid.*

[75] David Monciardini, 'The 'Coalition of the Unlikely' Driving the EU Regulatory Process of Non-Financial Reporting' (2016) 36(1) *Social and Environmental Accountability Journal* 76.

[76] European Commission (n 71).

eight Member States have decided to introduce an explicit reference to pension funds in their transposition of the EU directive.[77] Thirdly, financial investors themselves may have a number of employers and a financial turnover that passes the threshold for application of the Directive as required by Article 1(1). In the case of Norway, for example, the draft proposal for the national transposition of the Directive extends the duty to all companies with more than 500 employees and a net turnover of more than 40 million or a balance sheet total of over 20 million. In the absence of any exception for the Sovereign Wealth Fund, we could thus imagine that the largest shareholder in the world would have to submit a statement in line with the indications of the Directive.

The second reason why the Directive should be explored as a possible 'legal chokehold' in the complexity of the financialised food system is qualitative. Although not specifically mentioned in the Directive, Articles 1 and 3 contain broad references to the duty of disclosing 'as a minimum, environmental, social and employee matters, respect for human rights, anti-corruption and bribery matters' which suggests that companies may be required to account for and reveal the material and potential impact of: labour practices including child labour and forced labour; precarious work; wages; unsafe working conditions including building safety, protective equipment, workers' health, trafficking in human beings and other human rights matters; greenhouse gas emissions; other types of water and environmental pollution; deforestation and other biodiversity-related risks.[78] The non-financial declaration would thus act as a map of the tensions and criticalities of the whole chain and a possible leverage for systemic interventions that go beyond punctual solutions.

Thirdly, the Directive and the Guidelines suggest that disclosure should be systemic and take the transnational nature of production seriously. According to the texts, undertakings have to adopt a chain-based approach to disclosure and present both positive and adverse material impacts of their operations.[79] In the case of non-financial companies, the Guidelines clearly require that

[77] CSR Europe and GRI, (2017) Member State Implementation of Directive 2014/95/EU. A comprehensive overview of how Member States are implementing the EU Directive on Non-financial and Diversity Information, Policy and Reporting. The countries are Bulgaria, Croatia, Lithuania, Poland, Portugal, Romania, Slovenia and Spain. Iceland too, as a member of the EEA, has included pension funds in its transposition of the Directive.

[78] Article 1, Directive 95/2014.

[79] The Directive discusses the chains-based approach in Recitals 6 and 8. Recital 8 of the Directive also indicates that

> the severity of such impacts should be judged by their scale and gravity. The risks of adverse impact may stem from undertaking's own activity or may be linked to its operations, and where relevant and proportionate, its products, services and business relationships, including its supply and subcontracting chains.

The 2017 Guidelines on non-financial reporting discuss the assessment of the chain in the Key Principles on disclosure of material information (section 3).

they assess the whole network of production and, whenever the information is relevant, proportionate and significative,[80] disclose all the material risks (actual or potential) that exist across different levels of production.[81] In the case of a financial institution like pension funds, chain-based approach and the disclosure requirement could be interpreted as an obligation to account for and reveal all the potential or present adverse material impacts of companies that receive equity or debt investments.[82] This is clarified by the Guidelines, which states that

> [a] bank may consider that its own water consumption in offices and branches is not a material issue to be included in its management report. In contrast, the bank may assess that the social and environmental impacts of projects that it funds and its role in supporting the real economy of a city, a region or a country are material information.[83]

Although the Guidelines present a positive example, there is no reason why financial institutions should not equally communicate information concerning the excessive use of water, the impact on biodiversity, the land consumption, the risk for human rights, and several other material situations linked to one of their investments.

If we transpose this example to large financial institutions we may conclude that the Directive—depending on the way in which it has been implemented by the Member States—may be interpreted not only as an opportunity for financial investors to learn about companies and define their investment strategies, but as a legal duty for pension funds, hedge funds, sovereign wealth funds, insurance companies, etc. to publicly disclose information concerning all the potential and actual risks hidden behind their existing investments. Of course, a lot depends on national legislations and their substantive and procedural content. Not surprisingly, the United Kingdom as an epicentre of global finance has a very limited list of public interest entities (listed companies, credit institutions and insurance understandings).

With the appropriate legal framework in place, in the future we could witness the Swedish and the Norwegian Pension Fund, the University Superannuation Scheme (UK), Alecta or the BT Group producing non-financial reports containing the significant material impacts of their investments. Then it would be up to accountants, Member State authorities and civil

---

80 European Commission (n 71).

81 *Ibid*, 5 ff.

82 The Commission Guidelines use the case of a bank to explain what it means in relation to materiality and key performance indicators (KPI). In the text, we read that

> A bank may consider that its own water consumption in offices and branches is not a material issue to be included in its management report. In contrast, the bank may assess that the social and environmental impacts of projects that it funds and its role in supporting the real economy of a city, a region or a country are material information.

European Commission (n 68) 6.

83 *Ibid*, 6.

society organisations to check the declarations and decide how they could be leveraged to sanction or prevent possible violations of the right to food, biodiversity, the environment (for example, deforestation), access and use of water (for example, the existence of a struggle with local communities for the resource),[84] workers' rights (for example accusations against the chocolate industry of benefitting from slave labour in its supply chain)[85] and other similar circumstances.

In addition, the Directive may have more 'teeth' than a traditional corporate social responsibility measure would have. Although the EU document is silent in terms of sanctions, all Member States beside Denmark, Estonia, The Netherlands and Spain have introduced non-compliance penalties. In the case of Italy, for example, the law that implements the Directive introduces sanctions as high as 150,000 Euros for the omission of relevant information, non-compliance, or failure to submit within the timeframe, to be paid by the physical person who is responsible for the declaration.[86] It is possible to imagine, although hard to see happening in practice, that the publication of the next non-financial reports of the largest financial actors in Europe will be followed with attention by civil society organisations, academics and activist lawyers interested in assessing gaps and misreporting, and that this could trigger the intervention of the national competent authorities and add an extra incentive for a behavioural change.

Of course, it is hard to see how institutional investors who own shares in 9,000 companies will be autonomously reporting any relevant material condition or potential risk. As a matter of fact, 'capital … will not voluntarily adopt restrictions and it will not bind itself to a company in the name of stewardship or an ecological and just food system'.[87] In addition, it would be naïve not to be aware of the limits. Throughout the Directive, the use of notions like 'proportionate', 'relevant' and 'significant', for example, leaves a great amount of discretion with the companies, in particular in those cases where there is little transparency about the suppliers and where the cost of obtaining the information would be particularly high. Similarly, not all the Member States have endorsed a mandatory approach to the content of the Directive, with countries like the United Kingdom (which is central to the global financial world) endorsing the principle of 'comply or explain' which provides companies with the possibility of not fulfilling the disclosure requirements yet

[84] David Agren, 'Mexico Protesters Fear US-Owned Brewery will Drain their Land Dry' (*The Guardian*, 4 February 2018), online: < https://waronwant.org/media/coca-cola-drinking-world-dry>.

[85] Emiko Terazono, 'Chocolate Industry Accused of Failure on Child Labour' (*Financial Times*, 18 April 2018), online: <www.ft.com/content/eb58ba84-425f-11e8-803a-295c97e6fd0b>; Rachael Revesz, 'Nestle is Being Sued for Allegedly Using Child Slaves on Cocoa Farms' (*Independent*, 11 January 2016), online: <www.independent.co.uk/news/world/americas/nestle-is-being-sued-for-allegedly-using-child-slaves-on-cocoa-farms-a6806646.html>.

[86] Legislative Decree 30 December 2016, n. 254.

[87] Lorraine Talbot (n 12) 816.

remaining in compliance by merely justifying the departure from the standard.[88] Moreover, Article 1(1)(e) of the Directive introduces the safe harbour exception, according to which

> Member States may allow information relating to impending developments or matters in the course of negotiation to be omitted in exceptional cases where, in the duly justified opinion of the members of the administrative, management and supervisory bodies ... the disclosure of such information would be seriously prejudicial to the commercial position of the undertaking, provided that such omission does not prevent a fair and balanced understanding of the undertaking's development, performance, position and impact of its activity.

In the context of financial investors and the disclosure of information connected with their investment strategies, portfolio composition and financial performances, there is little doubt that this 'safety exit' could significantly reduce the Directive's effectiveness. Yet, the intervention of the Member States, civil society, watchdogs and international organisations interested in the respect of social and environmental rights (including at the regional and United Nations' level) may play an important role in strengthening the existing framework, addressing its limits and pushing for a quicker and more effective transition away from investments that generate returns through the exploitation of people and the planet.

V. Conclusions: towards a sustainable financialised food system or a de-financialised food system?

Financialisation is increasingly redefining the food sector and intensifying processes of homogenisation, deprivation and appropriation. Although the effects of an increased financial pressure on the food chain are clearly perceived by people and the planet, financial connections are often hidden behind complex legal and economic structures like special purpose vehicles (SPV)[89] that shield the identities of the final beneficiaries and increase the distance between violations and accountability. If we adopt the idea of 'root causes' coined by Susan Marks,[90] finance as the underling driver of food insecurity, land dispossession, loss of biodiversity and jobs, etc., often operates behind the logos of corporations, fiscal havens, SPVs and intermediaries.

---

[88] CSR Europe and GRI (n 75).

[89] The term 'Special Purpose Vehicle' identifies legal entities that are created within the context of a global enterprise (corporate group, global value chains, etc) and are often used for financial and accounting purposes, such as shielding assets, hiding debt or realising specific investments. SPVs can be kept off the balance sheet of parent companies and corporate groups consolidated accounts, which means that its assets, liabilities and equity are often invisible to investors and third parties, reducing transparency, accountability and the effectiveness of the instruments like the Directive.

[90] Susan Marks, 'Human Rights and Root Causes' (2011) 74(1) *Modern Law Review* 57.

To give an example, the largest US teachers' pension fund, TIAA-CREF, doubled the amount of land that it owned in Brazil between 2012 and 2015. However, it did not do it by direct purchase (forbidden in Brazil), but by funding Radar Corporation, a Brazil-based company that appeared as the sole and legitimate owner. Similarly, Brazilian law firms were recently denounced for aiding the Canadian group Brookfield to invest the funds from its Global Agricultural Investment Fund in a way that eluded the limit on foreign ownership of land in Brazil: instead of buying equity or land, they bought convertible bonds (a financial instrument) issued by the Brazilian company Emauba and obtained in exchange the guarantee of the payment of 98.78% of the liquid profit generated by the company and the possibility of converting the bonds into shares when the ban on foreign ownership would be lifted. Financial and legal instruments become the way to avoid legal constraints and cover the roots of the problem.[91]

In the struggle to think about countermeasures and possible forms of intervention within the complex conundrum of financial investments, transparency certainly plays a central role. The ability to map financial ties is essential to open the possibility to leverage them, engage with legal and political arguments and obtain some transformations. Although we know that around 80% of the global equity market is held by financial institutions[92] and that BlackRock, Vanguard, Fidelity, and State Street now own around 88% of all stock in S&P 500 corporations,[93] we lack a clear understanding of the way in which financial capital is intervening all along the food chain and how it is horizontally and vertically integrated within it. As discussed in this article, initiatives have been launched both from within and without the financial sector in order to counter the increasing relevance of financial actors: public authorities have drafted ad hoc regulations on acquisition of land and derivative trading, networks have been established that promote voluntary principles for responsible investments and activists have used both naming and shaming and the fiduciary duties of trustees to push for engagement and divestment from unsustainable sectors.

In this picture, some (relatively unexpected) support may be offered by the implementation of the EU Directive 95/2014 and the introduction by each Member State of rules on the disclosure of non-financial issues (and diversity information) in annual reports from 2018 onwards. According to the official purpose of the Directive, transparency and publicity would be used by investors to improve their portfolios and choose investments that have a better ESG profile and therefore a higher probability of generating long-term return.

---

91 *Ibid.*

92 McGrath et al. (n 8).

93 Jan Fichtner, Eelke M Heemskerk and Javier Garcia-Bernardo, 'Hidden Power of the Big Three? Passive Index Funds, Re-Concentration of Corporate Ownership, and New Financial Risk' (2017) 19(2) *Business and Politics* 298.

However, Member States can also decide that these requirements apply to investors and can provide sanctions in case of mis-compliance. In some cases, they already do so.[94] Instead of helping investors to define their investment strategies, external stakeholders such as NGOs, civil society and legal activists could thus use the data disclosed by financial investors to scrutinise and challenge the role that their investments have in consolidating an unsustainable transnational food chain. However, this would require the institutional recognition of these actors' role in engaging with finance, the provision of a straightforward system that would facilitate their role as watchdogs, and the 'recognition of a strong hierarchical logic between all the elements commonly identified as pertaining to sustainable development,'[95] with democratic, open and effective governance at the centre rather than financial performances.

Yet, too much optimism would be misplaced for several reasons. To start with, corporate governance scholars have long pointed to the limits and flaws of engaging with institutional investors to transform them into stewards of the good functioning of global capitalism.[96] Similarly, the unilateral decision to engage (or withhold funds) with companies that operate in violation of legal or normative standards may reduce the unsustainability of the food chain but may also produce unexpected negative effects along the chain outside the control and interest of the investor.[97] For example, when a loan is not renewed or shares are sold, jobs on the ground can be lost, the national Gross Domestic Product may not grow at the same pace, a less sustainable investor may replace the previous one. In addition, the need to generate revenues is such that resources taken away from specific projects may be reinvested in equally problematic sectors (maybe less visible or away from public pressure). Equally, the decision to engage with a company instead of divesting may lead to the investors' capture and lock it into situations where it is too costly for the company to improve its performances and the needed ESG investments are not realised because of the impact they may have on the expected return.

Moreover the decision to engage with finance and leverage its vocabulary and tools (accounting, ESG, materiality, reporting, etc.) generates an epistemological short circuit that cannot be simply solved by unilaterally implementing higher standards with the hope that they trickle down throughout the whole food chain or by preventing one project from happening. In addition, and needless to say, any measure undertaken within the paradigm

---

[94] CSR Europe and GRI (n 75).

[95] Timothy Cadman, 'Evaluating the Governance of Responsible Investment Institutions: An Environmental and Social Perspective' (2011) 1(1) *Journal of Sustainable Finance and Investment* 20, 27.

[96] See, e.g., Talbot (n 12); Villiers (n 12).

[97] Dan Danielsen, 'Local Rules and a Global Economy: An Economic Policy Perspective' (2010) 1(1) *Transnational Legal Theory* 49; Tomaso Ferrando, 'Land Rights at the time of Global Production: Leveraging Multi-Spatiality and 'Legal Chokeholds'' (2017) 2(2) *Business and Human Rights Journal* 275.

of sustainable finance would be incapable of getting rid of finance itself. Thus, the tension and clashes between the industrial and global ideal world of BlackRock and the local and non-commodified framework of La Via Campesina (the largest peasants' organisation of the world) would not disappear. On the contrary, movements and organisations may end up legitimising the 'financial way of looking at the food system' and accept that nature, people, biodiversity, labour conditions, etc. have a price tag and can be expressed in terms of ROI. An acritical engagement with finance would not address the underlying incompatibility between the vision of the food system as a complex construction of socio-ecological relationships that is essential both for people and nature and the idea that it can be the place of rent-seeking, extractive practices and remuneration of distant financial capital.

This should not come as a surprise but requires critical actors (including academics) to question whether the improvement of environmental and social performances of invested corporations justifies the rehabilitation of the financial system that was at the centre of the global meltdown of 2008 and the speculation on food commodities that skyrocketed the price of food all over the world. Is it truly possible to consider financial capital and financial actors as potential allies in the transition away from the global and unsustainable food system that they have contributed to and that they made their fortune from? Shall civil society, academics and activists put in energy and time trying to nudge financial actors who currently

> do not understand nor reward sustainable behaviour either because the markets are inefficient and do not reward good behaviour, or because market failure means that they do not need to worry about the very-long-term costs as they are outside of their investment time horizons?[98]

Is it worth translating the socio-environmental issues that characterised the food system in terms of externalities and accounting procedures, if this means financing improvements but also justifying the extraction of financial rent from it? The tensions are evident, and everyone interested in engaging with the EU Directive and the EU framework on sustainable finance should be aware of them and of the systemic implications of their decisions.

If we were optimistic, a solution may lie in between the complete rejection of sustainable finance and its full endorsement. Although hard to carve out, a new window of opportunity may have been opened by the mandatory nature of the disclosure introduced with the 2014 EU Directive, the application of the requirements to financial actors like pension funds and banks, the strengthening of the 'financial watchdog' role of civil society and the implementation by each Member State of robust and accessible mechanisms of monitoring and

---

[98] Steve Waygood, 'How do the Capital Markets Undermine Sustainable Development? What can be Done to Correct This?' (2011) 1(1) *Journal of Sustainable Finance and Investment* 81, 83.

sanctioning. If actors were to combine these elements in a systemic strategy, they would leverage the transparency and visibility of the transnational financialised food system not to improve financial performances but to give visibility to the nexus of causality between financial capital and unsustainable food chains. Instead of legitimising finance and its vision of the world, a stronger understanding of the financial complexity of the food system would expose the role of finance and financialisation in defining the food system beyond commodity speculation. Furthermore, it may help mapping actors and responsibilities, so that concrete legal, political and advocacy interventions could be devised. The idea that ESG accounting and disclosure will automatically improve the global economy while making finance actors more resilient is imperfect and must be rethought and improved. Yet, if properly understood and leveraged, it opens new spaces for the political, legal, financial and cultural challenges of rent-seeking capitalism and the planned misery that is inherent to financialisation and increasingly permeates transnational food chains.[99]

Disclosure statement

No potential conflict of interest was reported by the author.

[99] Marks, *Root Causes*, (n 88).

The World Trade Organization between law and politics: negotiating a solution for public stockholding for food security purposes

Matias E Margulis

ABSTRACT

This article examines efforts by member states of the World Trade Organization (WTO) to modify international trade laws to further accommodate public food stockholding for food security programmes operated by developing countries. While WTO members have negotiated a temporary Peace Clause to minimise the threat of a trade dispute for countries whose public food stockholding violates their international trade commitments, negotiations to modify existing WTO law have been fraught with political discord. I argue that states are using the WTO's negotiating function to address perceived conflicts between international trade law and national food security goals rather than pursuing a solution through legal adjudication. The case of public food stockholding reveals important dynamics about the WTO-food relationship security that are overlooked by approaches primarily concerned with supra-national constraints on national policy and the fragmentation of international law.

Introduction

This article examines recent efforts by the member states of the World Trade Organization (WTO) to modify international trade laws to ensure compatibility with public food stockholding. In response to rising levels of hunger and increased volatility of world food prices, many states in Asia and Africa have established or expanded public food stockholding—which involves governments purchasing, stockpiling and distributing essential food staples such as rice and wheat—as a form of self-insurance to support domestic food security. While the number of developing countries turning to public food stockholding has increased, it has simultaneously become one of the most contested trade policy issues at the WTO. Developed and developing countries disagree on the extent to which WTO rules should be modified to reduce the risk that some developing countries, such as India, will violate international trade rules in the pursuit of public food stockholding.

WTO member states have been in negotiations to end a situation of legal uncertainty surrounding public food stockholding. States agreed to a Peace Clause in 2013 at the WTO Bali Ministerial in which they temporarily waived the right to launch disputes against countries whose public food stockholding programmes led them to violate WTO rules on agricultural subsidy spending.[1] Yet the Peace Clause is only considered a stop gap by WTO members and the larger goal is to arrive at a so-called 'permanent solution' that would result in the rewriting of existing international trade rules to ensure that all public food stockholding programmes are WTO compliant.[2] Yet negotiations for a permanent solution have been fraught with political discord. WTO members missed a series of self-imposed deadlines in 2015 and 2017 to deliver a permanent solution because of political deadlock among developing and developed countries. As a result, the situation that currently exists is one where governments that are currently operating, seeking to expand or planning new public food stockholding programmes continue to face legal uncertainty about the consistency of their programmes with the law of the WTO. The lack of legal clarity surrounding public food stockholding at the WTO has been cited as problematic by the former United Nations (UN) Special Rapporteur on the right to food because of the 'chilling effect' uncertainty may have on states' efforts to improve food security.[3] Similar situations of legal uncertainty at the WTO, for example, have been argued to lead states to pursue less ambitious environmental protection policies because of the perceived risks of violating trade rules.[4] Therefore, there is a palpable concern that legal uncertainty at the WTO may discourage states from enacting new food security policies or convince them to pursue less ambitious goals in food security terms than they would otherwise have done.

The existing scholarly literature on public food stockholding at the WTO has been primarily concerned with the potential conflicts between international and domestic legal regimes[5] yet has overlooked the role of inter-

---

[1] WTO, *Public Stockholding for Food Security Purposes. Ministerial Decision of 7 December 2013*. Online: <https://www.wto.org/english/thewto_e/minist_e/mc9_e/desci38_e.htm>.

[2] *Ibid.*

[3] Olivier De Schutter, *The World Trade Organization and the Post-Global Food Crisis Agenda: Putting Food Security First in the International Trade System* (2011) online: <https://www.wto.org/english/news_e/news11_e/deschutter_2011_e.pdf> 3.

[4] Robyn Eckersley, 'The Big Chill: The WTO and Multilateral Environmental Agreements' (2004) 4 *Global Environmental Politics* 24, 29–32; See also, Ken Conca, 'The WTO and the Undermining of Global Environmental Governance' (2000) 7 *Review of International Political Economy* 484.

[5] See James J. Nedumpara, 'India's Food Security Concerns and the WTO Bali Ministerial Decision' (2014) 9 *Global Trade and Customs Journal* 177; Sannoy Das, 'Food Security Amendments to the WTO Green Box: A Critical Re-Examination' (2016) 50 *Journal of World Trade* 11.

state bargaining in seeking to accommodate national food security goals at the WTO. In this article, I argue that states have turned to politics rather than law to address legal uncertainty about public food stockholding. By this I mean that states have chosen 'politics' by pursuing a consensus-based solution that involves working through the WTO's negotiation function. This process is shaped by bargaining and accommodation among states with heterogenous preferences and power capabilities. I distinguish this from a solution pursued through 'law', which would involve states turning to adjudication via a supra-national court or other delegated agent that is empowered to decide and instruct them on the appropriate relationship between their international trade obligations and national policy goals.[6] I contend that the turn to politics by states in the case of public food stockholding is crucial to understanding the evolving WTO-food security relationship. In particular, the politics of public food stockholding suggest that the challenge identified by states is not one of addressing conflicts between legal regimes, but instead is one of accommodating a shifting balance of political and economic power among states and the new status of global food security as an international consensus goal.

The WTO-food security relationship

The relationship between the WTO and food security is a topic of significant debate among scholars (not only of International Law but also of Economics, Political Science and Development Studies), policymakers, practitioners and civil society organisations.[7] Put in its simplest form, at the heart of this debate is whether agricultural trade liberalisation supports or undermines national food security. There is no consensus to this debate. It is not limited to the 1995 *Agreement on Agriculture* (AoA), which sets the rules for international food trade, but also extends to the WTO's *Agreement on*

[6] I recognise that the distinction between politics and law is not always straightforward and that they are constitutive of one another. It is through politics that states design and establish international legal orders and institutions. The practice of international law-making and its implementation over time routinely leads to outcomes that collide with the preferences of states, thus subsequently generating new politics.

[7] See: Jim Greenfield, Maurizio de Nigris and Panos Konandreas, 'The Uruguay Round Agreement on Agriculture: Food Security Implications for Developing Countries' (1999) 21 *Food Policy* 365; FAO, *Experience with the Implementation of the Uruguay Round Agreement on Agriculture* (FAO, 2001); Carmen G Gonzalez, 'Institutionalizing Inequality: The WTO Agreement on Agriculture, Food Security, and Developing Countries' (2002) 27 *Columbia Journal of Environmental Law* 433; FAO, *Trade and Food Security: Conceptualizing the Linkages* (FAO, 2003); Eugenio Diaz-Bonilla, Marcelle Thomas and Sherman Robinson, 'Trade, Food Security and WTO Negotiations: Some Reflections on Boxes and Their Content' in *Agricultural Trade and Poverty: Making Policy Analysis Count* (OECD, 2003) 59–104; Peter M. Rosset, *Food is Different* (Fernwood Publishing, 2006); Jennifer Clapp, 'WTO Agriculture Negotiations: Implications for the Global South' (2006) 27 *Third World Quarterly* 563; Gerardo Otero, Gabriela Pechlaner and Efe Can Gürcan, 'The Political Economy of "Food Security" and Trade: Uneven and Combined Dependency' (2013) 78 *Rural Sociology* 263; Matias E Margulis, 'The Regime Complex for Food Security: Implications for the Global Hunger Challenge' (2013) 19 *Global Governance* 53.

Sanitary and Phytosanitary Measures (SPS) and *Agreement on Trade-Related Aspects of Intellectual Property Rights* (TRIPS), the latter of which is associated with the closure of a public commons for seed saving and distribution. In this section I consider how critical legal scholarship has conceptualised the WTO-food security relationship. Given the limited space, I provide a stylised overview of these perspectives, which I aggregate under two broad labels: supra-national constraints on national policy; and, the fragmentation of international law.

Supra-national constraints on national policy

One way to conceptualise the WTO-food security relationship is to consider the constraints imposed by WTO law on the policies pursued by states. The WTO is widely recognised as one of the most powerful international legal regimes wherein states take binding commitments to liberalise their trade policies over time, with commitments enforced by a dispute settlement system.

Supra-national constraints on food security may exist because of the binding nature of WTO law. Market outcomes resulting from binding international trade rules on agriculture are often identified as an important mechanism through which the WTO influences food security. Take the case of agricultural tariff liberalisation. Under the AoA, all WTO members were required to convert all non-trade barriers into tariffs, and bind and reduce all agricultural tariffs over a period of time.[8] A prominent critique of agricultural tariff reduction under the AoA is that it was highly unbalanced; the rules written in a way that favoured major agricultural exporting developed countries, leading to greater food import dependency among developing countries as lower tariffs led to cheaper food imports and simultaneously disincentivised domestic food production.[9] Seen from this perspective, WTO rules can be understood to lock-in policy reforms that may have negative consequences for national food security.[10]

WTO rules may also constrain states' ability to pursue food security by limiting their options to respond to unfavourable market conditions. Recall that a key goal of the AoA is to reduce state intervention in agricultural markets and

[8] This included an average tariff reduction of 36% over six years for developed countries and an average reduction of 24% over 10 years for developing countries. Least developed countries (LDCs) were not required to make reductions.

[9] Office of the High Commissioner for Human Rights, *Globalization and Its Impact on the Full Enjoyment of Human Rights: Report of the High Commissioner for Human Rights Submitted in Accordance with Commission on Human Rights Resolution 2001/32* (OHCHR, 2002); J. Michael Finger and Julio J. Nogués, 'The Unbalanced Uruguay Round Outcome: The New Areas in Future WTO Negotiations' (2002) 25 *World Economy* 321; Olivier De Schutter, *Mission to the World Trade Organization* (Human Rights Council, 2009); Jennifer Clapp, 'Food Security and Contested Agricultural Trade Norms' (2015) 11 *Journal of International Law and International Relations* 104.

[10] Anne Orford, 'Food Security, Free Trade, and the Battle for the State' (2015) 11 *Journal of International Law and International Relations* 1, 52–55.

trade. Trade rules have become increasingly about regulating domestic policy and thus the scope for state intervention. One issue that has received a lot of attention is whether developing countries have the right to temporarily raise tariffs beyond the bound levels in their WTO commitments in response to import surges.[11] Import surges—such as occur when local markets experience the dumping of cheap, subsidised agricultural products from abroad—have significant, long-term destabilising effects on domestic food production by threatening the livelihoods of small-scale farmers in poor developing countries. Small-scale farmers produce most of the food in developing countries, yet they lack the financial and institutional resources (including government support) to cope with cheap imports and the ensuing economic hardship compared to farmers in developed countries.[12] Raising tariffs to increase the price of imports is a standard policy tool utilised by states concerned about the effects of cheap imports on domestic producers. However, under current WTO rules most developing countries do not have the right to unilaterally increase agricultural tariffs beyond bound levels during an import surge. This is in sharp contrast with developed countries that have recourse to a Special Agricultural Safeguard under the AoA, which grants them the right to unilaterally apply tariff rates above bound levels during an import surge.[13] This asymmetry in the rules of the AoA in the case of import surges constrains developing countries' capacity to protect their food security. This is an illustration of what Carmen Gonzalez has dubbed the 'institutionalized inequality' of the AoA.[14]

The fragmentation of international law

The WTO-food security relationship is also approached from the fragmentation of international law perspective. The international legal system is said to be fragmented because disparate bodies of international law evolve in isolation from one another and, in doing so, may produce norm and treaty conflicts.[15] WTO law in particular is identified as a major driver of fragmentation of the international legal system at the expense of general, overarching

[11] Gonzalez (n 7), 476–480.

[12] Kevin Watkins and Joachim Von Braun, 'Time to Stop Dumping on the World's Poor' in *IFPRI Annual Report, 2002–2003* (IFPRI, 2003); Chris Downes, 'Must the Losers of Free Trade Go Hungry-Reconciling WTO Obligations and the Right to Food' (2006) 47 *Vanderbilt Journal of International Law* 619, 635–636; Carmen G. Gonzalez, 'International Economic Law and the Right to Food' in Nadia C. S. Lambek and others (eds), *Rethinking Food Systems: Structural Challenges, New Strategies and the Law* (Springer Netherlands, 2014), 165–193; Sarah Joseph, *Blame It on the WTO? A Human Rights Critique* (Oxford University Press, 2011). Developing countries have attempted to correct this situation by negotiating for a Special Safeguard Mechanism (SSM), which would permit them to raise tariffs to protect food security and rural livelihoods. While WTO members agree in principle to the legitimacy of the SSM as a policy tool for developing countries, the collapse of the Doha Round negotiations have left the SSM in a state of limbo.

[13] WTO, An 'Unofficial Guide to Agricultural Safeguards' (November 2018), online: <https://www.wto.org/english/tratop_e/agric_e/guide_agric_safeg_e.htm>.

[14] Gonzalez (no 7), 476–480.

systems of international public law. This has led to an ongoing academic and practitioner debate about the divergence between WTO law and international public law, and to the extent that harmonisation is possible using both legal and political processes.[16] For the vantage point of critics, the WTO's liberal trade bias is often argued to be in conflict with the norms and rules of other international legal regimes.[17] Under these conditions, states may face legal uncertainty on how to reconcile apparently contradictory international norms and treaty obligations.[18] In the case of food security, concerns relating to the fragmentation of international law have been raised about the potential for norm and treaty conflicts between WTO law and states' obligations under other international treaties, especially those that apply to relevant economic and social rights such as food, health and development.[19] Concerns that WTO law may undermine food security have been raised by the UN High Commissioner for Human Rights and UN Special Rapporteurs on the right to food, who are charged with advancing a human rights-based approach to food security.[20]

One of the potential norm conflicts frequently identified is in regard to competing interpretations about the role of the state and its responsibility

---

[15] See: International Law Commission, *Conclusions of the Work of the Study Group on the Fragmentation of International Law: Difficulties Arising from the Diversification and Expansion of International Law* (ILC, 2006); International Law Commission, *Fragmentation of International Law: Diffiuclties Arising from the Diversification and Expansion of International Law* (ILC, 2006); Anja Lindroos and Michael Mehling, 'Dispelling the Chimera of "Self-Contained Regimes" International Law and the WTO' (2005) 16 *European Journal of International Law* 857; Bruno Simma and Dirk Pulkowski, 'Of Planets and the Universe: Self-contained Regimes in International Law' (2006) 17 *European Journal of International Law* 483.

[16] See: Joost Pauwelyn, 'The Role of Public International Law in the WTO: How Far Can We Go?' (2001) 95 *American Journal of International Law* 535; Mcej Bronckers, 'More Power to the WTO?' (2001) 4 *Journal of International Economic Law* 41. Kenneth Abbott and Duncan Snidal, 'Hard and Soft law in International Governance' (2000) 54 *International Organization* 421; Gregory C Shaffer and Mark A Pollack, 'Hard vs. Soft Law: Alternatives, Complements, and Antagonists in International Governance' (2009) 94 *Minnesota Law Review* 706; Frank Biermann, Philipp Pattberg, Harro van Asselt and Fariborz Zelli, 'The Fragmentation of Global Governance Architectures: A Framework for Analysis' (2009) 9 *Global Environmental Politics* 14; Andreas Fischer-Lescano and Gunther Teubner, 'Regime-Collisions: The Vain Search for Legal Unity in the Fragmentation of Global Law' (2003) 25 *Michigan Journal of International Law* 999; Ernst-Ulrich Petersmann, 'From Fragmentation to Constitutionalisation of International Economic Law? Comments on Schneiderman's "Constitutionalism"' in Marc Bungenberg and others (eds), *European Yearbook of International Economic Law 2016* (Springer International Publishing, 2016), 45–46.

[17] See: Erich Vranes, 'The Definition of "Norm Conflict" in International Law and Legal Theory' (2006) 17 *European Journal of International Law* 395; Christine Kaufmann and Simone Heri, 'Liberalizing Trade in Agriculture and Food Security-Mission Impossible' (2007) 40 *Vanderbilt Journal of Transnational Law* 1039; Andrew Lang, 'Twenty Years of the WTO Appellate Body's "Fragmentation Jurisprudence"' (2015) 14 *Journal of International Trade Law and Policy* 116.

[18] Vranes (n 17), 398–399; Margulis (n 7), 61–63; See also Joost Pauwelyn, 'A Typology of Multilateral Treaty Obligations: Are WTO Obligations Bilateral or Collective in Nature?' (2003) 14 *European Journal of International Law* 907; G. Kristen Rosendal, 'Impacts of Overlapping International Regimes: The Case of Biodiversity' (2001) 7 *Global Governance* 95.

[19] Rhonda Ferguson, *The Right to Food and the World Trade Organization's Rules on Agriculture: Conflicting, Compatible, or Complementary?* (Brill Nijhoff, 2018); James Harrison, *The Human Rights Impact of the World Trade Organisation* (Hart Publishing, 2007); Joseph (n 12).

[20] See: OHCHR, *Human Rights and Trade* (OHCHR, 2003); OHCHR, *Human Rights and the World Trade Agreements: Using General Exception Clauses to Protect Human Rights* (OHCHR, 2005); De Schutter, *Mission to the World Trade Organization* (Human Rights Council, 2008); De Schutter (n 3).

to intervene in the market to achieve food security. The WTO's goal is to open national agricultural markets to international economic competition, which inevitably produces winners and losers. In poor developing countries, such losers may be small-scale farmers who lose their livelihoods and experience an increase in their vulnerability to food insecurity.[21] This outcome is not considered inherently problematic at the WTO based on the system's logic that economic dislocation from liberalisation is inevitable and outweighed by the net global welfare gains accrued from freer trade. The WTO's economistic value system stands in sharp contrast to that of the international human right system with its norm that states should take progressive measures to respect, protect and fulfil human rights such as the right to food. In other words, states have a duty to prevent outcomes that impair the enjoyment of human rights. Indeed, states are expected to take affirmative actions to remedy the situation of the 'losers' if these are vulnerable groups such as resource-poor farmers and labourers.[22] These competing understandings about the role of the state from a trade and human rights approach was identified by the High Commissioner for Human Rights as thus:

> Human rights law concerns itself in particular with the situation of the individuals and groups who might suffer during the reform process. Indeed, this is one of the key issues concerning globalization and human rights. Even where the net social benefit from trade liberalization favours the majority in a certain country, the principle of non-discrimination under human rights law requires immediate action to protect the human rights of those who do not benefit. In the case of the AoA, this means that States should use existing flexibilities in the Agreement where they exist, and WTO members should consider improving or adding flexibilities where appropriate.[23]

While WTO law does not *prevent* states from potentially compensating groups whose food insecurity worsens as a result of liberalisation, the international human rights regime *requires* that states take pro-active steps to compensate losers if their human right to food has been materially diminished. These potentially competing interpretations about the role of states manifests sharply in legal debates about how and when states should pursue agricultural trade liberalisation and the extent of their responsibilities to avert and/or mitigate negative consequences for food insecure populations.[24]

In addition to debates about potential norm conflicts between WTO rules and the international human rights obligations of states, a more practical

[21] *Ibid.*
[22] Kaufmann and Heri (n 17).
[23] OHCHR, *Globalization and Its Impact on the Full Enjoyment of Human Rights: Report of the High Commissioner for Human Rights Submitted in Accordance with Commission on Human Rights Resolution 2001/32* (OHCR, 2001), 13–15.
[24] Kaufmann and Heri (n 17), 1056.

concern about the fragmentation of international law is how it influences the actual behaviour of states in multilateral trade negotiations. According to the former UN Special Rapporteur on the right to food, Olivier De Schutter, the fragmentation of international law makes it complex and difficult for states to coordinate their international human rights obligations and trade commitments. The lack of coordination results in a situation where 'trade negotiators either are not aware of the human rights obligations of the Governments they represent, or they do not identify the implications for their position in trade negotiations'.[25] When states behave incoherently in the international arena in this way they disregard their obligations to protect, respect and fulfil the human right to food when entering into multilateral trade agreements. Such a situation leads states to treat trade commitments 'as equivalent in normative force' to existing human rights obligations, which De Schutter has argued to be erroneous on the basis that human rights obligations 'have the status of peremptory norms of international law' and thus 'should prevail over any other international commitments'.[26]

International legal scholars and the UN human rights system have advanced multiple solutions to address potential norm and treaty conflicts between the WTO and international human rights. This includes that states: incorporate the human right to food in their trade policy positions such as undertaking *ex ante* human rights impact assessments; evaluate the consistency of trade agreements with states' human rights obligations; seek further legal clarification from international human rights bodies; and, explore the use of exceptions and sunset clauses.[27] Others emphasise the need for trade negotiations to seek normative guidance from international legal documents such as the Committee on Economic Social Rights' *General Comment No. 12 on the Right to Food* or the UN *Voluntary Guidelines to Support the Progressive Realization of the Right to Adequate Food in the Context of National Food Security*.[28] Lastly, there is optimism that 'harmonization through interpretation' may resolve norm and treaty conflicts between the AoA and the human right to food through adjudication in reference to the *Vienna Convention on the Law of Treaties*.[29]

---

[25] De Schutter (n 3), 15–16.

[26] *Ibid.*

[27] See: OHCHR (n 23); Harrison (n 19); Olivier De Schutter, *A Human Rights Approach to Trade and Investment Policies* (2008) online: <https://www.iatp.org/documents/a-human-rights-approach-to-trade-and-investment-policies>.

[28] See: Sven Söllner, 'The "Breakthrough" of the Right to Food: The Meaning of General Comment no. 12 and the Voluntary Guidelines for the Interpretation of the Human Right to Food' (2007) 11 *Max Planck Yearbook of United Nations Law* 391.

[29] See: Kerstin Mechlem, 'Harmonizing Trade in Agriculture and Human Rights: Options for the Integration of the Right to Food into the Agreement on Agriculture' (2006) 10 *Max Planck Yearbook of United Nations Law* (2006) 127; De Schutter (n 27).

What is public food stockholding?

Public food stockholding refers to state-managed programmes of purchasing, storing and distributing agricultural commodities. Sometimes referred to as public food reserves or domestic food aid, public food stockholding is used by governments to achieve a mix of policy goals, including stabilising domestic food prices and supplies, providing subsidised food to targeted populations, and supporting rural livelihoods.

Establishing public food stockholding in developing countries was one of the major objectives of the post-war international food regime.[30] It is not just developing countries that have experimented with public food stockholding; until recently the US operated the Food Security Wheat Reserve for 'guaranteeing a supply of wheat in times of tight supplies or unanticipated need'.[31] Yet public food stockholding as a policy idea went out of favour in the 1980s and 1990s under structural adjustment policies and due to shifts in ideological currents that saw policymakers favour freer trade and the private sector to coordinate world food supply and prices.[32]

Interest in public food stockholding was revived during the 2007–2008 global food crisis. Spurred by a combination of national biofuel mandates, financial speculation in agricultural commodities, high oil prices and unilateral export restrictions, the global food crisis was characterised by skyrocketing prices for staple food grains, increasing the number of hungry people worldwide to over one billion and precipitating food riots in the developing world.[33] The crisis prompted governments—especially those states with high levels of food insecurity and vulnerable to external shocks—to rethink their policies for food security, including putting an increased emphasis on

[30] The idea to establish an international food reserves was proposed in 1946 by Sir John Boyd Orr, the first Director-General of the Food and Agriculture Organization of the United Nations. This plan for a 'World Food Board' was ultimately rejected by the US and Great Britain. See Amy L.S. Staples, 'To Win the Peace: The Food and Agriculture Organization, Sir John Boyd Orr, and the World Food Board Proposals' (2003) 28 *Peace & Change* 495.

[31] Charles E. Hanrahan, *The Bill Emerson Humanitarian Trust: Background and Current Issues* (Congressional Research Service, 2003), 3.

[32] See: Sophia Murphy, *Strategic Grain Reserves in an Era of Volatility* (Institute for Agriculture Trade Policy, 2009) 7–8; Jennifer Clapp, 'Food Self-Sufficiency: Making Sense of It, and When It Makes Sense' (2017) 66 *Food Policy* 88; Matias E. Margulis, 'The Forgotten History of Food Security in the Multilateral Trading System' (2017) 16 *World Trade Review* 25; Carsten Daugbjerg, Arild Aurvåg Farsund and Oluf Langhelle, 'The Resilience of Paradigm Mixes: Food Security in a Post-Exceptionalist Trade Regime' (2017) 24 *Journal of European Public Policy* 1698.

[33] See: Derek Headey and Shenggen Fan, 'Anatomy of a Crisis: The Causes and Consequences of Surging Food Prices' (2008) 39 *Agricultural Economics* 375; Jennifer Clapp, 'Food Price Volatility and Vulnerability in the Global South: Considering the Global Economic Context' (2009) 30 *Third World Quarterly* 1183; Matias Margulis, 'Multilateral Responses to the Global Food Crisis' (2009) 4 *CABI Reviews: Perspectives in Agriculture, Veterinary Science, Nutrition and Natural Resources* 1; Pedro Conceição and Ronald U. Mendoza, 'Anatomy of the Global Food Crisis' (2009) 30 *Third World Quarterly* 1159; Philip McMichael, 'A Food Regime Analysis of the World Food Crisis' (2009) 26 *Agriculture and Human Values* 281; Lucy Jarosz, 'Energy, Climate Change, Meat, and Markets: Mapping the Coordinates of the Current World Food Crisis' (2009) 3 *Geography Compass* 2065; Timothy Lang, 'Crisis? What Crisis? The Normality of the Current Food Crisis' (2010) 10 *Journal of Agrarian Change* 87.

domestic food production.[34] In this context, dozens of governments in Asia, Africa and the Middle East announced or expressed interest in public food stockholding.[35] The most significant programme was launched by the Indian government in 2013 when it passed the *National Food Security Act*.[36] The Act entitles two-thirds of its national population of 1.3 billion people to 5 kilogrammes of staple grains per person per month at a low subsidised price.[37] Other countries, such as Kenya and Malawi, significantly expanded the size of existing stockholding programmes (in some cases doubling) in response to the crisis. In Rwanda, the government re-introduced public food stockholding.[38]

Political discord over public food stockholding at the WTO

While the number of states introducing or expanding public food stockholding has grown in recent years, the question of the legality of such programmes under the law of the WTO has come under scrutiny. In 2013, the US, EU, Canada and Australia, argued that countries operating public food stockholding programmes, such as India, were close to exceeding their WTO-mandated levels of government spending on agricultural subsidies.[39] The US, EU, Canada and Australia, all of which are major agricultural exporters, view food stockholding programmes as disguised protectionism and undermining the goal of the WTO to advance agricultural trade liberalisation. Agricultural exporters fear public food stockholding will lead to lost commercial

[34] See: Eve Fouilleux, Nicolas Bricas and Arlène Alpha, '"Feeding 9 Billion People": Global Food Security Debates and the Productionist Trap' (2017) 24 *Journal of European Public Policy* 1658. Renewed interest in public food stockholding is not just at the national scale. In 2012 Japan, China, South Korea and other Asian nations established the Association of Southeast Asian Nations (ASEAN) Plus Three Emergency Rice Reserve to enhance food security in the region. The Economic Community of West African States (ECOWAS) agreed in 2013 to establish a regional food security reserve to promote a regional response to future food crises. This regional reserve became operational in 2017 following its first delivery of cereals to address a food crisis in the north-eastern Nigeria. Public food stockholding has also been the subject of global-level debates at the Group of Twenty (G-20), a club of advanced industrial and emerging economies, United Nations Conference of Trade and Development (UNCTAD) and the High Level Panel of Experts on Food Security and Nutrition in the context of identifying global solutions to address food price volatility.

[35] Murphy (n 32); Brian Wright and Carlo Cafiero, 'Grain Reserves and Food Security in the Middle East and North Africa' (2011) 3 *Food Security* 61; Mulat Demeke and others, *Food and Agriculture Policy Decisions: Trends, Emerging Issues and Policy Alignments since the 2007/08 Food Security Crisis* (FAO, 2014); Matias E. Margulis, 'A New Grey Zone in Global Trade Governance? Recent Developments on Food Security at the WTO' in Daniel Drache and Lesley A. Jacobs (eds), *Grey Zones in International Economic Law and Global Governance: Crises and Resilience* (UBC Press, 2018) 159–182; Sophia Murphy, 'Food Security and International Trade: Risk, Trust and Rules' (2015) 2 *Canadian Food Studies/La Revue canadienne des études sur l'alimentation* 88.

[36] Government of India, Ministry of Law and Justice. *National Food Security Act*, 2013.

[37] Department of Food and Public Distribution. Government of India (2017) online: <http://dfpd.nic.in/Salient-features-National-Food-Security-Act.htm>.

[38] Demeke and others (n 35), 75.

[39] WTO, 'Farm Produce Stockholding Worries Members who Fear Impact on Trade and Incomes' (2013) online: <https://www.wto.org/english/news_e/news13_e/agcom_26sep13_e.htm>.

opportunities as developing countries encourage domestic food production at the expense of imports. In addition to their commercial interests, many developed countries are concerned that public food stockholding policies are indicative of a pendulum shift towards food self-sufficiency in developing countries, which they regard as incompatible with the norm of free trade.[40]

The controversy unfolding over public food stockholding at the WTO is a complex one and it is difficult to address all the nuances in the space available here. My main contention is that to view events at the WTO as evidence of supra-national constraints on national food security policies or a conflict between international legal regimes is to miss the intricacies of important shifts in the politics shaping the WTO-food security relationship.

Firstly, recent developments on public food stockholding should not be conflated as a debate about supra-national constraints on national policy. This is because public stockholding for food security purposes *is permitted* under the rules of the AoA.[41] There is nothing to prevent states from operating public food stockholding. The only 'constraint' on public food stockholding programmes is that they meet the WTO's criteria of not distorting agricultural trade or affect production. Article 3 in Annex 2 of the AoA specifies that in order to meet this condition, the costs of running public food stockholding should be identified in national legislation and that stocks correspond to predetermined food security targets. The AoA also requires that government purchases of food stuffs 'be made at current market prices and sales from food security stocks shall be made at no less than the current domestic market price for the product and quality in question'.[42] However, the AoA permits states to provide subsidised food to 'eligible recipients' such as the poor at market or at subsidised prices as long as government purchases of foodstuffs be 'made at current market prices and the financing and administration of the aid shall be transparent'.[43] As long as programmes meet the conditions specified in the AoA, there is no limit on the size and scope of public food stockholding for food security purposes.

What then is the disagreement over public food stockholding at the WTO all about? The disagreement among developed and developing countries largely revolves around the issue of whether existing rules in the AoA are sufficiently flexible, or need to be rewritten to accommodate the recent expansion of public stockholding by developing countries, especially India's massive programme under its *National Food Security Act*. Some countries, including India, have argued that the current requirement in the AoA to purchase agricultural commodities at market prices is especially problematic for the running of their public food stockholding programmes. Many governments

---

[40] Murphy (n 35); Clapp (n 32).
[41] Article 1, Annex 2 of the *Agreement on Agriculture*.
[42] Article 3, Annex 2 of the *Agreement on Agriculture*.
[43] Article 1, Annex 2 of the *Agreement on Agriculture*.

wish to intentionally purchase food stuffs at fixed prices rather than market prices (known as administered prices), for example, when a policy goal is to incentivise domestic food production. Purchases at administered prices above market prices guarantees farmers a profitable price for their crops and thus a predictable income, thereby reducing the inherent risks of agricultural production and encouraging farmers to plant more crops than they would have otherwise and to make other production-related investments.

Government purchases of agricultural commodities at administered prices is a long-established practice, and while the market efficiency and potential for market distortions of this practice is a subject of scholarly debate among trade economists,[44] the relevant point for this article is that doing so puts some developing countries at risk of violating their international trade commitments on agricultural subsidy spending at the WTO. The architecture of the AoA is built around the core objective of discouraging states from using policies that may distort patterns of international trade and production. This includes curbing government spending on agricultural subsidies.[45]

Each WTO member state has a specified, legally-binding annual limit under the AoA on the value and volume of agricultural subsidies it may provide.[46] While most developed countries successfully negotiated relatively high agricultural subsidy spending limits under the AoA during the Uruguay Round (1986–1994) of multilateral trade negotiations, most developing countries negotiated for very low levels of spending on such subsidies.[47] This fundamental asymmetry in the AoA is a product of history. In the late 1980s, when governments were negotiating their WTO limits on agricultural subsidy spending, most developing countries were facing severe economic difficulties and retrenching public spending on agriculture as part of structural adjustment policies. Given the severity of their fiscal challenges at the time, most developing countries did not envisage they would be in a future position to significantly increase spending on agriculture and thus did not negotiate for high subsidy spending limits. However, as developing countries have implemented public stockholding to achieve food security in recent years,

[44] See: Christopher L. Gilbert, 'International Agreements to Manage Food Price Volatility' (2012) 1 *Global Food Security* 134; Franck Galtier, 'Managing Food Price Instability: Critical Assessment of the Dominant Doctrine' (2013) 2 *Global Food Security* 72; C. Peter Timmer, 'Food Security in Asia and the Pacific: The Rapidly Changing Role of Rice' (2014) 1 *Asia & the Pacific Policy Studies* 73; Francesco Laio, Luca Ridolfi and Paolo D'Odorico, 'The Past and Future of Food Stocks' (2016) 11 *Environmental Research Letters* 035010.

[45] The AoA defines different categories of agricultural subsidies and constrains their use in relation to the distorting effects on trade and production. This includes 'Green box' subsidies that are understood to have no or minimally-trade distorting effects and that may be provided without any spending limits. 'Blue box' subsidies have some trade-distorting effects but do not affect production that are permitted but subject to spending limits. 'Amber box' subsidies are considered to distort production and trade and therefore subject to strict spending limits.

[46] WTO, 'Supporting Tables for Commitments on Agricultural Subsidization' (2018) online: <https://www.wto.org/english/tratop_e/agric_e/supporting_tables_e.htm>.

[47] Gonzalez (n 7); Margulis (n 35).

many states now find themselves at risk of exceeding their permissible levels on agricultural subsidy spending at the WTO.[48] This situation matters because WTO rules are 'hard' ones: if governments exceed their agricultural subsidy spending limits, they may be deemed to be in violation of WTO law and thus be vulnerable to trade sanctions carrying significant economic costs.[49] This situation is not a hypothetical one: a recent study of developing country WTO members with public food stockholding programmes found that India, Turkey, the Philippines and Egypt are exceeding their agricultural subsidy limits.[50]

Developing countries operating public food stockholding programmes have publicly acknowledged that they are potentially at risk of exceeding their agricultural subsidy limits and thus violating WTO law. However, they argue that the problem lies not with their programmes, which they maintain are legitimate policies to achieve national food security, but instead with existing WTO law.[51] Following this line of argument, the Group of 33 (G-33), a bargaining coalition of thirty-plus developing countries led by India and including China, has been driving efforts to renegotiate WTO law to make it more compatible with contemporary public food stockholding practices.[52] The G-33's attempts to change WTO law has been fraught with political discord. The 2013 WTO Ministerial meeting in Bali, Indonesia—where public food stockholding was the top issue on the agenda for trade ministers—nearly collapsed due to disagreement between developed and developing countries on how to further accommodate public food stockholding under WTO law. Only an eleventh-hour US-India compromise, which required an extraordinary meeting between President Obama and Prime Minister Modi after India threatened to veto a new WTO agreement on trade facilitation if there was no progress on food stockholding, led to an agreement on a temporary Peace Clause. Under the temporary Peace Clause, WTO member states agreed not to initiate legal challenges against a fellow WTO member state if its spending on public food stockholding exceeds its agricultural subsidy limits.[53] The Peace Clause was a temporary measure as WTO members agreed that it would expire in 2017.

Although the Peace Clause addresses the threat of an immediate trade dispute, WTO member states committed themselves to negotiate a permanent solution to ensure the consistency of public food stockholding with WTO

[48] Margulis (n 35), 165–167.

[49] John H. Barton and others, *The Evolution of the Trade Regime: Politics, Law, and Economics of the GATT and the WTO* (Princeton University Press, 2010).

[50] Panos Konandreas and George Mermigkas, *WTO Domestic Support Disciplines: Options for Alleviating Constraints to Stockholding in Developing Countries in the Follow-up to Bali* (FAO, 2014).

[51] Das (n 5); South Centre, *Subsidies and Food Security in WTO: A Permanent Solution is Still Pending* (South Centre, 2014); Christian Häberli, *After Bali: WTO Rules Applying to Public Food Reserves* (FAO, 2014).

[52] The G-33 currently includes 48 developing country members.

[53] WTO (n 1).

law.[54] The G-33 has advanced several proposals to achieve a permanent solution. The G-33 at one point proposed a technical fix that would revise the methodology for calculating the level of agricultural subsidy spending with respect to public food stockholding in the AoA. Developing countries have argued since the early 2000s that the current formula used to calculate agricultural subsidies, which requires governments to calculate the subsidy element by using reference prices from 1986 to 1988 (when international food prices were low) and that does not adequately factor in inflation, results in exaggerated reported levels of agricultural subsidy spending by developing countries. The G-33 has argued that their technical fix would result in a more accurate measurement of the level of spending on agricultural subsidies. If this alternative methodology was to be adopted by WTO members, it is claimed that it would result in far lower reported figures of spending on agricultural subsidies by developing countries.[55] This revised methodology would thus have the intended effect of ensuring countries such as India would not be in breach of their binding subsidy limits under the AoA because of spending on public food stockholding. While this technical fix has wide support among WTO members, the G-33 was unable to translate this into agreement because the US was unwilling to agree to a bespoke change to the AoA without further trade concessions from developing countries on agriculture reform.[56]

States failed to agree a permanent solution for public food stockholding at the Nairobi Ministerial meeting in 2015.[57] However, trade ministers confirmed in Nairobi that the Peace Clause would not expire in 2017 and thus remains in force until a permanent solution is found.[58] Since the Nairobi ministerial meeting, developed and developing countries' positions on public food stockholding have grown further apart. In response to slow progress on a permanent solution, the G-33 changed its bargaining approach. While it continues to advocate for the technical fix, the G-33 put forward a proposal in 2017 calling for all government spending on public stockholding for food security purposes—regardless if made at market or administered prices—to be treated as non-trade distorting support and thus exempt from counting towards a country's agricultural subsidy spending limits at the WTO.[59] This proposal is regarded as a more radical approach as it seeks a

[54] Rorden Wilkinson, Erin N. Hannah and James Scott, 'The WTO in Nairobi: The Demise of the Doha Development Agenda and the Future of the Multilateral Trading System' (2016) 7 *Global Policy* 247.

[55] WTO (n 1); See also: Das (n 5); Alan Matthews, 'Trade Rules, Food Security and the Multilateral Trade Negotiations' (2014) 41 *European Review of Agricultural Economics* 511.

[56] See: J.P. Singh and Surupa Gupta, 'Agriculture and Its Discontents: Coalitional Politics at the WTO with Special Reference to India's Food Security Interests' (2016) 21 *International Negotiation* 295; Amrita Narlikar and Diana Tussie, 'Breakthrough at Bali? Explanations, Aftermath, Implications' (2016) 21 *International Negotiation* 209.

[57] Wilkinson, Hannah and Scott (n 54).

[58] WTO, *Public Stockholding for Food Security Purposes: Ministerial Decision of 19 December 2015* (2015) online: <https://www.wto.org/english/thewto_e/minist_e/mc10_e/l979_e.htm>.

blanket exemption for developing countries from existing WTO agricultural subsidy spending commitments on the grounds of food security. The G-33 proposal has proven to be highly controversial. It was rejected by developed countries, who regarded the idea of reclassifying spending on public food stockholding as non-trade distorting support as an unacceptable change to the AoA.[60] Developed and developing countries remain deadlocked over public food stockholding. This was illustrated again at the WTO Ministerial meeting in December 2017 in Buenos Aires, at which India blamed the US for thwarting talks on public food stockholding.[61]

Repeated failures and the lack of forward progress in the negotiations demonstrates the difficulty in reaching a permanent solution for public food stockholding at the WTO. Public food stockholding remains a major source of political friction and the question of its legality under WTO trade rules remain a significant and unresolved problem in global trade politics. Nevertheless, states have not called time on the negotiations and continue to negotiate towards a permanent solution.

Concluding thoughts: from law to politics

States have thus far negotiated a partial solution to address concerns about the legal uncertainty surrounding public food stockholding at the WTO. States reached an agreement on a Peace Clause to ensure no developing country is subject to a trade dispute for exceeding agricultural subsidy spending limits but have yet to agree on how to rewrite existing WTO rules to address the concerns of countries such as India, who wish to purchase and sell foodstuffs for public food stockholding at administered prices without exceeding agricultural subsidy spending limits. While legitimate concerns remain about the long-term chilling effect caused by legal uncertainty at the WTO over public food stockholding, the fact that states have chosen to engage in political bargaining rather than legal adjudication illustrates important and changing dynamics in the WTO-food security relationship.

The politics of public food stockholding at the WTO does not fit with a narrative of supra-national constrains on the food security policies of developing countries. WTO rules do not prevent developing countries from pursuing public food stockholding. This policy is entirely permissible in the AoA. There are also no asymmetries here as with the rules relating to

---

59 Non-trade distorting agricultural support falls under the "Green Box" in the AoA. The G-33 report is not publicly available, see WTO, 'New Proposals in Agriculture Talks Form "Tangible Steps" Forward' (2017) online: <https://www.wto.org/english/news_e/news17_e/agng_19jul17_e.htm>.

60 *Ibid.*

61 See Erin Hannah, James Scott and Rorden Wilkinson, 'The WTO in Buenos Aires: The Outcome and Its Significance for the Future of the Multilateral Trading System' (2018) 41 *The World Economy* 2578.

import surges, as discussed earlier. Existing WTO law, which has been in place since 1995, did not stop developing countries from pursuing public food stockholding before or after the 2007–2008 global food crisis. A real concern with WTO law arose only when it became apparent that a small number of developing countries but especially India, which is a powerful player at the WTO, were close to exceeding their agricultural subsidy limits. Therefore, I contend that the politics of public stockholding are thus not about supra-national constraints on national policy *per se* but instead about the problems faced by a small number of developing countries at risk of violating their WTO subsidy commitments. The solution will require states agreeing to either modify how agricultural subsidies are calculated and/or permitting certain developing countries such as India to increase their agricultural subsidy spending limits. This will involve more bargaining and compromise among developed and developing countries to find a consensus solution.

The long-standing argument that WTO rules constrain the food security policies of developing countries is premised on the experience of developing countries during the Uruguay Round (1986–1994) of multilateral trade negotiations that produced the AoA. Many regard the AoA to have principally benefitted the interests of major agricultural exporting countries such as the US, EU, Canada and Australia while having imposed major costs on the developing world.[62] Yet a major change is evident in the politics of public food stockholding at the WTO in that it has taken place during a transformative shift in the global balance of power among states. At present emerging economies such as India, China and Brazil are powerful players in the international trade regime and are shaping the agenda and law of the WTO.[63] Developing countries working together in the G-33 have been successful in making public food stockholding a key issue in the WTO negotiations and keeping it at the top of the agenda. In short, developing countries are exerting their influence in the negotiations and becoming rule-makers at the WTO. It is notable that the two key players in the political battle over public food stockholding have been India, an emerging power, and the US, an established power. These changing power dynamics at the WTO suggest a shift towards a polycentric trade regime where economic and political power is no longer enjoyed exclusively by a small number of developed countries in the North but is more diffused among a greater number of states, including the emerging economies

[62] See Gonzalez (n 7); Finger and Nogués (n 9).

[63] See: Kristen Hopewell, *Breaking the WTO: How Emerging Powers Disrupted the Neoliberal Project* (Stanford University Press 2016); Kristen Hopewell, 'Different Paths to Power: The Rise of Brazil, India and China at the World Trade Organization' (2015) 22 *Review of International Political Economy* 311; Charalampos Efstathopoulos, 'Leadership in the WTO: Brazil, India and the Doha Development Agenda' (2012) 25 *Cambridge Review of International Affairs* 269; Amrita Narlikar, 'New Powers in the Club: The Challenges of Global Trade Governance' (2010) 86 *International Affairs* 717.

of the developing world.[64] The changing balance of economic and political power is important because it suggests that the trade interests of developing countries, including food security, are much less likely be ridden roughshod over by developed countries at the WTO compared to the past.

From a distance, the involvement by actors such as the UN Special Rapporteur on the right to food and global civil society on the margins of the WTO negotiations on public food stockholding might suggest that there is an inherent conflict between international trade law and the human right to food. Yet no WTO member has invoked the need to respect international human rights treaties or obligations to justify or strengthen their bargaining position on food security issues in the negotiations, even when they could have done so.[65] Nor have developing countries entertained the option of forum-shifting the negotiations on public food stockholding to another supra-national institution that would be more favourable to claims about the potential conflict between trade liberalisation and the right to food such as the UN Committee for World Food Security, UN Human Rights Council or the International Court of Justice. While states may disagree on how best to modify WTO law in relation to public food stockholding, the current consensus among them appears to be that this is a matter to be resolved exclusively through political bargaining at the WTO rather than through adjudication. Indeed, the Peace Clause signals the preference of WTO member states to avoid decision-making on public food stockholding being subject to adjudication.

The politics of public food stockholding have yielded a significant outcome. Despite a lack of a permanent solution, the agreement on the Peace Clause is notable and significant. It represents a tacit acceptance by WTO member states that legitimate food security objectives are grounds to deviate from binding international trade commitments. Recall that the Peace Clause makes non-actionable a violation of agricultural subsidy spending limits caused by spending on public food stockholding. This marks a break with how states have previously treated the provisions in the AoA. The main purpose of the AoA is to cap agricultural subsidy spending by states and enforce these commitments through the WTO's dispute settlement mechanism. The flexibility demonstrated by states to waive certain obligations under the AoA on food security grounds illustrate that political bargaining can make WTO rules more malleable than often appreciated. Therefore, it is not helpful to conceive of WTO law to be 'constitutional' like that of other international legal regimes, where it is very difficult and complex to

---

[64] See: Matias E Margulis, 'Trading Out of the Global Food Crisis? The WTO and the Geopolitics of Agro-Power' (2014) 19 *Geopolitics* 322, 325–328; Matias E. Margulis, Nora McKeon and Saturnino M. Borras, 'Land Grabbing and Global Governance: Critical Perspectives' (2013) 10 *Globalizations* 1, 18; James H. Mittelman, 'Global Bricolage: Emerging Market Powers and Polycentric Governance' (2013) 34 *Third World Quarterly* 23.

[65] In the early 2000s Nordic states evoked the human right to food at the WTO in defence of certain agricultural policies but never followed through on placing this on the negotiation agenda of the WTO Doha Round.

change the content of treaties, for example, such as international human rights agreements.[66] The nature of WTO agreements, with their built-in agendas of continual negotiation and political accommodation, means that the substantive content of multilateral trade agreements are potentially highly changeable over time. States have frequently deviated from WTO rules on food policy grounds in the past when it suited their interests.[67] We are now seeing this again in the negotiations on public food stockholding which follows earlier patterns of permissive deviation from the rules. However, this time, the changes have been driven by developing countries rather than developed countries.

A second contingent factor reshaping the WTO-food security relationship are developments in the global and national food policy environments that have resulted in a greater permeability of the WTO to food security issues than has been previously thought possible. Unlike the era in which the AoA was negotiated where states were primarily seeking to retrench support to the agricultural sector, the present context is one where many developing countries, increasingly supported by international institutions and new political projects such as the Sustainable Development Goals, are scaling up national policies and investment in the agricultural sector to support food security. Compared to the era of the Washington Consensus of the 1980s, the current policy environment is one where food security has the status of a global consensus goal. The policy environment significantly contributes to legitimating actions in the name of food security by state *and* non-state actors. This makes the WTO as an institution relatively more receptive to food security concerns compared to when the AoA was originally negotiated. This partly explains why developing countries' concerns about public food stockholding have dominated and remained on the WTO agenda. Alongside the changing balance of power and greater role of developing countries in shaping the agenda and rules of the WTO, these developments portend an era of potentially improved coherence between international trade and food security goals.

Acknowledgments

I thank the editors and anonymous reviewer for their helpful comments.

Disclosure statement

No potential conflict of interest was reported by the author.

ORCID

Matias E Margulis http://orcid.org/0000-0003-0931-6581

---

[66] Jeffrey L. Dunoff, 'Constitutional Conceits: The WTO's "Constitution" and the Discipline of International Law' (2006) 17 *European Journal of International Law* 647, 657–661.

[67] Daugbjerg, Farsund and Langhelle (n 32).

Transnational legal methodology and domestic markets for food

Amy J. Cohen

ABSTRACT

Transnational legal scholars often describe how today transnational private ordering may evade, even weaken, state power. This article, by contrast, explores how transnational private ordering and state power can function as complements as much as antagonists. More specifically, it analyses an ongoing legal conflict in India over the regulation of new large supermarket chains according to what Peer Zumbansen calls transnational legal methodology—that is, a method of legal analysis that theorises the transnational and domestic, like the state and the market, not as opposites but rather as alternative, even potentially homologous, ways of describing the distribution of authority, resources, and power. In so doing, the article also suggests that food—a global market commodity constitutive of national sovereignty—is especially good to think with for transnational legal theory.

Our symposium is motivated by the idea that food is a generative category for transnational legal analysis. Transnational legal scholars all agree that state law is too limited a frame to fruitfully analyse many of the social, political, and economic problems that today transcend national boundaries.[1] Indeed, several scholars describe the state as fragmenting or fracturing in the face of new transnational orders.[2] In this respect, food offers much for the

[1] Gregory Shaffer, 'Theorizing Transnational Legal Ordering' (2016) 12 *Annual Review of Law and Social Science* 231, 246.

[2] For example, in his recent annual review, Gregory Shaffer describes a group of transnational legal scholars that 'maintain the state lacks the will, capacity, or efficiency to create, apply, and enforce law for the coordination and regulation of behavior' and that examine 'the role of commercial actors in lawmaking and enforcement today.' *Ibid* at 233. These scholars theorize 'the marginalization of state law and the autonomy of private legal ordering in light of the complexity of modern society and the decline of state capacities.' To be sure, many other transnational legal scholars describe mutually constitutive (and quite complex) relationships between transnational private commercial regulation and state law. See, eg, *Ibid*, 236; Stephan Wood, Kenneth W. Abbott, Julia Black, Burkard Eberlein, and Errol Meidinger, 'The Interactive Dynamics of Transnational Business Governance: A Challenge for Transnational Legal Theory' (2015) 6 *Transnational Legal Theory* 333; Robert Wai, 'The Interlegality of Transnational Private Law' (2008) 71 *Law and Contemporary Problems* 107; Ralf Michaels, 'The True Lex Mercatoria: Law Beyond the State' (2007) 14 *Indiana Journal of Global Legal Studies* 447.

transnational legal theorist to study. Today, multinational corporations (MNCs) such as global retailers reach deep into the food systems of developing economies, governing many countries' farmers and agricultural markets through private standards encoded in new contract-based regulatory regimes.[3] Indeed, rural sociologist Philip McMichael describes 'a trajectory of "world agriculture"' embodied in what he calls today's global 'corporate food regime'.[4] Resistance to world agriculture is likewise transnational. Global networks of small producers now claim rights to 'food sovereignty' against both state and corporate power.[5] In both cases, analysts productively theorise the state as coexisting alongside, or even competing with, multiple forms of private authority.

Our journal convener, Peer Zumbansen, however, uses the phrase transnational legal theory to capture not only how transnational legal actors and networks potentially decentre the state. He also proposes to understand transnational legal analysis as *methodology*—one that 'reflexively collapses and critically engages the boundaries between domestic and international legal (economic, social, cultural, political) problems and demands an assessment of the inner connections and resemblances in their alleged differences'.[6] Such alleged differences, Zumbansen cautions further, do not reflect necessary oppositions between 'domestic and international qualities'.[7] To the contrary, he argues that many of our familiar dichotomies—domestic/international, public/private, state/market—reflect 'merely the exertion of definitional and conceptual sovereignty over an otherwise untameable power'.[8] From this perspective, the transnational legal analyst might, for example, study not simply how developing states compete with MNCs for authority and power, but also how such states may seek to *use* commercial private regulation to strengthen their own capacity to distribute essential domestic goods and services. In other

[3] See generally Amy J. Cohen 'Supermarkets in India: Struggles over the Organization of Agricultural Markets and Food Supply Chains' (2013) 68 *University of Miami Law Review* 19; Doris Fuchs, Agni Kalfagianni, and Maarten Arentsen, 'Retail Power, Private Standards, and Sustainability in the Global Food System' in Jennifer Clapp and Doris Fuchs (eds), *Corporate Power in Global Agrifood Governance* (MIT Press, 2009) 29–60; Spencer Henson and John Humphrey, 'Private Standards in Global Agri-food Chains' in Axel Marx, Miet Maertens, Johan Swinnen and Jan Wouters (eds), *Private Standards and Global Governance: Economic, Legal and Political Perspectives* (Edward Elgar, 2012) 98–113; Thomas Reardon, C. Peter Timmer, Christopher B. Barrett and Julio Berdegué, 'The Rise of Supermarkets in Africa, Asia, and Latin America' (2003) 85 *American Journal of Agricultural Economics* 1140.

[4] Philip McMichael, 'Global Development and the Corporate Food Regime' in Frederick H. Buttel and Philip McMichael (eds), *New Directions in the Sociology of Global Development* (Emerald Group Publishing Limited, 2005), 265–99, 272.

[5] *Ibid.* See, eg, Hannah Wittman, Annette Aurelie Desmarais, and Nettie Wiebe (eds), *Food Sovereignty: Reconnecting Food, Nature & Community* (Food First, 2010); Priscilla Claeys, *Human Rights and the Food Sovereignty Movement: Reclaiming Control* (Routledge, 2015); Michael Fakhri and Nathan Bellinger, 'The Intersection between Food Sovereignty and Law' (2013) 26 *American Bar Association Natural Resources & Environment* 2.

[6] Peer Zumbansen, 'Transnational Law, *Evolving*' in Jan M. Smits (ed.), *Elgar Encyclopedia of Comparative Law* (Edward Elgar, 2nd ed. 2012) 899–925, 904.

[7] *Ibid.*

[8] *Ibid*, 904–5.

words, for Zumbansen, transnational legal theory requires the analyst to understand the transnational and domestic, like the state and the market, as alternative, even potentially homologous, ways of describing the distribution of authority, resources, and power.

Here, too, food is good to think with. Food is simultaneously a public good and a market commodity. To ensure authority and legitimacy to rule, states must provide adequate food to their inhabitants. States that fail to ensure the distribution of food at a politically acceptable price often face domestic unrest and foreign influence and intervention.[9] At the same time, most nation states today distribute food primarily through markets—*markets* thus constitute crucial tests of political legitimacy, especially in developing and transitioning economies 'where alternative mechanisms of allocation and distribution, such as communism, authoritarianism or central planning, are deemed to have failed'.[10] Recall the food riots in numerous countries around the world between 2006 and 2008, which reflected food shortages and price spikes—recurring instability precipitated not only by climate change but also by food price speculation and the effect of the global biofuel industry on food prices.[11] These riots dramatically illustrate the potential for political unrest when states cannot mediate between volatile transnational commodity markets and their own domestic markets for food. And yet transnational legal methodology also helps to reveal how state actors may purposefully privilege transnational market orders—against domestic capital—precisely because transnational economic orders appear to strengthen, not simply fracture or constrain, public governance and state control.

In the remainder of this brief article, I will attempt to illustrate this argument with a suggestive and ongoing legal dispute in India, involving small retail traders who deal in grain, new corporate supermarket chains, and the state of Karnataka. My analysis is based on the case briefs as well as interviews with lawyers, plaintiffs, and government officials conducted in Bangalore in the spring of 2017. In this dispute, no actor crosses national borders or invokes sources of authority beyond Indian constitutional and regulatory law. From the perspective of 'domestic' legal analysis, then, we might attempt to decipher simply how a state court does or should declare winners and losers according to national law. But this familiar form of case interpretation misses larger questions relevant to transnational legal theory: namely, what kind of market order is the Indian state trying to create as it

[9] See, eg, E P Thompson, 'The Moral Economy of the English Crowd' (1971) 50 *Past and Present* 76; John H. Perkins, *Geopolitics and the Green Revolution: Wheat, Genes, and the Cold War* (Oxford University Press, 1997); John Walton and David Seddon (eds), *Free Markets and Food Riots: The Politics of Global Adjustment* (Wiley-Blackwell, 1994).

[10] Amy J. Cohen and Jason Jackson, 'Governing Through Markets: Multinational Firms in the Indian Bazaar' (unpublished manuscript on file with author).

[11] *See* Anne Orford, 'Food Security, Free Trade, and the Battle for the State' (2015) 11 *Journal of International Law and International Relations* 1, 2–3.

chooses between transnational capital (new large supermarkets) and local capital (small retail traders), and what do these choices suggest about its efforts to exert symbolic and economic sovereignty in a transnational world?

*

In 2014, the state government of Karnataka relaxed storage caps on the amount of foodgrains that large supermarkets—but not small retail shops—could stock.[12] The government did so to facilitate the new 'farm to fork' supply chain practices and economies of scale that large retail companies promise to install. In response, small retailers filed an equal protection challenge in the Karnataka High Court under the Indian constitution, arguing that the state could not rationally justify its discrimination between large and small firms.

The Indian state has traditionally used commodity controls, including storage caps, to influence food prices.[13] The theory is that in times of shortage local market actors hoard commodities, artificially spiking food prices with potentially politically and socially devastating consequences. Especially in the wake of famine-stricken colonial rule (think, for example, of the 1942–1943 Bengal famine[14]), nationalist state planners aimed to consolidate political authority and economic sovereignty by creating morally legitimate agricultural markets with strict legal limits on profiteering.[15] To this day, the Indian government uses storage caps to prevent hoarding and speculation, and it enforces these caps by periodically raiding wholesale markets, confiscating excess grain, compelling market sales, and fining offenders for exceeding holding limits.

New supermarket chains, which today play a small but growing role in the Indian retail market, consider this untenable government interference in their business. They insist that there is no need for the government to use with them the same heavy-handed tactics it deploys to make sure small traders honour the storage caps.[16] As a lawyer who represents the Retail Association of India (RAI), a consortium of large retail chains, told me, 'We can't hoard. We have computerized records of anything that is purchased or in stock with us, it can be verified and checked at any given point of time.' This is in

---

[12] Notification No SE202 MRE 2013, Bangalore Dt 26/02/204 published in the Karnataka Gazette, No 204 Wednesday, March 5, 2015 (translated from Kannada by Pattabhi Raman).

[13] See, eg, Essential Commodities Act, 1955.

[14] Amartya Sen, *Poverty and Famines: An Essay on Entitlement and Deprivation* (Oxford University Press, 1981). When war inflation drove up the price of food more that the wage of labour, especially agricultural labourers in rural Bengal could not afford to purchase food that was available via markets. *Ibid*, 75–81. The famine that followed, and claimed over 3 million lives, reflected multiple factors that included financially profitable 'speculative withdrawal[s]' and 'panic hoardings' of rice. *Ibid*, 76.

[15] See Cohen and Jackson (n 10); see also Benjamin Siegel, *Hungry Nation: Food, Famine and the Making of Modern India* (Cambridge University Press, 2018).

[16] See, eg, Plaintiffs' Brief before the High Court of Karnataka, Reliance Retail Limited versus State and Others, writ petition no. 49626 (2015), 2 (challenging a 'raid on the premises of Reliance Market and [the seizure of] Pulses on the ground that ... the quantities kept in the premises are in excess of the limits prescribed under [national and state law]').

contrast, he continued, to small informal market actors where 'there are no bills, it's on trust and it's all cash-based transactions, so if [a traditional retail trader] buy[s] such a huge quantity … there will be no record and it can be stocked somewhere else outside'.[17]

In making this argument, the RAI lawyer implicitly invoked a longstanding moral-cultural discourse in India: the idea that for centuries, entrenched networks of indigenous traders have dominated food markets, using kinship relations to dictate the flow of goods and market information. These are informal, patronage-based, and socially-regulated conventions of market governance that create markets that appear opaque, inefficient, and unethical to state actors and that, crucially, seem resistant to formal state control.[18] In contrast, new large retail companies—financed domestically or now also sometimes through partnerships with multinational retailers—endeavour to mimic the logistics and supply chain management systems common in the West: legible formal contractual relations, private standards steeped in principles of supply chain 'traceability', and third-party accreditation and audit schemes.[19] The formalism of their operations means, the RAI lawyer argued, that large retailers are market actors of a qualitatively different kind. Indian policymakers repeat this claim. For example, Ashok Gulati, a Delhi-based agricultural economist and the former chairman of the Commission for Agricultural Costs and Prices, observes that multinational retail corporations behave according to legal rules because their market transactions are so visible to regulators, unlike small-scale traders whose market malpractices are notoriously hard for state actors to 'see':[20] 'Small capital can get away with malpractices but big capital cannot. Twenty people will be there watching him.'[21] For this reason, the RAI lawyer submitted, big and small capital need not be subject to the same systems of regulation.

But when, in 2014, Karnataka therefore decided to permit supermarkets to stock five times as much commodity as retail traders that owned single shops, it was the 'informal' sector that petitioned the High Court, arguing that the new classifications violated the equal protection clause of the Indian Constitution. 'There is no difference,' their lawyer explained, 'between the Retail traders and the hyper market in as much as both are retail traders having obtained retail license[s] selling to the consumer. Hence fixing 500 quintals

[17] Interview with Ajoy Kumar Patil, Advocate, Retailers Association of India, Bangalore, India, April 30, 2017.

[18] Cohen and Jackson (n 10); see also Ritu Birla, *Stages of Capital: Law, Culture, and Market Governance in Late Colonial India* (Duke University Press, 2009); Rohit De, *Mr. Bagla's Baggage: Commodity Control, Capitalists and the Making of Administrative Law* (Mimeo, 2014).

[19] See, eg, Cohen (n 3).

[20] James Scott, *Seeing Like a State: How Certain Schemes to Improve the Human Condition Have Failed* (Yale University Press, 1998).

[21] Interview with Ashok Gulati, Infosys Chair Professor for Agriculture, Indian Council for Research on International Economic Relations (ICRIER), New Delhi, July 4, 2017.

for Hyper/Super markets and 100 quintals for Retail traders is illogical, unscientific and also discriminatory'.[22] Likewise plaintiffs told me, the state cannot legally 'differentiate between us and the MNCs' when both hold the same retail license.[23]

In his arguments before the Court, the RAI lawyer stressed (among other arguments) the social functions of supermarkets and the benefits of globalisation to justify why the state should deviate from the principle of formal equality.[24] Unlike small retail traders, supermarkets perform multiple kinds of market functions, including 'promoting and facilitating world class logistics and warehouse chain[s]'[25] like those 'fully evolved and developed in advanced economies of the world, especially in western countries'.[26] An 'organized retail company', the RAI lawyer continued, operates 'as several market functionaries like Trader and/or Direct Purchase Center and/or Stockiest and/or Processor', working nimbly across multiple points of a vertically coordinated supply chain.[27]

I imagine that this argument for supermarket flexibility especially burned the plaintiffs. But to understand why we must look beyond the written submissions in this case. The plaintiffs once held licenses to trade in a wholesale market conveniently located near an entrance to the city—trading licenses that enabled them to deal in up to 2000 quintals of grain. When the state government decided to relocate this particular market further north, these plaintiffs were holdouts: stubborn grain traders who refused to move from the market's original location, squatting on government land until, through a combination of protests and political and legal pressure, they were formally granted retail but not renewed trading licenses (retail licenses, again, that

[22] Plaintiffs' Brief submitted to the High Court of Karnataka at Bangalore, Writ Petition No. 28897-901 between Nath and Company and others versus Union of India and Others (2014) 8 para 4.

[23] Interview with plaintiff, Bangalore, India, June 3, 2017.

[24] It is worth noting that these legal positions exactly invert the arguments made in the early twentieth century before the United States Supreme Court when chain retail stores claimed formal equality in order to challenge regulations meant to benefit single stores. To briefly summarise, opponents of chain stores enacted state legislation that required, for example, graduated licenses fees or increased taxes based on how many stores a corporation owned or the extent of a corporation's geographical reach. Supreme Court jurists, applying classical formal legal principles, struck down these legislative restrictions as impermissibly interfering with the rights of all market actors to buy and sell on formally equal terms. That is, until 1931 when the Court reviewed a number of social facts about the purchasing and management practices of chains and concluded that the state had drawn a qualitative distinction between the chains and single stores—and one that was legitimate to advance social welfare. *State Bd. of Tax Comm'rs v. Jackson*, 283 U.S. 527 (1931). This logic, however, soon gave way to a different set of arguments favouring retail consolidation. For a wonderful elaboration of this history, see Richard C. Schragger, 'The Anti-Chain Store Movement, Localist Ideology, and the Remnants of the Progressive Constitution 1920–1940' (2005) 90 *Iowa Law Review* 1011. See also Amy J. Cohen, 'The Law and Political Economy of Contemporary Food: Some Reflections on the Local and the Small' (2015) 78 *Law and Contemporary Problems* 101.

[25] Impleaded brief for the Retail Association of India submitted to the to the High Court of Karnataka at Bangalore, Writ Petition No. 28897-901 between Nath and Company and others versus Union of India and Others (2014) 9, para 8 (quoting the Retail Trade Policy of Karnataka).

[26] *Ibid*, 4 para 4.

[27] *Ibid*, 6, para 5.

came with a 100-quintal cap). Although the plaintiffs simply demanded formal equality before the court, what they would ideally want is renewed permission to deal in larger quantities of grain and to pursue more flexible and diverse forms of trade. As field economist Barbara Harriss-White has illustrated, indigenous merchant capital too 'may buy, sell, broker, store, transport, process, produce, finance production, and finance trade. There are two to the 9th possible combinations of these nine activities and there are other activities'.[28] Or to put this observation another way, the 100-quintal storage cap limits plaintiffs to the single market function of small end-consumer sales when, just like corporate retail capital, they too desire to pursue multiple market functions across the supply chain.

And therein lied the dilemma for state regulators. The government officials I spoke with worried generally that if the state raises storage caps for small retail traders, then some small retail firms could potentially double as wholesale firms, transforming retail markets into spaces where wholesale trading also occurs. In Karnataka, wholesale markets are 'regulated', which means that administrative and elected state officials adjudicate disputes about market malpractices, assess taxes and service fees on sales, and collect daily information about commodity quantity and price.[29] Retail markets, by contrast, are unregulated. As such, liberalising storage caps for small retailers could mean grain trading that happens in markets beyond official state control. One government lawyer told me that he appreciated the plaintiffs' classical legal principle: that formally equal actors (retail traders with the same government licence) should buy and sell on formally equal terms. But the stakes of equalising the caps (say simply 500 quintals for all retail traders, large or small) let alone lifting them entirely for everyone are more complex. Government officials must resolve, on the one hand, how to pursue market liberalisation in order to facilitate the growth of large capital without, on the other hand, undermining their always fragile and incomplete oversight over small firms.

*

This desire—to facilitate market liberalisation for big/globalising/transnational forms of capital while maintaining state regulation for small/indigenous/local ones—may strike some legal analysts as contradictory, even unjust, when analysed under domestic legal rules and principles, such as under a formal reading of the Indian constitution.[30] Transnational legal analysis does not resolve this injustice, but it does offer an alternate framework for theorising it. Following Zumbansen,

---

[28] Barbara Harriss-White, *Rural Commercial Capital: Agricultural Markets in West Bengal* (Oxford University Press, 2008), 26.

[29] For more detail on regulated markets in India, see Barbara Harriss, 'Inaction, Interaction and Action: Regulated Agricultural Markets in Tamil Nadu' (1980) *Social Scientist* 9, 96. See also Cohen (n 3).

[30] Cf. n 24 on how the principle of formal equality was mobilized in the American case.

transnational legal analysis invites us to understand regulation *and* liberalisation as alternative mechanisms for the state to assert authority and control over markets for food. And it likewise invites us to consider how powerful transnational actors may appear to strengthen state power and not simply undermine it.

I develop these arguments about the perceived promises of transnational retail corporations in India—arguments meant to be partial and suggestive—in an article with political economist Jason Jackson. We venture that against recalcitrant, delegitimised indigenous traders that for centuries have appeared resistant to formal state control, new large corporations promise to enhance the ability of Indian regulators to 'see', and hence govern, markets for food.[31] Indeed, practices like private standards, auditing, and monitoring make corporate capital appear state-like. Corporate retailers, in other words, supply their own forms of private market 'governance' including contract-based standards and norms—and, crucially, standards and norms that are supposed to travel legibly across markets, borders, and scale. But Indian policymakers do not therefore necessarily perceive large retail chains as competing with the state (as debates about private versus public governance can suggest). Instead, they often describe large retail chains as more amenable to modern forms of state authority encoded in public regulation and state law. For example, Ramesh Chand, a member of the NITI Aayog (which was formally the Planning Commission of India and is now a think-tank for the federal government) explained that 'a big organized licensed firm is subject to the scrutiny of law more than a small firm'.[32] Or as his colleague, the advisor for agriculture at the NITI Aayog, added, 'monitoring thousands is rather difficult [compared to] one'.[33]

In order to create the conditions for large capital to consolidate the market in this way, policymakers must of course enact new liberalising legal rules. Indeed, in 2017, the NITI Aayog proposed jettisoning storage caps entirely. As one official explained, 'removing stock restrictions from agriculture commodities will lead to organised trading, improve scale and logistics benefit[s] and bring about more capital into trade with [a] handful of big traders competing with each other'.[34] But given the decentralised structure of agricultural marketing laws in India, if removing storage caps also boosts small and medium sized firms, then it will be individual states, far more than policymakers in Delhi, that must determine how to

[31] Cohen and Jackson (n 10); Scott (n 16).

[32] Interview with Ramesh Chand, Member, NITI Aayog (National Institute for Transforming India), New Delhi, July 7, 2017.

[33] Interview with JP Mishra, Advisor (Agriculture), NITI Aayog (National Institute for Transforming India), New Delhi, July 4, 2017.

[34] Yogima Sharma, 'Remove Agriculture from Essential Commodities Act: Niti Aayog' *The Economic Times*, (28 August 2017), online: <https://economictimes.indiatimes.com/news/economy/policy/remove-agriculture-from-essential-commodities-act-niti-aayog/articleshow/60250348.cms>.

police these smaller 'informal' market actors as they attempt to accumulate capital and grow. Hence the legal dilemma confronting Karnataka in the case I described. Government officials who defend the classifications likely desire more than simply creating the conditions for new 'free markets' to work. They likely aim to enhance their own regulatory authority over food markets by working *through* private market ordering, but crucially through private ordering of the right kind—one that is *already* transnational-ising and modernising.[35]

*

Anne Orford recently illustrated how today's dominant policy consensus —that food security is a transnational problem that requires transnational solutions in the form of global 'free-market' integration and liberalisation —undercuts the ability and political legitimacy of states to care for the welfare (and freedom) of local populations.[36] This argument is significant. But as Zumbansen suggests, 'stor[ies] about the erosion of the welfare state under the conditions of globalization', often rest on a particular Western imaginary, namely, an 'idea of the state not only as a still relatively stable institutional environment but also as a reliable guarantor of public good delivery'.[37] Many postcolonial democracies, however, have never achieved 'a single, vertically integrated sovereignty sustained by a highly centralized state'.[38]

In India, longstanding struggles by state planners to aggregate and control agricultural markets dominated by decentralised merchant capital illustrate this point well—not only because agricultural markets distribute essential goods, but also because different kinds of food markets constitute different institutional and ideological mechanisms of political authority.[39] For this reason, I have argued that at the heart of a seemingly local conflict over grain trading, we can glimpse significant transnationalising forces at work—forces that illustrate how state power and transnational economic ordering function as complements as much as antagonists. Or to frame this point as a matter of transnational legal method, rather than read a domestic legal case as a competition between different market actors to be adjudicated by state law, I instead asked what this case reveals about the Indian state's desire for transnational capital in order to enhance its own governance and control over politically significant domestic markets for food.

---

[35] Cohen and Jackson (n 10).

[36] Orford (n 11).

[37] Peer Zumbansen, 'Where the Wild Things Are: Journeys to Transnational Legal Orders, and Back' (2016) 1 *UC Irvine Journal of International, Transnational, and Comparative Law* 161, 166.

[38] John L. Comaroff and Jean Comaroff, 'Law and Disorder in the Postcolony: An Introduction' in Jean Comaroff and John L. Comaroff (eds), *Law and Disorder in the Postcolony* (University of Chicago Press, 2006) 1–57, 35.

[39] Cohen and Jackson (n 10).

Acknowledgements

Many thanks to Ilana Gershon, Genevieve Lakier, an anonymous reviewer, and especially Matthew Canfield for comments and conversations, and to the journal editors for creating this symposium issue

Disclosure statement

No potential conflict of interest was reported by the author.

Commodity derivatives, contract law, and food security

Anna Chadwick

ABSTRACT
Speculation in commodity derivative markets has been linked to the causation of the 2007–11 global food crisis. Derivatives have also been implicated in the causation of the global financial crisis. Much of the legal scholarship on derivatives is concerned with how best to regulate their use. Other work has pointed to the role of transnational actors, such as the International Swaps and Derivatives Association (ISDA), in facilitating the growth of the global derivatives market. What is missing in this scholarship is an account of how the norms of contract law have been altered, extended, and even distorted to create a new generation of financial assets linked to food prices. In this paper, I begin a project of examining how the trade in commodity derivatives has disrupted some of the established principles of contract law, and I reflect on the significance of my findings for the debate about derivatives regulation.

1. Introduction

In the period between 2006 and the second quarter of 2008, the prices of maize, rice, and wheat on international commodity markets more than doubled.[1] These three staple grains account for almost half of the calories that are consumed by poor households in the Global South.[2] Consequently, as basic food prices spiralled higher, riots and protests broke out in in more than twenty-five countries worldwide.[3] The World Bank has estimated that the global food crisis pushed up to an additional 105 million people deeper into poverty in 2008 alone.[4] Although grain prices did drop in 2009, by

[1] Donald Mitchell, 'A Note on Rising Food Prices' (2008) World Bank Policy Research Working Paper WPS 4682, online: <https://openknowledge.worldbank.org/bitstream/handle/10986/6820/WP4682.pdf?sequence=1&isAllowed=y> 3.

[2] David Lobell et al., 'Prioritizing Climate Change Adaption Needs for Food Security in 2030' (2008) 319 (5863) *Science* 607, 608.

[3] Ray Bush, 'Food Riots: Poverty, Power and Protest' (2010) 10(1) *Journal of Agrarian Change* 119.

[4] Ivanic Maros and Will Martin, 'Implications of Higher Global Food Prices for Poverty in Low-income Countries' (2008) World Bank Policy Research Working Paper WPS 4594, online <http://documents.worldbank.org/curated/en/253001468150585777/Implications-of-higher-global-food-prices-for-poverty-in-low-income-countries>.

2010 they surged once again reaching dangerous new heights.[5] A survey of food consumption patterns in some of the countries worst affected by the crisis—the Central African Republic, Ethiopia, Liberia and Sierra Leone—found substantial evidence of restricted dietary diversity and food intake reductions among poor households.[6] As well as increasing the risk of micronutrient deficiencies among poor communities, the rising cost of food forced many families to reduce spending on healthcare and education, with damaging long-term effects for children in particular.[7]

Numerous factors have been advanced to explain this episode of extreme food price volatility. A growing global population, climatic events impacting harvests, high prices for oil, and the promotion of crop-intensive biofuels all feature in accounts of what happened to food prices during this period.[8] Undoubtedly, each of these factors played a role. Nevertheless, several studies have underlined that the food price volatility of 2007–11 cannot be explained by supply and demand fundamentals alone.[9] Since 2008, claims have emerged that part of the responsibility for the crisis lies with the creation of a new market in commodity derivative contracts that has enabled financial actors to speculate on agricultural commodity prices. In recent years, a coalition of NGOs including Oxfam, Global Justice Now (GJN), World Economy Ecology and Develoment (WEED), and The Centre for Research on Multinational Corporations (SOMO) has been lobbying governments to address the threat posed to food prices by banks, hedge funds, and pension funds who, to employ the characterisation of GJN, have been 'betting on food prices in financial markets' and 'causing drastic price swings in staple foods such as wheat, maize and soy'.[10]

In the years leading up to the global food crisis, levels of financial investment in commodity derivatives increased substantially, rising from less than $100bn in 2005 to over $400bn in 2011.[11] NGOs have gathered a

---

[5] Food and Agriculture Organization, *World Food Prices Reach New Historic Peak* (3 February 2011), FAO Media Centre website, online: <www.fao.org/news/story/en/item/50519/icode/>.

[6] Samuel H. Swan, Sierd Hadley, and Bernardette Cichon, 'Crisis Behind Closed Doors: Global Food Crisis and Local Hunger' (2010) 10(1) *Journal of Agrarian Change* 107.

[7] *Ibid.*

[8] Food and Agriculture Organization, *Report on The State of Agricultural Commodity Markets: High Food Prices and the Food Crisis – Experiences and Lessons Learned* (2009), online: <www.fao.org/docrep/pdf/012/i0854e/i0854e.pdf>; Anuradha Mittal, United Nations Conference on Trade and Development (UNCTAD), *The 2008 Food Price Crisis: Rethinking Food Security Policies* (2009) G24 Discussion Paper Series 56, online: <https://core.ac.uk/download/pdf/6993863.pdf>.

[9] Food and Agriculture Organization, *Volatility in Agricultural Commodities: An Update* (2008), FAO Food Outlook, online: <www.fao.org/docrep/010/ai466e/ai466e13.htm>; Miguel Robles, Maximo Torero, and Joachim von Braun, International Food Policy Research Institute, International Food Policy Research Institute, *When Speculation Matters* (2009) Issue Brief 57, online: <www.cftc.gov/sites/default/files/idc/groups/public/@swaps/documents/file/plstudy_40_ifpri.pdf>.

[10] Global Justice Now, *Food Speculation*, online: <www.globaljustice.org.uk/food-speculation>.

[11] Marc-Olivier Herman, Ruth Kelly, and Robert Nash, Oxfam, *Not a Game: Speculation vs. Food Security* (2011) Oxfam Issues Briefing, online: <www.oxfam.org/en/research/not-game-speculation-vs-food-security>, 5.

compelling body of evidence to back up their claims about the relationship between speculation and price volatility. Their reports contain evidence of statistical correlations between rising levels of investment and price movements in underlying markets, accounts of historical episodes of price instability linked to speculative activity, and interviews with financial traders who have testified to the changes they have witnessed in commodity markets in the last decade.[12] Not surprisingly, financial institutions have denied the possibility that their involvement in commodity derivative markets could have had the kind of impact suggested by NGOs.[13] While this remains a controversial debate, a series of investigations launched by the US Congress resulted in an affirmative finding that excessive levels of speculation in commodity derivatives was a cause of the price volatility.[14] G20 governments have been persuaded to take action, and, spearheaded by the US and the EU, have moved to introduce new regulations to restrict excessive levels of financial investment in commodity derivative markets.

In this article, I explore a hitherto neglected aspect of the trade in commodity derivatives, which is the way in which derivative contracts are in tension with some of the established principles of contract law. In Part I of the article, I provide a brief introduction to commodity derivative markets, and I explain how the significance of law in this context is conceptualised in existing legal scholarship. In Part II, I focus on a number of ways in which derivatives upset some of the key principles of contract law. In doing so, I problematise the pervasive tendency to think of contract as a neutral vehicle to facilitate financial transactions, and I offer a counterpoint to the prevalent view that the threat posed to food prices by commodity derivatives can be addressed by curbing excessive volumes of speculative trading in these markets. Instead, I aim to demonstrate that it is the nature of these atypical contracts that has enabled financial actors to influence price directions in food commodity markets in the way that they have. This finding has implications for current debates on how to regulate derivatives, as I discuss in the concluding section of the article.

2. Commodity derivatives from legal perspectives

Derivatives are financial contracts that enable a market actor to adopt a position in a market for an underlying asset and to use that position make a profit

[12] The Institute for Agriculture and Trade Policy (IATP) provides a helpful compendium of much of this work, see Ben Lilliston and Andrew Ranallo (eds), IATP, *Excessive Speculation in Agriculture Commodities: Selected Writings from 2008–2011* (2011) online: <www20.iadb.org/intal/catalogo/PE/2011/08247.pdf>.

[13] Deutsche Bank supported its decision to continue investing in commodity derivatives in 2014, arguing that 'there is no convincing evidence that the products we offer have a de-stabilizing impact on prices and cause more people to go hungry.' Deutsche Bank, *Our Position: The Key Questions and Answers*, online: <www.db.com/cr/en/concrete-current-questions-and-answers-may-2014.htm>.

[14] United States Senate, *Excessive Speculation in the Wheat Market, Majority and Minority Staff Report* (2009) Permanent Subcommittee on Investigations, Washington, DC: US Senate.

or a loss, or to hedge against risk, depending on how the market for the asset behaves in the future. The assets underpinning derivatives contracts can be tangible, like property and commodities (grain, metals, fuels), or they can be intangible, such as stocks, currencies, and interest rates.[15] Derivatives come in an array of different forms, including forwards, futures, options and swaps, all of which afford contracting parties different constellations of rights and obligations concerning the underlying asset. Many of these instruments are now linked to abstract financial indices, such as the S&P/ASX 200 index, and are priced using complex mathematical formulae. At root, however, derivatives have been developed from a more basic instrument known as a 'futures contract'. A futures contract is a standardised contract through which two parties agree to exchange a fixed amount of a given commodity at an agreed date in the future for a sum of money negotiated in the present. Futures contracts allow parties to lock in a price at which to make an exchange in the future, thereby allowing farmers and manufacturers the means to avoid potentially disruptive price changes. Commodity futures contracts have a long history, and have been used for centuries as both a mechanism of agricultural insurance and as vehicles to facilitate profitable speculation.

For a long period of history, futures contracts were only legally sold via institutions known as 'futures exchanges'. The most famous example of a futures exchange is the Chicago Board of Trade. This institution pioneered an organised trade in agricultural futures contracts in the US in the nineteenth century, and was a prototype for the development of other futures exchanges around the world.[16] Since the 2000s, however, a new market in 'over-the-counter' (OTC) derivatives has overtaken the trade in exchange-traded futures contracts. OTC transactions are carried out bilaterally, between private parties, and are transacted outside of formal futures exchanges. OTC derivatives are principally traded by large banks and hedge funds, who, together with their lawyers, are responsible for developing the 'exotic' credit and interest rate derivatives that were instrumental in bringing about the global financial crisis. Financial institutions have also created a more sophisticated range of financial instruments linked to commodity prices, such as 'commodity index funds', and 'commodity exchange-traded funds' (ETFs). These products enable a wide range of actors to gain profitable exposure to price movements in underlying commodity markets without having to engage directly in 'costly and fiddly direct trading' in the futures market.[17]

[15] Michael Chui, Bank for International Settlements, *Derivatives Markets, Products and Participants: An Overview*, (2012) IFC Bulletin 35 online: <www.bis.org/ifc/publ/ifcb35a.pdf>.

[16] Ann Berg, 'The Rise of Commodity Speculation: From Villainous to Venerable' in Adam Prakash (ed), *Safeguarding Food Security in Volatile Global Markets* (FAO, 2011) online: <www.fao.org/docrep/013/i2107e/i2107e.pdf>.

[17] World Development Movement, *Dangerous Futures: How are pensions fuel hunger* (2013) online: <www.globaljustice.org.uk/sites/default/files/files/resources/pension_report_final.pdf> 9.

Credit derivatives, in particular, are now widely recognised as having played a leading role in the causation of the global financial crisis, principally by creating opaque webs of poorly collateralised debt between financial institutions who then relied on these elaborate forms of insurance to pursue speculative investment strategies with their own capital.[18] Taken together with the evidence of a connection between commodity derivatives and the global food crisis, pressure has mounted on policymakers to take action. In order to prevent a repeat of the global financial crisis, G20 governments have committed to enact new regulations that require institutions trading in derivatives to go through a more rigorous and transparent process in order to effect transactions. The *Dodd Frank Act 2010* (Dodd Frank) in the US, and the new rules under the European Market Infrastructure Regulation and second Market in Financial Instruments Directive II (EMIR-MiFID II) in Europe require banks and hedge funds to trade derivatives through regulated institutions known as clearing houses, to post greater collateral for their trades, and to report transaction data to government regulatory agencies.[19] NGOs concerned about practices of food speculation have also been successful in persuading policymakers to develop 'position limits' to restrict excessive levels of financial speculation in commodity derivative markets.[20] Position limits place an upper limit on the number of contracts other than 'bona fide hedging' positions which an investor, or combined group of investors, may hold for a specific commodity.[21] In the US, investors have been limited to controlling 25 percent of a given contract. In the EU, 25 percent is the recommended level set by the EU regulator, the European Securities and Markets Authority (ESMA), but national governments can make adjustments to the limits.[22]

Implementing the technical rules that give effect to the framework agreements of Dodd Frank and Emir-MiFID II has been a fraught process. A lawsuit challenging the US position limits on the grounds of limited evidence connecting speculative trading to commodity price volatility resulted in the US limits being struck down. However, new rules that are largely similar to the original measures have

[18] Financial Crisis Inquiry Commission Hearing, 'The Role of Derivatives in the Global Financial Crisis', Testimony of Michael Greenberger before the Financial Crisis Inquiry Commission Hearing (Washington DC, 30 June 2010) online: <http://digitalcommons.law.umaryland.edu/cgi/viewcontent.cgi?article=1036&context=cong_test>.

[19] The Dodd-Frank Wall Street Reform and Consumer Protection Act of 2010, Pub.L. 111–203, H.R. 4173 [Dodd-Frank]; The Regulation (EU) No 648/2012 of the European Parliament and of the Council of 4 July 2012 on OTC derivatives, central counterparties (CCPs) and trade repositories (TRs) [EMIR]; Directive 2014/65/EU of the European Parliament and of the Council of 15 May 2014 on markets in financial instruments and amending Directive 2002/92/EC and Directive 2011/61/EU [MiFID II].

[20] Dodd-Frank s 737; MiFID II s 125-131.

[21] Due to the benefits that bespoke OTC derivatives afford to commercial participants, regulators are concerned not to prevent commercial hedgers from using OTC derivatives for hedging purposes.

[22] ESMA, *Opinion: Draft Regulatory Technical Standards on Methodology for Calculation and the Application of Position Limits for Commodity Derivatives Traded on Trading Venues and Economically Equivalent OTC contracts* (2016), ESMA/2016/668, online: <www.esma.europa.eu/sites/default/files/library/2016-668_opinion_on_draft_rts_21.pdf> 7, para 25.

been reinstated.[23] Campaigners have welcomed the regulations, and are currently working to ensure that the rules are not watered down by the financial lobby. As GJN has stated, 'despite some weaknesses the agreement represents huge progress, meaning that for the first time the EU has rules to tackle food speculation'.[24] Unfortunately, however, there is cause to question this optimism. As I have discussed in other work, there is reason to consider that the regulations are unlikely to be effective in shielding commodity prices from speculative interference.[25] Position limits attempt to restrict the volume of speculative transactions that a single trader or financial institution can make in a market for a given commodity derivative contract, but this fails to account for the cumulative impact of dispersed market actors 'herding' together to influence price directions in commodity markets—a phenomenon described in the work of people in the behavioural school of economics, notably Robert Shiller.[26] More broadly, scholarship from the influential Social Studies of Finance (SSF) suggests that it may no longer be possible to convincingly distinguish between the 'real' or 'fundamental' values of food commodities and the prices of commodity derivative contracts. Work by Donald MacKenzie and Donatella Alessandrini encourages a reconceptualisation of the financial formulas that purport to 'measure' or 'record' value, and points towards a new understanding of derivatives as complex assemblages of technology, institutional practice, and economic assumption that 'do something to the value that they are supposed to measure'.[27] Viewed through an SSF lens of analysis, purging commodity derivative markets of 'excessive' volumes of speculation may do little to address the new market reality in which market actors who are assumed by economic theory to be 'discovering' commodity prices are, in fact, helping to produce those prices; prices that reflect the sentiments of financial markets, as opposed to fundamentals for grain or other commodities.

Much of the legal scholarship on commodity derivatives since 2010 has centred on the question of how best to regulate their use. Debate continues over how to ensure regulatory harmonisation, how to promote effective compliance, and to what extent the US and European measures can have extraterritorial effect.[28] Other legal scholarship on derivatives explores the operations

---

[23] See *International Swaps and Derivatives Association, et v. United States Commodity Futures Trading Commission*, Civil Action No. 11-CV-2146 (District Court For The District Of Columbia, 28 September 2012). For an insightful analysis of the case, see further James. W. Williams, 'Dodging Dodd- Frank: Excessive Speculation, Commodities Markets, and the Burden of Proof' (2015) 37 *Law & Policy* 119.

[24] Global Justice Now (n 10).

[25] Anna Chadwick, 'Regulating Excessive Speculation: Commoodity Derivatives and the Global Food Crisis' (2017) 66(3) *International & Comparative Law Quarterly* 625.

[26] Robert J Shiller, *Irrational exuberance* (Princeton University Press, 3rd edn 2015).

[27] Donatella Alessandrini, 'Financial Derivatives and the Challenge of Performation: Where Continegency Meets Contestability' in Emile Cloatre and Martin Pickersgill (eds), *Knowledge, Technology and Law* (Routledge, 2014) 154; Donald MacKenzie, *An Engine, Not a Camera: How Financial Models Shape Markets* (MIT Press, 2006); Edward Lipuma, 'Ritual in Financial Life' in Benjamin Lee and Randy Martin (eds), *Derivatives and the Wealth of Societies* (The University of Chicago Press, 2016) 37.

[28] Christian Johnson, 'Regulatory Arbitrage, Extraterritorial Jurisdiction, and Dodd-Frank: The Implications of US Global OTC Derivative Regulation' (2014) 14(2) *Nevada Law Journal* 542.

of the International Swaps and Derivatives Association (ISDA) and its role as a 'global' 'private' law-maker. In the main, this body of work is concerned to describe the evolution of new forms of transnational governance, and to consider whether the ISDA regime is an autonomous and anational legal system.[29] Scholars have sought to connect the activities of ISDA to broader developments in transnational law, investigating whether the contractual documentation, guidelines, and boilerplate legislation produced by ISDA to facilitate a global trade in derivatives really ever 'takes off' from the national legal system, or whether it is, in fact, dependent on domestic legal regimes to function.[30] The answer from John Biggins, Joanna Braithwaite, and a number of other scholars is clear: financial actors are dependent on national courts and domestic law, and particularly the common law regimes of the US and the UK (the jurisdictions nominated by ISDA to govern disputes) in order to function.[31] Nevertheless, while contract law is central to transnational scholarship on derivatives markets, the focus is overwhelmingly on contractual standardisation and what the actions of innovative actors like ISDA reveal about the changing role of the state with respect to the governance of financial markets. As with the practitioners-guides to 'the law on derivatives', contract law tends to emerge from this debate as a mechanism for managing legal and market risk—albeit in standardised form.[32] Little attention is being paid to how these financial contracts may actually extend, innovate, or disrupt established principles of contract law, or to how contract law may be implicated in the socially-harmful effects of derivatives trading.

I now turn to consider the relevance of contractual innovation in the trading of commodity derivatives. I confine my analysis to principles of contract law from common law jurisdictions, as it is the common law jurisdictions of England and the State of New York that underpin the transnational contract documentation of ISDA.

3. Commodity derivatives and innovative contract law

New types of derivatives linked to commodity prices, such as index funds and commodity ETFs, cater to investors seeking to profit from price changes in underlying markets. These instruments are typically retailed by large banks, such as Barclays and JP Morgan, or 'boutique investment management

[29] Gabriel Rauterberg and Andrew Verstein, 'Assessing Transnational Private Regulation of the OTC Derivatives Market: ISDA, the BBA, and the Future of Financial Reform' (2013) 54(1) *Virginia Journal of International Law* 9.

[30] John Biggins, '"Targeted Touchdown" and "Partial Liftoff": Post-Crisis Dispute Resolution in the OTC Derivatives Markets and the Challenge for ISDA' (2012) 13(2) *German Law Journal* 1297.

[31] *Ibid*; Joanne, P Braithwaite, 'Standard Form Contracts as Transnational Law: Evidence from the Derivatives Markets' (2012) 75(5) *The Modern Law Review* 779.

[32] Alistair Hudson, *The Law on Derivatives* (Sweet&Maxwell, 2012); Schuyler K Henderson, *Henderson on Derivatives* (Butterworths, 2nd edn, 2010).

firms', such as Invesco PowerShares.[33] ETFs are traded on securities exchanges and are backed by physical commodities or long futures positions held in a trust.[34] Commodity index funds are funds that enter into swap contracts that track published commodity indexes such as the S&P Goldman Sachs Commodity Index or the Dow Jones AIG Commodity Index.[35] The vast majority of commodity index trading by banks and funds is conducted off-exchange using OTC derivative contracts. Significantly, however, many institutions engaging in index trading provide investors with 'exposure' to commodities by buying and selling exchange-traded futures contracts to replicate the performance of a basket of commodities including fuels, metals, and agricultural commodities.[36] Financial investment in commodities often entails the use of combinations of OTC derivatives and exchange-traded futures to create exposure to underlying commodity prices.

As the weighty tomes on how to manage risk associated with derivatives and the prevalence of ISDA's standardised derivatives documentation would testify, contract law is integral to the operation of derivatives markets. That being the case, there remains substantial ambiguity as to how to classify derivatives contracts. Derivatives are commonly defined as 'contractual agreements that obligate parties to exchange assets or cash flows'.[37] However, as Hudson, a leading scholar on the law on derivatives notes there are six possible ways of interpreting derivatives contracts, namely, as financial forwards, as executory contracts, as mutual debts, as repayments, as condition precedents, and as disjointed options.[38] Davrados has also pointed to the tendency to ignore the matter of the precise legal characterisation of derivatives, observing that the issue is frequently dismissed because 'it is seemingly obvious that these financial instruments fall within the category of peculiar (sui generis) financial trade contracts, without the need for any further qualification whatsoever'.[39]

---

33 Shelia Olson, Investopedia, 'Top 3 Commodities ETFs for 2018' (2018), online: <www.investopedia.com/investing/commodities-etfs/>.

34 Long positions are positions taken in expectation that the value of the commodity rises. Commodity Futures Trading Commission, 'Staff Report on Commodity Swap Dealers & Index Traders with Commission Recommendations' (2008) online: <http://www.cftc.gov/idc/groups/public/@newsroom/documents/file/cftcstaffreportonswapdealers09.pdf> 11–13.

35 *Ibid*, 13.

36 The main futures markets for agricultural commodities are located in the US. The Chicago Mercantile Exchange (CME) is the leading exchange for several commodities. Exchanges for agricultural commodities have traditionally been less active in the EU, as the Common Agricultural Policy functioned to offer European farmers guaranteed prices, but this has changed with reforms to the CAP, sparking a new wave of activity in European futures markets. European Commission, *Agricultural Commodity Derivative Markets: The Way Ahead* (2009) European Commission Staff Working Document, COM(2009)591, online: <http://ec.europa.eu/economy_finance/publications/pages/publication16071_en.pdf> 5.

37 Alan N Rechtschaffen, *Capital Markets, Derivatives and the Law: Evolution after Crisis* (Oxford University Press, 2nd edn 2014) 50.

38 Alastair Hudson, *The Law on Financial Derivatives* (Sweet & Maxwell, 2nd edn 1998) 62–75.

39 Nikolaos Davrados, 'OTC Derivatives and the Conflict of Laws' (2012) 65(1) *Revue Hellénique de Droit International* 181, 190.

While these critiques clearly apply to more complex types of derivatives, one might think that the classification of the humble 'futures contracts' might be more straightforward. In reality, probing into the mechanisms of contemporary trading on futures exchanges exposes some unusual characteristics of these contracts. One such characteristic is that exchange-traded futures contracts are highly standardised, and the quantities of commodities to be bought and sold, contract length, and delivery dates are already predetermined. Often the only variable to be agreed on by the parties is the price. Furthermore, futures contracts are subject to a distinctive regime of time-allotted trading with contracts typically being divided into several (usually four or more) expiry dates throughout the year. Each of the futures contracts is active (can be traded) for a specific amount of time. The contract then expires, and cannot be traded any more.[40] The high levels of standardisation and time-allotted trading featured in futures trading make this practice distinct from other forms of contractual negotiation. Perhaps most significantly, however, in spite of the highly prescriptive terms of the contracts, the vast majority of futures contracts do not result in the delivery of tangible commodities.[41] This is a long-standing feature of futures trading. It was reported in 1971, for example, that approximately 99 percent of wheat futures traded in the Chicago Board of Trade were liquidated before making delivery.[42]

The mechanisms of futures trading highlight the unconventional relationship between derivatives and norms of ordinary contract law. As Johnson and Hazen, two legal scholars writing on derivatives regulation, have put it futures trading is 'one of humanity's 'more impenetrable' concepts in that it 'involves selling what one does not own and, as a rule, buying what one does not want. It is shrouded in terminology that conceals its meaning'.[43] To strike such a bargain would appear to flout some of the well-established principles of contract law. Making an agreement for the purpose of selling what you do not own has all the hallmarks of misrepresentation: you are making a false statement of fact and inducing your contractual partner to enter into a contract based on the false representation that you have a quantity of grain, or currency, or shares to sell, when in fact you do not.[44] Similarly, committing to buy something you do not intend to take possession of suggests an intention to breach the agreement from the very beginning. Since when was offering to buy a bushel of wheat and then failing to pay for it, or offering to sell a bushel

---

[40] Adam Milton, The Balance, 'Guide to Futures Market Expiration Dates' (2018), online: <www.thebalance.com/guide-to-futures-market-expiration-dates-1031175>.

[41] Andrew Hecht, The Balance, 'Basis Risk: The Spread Between Futures and Physical Prices' (2018), online: <www.thebalance.com/futures-prices-versus-physical-prices-808962>.

[42] *Cargill, Inc v Hardin* , 452 F 2d 1154, 1157 (US Court of Appeal, 8th Cir, 7 December 1971).

[43] Philip McBride Johnson and Thomas Lee Hazen, *Derivatives Regulation* (Aspen Publishers, 2004) 1397.

[44] Smith describing the conditions for misrepresentation in contract law. Patrick Selim Atiyah and Stephen A Smith, *Atiyah's Introduction to the Law of Contract* (Oxford University Press, 6th edn 2006) 254.

of corn, and then failing to deliver it, no longer considered a breach of contract?

A possible reply to this argument is that it is predicated on the flawed premise that futures contracts are like contracts for the sale of goods. In fact, as Davrados points out, a derivative cannot be safely labelled a sales contract because the traditional concept of a sale is understood as the transfer of an already existing object or right under the law.[45] In the UK, a sales contract assumes that a trader has rights in the goods to be transferred.[46] Similarly, in the US, a 'sale' consists in the passing of title from the seller to the buyer for a price.[47] The peculiarity of a derivatives contract, Davrados underlines, 'stems from the fact that the object of the contract (the financial position) is not pre-existent, but is created from the contract itself.[48] Indeed, futures contracts are defined and regulated as a distinct type of contract under both the *Financial Services and Markets Act 2000* in the UK, and the *Commodities Exchange Act* in the US.[49] Nevertheless, even if we accept they are a new category of contracts to which ordinary principles relating to misrepresentation and breach do not apply, many types of futures and derivatives still fall foul of other fundamental requirements of contract law relating to certainty and completeness.

As Christopher Chen exposes in his analysis of several US and UK cases, it is not easy to separate commercial sales from commodity futures contracts used for investment purposes.[50] As it is quite common to see commercial contracts with a delivery date some time in the future, he argues, the distinction between regulated futures contracts and unregulated commercial contracts is precarious.[51] Chen notes that some commentators have suggested that intention to deliver the physical commodities should be the factors distinguishing these types of contracts; however, as his analysis reveals, such an approach puts the certainty and specificity of the contract into question. Every commodity futures contract traded on the Chicago Board of Trade calls for delivery, and every trader has the right to hold the contract through expiration and to deliver or receive the cash commodity. This means that it is only possible to know whether delivery has been made in hindsight.[52] Hence, it is left to courts to try to establish the intentions of the parties after the fact. Perversely, in the

---

[45] Davrados (n 39) 89.

[46] See *Consumer Rights Act 2015*, c 2 s 5 'Sales Contracts'.

[47] *Uniform Commercial Code* (2002), art 2 Sales s 2-401.

[48] Davrados (n 39) 89.

[49] In the UK 'futures' is a kind of regulated investment. The term 'futures' is defined as 'rights under a contract for the sale of a commodity or property of any other description under which delivery is to be made at a future date and at a price agreed on when the contract is made'. If it is traded on an exchange, it is assumed to be a futures contract traded for investment purposes. *Financial Services and Markets Act 2000* (Regulatory Activities) Order 2001 SI 2001/544 art 84(1); FSMA 2000 §285 et seq.

[50] Christopher Chao-hung Chen, 'The Boundary of Futures Regulation: From U.K. And U.S. Judgments Regarding Commodity Forward Contracts' (2009) 6(1) *Soochow Law Journal* 165, 170.

[51] *Ibid.*

[52] *Ibid*, 184.

event that it is found that parties did not intend delivery, this would mean that the court would have to make a finding that contradicted the express written terms of the parties' contract. This situation undermines the requirement of certainty that is traditionally understood to be needed in order to effectuate a valid contract. The parties cannot rely on their written agreement to determine whether they have a contract for the sale of goods dated in the future, or a futures contract that does not require the delivery of goods.

Attempting to distinguish between futures contracts and contracts for the sale of goods based on an intention to deliver the physical commodity raises further issues when one considers how common law courts go about determining the intentions of the parties. Under common law approaches to contracts, judges do not insist on a harmony of subjective intentions with respect to the necessary agreement to form contractual relations. Rather, parties are held to have agreed to what a reasonable man would infer from their communications with respect to their contract. This further complicates the situation of parties trading commodity futures contracts. The mismatch between the stated terms of the contract and the true intentions of the parties could perhaps be salvaged by contractual reading focused on the actual subjective intentions of the parties. For example, say both parties knew that neither of them possessed nor intended to sell or take delivery of the grain in question. They could be understood as having agreed on the actual nature of their bargain in spite of the written terms of their contract. Under the common law, by contrast, the parties should be held to what a reasonable man would have understood from their negotiations. 'The words and acts of the parties are themselves the basis of contractual liability' Williston underlines, 'and not merely evidence of a mental attitude required by the law'.[53] This would suggest that in order for a futures transaction in which neither party actually intends to sell or to take delivery of the grain to be a valid contract, the parties should have communicated to one another that their real intentions did not correspond to the written terms of the contract that they agreed upon together. Otherwise, the only contract that exists is a contract for the sale, purchase, and delivery of grain; there is no contract for the exchange of payments based on the market price of grain. To put it another way, if the real intention of the parties to contract to exchange payments based on the market price of grain is nowhere in evidence, then to what terms can the parties be held to have agreed by the hypothetical reasonable man?

Chen offers an alternative criterion to distinguish between futures contracts and sale of goods contracts. In his view, the boundary should depend not on the intentions of the parties, but on 'whether a trading scheme offers a factual facility to offset contrary trades between two or among multiple parties'.[54] The practice of 'offsetting' is commonplace in exchange-

[53] Samuel Williston, 'Mutual Assent in the Formation of Contracts' (1919) 14(2) *Illinois Law Review* 85, 87.
[54] Chen (n 50) 165.

traded futures markets. In order to offset the position that they hold in a market for a given contract, traders close out their market positions by entering into an equal and opposite position in the market, bringing their net position in the market back to zero (ie, if an investor contracted to sell six October corn contracts, then he must buy six October corn contracts to truly offset the position).[55] Closing out transactions in this way is known as 'liquidating', 'offsetting', or 'reversing' the position. As long as the trader competently liquidates their position, they will not be obligated to deliver the commodity or asset, nor will they be obligated to take delivery.[56] As the transactions go through an intermediary, 'the net position is what's important'.[57] Chen identifies the practice of offsetting as characteristic of futures trading, and posits that the ambiguity between these terminologically identical contracts can be resolved by reference to the existence of 'a factual facility to offset contrary trades'.[58] However, Chen's approach does not adequately attend to the tensions between futures trading and accepted doctrines of contract law. In Chen's formulation, the nature of the contract and the agreement between the parties is made to depend on the existence of a factual facility for offsetting transactions, that is, a factual state that is external to the contract itself. As discussed above, under the common law, parties should be held to what a reasonable man would have understood from their negotiations, with a critical role for the words and acts of the parties. Making the rights and obligations of the contract hinge on the existence of a criterion external to the contract at least raises the question as to whether the contract satisfies normative requirements of completeness and certainty.[59]

Settling futures contract with a cash payment (instead of the delivery of the commodity contracted for) has been a prevalent practice since standardised futures contracts began to be bought and sold as articles of value on the Chicago Board of Trade. A practical solution has thus been found to address the mismatch between stated terms of futures contracts and the parties' actual economic position and their true contractual intentions. Nevertheless, the question as to if and how futures contracts, and, now, a host of other derivatives contracts, can be reconciled with traditional understandings of a contract entailing a meeting of minds remains unanswered.[60] Thinking about the derivatives as comprising a vast network of legal obligations the

[55] Investopedia, *Offsetting Contracts, Settlements and Delivery*, online: <www.investopedia.com/exam-guide/series-3/studyguide/chapter4/offsetting-contracts-settlements-delivery.asp>.

[56] *Ibid.*

[57] *Ibid.*

[58] Chen (n 50) 165.

[59] For a discussion of these requirements, see Elizabeth Macdonald and Ruth Atkins, 'Certainty and Completeness' in Elizabeth Macdonald and Ruth Atkins (eds), *Koffman & Macdonald's Law of Contract* (Oxford University Press, 8th edn 2014).

[60] As Choi and Gulati have noted, '[t]he traditional model of contract interpretation focuses on the "meeting of the minds". Stephen J Choi and G Mitu Gulati, 'Contract as Statute' (2006) 104(5) *Michigan Law Review* 1129, 1130.

written terms of which do not accurately reflect the true intentions of the parties highlights the inconsistencies between the operations of this market and traditional doctrines of contract law. In addition, the practice of off-setting has only been made practicable by the development of another innovative contractual technique: novation. Novation is the act of either replacing a party in contract with another or replacing one contractual obligation with another, requiring the consent of all parties involved. As Chen's analysis highlights, it is through a series of novations that futures contracts are able to be offset, thereby avoiding the need for delivery.[61] Futures exchanges, or, in other cases, institutions known as 'clearing houses', interpose themselves between the two parties making the trade effectively becoming the buyer to every seller and the seller to every buyer meaning that the original contracting parties no longer have a direct obligation to one another regarding delivery.[62] Novation, as Braithwaite underlines, is 'notable as the only means in English law whereby the benefits and burdens of a contract may effectively be transferred to a third party'.[63] For centuries, society has placed high value on the liquidity of property, but not, traditionally, on the liquidity of contracts. The doctrine of privity of contract has traditionally held that contractual rights are only binding on and enforceable by the immediate parties to the contract.[64] Once again, the trading of futures contracts is premised on a departure from this norm.

Only by virtue of the innovative contractual techniques of offsetting and novation have financial actors been able to enter into hundreds of different derivative transactions in which they purport to buy and sell what they do not own, simulating the buying and selling of commodities and assets in underlying markets and then exiting the market with an economic benefit (or loss). The fact that the ownership is only simulated, however, does not make the effect that all of this financial market 'positioning' has in the underlying economy any less real. This article has already impressed that commodity derivatives exceed existing categories of contract, require the suspension of ordinary rules concerning misrepresentation, breach, certainty, completeness, and privity of contract, and depend on innovative contractual techniques to be effectuated. The final and perhaps most fundamental point that I wish to raise about these financial contracts is whether they should be conceptualised as contracts at all.

A key distinction between derivatives and securities (eg, stocks and bonds) is that derivatives do not create proprietal interests in the assets from which they derive their value. Yet, through the innovative approach to contract

---

[61] Chen (n 50) 186.

[62] Niti Nandini Chatnani, *Commodity Markets: Operations, Instruments, and Applications* (Tata McGraw-Hill Education, 2010) 93.

[63] Joanne P Braithwaite, 'Private Law and the Public Sector's Central Counterparty Prescription for the Derivatives Markets' (2011) LSE Law, Society and Economy Working Papers 2/2011, online: <http://eprints.lse.ac.uk/38467/1/WPS2011-02_Braithwaite.pdf> 14.

[64] Atiyah and Smith (n 44) 337.

taken in the development of these markets, financial institutions are able to create a 'position' in a market for an underlying commodity in which they have no pre-existing property, rights, or claims, and to benefit from changes in the price of that commodity as if they owned it. Traditionally, regimes of property law have enabled only those persons that bear the responsibilities and obligations of physical ownership to enjoy the economic benefit of a property or commodity. The development of derivatives has enabled innumerable parties to enter into contracts that derive their value from underlying commodities that neither party owns. While it is not the owner of the real commodities that pays the parties to a derivative transaction, derivatives nonetheless enable parties to simulate the ownership of existing commodities and to benefit, or to make a loss, from changes in their price. In the case of commodity index funds, it is possible to simulate ownership of multiple commodities all at the same time. Legally speaking, definitions of property ownership demand a number of features such as exclusive rights of possession, burdens of ownership, and actionability against all the world, as opposed to against an identifiable contractual party, that derivatives, at least on the face of it, would not appear to meet.[65] This article will not seek to substantiate a claim that derivatives are a new form of property. However, I do want to suggest that derivatives blur the lines between traditional conceptions of contract and property.

So why does this matter with respect to the debate about food commodity speculation? It matters because the ability of financial investors to speculate on the future direction of food prices has depended on their ability to misrepresent their true economic position with respect to underlying agricultural commodities, and to enjoy a productive ambiguity with respect to their contractual intentions with respect to the agricultural commodity. Derivative markets are widely positioned as arenas in which the prices of underling assets and commodities are 'discovered'. This means that the actions of financial traders with respect to commodity derivative contracts are frequently interpreted in the broader economy as containing information about supply and demand for the commodities underpinning the contracts. The written terms of futures contracts enable financial actors to manifest intent to buy and sell quantities of grain and other commodities, and, thereby, to influence *market perceptions* of supply and demand for commodities, which in turn influences market prices—hence how speculative activity in commodity derivative markets influences price directions in physical markets for agricultural commodities.

[65] For a discussion of the distinctions between property and contract and their relevance with respect to financial assets see David Pearce, 'Property and Contract: Where Are We?' in Alastair Hudson (ed), *New Perspectives on Property Law, Obligations and Restitution* (Cavendish Publishing Limited, 2004); Tamar Frankel, 'Securitization: The Conflict Between Personal and Market Law (Contract and Property)' (1999) 18 *Annual Review of Banking Law* 197.

4. Conclusion

Commodity derivatives, as with other financial instruments, have no existence outside of their contractual form. Both exchange-traded futures and the more complex financial derivatives that are traded in contemporary markets are intrinsically dependent on contract law in order to be effective as transactions. Yet, the very nature of these instruments would appear to contradict some of the foundational principles of contract doctrine. This has implications for current debates on the regulation of derivatives, since policymakers appear largely content to introduce procedural mechanisms to make derivatives trading less systemically risky, to give regulators greater powers of scrutiny and oversight, and to try to prevent market actors adopting monopoly-like positions in commodity derivative markets in order to stop them from 'manipulating' prices. This brief foray into the contractual dimensions of derivatives trading would suggest that there is an urgent need to problematise the kinds of entitlements and powers that parties entering into derivative contracts are wielding in the first place. It may be that it is the nature of these 'contracts', and not the volume in which they are traded, that poses a threat to food prices. I would argue that instead of fixating on position limits, ensuring the food security of future generations might require contesting some of the extensive liberties that the financial services industry has been taking with respect to contract law.

Disclosure statement

No potential conflict of interest was reported by the author.

The rise of new rights for peasants. From reliance on NGO intermediaries to direct representation

Priscilla Claeys

ABSTRACT

The UN Declaration on the Rights of Peasants and other people working in rural areas, adopted by the UN General Assembly in December 2018, recognises new human rights to peasants and other people working in rural areas. The recognition of these rights (such as the right to land, seeds or biodiversity) in international law responds to a normative gap identified by the affected themselves and contributes to the project of 'decolonising' human rights. This international law-making process constitutes an important innovation in that it was requested by and developed with the active involvement of La Via Campesina activists—and other transnational movements representing other categories of rural food producers—who have positioned themselves as 'law makers'. In this paper, I argue that a commitment to 'human rights from below' must account for and support the direct engagement, in international law-making, of transnational social movements representing the affected and speaking on their own behalf.

Peasants, agricultural workers, landless, fisherfolk, shepherds, pastoralists and Indigenous Peoples have worked the land and fed humanity for millennia. Yet, according to the United Nations (UN), people living and working in rural areas account for 70% of the world's poor, with women and girls representing 60% of those affected by chronic hunger and malnutrition.[1] More than ever, rural communities are threatened by a predatory food and economic system. They see their rights violated and have no access to justice.

United to defend food sovereignty, the peasant organisations gathered in the transnational agrarian movement La Via Campesina (LVC) turned to the UN in the late 2000s to demand a new international legal instrument recognising their rights.[2] The UN Human Rights Council (HRC) responded to this call in 2012 with the creation of an open-ended[3] intergovernmental

---

[1] FAO, IFAD, & WFP, 'State of Food Insecurity in the World. In Brief' (2015).

[2] Priscilla Claeys, 'The Creation of New Rights by the Food Sovereignty Movement: The Challenge of Institutionalizing Subversion' (2012) 46(5) *Sociology* 844.

working group (OEIWG) tasked with negotiating a UN Declaration on the Rights of Peasants and others working in rural areas (hereafter UNDROP). Six years later, in September 2018, the HRC adopted the UNDROP by a majority.[4] The global food crisis of 2007–2008 prompted the HRC to take action. It had brought attention to the challenges facing the rural world and provided an opportunity for peasant movements to highlight the contributions of small-scale farmers to global food security and adaptation to climate change.[5]

The UNDROP, the negotiation of which I have studied and supported in various capacities,[6] recognises new human rights to peasants and other people working in rural areas, extending the protection of human rights to a new social group.[7] At the heart of the draft Declaration are the right to land and other natural resources, the right to seeds, the right to biodiversity, the right to a decent income and livelihood as well as the means of production, and the right to food sovereignty. The recognition of these rights in international law contributes to the project of 'decolonising' human rights[8] by responding to a normative gap identified by the affected themselves and recognising new rights that are framed as collective human rights.

The process of elaboration of this new international legal instrument constitutes an important innovation in that it was initiated, framed and requested by the transnational social movement LVC. LVC represents 200 million peasant farmers across 73 countries (through more than 164 organisations) and is well known for its 20 years of struggles against trade liberalisation and the World Trade Organization (WTO), Genetically Modified Organisms (GMOs) and land grabbing. The draft Declaration which has served as a basis for discussion at the HRC was developed by LVC activists, who have positioned themselves as

---

[3] This means that all UN Member and Observer States, intergovernmental organisations and non-governmental organisations with ECOSOC consultative status may attend public meetings of the working group.

[4] With 3 votes against (Australia, Hungary and the United Kingdom), 11 abstentions (including Germany, Brazil and Spain) and 33 votes in favour (including Switzerland, Middle-East and North African, Latin American and African States).

[5] La Via Campesina, *Small Scale Sustainable Farmers Are Cooling Down The Earth* (2009), online: <https://viacampesina.org/en/la-via-campesina-position-paper-small-scale-sustenable-farmers-are-cooling-down-the-earth/>.

[6] Notably as scholar-activist and Senior Research Fellow (2016-) at the Centre for Agroecology, Water and Resilience at Coventry University (UK), invited expert to the fourth session (2017) of the Open-Ended Intergovernmental Working Group on the Rights of Peasants, consultant for the UN Office of the High Commissioner for Human Rights in charge of writing a study on the Normative sources and rationale underlying the draft declaration on the rights of peasants and other people working in rural areas (A/HRC/WG.15/4/3, published on 4 May 2017), staff (3-month) at the UN Office of the High Commissioner for Human Rights in charge of organising the third session (2016) of the Open-Ended Intergovernmental Working Group on the Rights of Peasants, PhD student and Senior Advisor to the UN Special Rapporteur on the right to food (2008–2014) and member of Fian International (since 2003).

[7] Clifford Bob, *The International Struggle for New Human Rights* (University of Pennsylvania Press, 2010).

[8] José-Manuel Barreto, 'Decolonial Strategies and Dialogue in the Human Rights Field: A Manifesto' (2012) 3(1) *Transnational Legal Theory* 1.

'law makers'.[9] International law-making processes increasingly involve consulting a diversity of non-state actors, from transnational corporations to non-governmental organisations (NGOs).[10] However, the direct involvement of social movements in international law-making is rare[11] and the emblematic case of the UN Declaration on the Rights of Indigenous Peoples remains a unique example of rights-holders participating significantly in the design and negotiation of an international legal instrument. It is certainly unusual practice at the HRC where standard-setting remains dominated by states.[12] It is also ill-studied and, as I show in this paper, unaccounted for in the frameworks that scholars have developed to analyse the participation of the 'affected'[13] in human rights development, elaboration and interpretation.

This paper is structured as follows. In the first section, I set the stage by providing a short summary of how peasant movements framed rights-based claims in the late 1990s, in response to the introduction of neoliberal policies in food and agriculture. This led to the drafting of a number of Charters or Declarations in which they compiled their demands. In the second section, I explore how LVC activists succeeded in putting their claims on the international agenda in the late 2000s. To this end, in the third section, I discuss the framework designed by Clifford Bob to study the emergence of new human rights, in dialogue with the framework elaborated by Koen De Feyter and Gaby Oré Aguilar to study the local relevance of human rights. Although these frameworks have distinct purposes, they are similar in their assumption that local disempowered 'communities' or groups depend on local, national and international NGOs—described as intermediaries or gatekeepers—to attract international attention to their claims. In contrast, I show in the fourth section that LVC played a central role in not only framing their rights-based claims but establishing the strategic alliances it required with states (as well as with small NGOs and human rights experts) to get the attention of the HRC. LVC did not entirely bypass gatekeepers but worked with them on its own terms. It also demonstrated its ability to engage directly

---

9 Balakrishnan Rajagopal, *International Law from Below: Development, Social Movements, and Third World Resistance* (Cambridge University Press, 2003).

10 Jean d'Aspremont (ed), *Participants in the International Legal System: Multiple Perspectives on Non-State Actors in International Law* (Routledge, 2011); Math Noortmann & Cedric Ryngaert, *Non-state Actor Dynamics in International Law: From Law-takers to Law-makers* (Ashgate Publishing, Ltd, 2010).

11 Tsutsui et al. convincingly argue that tensions between civil society and state actors have driven much of the development of human rights. They highlight how diverse CSOs have had a direct impact on the drafting or elaboration of key human rights instruments such as CERD, CEDAW or the Optional Protocol to the ICESCR. The authors, however, do not operate a strict distinction between social movements and NGOs. See Kiyoteru Tsutsui, Claire Whitlinger, and Alwyn Lim, 'International Human Rights Law and Social Movements: States' Resistance and Civil Society's Insistence' (2012) 8 (1) *Annual Review of Law and Social Science* 367.

12 The HRC however offers a number of avenues for civil society participation. See Lucia Nader, 'The role of NGOs in the UN Human Rights Council' (2007) 4(7) *Sur. Revista Internacional de Direitos Humanos* 6.

13 Josh Brem-Wilson, 'La Vía Campesina and the UN Committee on World Food Security: Affected Publics and Institutional Dynamics in the Nascent Transnational Public Sphere' (2016) *Review of International Studies* 302.

with states in the political and technical process of negotiating new global norms. In the conclusion, I argue that a commitment to human rights 'from below'[14] must account for and support the direct engagement, in international law-making, of transnational social movements representing the affected and speaking on their own behalf.

The creation of new human rights from below

The new rights contained in the UNDROP find their roots in local peasant struggles. Peasants have framed these rights in response to the new threats they experienced in the last decades, including agricultural trade liberalisation, transnational corporate power, the commoditisation and privatisation of land and natural resources and the development of intellectual property rights on seeds.

The initiative to draft a declaration was first developed by a national peasant union in Indonesia, Serikat Petani Indonesia (SPI), an LVC member organisation.[15] In the late 1990s, as part of a participatory research action project conducted by the International Institute for Environment and Development (IIED),[16] a Peasant Rights' Charter was elaborated through village workshops. Initially conceived of as a tool to oppose the 'green revolution', the Charter recognised 61 rights to 'peasants and their families, personally or as group' in the following eight areas: livelihood, resource control (land, biological diversity), production (including technology choices), consumption (including what to produce), marketing (market access, quality protection and property rights), political and social arenas, reproduction (including both human reproduction and biodiversity) and freedom of expression (language, culture, religion and arts). The 1999 Charter contained a short definition of peasants as rights-holders and envisioned that these rights would be both achieved by peasants themselves and implemented by the state and/or national/international organisations.[17]

In the early 2000s, the farmer organisation SPI initiated discussions about peasants' rights within the South East Asian and East Asian region. At a regional conference in 2002, members of LVC in the region adopted a 'Declaration about the protection of the peasant right', which included a preamble[18] and 10 main articles: 1) right to life and proper living standard, 2)

[14] Balakrishnan Rajagopal, *International Law from Below: Development, Social Movements, and Third World Resistance* (Cambridge University Press, 2003).

[15] Heri Purwanto, 'Local To Global; How Serikat Petani Indonesia Has Accelerated The Movement For Agrarian Reform', in *La Via Campesina's Open Book: Celebrating 20 Years of Struggle and Hope* (Vía Campesina, 2013).

[16] Mansour Fakih, Toto Rahardjo, & Michel Pimbert, *Community Integrated Pest Management in Indonesia. Institutionalising Participation and People Centred Approaches* (IIED, 2003).

[17] *Ibid*, annex 5, 153.

[18] The 2002 Declaration recognised 76 different rights to 'peasant men and women and their family', no longer alluding to the role of states in implementing these rights nor offering a definition of peasants as

right to agrarian resources 3) right to seeds, 4) right to capital and means of agricultural production, 5) right to access to information and agricultural technology, 6) right to freedom in determining price and market for agricultural production, 7) right to protection of agricultural values, 8) right to biological diversity, 9) right to environmental preservation, and 10) right to freedom of association.

In 2008, LVC adopted a revised version of this Declaration, after consulting with other regions.[19] The same year, the movement launched a Global Campaign for a Declaration of Peasant Rights at LVC's fifth international conference in Maputo,[20] and organised an international conference on the Rights of Peasants in Jakarta. The 2008 Declaration entitled 'Declaration of Rights of Peasants—Women and Men', included a definition of peasants as rights-holders in article 1, and recognised 84 rights grouped in 12 articles.[21] The 2008 Declaration[22] identified the neoliberal policies of the International Monetary Fund (IMF) and the WTO, structural adjustment programmes, free trade agreements and transnational corporations as responsible for the increase in violations of peasants' rights and blamed the 'capitalist logic of accumulation' for dismantling peasant agriculture. It contained three references to food sovereignty[23] and 7 references[24] to the collective nature of the rights of peasants. The text recognises these rights to peasants 'individually or collectively'.[25] On 6 April 2009, Henry Saragih from Indonesia, then

rights-holders. This document is on file with the author. For more information, see Priscilla Claeys, *Human Rights and the Food Sovereignty Movement: Reclaiming Control* (Routledge, 2015).

[19] La Via Campesina, *Declaration of Rights of Peasants – Women and Men* (2009), online: <https://viacampesina.net/downloads/PDF/EN-3.pdf>.

[20] La Via Campesina, 'Declaration of Maputo (Declaration of the 5th International Conference of Via Campesina, Maputo, Mozambique)' (2008), online: <https://viacampesina.org/en/declaration-of-maputo-v-international-conference-of-la-via-campesina/>.

[21] These 12 articles were: 2) rights of peasants, 'as a collective or as individuals', to all human rights and fundamental freedoms recognised in the Universal Declaration of Human Rights and IHRL, including non-discrimination and participation in decision-making, 3) right to life and adequate standard of living, 4) right to land and territory, 5) right to seeds and traditional agricultural knowledge and practice, 6) right to means of agricultural production, 7) right to information and agricultural technology, 8) right to determine price and market for agricultural production, 9) right to protection of agricultural values, 10) right to biological diversity, 11) right to preserve the environment, 12) freedom of association, opinion and expression, and 13) right to access to justice.

[22] The 2009 Declaration included a reference to the need to include state obligations and monitoring mechanisms in the text and eventually turn the Declaration into a legally-binding Convention.

[23] The first reference to food sovereignty was contained in in article iv.11, which read: Peasants (women and men) have the right to agricultural land that can be irrigated to ensure food sovereignty for growing population; the second reference was contained in article v.9, which read: 'Peasants have the right to food sovereignty'; and the third reference was contained in article viii.9, which read: 'Peasants (women and men) have the right to develop community-based commercialization systems in order to guarantee food sovereignty'.

[24] An additional reference to collective rights was included in article 9, which recognised the 'right of peasants to be respected for their spirituality', 'as individuals and as peoples'.

[25] This formulation is the most commonly used in the text and is found in articles v.6, viii.5, x.2, x.5 and xii.3. In addition, alternative formulations are used such as 'collectively or individually' in article iv.1 and 'as a collective or as individuals' in article ii.1.

Secretary General of LVC, presented the Declaration on the Rights of Peasants to the UN General Assembly as a response to the global food crisis.[26]

Getting peasants' rights on the international agenda

In 2012, seising the 'legal opportunity'[27] that the global food crisis had opened up, LVC succeeded in getting the issue of the rights of peasants on the HRC agenda. This was made possible through a number of strategic alliances that LVC had established in the previous decade with right to food experts—including the UN Special Rapporteur on the right to food, Olivier De Schutter,[28] his predecessor Jean Ziegler, then sitting on the Advisory Committee to the HRC,[29] and Ziegler's former Special Advisor, Christophe Golay, an academic based at the Geneva Academy of International Humanitarian Law and Human Rights—as well as small international NGOs—mainly the human rights organisation FIAN International[30] and the small progressive think-thank Centre Europe-Tiers Monde—CETIM.[31] With their support,

[26] Henry Saragih, 'Via Campesina statement at the UN General Assembly on The Global Food Crisis and the Right to Food' (United Nations General Assembly, New York, 6 April 2009), online: <https://viacampesina.org/en/via-campesina-statement-at-the-un-general-assembly-on-the-global-food-crisis-and-the-right-to-food>.

[27] The concept of legal opportunity comes from social movements' studies and builds on Tarrow's 'political opportunity structures'. See Sidney Tarrow, *Power in Movement: Social Movements and Contentious Politics* (Cambridge University Press, 1998). It provides a better understanding of the role of legal strategies in protest, notably because movements engaged in legal mobilisation are constrained in their interpretive schema as they must articulate their claims within preestablished legal categories. On this point, see Brian Doherty and Graeme Hayes, 'Having Your Day in Court: Judicial Opportunity and Tactical Choice in Anti-GMO Campaigns in France and the United Kingdom' (2014) 47 (1) *Comparative Political Studies* 3.

[28] On 22 May 2008, the UN Special Rapporteur on the right to food called for a special session of the HRC to discuss 'the negative impacts on the realization of the right to food of the worsening of the world food crisis, caused inter alia by soaring food prices'. This led to the adoption of Resolution 10/12 of the HRC, in the framework of which the Advisory Committee to the HRC contributed two studies, one on the right to food and one on the advancement of the rights of peasants (see below).

[29] The Advisory Committee to the HRC played a central role in initiating a formal process for discussing the rights of peasants within the HRC, using the right to food as a strategic entry point for discussing the discriminations faced by small-holder farmers. The Advisory Committee contributed two studies that provided background to the future work of the OEIWG tasked with negotiating a UN Declaration on the Rights of Peasants: a 2011 study on discrimination in the context of the right to food (A/HRC/16/40) which identified people working in rural areas among the people most vulnerable to hunger and malnutrition, and suffering from multiple forms of discrimination; a 2012 study on the advancement of the rights of peasants and other people working in rural areas (A/HRC/19/75) which recommended the HRC create a new special procedure (e.g a UN Special Rapporteur) to improve the protection of the rights of peasants and develop a new international human rights instrument on the rights of peasants and other people working in rural areas. The 2012 study already contained the La Via Campesina Declaration as an annex, which was a strategic move to give the Declaration visibility and legitimacy.

[30] FIAN and La Via Campesina jointly launched a Global Campaign for Agrarian Reform in 1999. Between 2004 and 2006, and in the framework of that campaign, FIAN helped LVC document cases of human rights abuses, mostly related to access to land. This led to the joint publications of three reports on the violations of peasants' human rights, in 2004, 2005 and 2006, which FIAN brought to the attention of the UN Commission on Human Rights (now the Council).

[31] The Geneva-based CETIM has a history of logistically supporting La Via Campesina's International Working Committee on Human Rights. In the early 2000s, CETIM helped organise the meetings of

LVC approached the Permanent Representation of Bolivia to the HRC and convinced the then Ambassador Angelica Navarro of the importance and legitimacy of their claims. Bolivia agreed to sponsor resolution 21/19 which, on the 11th October 2012, established the open-ended intergovernmental working group (OEIGWG) tasked with 'negotiating, finalising and submitting to the Human Rights Council a draft United Nations declaration on the rights of peasants and other people working in rural areas'.[32]

Analysing human rights from below

The rise of new rights is complex, contingent and contentious. In a co-edited volume called *The International Struggle for New Human Rights*, Clifford Bob analyses a number of efforts by several groups in the last decades to demand the recognition of new rights at the international level, with a view to understand the reasons for success or failure and draw lessons learned.[33] The book covers a large variety of groups, including children born of wartime rape, dalits, LGBTIQ people, people with HIV/AIDS, people with disabilities, and women and girls affected by genital mutilation. The book argues that, although some groups succeed, a great number of groups actually fail in even getting the international human rights movement to endorse their claims as human rights issues (let alone UN bodies). The main reason for this is that the big human rights organisations that dominate the human rights movement (such as Amnesty International and Human Rights Watch) operate as 'gatekeepers', deciding what counts as legitimate human rights claims.[34] Among the suggested reasons that may lead these organisations to turn down some claims are concerns associated with moving beyond the organisation's areas of expertise or explicit mandate, with potential negative impacts in terms of reputation, funding or membership.[35] This helps explain why these big human rights organisations have focused almost exclusively on civil and political rights, at the expense of economic, social and cultural rights (the category in which most of the new rights of peasants would fall).[36] It should be added that human rights advocates have, in

LVC's Working Committee in parallel with the relevant sessions of the UN Human Rights Commission. As early as 2001, in a joint statement with CETIM, La Via Campesina had requested that the then UN Human Rights Commission 'formulate and enact' a Declaration on the Rights of Peasants.

[32] For a detailed historical analysis of the interactions of these various actors with various bodies of the HRC, including the Advisory Committee, see Arne Vandenbogaerde, 'Localizing the Human Rights Council: A case study of the Declaration on the Rights of Peasants' (2017) 16(2) *Journal of Human Rights* 220.

[33] Clifford Bob, *The International Struggle for New Human Rights* (University of Pennsylvania Press, 2010).

[34] *Ibid*, 3, 8.

[35] Daniel Chong, 'Economic Rights and Extreme Poverty: Moving toward Subsistence', in Clifford Bob (ed), *The International Struggle for New Human Rights* (University of Pennsylvania Press, 2010) 116.

[36] Daniel Chong, 'Economic Rights and Extreme Poverty: Moving toward Subsistence', in Clifford Bob (ed), *The International Struggle for New Human Rights* (University of Pennsylvania Press, 2010) 108.

addition, expressed fears that the 'proliferation' of new rights might threaten the significance and value of existing human rights.[37]

The book provides a useful 4-step framework to analyse the creation of new human rights by various 'claimants': 1) politicised groups frame long-felt grievances as normative human rights claims; 2) they place these claims on the international agenda by convincing 'gatekeepers' in major human rights organisations to accept them; 3) states and international bodies, under the pressure of gatekeepers and aggrieved groups, accept the new norms; and 4) national institutions implement the norms.[38] I have discussed step 1—human rights framing by food sovereignty activist—in detail in my book *Human Rights and the Food Sovereignty Movement: Reclaiming Control*,[39] which explores how LVC and food sovereignty activists are contributing to the emergence of an alternative conception of human rights, that is less individualistic, anthropocentric, Western and liberal, and more collective, cosmopolitan and multi-cultural.[40] In this paper, I focus on step 2 (when claimants connect to international NGOs), with a view to shed light on some under-explored aspects of Bob's framework.

Bob's framework analyses the emergence of new human rights as determined by a number of hierarchical relations of power between local disempowered 'communities' or groups (who frame human rights claims), local NGOs (to which they need to turn for support), and national and international NGOs (who have the responsibility and networks needed to attract global attention to the human rights issue at stake). Step 2 of this framework looks at how claimants link up with gatekeepers, which are defined as 'entities at the core of the human rights movement, whose support for a claim can boost it substantially'.[41] Gatekeepers typically hold the best staffs and largest budgets. In this framework, a handful of NGOs as well as 'human rights intellectuals' play the key role of 'certifying new rights'.[42] Claimants are dependent on the benevolent intervention of local NGOs, supportive lawyers and international human rights organisations to get their claims on the international agenda.

---

[37] Philip Alston, 'Conjuring up New Human Rights: A Proposal for Quality Control' (1984) 78(3) *The American Journal of International Law* 607.

[38] Clifford Bob, *The International Struggle for New Human Rights* (University of Pennsylvania Press, 2010) 8–12.

[39] Priscilla Claeys, *Human Rights and the Food Sovereignty Movement: Reclaiming Control* (Routledge, 2015).

[40] Boaventura de Sousa Santos, 'Vers une conception multiculturelle des droits de l'homme' (1997) (35) *Droit et Société* 79; Boaventura de Sousa Santos & César A Rodríguez-Garavito, *Law and Globalization from Below: Towards a Cosmopolitan Legality* (Cambridge University Press, 2005); Priscilla Claeys, 'The Creation of New Rights by the Food Sovereignty Movement: The Challenge of Institutionalizing Subversion' (2012) 46(5) *Sociology* 844.

[41] 'Introduction: Fighting for New Rights' in Clifford Bob (ed), *The International Struggle for New Human Rights* (University of Pennsylvania Press, 2008) 6.

[42] *Ibid*, 4.

It is interesting to note that in their Localising Human Rights framework, Koen De Feyter and Gaby Oré Aguilar develop a similar hypothesis. Their research explores how human rights can become relevant to the most excluded individuals and communities (what they call the local relevance of human rights), and how these communities can participate in the development, elaboration and interpretation of human rights.[43] Their methodological framework considers the interactions between local communities on the one hand, and a network of human rights actors on the other. They argue that cooperation between community-based organisations, local human rights NGOs, international NGOs and allies in governmental and intergovernmental institutions is critical to the bottom-up approach to building human rights.[44] Acknowledging that local communities' views and interests can easily be dismissed or distorted in a setup that involves so many intermediaries, they also point to the importance of addressing issues of representation and of trying to ensure that 'the human rights experiences of communities set the agenda'.[45] Their framework builds on the research conducted by anthropologist Sally Engle-Merry on the role of NGO intermediaries located between 'local activism' and transnational human rights. Engle-Merry shows that NGO intermediaries do not only bring resources and networks. They also act as 'knowledge brokers' who 'translate' local community claims into claims that can be received by a broader public (and/or the state).[46]

From reliance on NGO intermediaries to direct representation

The case of the UNDROP presents a radically distinct trajectory from the one depicted in the frameworks discussed above. The Declaration was developed, pushed, and directly brought to the international level by the transnational agrarian movement LVC. While Engle Merry and other authors have documented how universal norms are appropriated and transformed in local struggles (what Engle Merry has called 'vernacularization'),[47] here we see human rights in their pre-codified form undertaking an institutional, bottom-up trajectory, from grassroots claims to newly recognised global norms.[48] LVC approached the HRC with an agenda it had internally and

[43] Koen De Feyter, Stephan Parmentier, Christiane Timmerman, & George Ulrich, *The Local Relevance of Human Rights* (Cambridge University Press, 2011).
[44] Koen De Feyter, Stephan Parmentier, Christiane Timmerman, & George Ulrich, *The Local Relevance of Human Rights* (Cambridge University Press, 2011) 115.
[45] 'Localising Human Rights' in Wolfgang Benedek, Koen De Feyter & Fabrizio Marrella (ed), *Economic Globalisation and Human Rights* (Cambridge University Press, 2007) 83.
[46] Sally Engle Merry, 'Transnational Human Rights and Local Activism: Mapping the Middle' (2006) 108(1) *American Anthropologist* 38.
[47] Peggy Levitt and Sally Engle Merry, 'Vernacularization on the Ground: Local Uses of Global Women's Rights in Peru, China, India and the United States' (2009) 9 (4) *Global Networks* 441.
[48] I have highlighted this in Priscilla Claeys, 'The Creation of New Rights by the Food Sovereignty Movement: The Challenge of Institutionalizing Subversion' (2012) 46(5) *Sociology* 844.

autonomously elaborated, and its own draft Declaration which reflected peasant worldviews and conceptions of human rights. The Advisory Committee to the HRC and a core group of states (Bolivia, Ecuador, Cuba and South Africa) considered peasant claims as legitimate[49] because they were brought by a strong and well recognised transnational social movement uniting small-scale farmers and peasant organisations speaking in their own name. The process gained further traction when several other rural constituencies joined in, partly as a result of LVC's efforts to reach out to other groups.[50] Of particular relevance were pastoralists (represented by the World Alliance for Mobile Indigenous Peoples (WAMIP)), fishers (World Forum of Fisher Peoples (WFFP)), Indigenous Peoples (International Indian Treaty Council (IITC)), agricultural workers (International Union of Food Workers (IUF)), and other peasant movements not affiliated with LVC (such as the *Fédération Internationale des Mouvements d'Adultes Ruraux Catholiques* (FIMARC) or the regional peasant network from Africa called the *Réseau des organisations paysannes et de producteurs de l'Afrique de l'Ouest* (ROPPA)). These other rural constituencies have brought in their specific concerns, needs and interests, and pointed to gaps in the original LVC text.

More needs to be said, however, about the role of NGOs. Indeed, LVC would likely not have succeeded in creating or seising this legal opportunity without the support of carefully selected NGOs and experts.[51] The emergence, in the late 1990s, of agrarian movements speaking on their own behalf in global governance arenas has been well documented. Their direct representation has challenged the traditional domination of NGOs in such spaces.[52] The 2009 reform of the UN Committee on World Food Security (CFS), for example, recognises an active role for civil society organisations as participants in food security debates, and its Civil Society Mechanism (which facilitates and coordinates civil society engagement in the CFS) prioritises social movements over NGOs.[53]

Such developments, however, are barely palpable at the HRC, where civil society involvement follows strict rules that considerably limit the direct representation of social movements. These rules, together with the technical nature of human rights debates, make strategic alliances with selected

49 Human Rights Council, 'Final study of the Human Rights Council Advisory Committee on the Advancement of the Rights of Peasants and Other People Working in Rural Areas (A/HR/19/75)' (2012).

50 It is worth noting here that there is no self-governed mechanism for organising and coordinating civil society participation at the UN Human Rights Council, contrary to what now exists at the UN Committee on World Food Security with the Civil Society Mechanism (CSM).

51 Christophe Golay, 'Legal Reflections on the Rights of Peasants and Other People Working in Rural Areas. Briefing paper prepared for the first session of the working group on the rights of peasants and other people working in rural areas, Geneva, 15–19 July 2013' (2013).

52 Nora McKeon, *The United Nations and Civil Society. Legitimating Global Governance-Whose Voice?* (Zed Books with the United Nations Research Institute for Social Development (UNRISD), 2009).

53 Jessica Duncan, *Global Food Security Governance: Civil Society Engagement in the Reformed Committee on World Food Security* (Routledge, 2015).

NGOs absolutely necessary for social movements wanting to engage with the HRC. In order to participate in HRC discussions, civil society organisations must obtain general or special consultative status.[54] The process takes about two years and is ill-conceived for social movements. Organisations have to register their profile, answer a questionnaire about their aims, projects and activities, and describe their structure, membership rules, and sources of income and expenditures. The application is then reviewed by the Committee on Non-Governmental Organizations, which is made of 19 states.[55]

In the absence of consultative status,[56] LVC has, since the beginning of the negotiation process, relied on two NGOs, FIAN and CETIM, to gain access to the HRC. These NGOs have also provided logistical, technical and legal support.[57] It should be noted here that the Bolivian Chair of the OEIWG on the Rights of Peasants has, in respect for the work and commitment of LVC, allowed agrarian activists to speak in their own name (that of their respective member organisations) during plenary discussions, and not as FIAN or CETIM as their badge indicates. Similarly, the official attendance list included in the report of each session of the OEIWG, and which traditionally mentions only organisations with consultative status, was extended (although not systematically) to include 'other non-governmental organizations' such as LVC.[58]

A complex picture emerges from this discussion. On the one hand, the autonomy, legitimacy and direct representation of agrarian movements in global governance have made it possible for grassroots human rights claims to emerge and travel up without the intermediary of NGOs. On the other hand, strategic alliances between transnational movements and NGOs remain important in light of the specific constraints to participating in the HRC. In such a context, one of the main challenges for social movement

---

[54] Consultative status provides NGOs the opportunity to formally participate in UN meetings, including speaking on the record publicly and organising side events on UN grounds.

[55] The Committee, which meets twice a year and analyses about 300 applications per session, has been the target of serious criticism for deferring applications for reasons that are unrelated to the criteria listed above and outlined in UN Resolution 1996/31. Organisations working on sexual orientation and gender identity, reproductive and sexual rights, minority rights and caste have been particularly vocal in denouncing this situation, as they represent the majority of such deferred applications, together with organisations working on forced disappearances and human rights in conflict situations, as well as on business and human rights.

[56] While other networks such as the international federation of rural adult catholic movements FIMARC or the international federation of organic movements IFOAM have been granted consultative status, La Via Campesina has registered its profile as an organisation but not applied.

[57] While I focus here on legal support that was provided directly to LVC, it should be noted that a group of legal experts, myself included, also worked at different times with the Permanent Mission of Bolivia, offering support with identifying agreed language i.e., other relevant international norms that could be used as basis for drafting new versions of the draft Declaration, in an effort to respond to the objections of states. Several of these experts were sympathetic to LVC's demands and ensured that such redrafting efforts would be in line with LVC's vision.

[58] In the reports of the first, fourth and fifth sessions, both organisations with consultative status and other NGOs are listed. In the report of the second and third sessions, only those with consultative status are mentioned.

activists, allied NGOs and human rights experts engaged in what they all see as a shared struggle is to work together in ways that enable social movements representatives to manage and control civil society participation in the process of negotiation. For NGOs and scholar activists, this means extending their support in ways that do not undermine the autonomy and self-organising power of social movements[59], and limiting the 'translation' impacts of their technical and legal support.

Conclusions

Since the creation of the OEIWG, five sessions were held in Geneva to discuss successive versions of the draft Declaration. These sessions were characterised by substantial participation of social movements, mainly peasant organisations, who seised this opportunity to 'build' their own human rights.[60] At these sessions, civil society organisations—LVC, FIMARC, FIAN International, CETIM, but also allies from other rural constituencies such as the pastoralists' network WAMIP, the fishers' network WFFP and the Indigenous Peoples' network IITC—advanced a number of arguments in defence of a new international human rights instrument. They pointed to the evolutionary character of international law, and its need to develop to respond to the challenges of a changing world.

At the first session of the OEIWG, in July 2013, a first reading of the draft Declaration took place. The draft presented by the Chair was the one elaborated by LVC and adopted by the Advisory Committee to the HRC[61] (A/HRC/19/75), with three minor changes to the 'original' Declaration. At the second session, in 2015, the Chair released a radically revised draft Declaration, with the dual objective of reinforcing its coherence with existing human rights standards and responding to the objections voiced by states.[62] At the third session, in 2016, the 2015 draft Declaration was made available in all six UN languages,[63] which enabled more substantive discussions. At the fourth session, in 2017, the Chair presented a new and shorter draft,[64] in a further effort to gather more support from HRC member states.

---

[59] This is less of a challenge at the CFS where the CSM mechanism ensures the balanced participation of distinct constituencies and assigns only a limited role to NGOs (although they do play facilitation roles).

[60] Priscilla Claeys, 'Food Sovereignty and the Recognition of New Rights for Peasants at the UN: A Critical Overview of La Via Campesina's Rights Claims over the Last 20 Years' (2015) 12(4) *Globalizations* 452.

[61] This draft was presented in the annex to the 2012 Final study of the HRC Advisory Committee on the advancement of the rights of peasants and other people working in rural areas.

[62] Christophe Golay, the Geneva Academy of International Humanitarian Law and Human Rights, *Negotiation of a United Nations Declaration on the Rights of Peasants and Other People Working in Rural Areas* (2015), Acadamy In-Brief No. 5.

[63] Human Rights Council, 'Draft Declaration on the Rights of Peasants and Other People Working in Rural Areas Presented by the Chair-rapporteur of the Working Group' (2016) A/HRC/WG.15/3/2.

[64] Human Rights Council, 'Draft Declaration on the Rights of Peasants and Other People Working in Rural Areas Presented by the Chair-rapporteur of the Working Group' (2017) A/HRC/WG.15/4/2.

In April 2018, the fifth and last session enabled discussions over yet another revised draft.[65] Over the summer of 2018, Bolivia conducted further bilateral and informal negotiations with a view to secure the support votes of a few additional states by making the latest necessary adjustments in the text, while remaining in constant dialogue with LVC. The result of these discussions was a considerably amended draft,[66] which Bolivia presented, together with the report of the fifth session, at the 39th session of the HRC on the 21st September 2018. A week later, Bolivia submitted the declaration to a vote and succeeded in gathering a majority of states to support the text. Following the adoption of the UNDROP at the UNHRC, Bolivia proceeded to put the Declaration on the agenda of the 73rd session of the UN General Assembly Committee on Social, Humanitarian & Cultural Issues (Third Committee) in New York.[67] The resolution (A/C.3/73/L.30), dated the 30th October 2018, called for the adoption of the UNDROP and requested the Secretary-General to include the text of the Declaration in the next edition of 'Human Rights: A Compilation of International Instruments'. The resolution was adopted on the 20th November 2018, with 119 yes, 7 no and 49 abstain. 18 countries did not vote. The formal adoption of the UNDROP by the UN General Assembly took place on the 17th December 2018, with 121 yes, 8 no and 54 abstain. Efforts will now focus on its dissemination and implementation.

In this paper, I shed light on some under-explored aspects of the framework developed by Bob for analysing the creation of new rights. With regard to step 2 (connecting to international NGOs), my analysis showed that, in the case of the UNDROP, the claimants were not local communities represented by intermediary local and international NGOs but agrarian activists organised at the transnational agrarian level and speaking on their own behalf. Their legitimacy and autonomy as social movement representatives enabled them to engage directly with states and to put their claims on the international agenda without requiring the certification of big gatekeeping NGOs. The support role played by human rights experts and small NGOs such as FIAN International and CETIM was nevertheless critical—in particular for access to the HRC and legal expertise—but it never threatened the ability of social movements to lead civil society's participation in the process. In light of this, I argue that the frameworks developed to date to analyse the process of the creation of new rights by social groups need to be updated to account for the emergence of transnational social movements

65 Human Rights Council, 'Draft Declaration on the Rights of Peasants and Other People Working in Rural Areas Presented by the Chair-rapporteur of the Working Group' (2018) A/HRC/WG.15/5/2.

66 Human Rights Council, 'Draft Declaration on the Rights of Peasants and Other People Working in Rural Areas Presented by the Chair-rapporteur of the Working Group' (2018) A/HRC/WG.15/5/3.

67 See United Nations, 'Social, Humanitarian & Cultural Issues (Third Committee). Documents Per Agenda Item' http://www.un.org/en/ga/third/73/documentslist.shtml (accessed 7 December 2018).

representing the affected and capable of engaging, directly and autonomously with states, in the political and technical process of creating new global human rights norms.

Acknowledgements

I am grateful to Matthew Canfield, Nadia Lambek, the anonymous reviewers and the journal editors for their useful comments on this article.

Disclosure statement

No potential conflict of interest was reported by the author.

ORCID

Priscilla Claeys http://orcid.org/0000-0003-1288-6008

Engendering the right to food? International human rights law, food security and the rural woman

Joanna Bourke Martignoni

ABSTRACT

International human rights bodies such as the UN Committee on the Elimination of Discrimination Against Women, the Special Rapporteur on the Right to Food and the UN Human Rights Council are increasingly engaging with issues of gender equality in connection with the rights to food, land and other natural resources. These monitoring mechanisms often partially attribute gender-based inequalities in land rights and food security to the influences of discriminatory local customary norms and harmful cultural practices as well as to broader questions of economic development, environmental degradation and unequal service delivery that are viewed as particularly affecting women in rural areas.

This paper interrogates the discourses of international human rights mechanisms in relation to the rural woman and her right to food. Focusing in particular on the history and development of Article 14 of the UN Convention on the Elimination of Discrimination Against Women, it examines the dominant narratives being constructed about gendered food insecurity and unequal land rights at the international level and the manner in which these are embodied through discussions of the role and status of rural women.

Introduction

> Rural women are active agents of economic and social change and environmental protection … They play crucial roles ensuring food and nutrition security, eradicating rural poverty and improving the well-being of their families yet continue to face serious challenges as a result of gender-based stereotypes and discrimination that deny them equitable access to opportunities, resources, assets and services.[1]

The figure of the 'rural woman' as a distinct subject of international human rights law and policies is tightly bound to the issue of food security. The discursive association of the rural woman with the right to food shapes laws and

[1] UN Women, 'The UN System: Working Together to Empower Rural Women', 2012, online: <www.un.org/womenwatch/feature/ruralwomen/>.

economic policies that seek to define and regulate 'productive' and 'reproductive' gender relations in agrarian settings.[2] International human rights law's construction of the food insecure rural woman has also served as a platform for the modernising project of global development, in particular through its promotion of technological and market-driven agro-industrial growth and its disapprobation of normative pluralism, which is viewed as perpetuating backward and localised 'traditional practices'.[3]

This article examines the manner in which the subject of the rural woman and her right to food are created and understood in international human rights law and its institutions. It seeks to problematise the binary categories of the public and the private spheres, tradition and modernity, local and global spaces and State and non-State forms of normativity that have been deployed in efforts to diagnose and remedy the problem of gendered food insecurity.[4] In particular, it interrogates discourses on local customs and traditions and their use as explanatory frameworks for gendered inequalities in access to food, land and natural resources. To do this, examples of the interpretive practice of international human rights institutions in connection with rural women and the rights to food and land have been compiled using the Universal Human Rights Index database and then analysed together with selected literature and empirical case studies on these topics.[5]

The discussion that follows is largely grounded in the work of the Committee on the Elimination of Discrimination Against Women (CEDAW) as it is the human rights monitoring mechanism that has issued the overwhelming majority of observations and recommendations in connection with rural women and rights to food, land and natural resources.[6] It should be

[2] See Seema Arora-Jonsson, 'Virtue and Vulnerability: Discourses on Women, Gender and Climate Change' (2011) 21 (2) *Global Environmental Change* 744. Mary Cobbett, 'Beyond "Victims" and "Heroines": Constructing "Girlhood" in International Development' (2014) 14 (4) *Progress in Development Studies*. Elizabeth Prügl, 'The Productivity of Gender', Unpublished DEMETER Project Paper Prepared for ICRD Bern, 4–6 September 2017 (on file with the author). Cheryl Doss, Ruth Meinzen-Dick, Agnes Quisumbing and Sophie Theis, 'Women in Agriculture: Four Myths' (2017) 16 *Global Food Security* 69 <http://dx.doi.org/10.1016/j.gfs.2017.10.001>.

[3] See Dorothy Hodgson, *Gender, Justice, and the Problem of Culture: From Customary Law to Human Rights in Tanzania* (Indiana University Press, 2017).

[4] On some of these binaries see, for example, Chandra Mohanty, 'Under Western Eyes: Feminist Scholarship and Colonial Discourses' (1988) 30 (1) *Feminist Review* 61. Dorothy Hodgson, *Gender, Justice, and the Problem of Culture: From Customary Law to Human Rights in Tanzania* (Indiana University Press, 2017). Sally Engle Merry, *Human Rights and Gender Violence: Translating International Law into Local Justice* (University of Chicago Press, 2006).

[5] United Nations Human Rights Index Index, 'Welcome to UHRI,' online: <https://uhri.ohchr.org/en/>. The data analysis is also informed by Prügl (n 2).

[6] In the data samples gathered, 78% of the observations and recommendations on rurality, food security and gender equality were issued by CEDAW, with the Committee on the Rights of the Child (CRC) making up the next biggest portion with 10% and the remaining recommendations coming from a variety of sources including the Committee on Economic, Social and Cultural Rights, the Special Procedures of the Human Rights Council such as the Special Rapporteur on Violence Against Women, the Working Group on the Elimination of Discrimination Against Women in Law and Practice, the Special Rapporteur on the Right to Food and the Special Rapporteur on Extreme Poverty, as well as recommendations made by States within the framework of the Universal Periodic Review process.

emphasised that the notion of 'gender' is used almost exclusively in international human rights discourse as a synonym for 'women' and this focus on rural women in connection with food security has important consequences for the manner in which power relations within agrarian communities are observed and analysed.[7]

The first section of the paper examines the way in which the rural woman is constructed through international human rights law and how this subject-definition is used to explain the problems of gendered food insecurity and 'underdevelopment' in agrarian societies. The second part looks at the causal linkages that are established or assumed by international human rights mechanisms in connection with gender equality, rural development and the rights to food, land and natural resources. The third section briefly sketches the dominant narratives that have been created by human rights monitoring bodies with respect to normative pluralism and its relationship with international law on gender equality and the rights to food, land and natural resources. The conclusions tie these strands together and focus on the remedies to gendered inequalities in access to food and land that are proposed by the international human rights monitoring system. It is argued that the disproportionate emphasis on customary law as a barrier to the realisation of the rights to food and land may be obscuring other, more influential, structural forms of gender inequality, while simultaneously failing to harness the positive role that local norms, actors and practices could potentially play in ensuring food security.

Defining the subject: the rural woman and food security

The rural woman and her role in agricultural development and food production emerged as recurrent and prominent themes at the Rome World Food Conference (1974) and during the Mexico World Conference on the International Women's Year (1975).[8] The resolutions adopted by these

[7] Doss et al (n 2). The authors note, 'The focus on women, rather than on gender, overlooks the contributions of men and the prevalence of "jointness" and negotiation within a household.'

[8] Universal Declaration on the Eradication of Hunger and Malnutrition, United Nations General Assembly Resolution 3180 (XXVIII) (16 November 1974) United Nations Document E/CONF.65/20, para 4 draws attention to the '... key role of women in agricultural production and the rural economy in many countries' and urges governments to '... ensure that appropriate education, extension programmes and financial facilities are made available to women on equal terms with men'. World Conference on the International Women's Year, UNGAR Res 3520 (XXX) (15 December 1975) UN Doc E/CONF.66/34. The Conference adopted Resolution 21 on the 'Condition of women in rural areas' which emphasised the role of women as food producers and the 'hitherto insufficient' acknowledgement of the contribution of rural women in 'procuring and preparing food for family consumption.' In its far-reaching recommendations, the resolution called on States to take steps to inter alia 'ensure legal parity and economic rights in the peasant family as an essential part of any rural development programme' and to design 'integrated rural development proposals' including 'fundamental structural changes in socio-economic institutions' such as the promotion of cooperative workers' and small landowners' associations along with the development of 'educational, health and welfare services, pricing, marketing and credit facilities and the strengthening of popular and elected participation in decision-making.'

conferences squarely positioned rural women at the heart of discussions on food security and created momentum for the inclusion of a provision acknowledging rural difference within the draft text for what would later become Article 14 of the Convention on the Elimination of All Forms of Discrimination Against Women (CEDAW Convention).[9] The attention given to rural women within the United Nations' system has exponentially increased since the adoption of the CEDAW Convention in 1979 to the extent that a decision was made by the General Assembly in 2007 to designate 15 October as the International Day of Rural Women.[10] Significantly, World Food Day is observed the following day.[11]

Most advocacy around women's rights at the time of the drafting of the CEDAW Convention during the mid-1970s was being done by urban civil society groups.[12] Available records of the Convention's negotiations do not refer to involvement by rural women's or peasant associations.[13] Discussions concerning a specific treaty provision on the rights of rural women emerged relatively late in the Convention's drafting process and were initiated by a representative from the Food and Agriculture Organization of the United Nations (FAO) and then supported by a core group of interested States including Egypt, India, Indonesia, Iran, Pakistan, Thailand and the United States.[14] The involvement of the FAO in advocacy around the need to recognise the rights of rural women was sparked by the organisation's interest in improving conditions for female plantation workers and in making links between recently adopted international policy documents on hunger and nutrition and those on women in agricultural development.[15] A further important factor that led to growing political support for rural development amongst States and international organisations was a desire to reverse rural-urban migration flows which had markedly increased during the 1970s.[16]

---

[9] Convention on the Elimination of All Forms of Discrimination Against Women, 1249 UN Treaty Series (18 December 1979) 13, online <http://www.un.org/womenwatch/daw/cedaw/states.htm>. The provision on rural women in Article 14 of the Convention marks the first attempt to define legally enforceable human rights for this social group. See, Lisa R. Pruitt, 'Deconstructing CEDAW's Article 14: Naming and Explaining Rural Difference' (2011) 17(2) *William & Mary Journal of Women and the Law* 390.

[10] UNGA, 'Improvement of the Situation of Women in Rural Areas' (2007) UN Doc A/RES/62/136.

[11] UNGA, 'World Food Day' (1980) UN Doc (A/RES/35/70).

[12] Johanna E Bond, 'Gender, Discourse and Customary Law in Africa,' (2010) 83 *Southern California Law Review* 509.

[13] Lars Adam Rehof, *Guide to the travaux préparatoires of the United Nations Convention on the Elimination of All Forms of Discrimination Against Women* (Martinus Nijhof, 1993). See also Fareda Banda, 'Article 14' in Marsha A Freeman, Christine Chinkin and Beate Rudolf (eds), *The UN Convention on the Elimination of All Forms of Discrimination Against Women: A Commentary* (Oxford University Press, 2012), 357–386.

[14] Pruitt (n 8) 355–356.

[15] Noreen Burrows, 'The 1979 Convention on the Elimination of All forms of Discrimination Against Women' (1985), 32(3) *Netherlands International Law Review* 419, 446.

[16] Report of the Secretary-General 'United Nations Decade for Women. Equality, Development and Peace: Women in Rural Areas,' (1977) UN Doc A/32/269, para 19, '… formulate and execute integrated government planning policies that provide for effective integration of women in rural development with a view to reducing their migration to urban areas, which only worsens the problem of marginality.'

The final version of the CEDAW Convention only directly refers to the right to food as one component of 'adequate living conditions' in Article 14 which deals with the rights of rural women.[17] Food and nutrition are mentioned in the preamble to the Convention in connection with women living in poverty and in Article 12 (2) on the right to health and the obligation to ensure adequate nutrition during pregnancy and lactation. The *travaux préparatoires* for the Convention reveal that some State delegations felt that the focus should be on poverty rather than rurality and that the provisions in the Convention should also encompass disadvantaged women in urban environments.[18] The drafting history of Article 14 also shows that it was agreed that while there was a need to ensure women's equal participation in agricultural development initiatives, rurality was not to be explicitly linked to '(under)development' in general.[19]

With the adoption of the CEDAW Convention in 1979, the rural woman emerged as a distinct subject of international law. Rural women are not only confined to Article 14 of the Convention, they are also referred to in the instrument's Article 10 on the right to education. The CEDAW Convention and subsequent practice of the Committee paint a particular picture of gendered rurality and the inequalities faced by rural women in relation to the rights to food and land.[20] In her study of the development of Article 14, Lisa Pruitt observes,

> Some of the needs and rights enumerated in Article 14 appear to be related to rurality itself, as well as to associated livelihoods such as agriculture. Some appear to recognize the less developed and perhaps more patriarchal character of rural places ... Article 14 sometimes appears to scale back or diminish for rural women the robustness or detail of a right recognized elsewhere in CEDAW, perhaps setting a lower or different standard for these same rights in rural contexts.[21]

In its recommendations to States on their periodic reporting under Article 14 of the Convention, the primary human rights violations experienced by rural women are identified by the CEDAW Committee as:

---

[17] CEDAW (n 8). The preamble to the Convention states that 'in situations of poverty women have the least access to food' and Article 12 (2) mentions the right of women to 'adequate nutrition during pregnancy and lactation.'

[18] Pruitt (n 8) footnote 42, 'Argentina proposed that Article 14 be more comprehensive to cover both women in rural areas and disadvantaged population groups in rural and urban areas.'

[19] *Ibid* 354–355.

[20] Many of the Concluding Observations by the CEDAW state that rural women, particularly women-headed households in rural areas, experience, 'precarious living conditions and lack of access to justice, health care, ownership of land, administration of property and inheritance, education, economic opportunities and community services'. See CEDAW, 'Concluding Observations on Burkina Faso' (5 November 2010) UN Doc CEDAW/C/BFA/CO/6; CEDAW, 'Concluding Observations on Papua New Guinea' (30 July 2010) UN Doc CEDAW/C/PNG/CO/3; CEDAW, 'Concluding Observations on Botswana' (26 March 2010) UN Doc CEDAW/C/BOT/CO/3; CEDAW, 'Concluding Observations on Malawi,' (5 February 2010) UN Doc CEDAW/C/MWI/CO/6; CEDAW, 'Concluding Observations on Madagascar,' (7 November 2008) UN Doc CEDAW/C/MDG/CO/5.

[21] Pruitt (n 8) 351.

- discrimination in access to services such as health care, social security and education due to geography, poverty and the lack of rural women's political representation;
- exclusion of women farmers from the formal economy with its agricultural technologies, markets, pricing mechanisms and credit services;
- discrimination in the 'private sphere' of the home and community with the idea that social conservatism and patriarchal ideas are more deeply entrenched in rural areas;
- lack of access to justice and formal legal remedies and exposure to harmful traditional practices, particularly in connection with equal rights to inherit, own and control land which are enforced through customary legal systems.[22]

As mentioned earlier, during the drafting of Article 14 of the CEDAW Convention, it was decided not to explicitly link development with rurality, however, this division between the South and the North resurfaces in the Committee's interpretive General Recommendation no. 34 on rural women which was adopted in 2016. The General Recommendation refers to the situation of rural women in 'developed' countries, particularly migrant agricultural workers and indigenous women, but covers them in a separate section that primarily focuses on a lack of service provision without mentioning social and cultural barriers to the enjoyment of equal land rights and food security.[23] The subtext of the narrative is, therefore, that the rural woman is located within a specific development context and requires 'modernisation' through her integration into the neo-liberal economy and the formal legal system in order to claim her equal rights.

---

[22] See, for example, CEDAW, 'General Recommendation no. 34 (2016) on the Rights of Rural Women' (4 March 2016) UN Doc CEDAW/C/GC/34. CEDAW, 'Concluding Observations on Zimbabwe,' UN Doc CEDAW/C/ZWE/CO/2-5, (CEDAW, 2012), para 37; CEDAW, Concluding Observations on Congo, CEDAW/C/CGO/CO/6, (CEDAW, 2012), para 37; CEDAW, 'Concluding Observations on Burundi,' (8 April 2008) UN Doc CEDAW/C/BDI/CO/4; CEDAW, 'Concluding Observations on Sierra Leone' (11 June 2007) UN Doc CEDAW/C/SLE/CO/5; CEDAW, 'Concluding Observations on Tanzania' (16 July 2008) UN Doc CEDAW/C/TZA/CO/6; CEDAW, Concluding Observations on Liberia, (7 August 2009) CEDAW/C/LBR/CO/6; CEDAW, Concluding Observations on Malawi, (5 February 2010) UN Doc CEDAW/C/MWI/CO/6; CEDAW, 'Concluding Observations on Papua New Guinea' (30 July 2010) UN Doc CEDAW/C/PNG/CO/3, para 17.

[23] CEDAW (n 21) paras 88–92. Note, however, the Committee's consideration of the third periodic report of Switzerland in 2009 observed 'laws governing inheritance of property often prevent widows from inheriting farms' and recommended that attention be paid to the 'economic empowerment' of rural women without any consideration of the socio-cultural barriers based on traditional norms that sustain discriminatory legislation. CEDAW, 'Concluding Observations on Switzerland' (7 August 2009) UN Doc CEDAW/C/CHE/CO/3, para 39–40. On the topic of discriminatory customs and traditions that impact women's land ownership in Europe and North America see: European Commission, 'Women in EU Agriculture and Rural Areas: Hard Work, Low Profile' in *EU Agricultural Economic Brief No 7* (June 2012); Hannah Alsgaard, 'Rural Inheritance : Gender Disparities in Farm Transmission' (2012) 88 *North Dakota Law Review* 347; Ann Grübstrom et al., 'Balancing Family Traditions and Business: Gendered Strategies for Achieving Future Resilience Amongst Agricultural Students' (2014) 35 *Journal of Rural Studies* 152.

The acknowledgement that 'rural women are not a homogenous group' along with the listing of a number of intersectional identity attributes in CEDAW's interpretive General Recommendation on the rights of rural women, does not substantially shift the focus of human rights discourse on rural women away from this essentialist standpoint.[24] Although the human rights approach is slightly less mired in the instrumentalist, human capital and productivity-based justifications for gender equality found in many of the international policy documents on women and agriculture, it mirrors their emphasis on women's 'intertwined subjectivities' as mothers and providers of food and nutrition for their families and communities.[25] The protection of the equal right to food for the rural woman is seemingly conditioned upon that right being responsibly exercised for the benefit of her family and for the environment.[26]

The next section discusses the way in which these ideas about the rural woman have influenced the framing of the relationships between food security, land rights and gender equality in international human rights law.[27]

Joining the dots: the rights to food, land and gender equality in rural communities

International organisations, civil society and the human rights system are increasingly insisting that gender equal rights over land and natural resources are key mechanisms for the achievement of food security.[28] The UN Committee on Economic, Social and Cultural Rights (CESCR) in its interpretive General Comment no. 12 on the right to adequate food (1999), notes that States have obligations to guarantee 'full and equal access to economic resources, particularly for women, including the right to inheritance and the ownership of land and other property, credit, natural resources and appropriate technology.'[29]

Land rights are therefore considered by various components of the international human rights system as key pre-requisites for food production as

[24] CEDAW (n 21) para 14. See also, Sylvia Chant, 'Women, Girls and World Poverty: Empowerment, Equality or Essentialism?' (2016) 38 (1) *International Development Planning Review* 1.

[25] Anne C. Bellows, Flavio L.S. Valente, Stefanie Lemke and Maria Daniela Nunez Burbano de Lara (eds), *Gender, Nutrition and the Human Right to Adequate Food. Toward an Inclusive Framework*, (Routledge, 2016).

[26] Seema Arora-Jonsson (n 2).

[27] Doss et al (n 2).

[28] UN Human Rights Council, 'Draft Declaration on the Rights of Peasants and Other People Working in Rural Areas' (6 March 2017) UN Doc A/HRC/WG.15/4/2; World Bank, *Gender in Agriculture Sourcebook* (World Bank, 2009); Food and Agriculture Organization of the United Nations, 'Women in Agriculture Closing the Gender Gap for Development' in *The State of Food and Agriculture 2010–2011* (FAO, 2011); International Development Law Organisation, 'Using Law to Strengthen Food Security and Land Rights for Women' in *Women, Food, Land: Exploring Rule of Law Linkages* (IDLO, 2016); Resource Equity and Landesa, *Gender and Collectively Held Land* (Resource Equity and Landesa, 2016).

[29] UN Committee on Economic, Social and Cultural Rights, 'General Comment no. 12 on the Right to Adequate Food' (1999) UN Doc E/C.12/1999/5, para 26.

well as mechanisms to provide women with access to additional income-earning opportunities through the sale of agricultural commodities and the ability to leverage land as collateral for further investments in both on and off farm livelihoods.[30] Interestingly, in their overview of available empirical evidence, Ruth Meinzen-Dick, Agnes Quisumbing, Cheryl Doss and Sophie Theis found that while there was a 'high level of agreement' concerning the positive correlation between women's land rights and food security, there was actually relatively weak data to support this view.[31]

The discourses of the human rights institutions concerning the concept of land tenure as well as the different ways in which ownership, control over, access to and use of land and natural resources play out in various contexts are characterised by a lack of precision and consistency. The 2016 CEDAW General Recommendation no. 34 on the rights of rural women has a section on land and resource rights in which it uses, but fails to define, the terms 'access', 'ownership', 'possession', 'occupation', 'control', 'management', 'administration' and 'transfer'.[32] The General Recommendation also brings in the notion of 'food sovereignty' and the idea that in this connection, rural women should have the 'authority to manage and control their natural resources.'[33]

What is apparent in many of the analyses developed by the human rights system is an emphasis on identified normative shortcomings—discriminatory customary and statutory laws, a lack of 'harmonization' of national and local norms with international human rights law, as well as an absence of access to remedies—as major impediments to gender equality in connection with rights to food, land and natural resources.[34] The UN Special Rapporteur on the

30 See, for example, CEDAW, 'Concluding Observations on Malawi' (24 November 2015) UN Doc CEDAW/C/MWI/CO/7, para. 42 states that 'the Committee is concerned that the delay in the passage of the customary land bill jeopardizes rural women's access to use of land for food crops and income-generating opportunities. It is also concerned that rural women are disproportionately affected by malnutrition and food insecurity.' See further, CEDAW, 'Concluding Observations on the Philippines' (25 July 2016) UN Doc CEDAW/C/PHL/CO/7-8, para 43; CEDAW, 'Concluding Observations on Senegal' (28 July 2015) UN Doc CEDAW/C/SEN/CO/3-7, para 32; CEDAW, Concluding Observations on Gabon, (11 March 15) UN Doc CEDAW/C/GAB/CO/6, para 36; CEDAW, Concluding Observations on Bolivia, (28 July 2015) UN Doc CEDAW/C/BOL/CO/5-6, para 32; CEDAW, Concluding Observations on Indonesia, (7 August 2012) UN Doc CEDAW/C/IDN/CO/6-7, para 45; CEDAW, Concluding Observations on the Solomon Islands, (14 November 2014) UN Doc CEDAW/C/SLB/CO/1-3, para 38; CEDAW, Concluding Observations on India, (24 July 2014) UN Doc CEDAW/C/IND/CO/4-5, para. 32; CEDAW, Concluding Observations on Honduras, (25 November 2016) UN Doc CEDAW/C/HND/CO/7-8, para 42.

31 Ruth Meinzen-Dick, Agnes Quisumbing, Cheryl Doss and Sophie Theis, 'Women's Land Rights as a Pathway to Poverty Reduction: Framework and Review of Available Evidence' (Agricultural Systems, 2017) <http://dx.doi.org/10.1016/j.agsy.2017.10.009>.

32 CEDAW (n 21) paras 55–59.

33 Ibid, para 64.

34 See, CEDAW, 'Concluding Observations on Burkina Faso' (5 November 2010) UN Doc CEDAW/C/BFA/CO/6; CEDAW, 'Concluding Observations on Papua New Guinea' (30 July 2010) UN Doc CEDAW/C/PNG/CO/3; CEDAW, 'Concluding Observations on Botswana' (26 March 2010) UN Doc CEDAW/C/BOT/CO/3; CEDAW, 'Concluding Observations on Malawi,' (5 February 2010) UN Doc CEDAW/C/MWI/CO/6; CEDAW, 'Concluding Observations on Madagascar,' (7 November 2008) UN Doc CEDAW/C/MDG/CO/5.

Right to Adequate Food noted in her 2016 report to the Human Rights Council

> Women additionally face numerous legal barriers in domestic law, which prevents them from fully realizing their right to food, including property rights, land rights and intellectual property rights. These legal barriers also prevent women from maintaining livelihoods that provide sustainable incomes necessary to purchase food, thus challenging women's right to food and ability to achieve food security.[35]

This characterisation of the difficulties faced by rural women in the realisation of the right to food through equal access to land is reiterated by the CEDAW Committee which, as previously noted, highlights the issues of 'discriminatory laws', the 'lack of harmonization of laws and their ineffective implementation at the national and local levels', along with 'discriminatory cultural attitudes and practices'.[36]

Normative pluralism, food, land and the rural woman: global confronts the local

The human rights system has, in the main, viewed normative and legal pluralism as impediments to the realisation of gender equality.[37] The complexity of the multiple and often contradictory norms and practices that exist in the interstices and interactions between State and non-State laws at different levels is something that many of the supra-national human rights institutions have struggled to adequately characterise.[38] Several authors have noted the standardising, prescriptive tendencies of international human rights law and the paradox that these are expressed within a paradigm that simultaneously claims to value and protect cultural diversity.[39]

---

[35] UN Human Rights Committee (UNHRC), 'Report of the Special Rapporteur on the Right to Food (2015) UN Doc A/HRC/31/51, para 17.

[36] CEDAW (n 21) para 56.

[37] William Twining, 'Normative and Legal Pluralism: A Global Perspective' (2010) 20 *Duke Journal of Comparative & International Law* 476, footnote 4: 'In this context "normative pluralism" broadly refers to the coexistence in the same time – space context of multiple systems of norms or rules or of institutionalized normative orders.' See for example, CEDAW (n 21) para 5: 'plural justice systems include multiple sources of law, whether formal or informal – State, non-State and mixed – that women may encounter when seeking to exercise their right of access to justice.' CEDAW (n 21) para 8, '... the parallel existence of often overlapping and conflicting statutory, customary, and religious laws and authorities.' See further; Nicole N Roughan, *Authorities: Conflicts, Cooperation, and Transnational Legal Theory* (Oxford University Press, 2013); Giselle Corradi, Eva Brems and Mark Goodale (eds), *Human Rights Encounter Legal Pluralism. Normative and Empirical Approaches* (Hart Publishing, 2017); International Council on Human Rights Policy, *When Legal Worlds Overlap: Human Rights, State and Non-State Law* (ICHRP, 2009); Sally Engle Merry, 'Legal Pluralism in Practice' (2013) 59(1) *McGill Law Journal*, 1.

[38] Corradi et al (n 35); International Council on Human Rights Policy (n 35); Merry (n 35); Helen Quane, 'Legal Pluralism and International Human Rights Law: Inherently Incompatible, Mutually Reinforcing or Something in Between?' (2013) 33 (4) *Oxford Journal of Legal Studies*, 675.

[39] Vicky C. Jackson, 'Feminisms, Pluralisms, and Transnationalism: On CEDAW and National Constitutions' in Kim Rubenstein and Katharine G. Young (eds), *The Public Law of Gender* (Cambridge University Press, 2016); Michael A. Helfand (ed), *Negotiating State and Non-State Law. The Challenge of Global and Local*

Discussions of normative pluralism are abundant in relation to gender equality and the rights to food, land and natural resources.[40] In fact, aside from recognition of the legal systems of indigenous peoples', it is rare to find references by the human rights monitoring bodies to plural legal or normative orders outside of debates on gender equality.[41] An examination of the meanings being attributed to legal or normative pluralism within the discourses of the United Nations' human rights monitoring mechanisms on gender equality and the rights to food and land reveals several recurring themes, along with a certain degree of ambiguity.[42]

As a general rule, 'plural', 'informal', 'parallel', 'traditional' and 'customary' legal systems are treated by the human rights monitoring mechanisms as socio-cultural obstacles to the implementation of the non-discrimination provisions contained in the Universal Bill of Rights and in the Convention on the Elimination of Discrimination Against Women as well as in national legislative instruments.[43] Most of the recommendations by monitoring bodies on customary and traditional norms cover a wide range of practices that are characterised as inherently discriminatory and in need of regulation through incorporation within modern statutory laws that have been 'harmonised' with international human rights guarantees.[44] Aside from the

Legal Pluralism (Cambridge University Press, 2015); Dorothy Hodgson, *Gender, justice, and the problem of culture: from customary law to human rights in Tanzania* (Indiana University Press, 2017); Emmanuel Melissaris, *Ubiquitous Law. Legal Theory and the Space for Legal Pluralism*, (Routledge, 2016).

40 See FAO, *Focus on Right to Food and Gender* (FAO, 2007), 2: 'In some countries, discrimination is reflected in customary law and in others the existence of a pluralist legal system challenges women's right to food'; FAO Legal Paper no. 4, *Legal pluralism: Women's land rights and gender equality in Mozambique* (FAO, 2017); Anne C. Bellows, Flavio L.S. Valente, Stefanie Lemke and Maria Daniela Nunez Burbano de Lara (eds), *Gender, Nutrition and the Human Right to Adequate Food. Toward an Inclusive Framework* (Routledge, 2016).

41 See the discussion by Eva Brems, 'Legal Pluralism as a Human Right and/or as a Human Rights Violation' in Giselle Corradi, Eva Brems and Mark Goodale (eds) *Human Rights Encounter Legal Pluralism. Normative and Empirical Approaches* (Hart Publishing, 2017); See further, Quane (n 36).

42 The analysis was conducted using advanced key word searches within the Universal Human Rights Index and the results were then exported into the qualitative data analysis application, Dedoose (www.dedoose.com).

43 See, for example, CEDAW, 'Concluding Observations on Rwanda' UN Doc CEDAW/C/RWA/CO/7-9 (2017), para 42, 'The implementation of Law No. 43/2013 is hampered by stereotypical attitudes towards ownership and inheritance by women and by the continued application of discriminatory customs.' See further, CEDAW, 'Concluding Observations on the Philippines' UN Doc CEDAW/C/PHL/CO/7-8 (2016), para 49 (c); CEDAW, 'Concluding Observations on Togo' UN Doc CEDAW/C/TGO/CO/6-7 (2012), para 40; CEDAW, 'Concluding Observations on Iraq' UN Doc CEDAW/C/IRQ/CO/4-6 (2014), para. 53, 'In line with its general recommendation No. 29 on the economic consequences of marriage, family relations and their dissolution, the Committee recalls that identity-based personal status laws and customs perpetuate discrimination against women and that the preservation of multiple legal systems is in itself discriminatory against women.'

44 See Sally Engle Merry, *Human Rights and Gender Violence: Translating International Law in Local Justice* (University of Chicago Press, 2009), 102: 'In the postcolonial era, the glamour of the modern is still juxtaposed to backward others, but now it includes those who are 'developing' but still burdened by culture. Transnational legal settings are producing culture, but it is a culture that relegates culture to the margins.' See also Rosa Freedman and Nicolas Lemay-Hébert (eds), *Hybridity: Law, Culture and Development* (Routledge, 2017); Brian Z Tamanaha, Caroline Sage and Michael Woolcock (eds), *Legal Pluralism and Development: Scholars and Practitioners in Dialogue* (Cambridge University Press, 2012).

occasional reference to issues connected to the implementation of human rights in federal systems, legal pluralism is framed as something that primarily affects communities in the global South.[45] The Concluding Observations on the third periodic report of Papua New Guinea issued by the CEDAW in 2010 are illustrative of the dominant narrative about the relationship between gender equality and customary law;

> while noting the plural legal system operating in Papua New Guinea, the Committee is concerned that even though customary law is subordinate to the Constitution and statutory laws, it is the main law applicable in the village courts, resulting in continuing discrimination against women.[46]

In connection with the rights to food, land and natural resources, this trend is also reflected. Traditional and customary norms are frequently, unless related to the rights of indigenous and tribal women to access 'ancestral lands and resources',[47] grouped together to form a mass of harmful practices that must be eliminated or, at the very least, modulated through their incorporation into formal, legislative instruments.

> [S]tereotypes contribute to the persistence of violence against women as well as harmful practices, including female genital mutilation, levirate and sororate, child marriage, polygamy, repudiation, and food prohibitions or taboos. The Committee is also concerned that the State party has not taken sufficient action to modify or eliminate such stereotypes and harmful practices.[48]

More ambiguous, however, are observations made by the monitoring mechanisms that simultaneously seek to limit the scope of customary norms due to their purported incompatibility with international human rights law, while also acknowledging that traditional systems of land tenure and 'secondary' or usufruct rights may have previously promoted gender

---

[45] See, for example, CEDAW, 'Concluding Observations on Switzerland' (7 August 2009) UN Doc CEDAW/C/CHE/CO/3.

[46] CEDAW, 'Concluding Observations on Papua New Guinea' (30 July 2010) UN Doc CEDAW/C/PNG/CO/3, para 17.

[47] See CEDAW, 'Concluding Observations on the Russian Federation' (20 November 2015) UN Doc CEDAW/C/RUS/CO/8, para 40 (b): 'Guarantee that indigenous women have full and unrestricted access to their ancestral lands and the resources on which they depend for food, water and health and to maintain and develop their distinct cultures and identities as peoples.' See also, CEDAW, 'Concluding Observations on Malawi' (24 November 2015) UN Doc CEDAW/C/MWI/CO/7, para. 43.

[48] CEDAW, 'Concluding Observations on Senegal' (28 July 2015) UN Doc CEDAW/C/SEN/CO/3-7, para 18. In a similar vein, see UNGA 'Report by the Special Rapporteur on Violence Against Women on her mission to Ghana' (2008) UN Doc A/HRC/7/6/Add.3, para 93, which urges the government to, 'denounce publicly and unequivocally all forms of violence against women and girls including marital rape, wife beating, child and other forced marriages, *trokosi*, FGM, humiliating widowhood rites and inheritance/property grabbing; elected politicians, officials, traditional authorities and other persons vested with public authority must not invoke any custom, tradition or religious consideration to justify or condone such violence; they should also discourage the practice of dowry and polygamy and publicly question the existence of harmful witchcraft.'

equality.[49] Such statements draw attention to the dynamic nature of local norms—something that the monitoring mechanisms frequently downplay or overlook—as well as to the fact that it appears to be interactions with systems of power at different levels that produce or reproduce gendered inequalities in rights to food and land, rather than the simple existence or persistence of customary laws themselves.[50]

The dominant narrative on legal pluralism being developed by the human rights mechanisms focuses on the 'problem' of local customary norms in connection with access to food, land and natural resources.[51] Customs and traditional practices are, in the main, framed as being inherently discriminatory against women and in need of reform and regulation through State-based legislative enactments and policies.[52] Local authorities are to be engaged by the State for the purposes of eliminating 'harmful' customs and replacing these with practices that align with transnational gender equality law and, to a large degree, with the dominant neo-liberal paradigm of market-based agricultural development.[53] In the process, societies—overwhelmingly in Africa but occasionally also in South and Central Asia and the Pacific—that recognise non-State norms, are implicitly characterised by the monitoring mechanisms as backward and resistant to the modernising project of transnational human rights.[54]

Diagnosing and remedying gendered inequalities in food and land rights

Gender equality demands have the potential to disrupt unequal power relations at different levels and provide a variety of mechanisms through which structural injustices in access to food, land and other natural resources

[49] See, for example, CEDAW, 'Concluding Observations on Micronesia' (9 March 2017) UN Doc CEDAW/C/FSM/CO/1-3, para 40, 'The Committee is further concerned about recent changes to the matrilineal inheritance system for land, which have placed women in a disadvantaged position in relation to ownership, acquisition, management and disposition of property.'

[50] See the lengthy and nuanced discussion of the evolving nature of gendered customary norms amongst Maasai groups in Tanzania in Dorothy Hodgson, *Gender, justice, and the problem of culture: from customary law to human rights in Tanzania* (Indiana University Press, 2017).

[51] See, CEDAW, 'Concluding Observations on Samoa' (7 August 2012) UN Doc 49, para 34; CEDAW, 'Concluding Observations on Zimbabwe' (23 March 2012) UN Doc CEDAW/C/ZWE/CO/2-5, para 35; CEDAW, 'Concluding Observations on Burkina Faso' (5 November 2010) UN Doc CEDAW/C/BFA/CO/6.

[52] Even in cases in which the mechanisms don't view custom as a barrier to gender equality, States are still urged to 'formalise' customary norms through legislative provisions and government policies. See, for example, CEDAW 'Concluding Observations on Malawi' (24 November 2015) UN Doc CEDAW/C/MWI/CO/7, para 43, 'The Committee recommends that the State party expedite the adoption of the customary land bill to ensure the protection of women's customary land rights, access to land, including for food crops and income generating opportunities, and control over productive resources, and promote their participation in decision-making regarding land allocation.'

[53] See, CEDAW, 'Concluding Observations on the Philippines' (25 July 2016) UN Doc CEDAW/C/PHL/CO/7-8, para 16 (b).

[54] Prügl (n 2). See also, Susanne Zwingel, *Translating International Women's Rights*, (Palgrave Macmillan, 2016), 86.

might be observed and redressed. The emergence of the rural woman as a subject of international law and policy in the 1970s has been intricately bound to the issue of gender-based inequalities in relation to food security. To date, however, the primary engagement of UN human rights mechanisms has been with those forms of discrimination and inequality that rural women face in the 'private' and 'local' spheres of the family and community without convincingly connecting these to global inequalities in food systems.[55] At the same time, the growing body of human rights jurisprudence and academic literature that discusses the political and economic forces driving the 'land rush' in different parts of the world and the impact that this is having on the right to food has tended to be largely gender blind.[56]

As outlined above, the international human rights monitoring mechanisms have generally viewed certain types of normative pluralism—namely local traditional customary practices—as inherently problematic for gender equality in the areas of food security and land rights whilst overlooking the opportunities that pluralism could provide for a more effective realisation of the right to adequate food.[57] The role of customary law is particularly important in regulating access and usufruct rights over collectively held land and other resources and it has been demonstrated in a number of countries that a nuanced, contextual understanding of customary norms may enable them to be successfully used to promote gender equality and food security.[58] In the same vein, following a lengthy civil society campaign, the Human Rights Council adopted the UN declaration on the rights of peasants and other people working in rural areas, which seeks, among other things, to reconcile respect for local traditional knowledge and rights over land and other resources with global gender equality guarantees.[59]

---

[55] See, Bina Agarwal, 'Gender and Land Rights Revisited: Exploring New Prospects via the State, Family and Market' (2003) 3 *Journal of Agrarian Change* 184.

[56] See, UNGA, 'Report by the Special Rapporteur on the Right to Adequate Food' (2010) UN Doc A/65/281; Saturnino M Borras, Ruth Hall, Ian Scoones, Ben White and Wendy Wolford, 'Towards a Better Understanding of Global Land Grabbing: An Editorial Introduction' (2011) 38(2) *The Journal of Peasant Studies* 209; World Bank, 'Module 4: Gender Issues in Land Policy and Administration' in *Gender in Agriculture Sourcebook* (World Bank, 2009), 137, 'A number of factors, including a growing market economy, increasing poverty, and commercial agriculture, are converting land into an asset, accentuating land scarcity, and privatizing (and individualizing) land rights.'

[57] See, Brian Z Tamanaha, Caroline Sage and Michael Woolcock (eds), *Legal Pluralism and Development: Scholars and Practitioners in Dialogue* (Cambridge University Press, 2012), 2; See also, Ruth Meinzen-Dick, 'Property Rights for Poverty Reduction?' in Department of Economic and Social Affairs Working Paper No. 91 (United Nations: Department of Economic and Social Affairs, 2009) UN Doc ST/ESA/2009/DWP/91, 6.

[58] See, for example, Landesa and Resource Equity, *Gender and Collectively Held Land. Good practices and lessons learned from six global case studies* (Resource Equity and Landesa Rural Development Institute, 2016); Elizabeth Daley and Birgit Englert, 'Securing Land Rights for Women' (2010) 4(1) *Journal of Eastern African Studies* 91; Naomi Kenney and Ana Paula de la o Campos, *Developing Gender Equitable Legal Frameworks for Land Tenure. A Legal Assessment Tool* (FAO, 2016)

[59] See UNHRC, 'United Nations Declaration on the Rights of Peasants and Other People Working in Rural Areas' (28 September, 2018) UN Doc A/HRC/39/L.16. Adopted by the Human Rights Council with 33 votes in favour, 11 abstentions and 3 against.

Moving away from the local level to address other factors that contribute to gendered food insecurity, the CEDAW Committee's interpretive General Recommendation on rural women refers to the 'macroeconomic roots' of gender inequality and calls upon States to adopt gender-sensitive trade, fiscal, investment and rural development policies.[60] It is clear that the Committee is concerned by the global power dynamics and structures that may be influencing the accessibility of food and land for women at the local level. The Committee's recommendations to States in this regard contain an injunction to 'address the negative and differential impacts' of economic policies including trade liberalisation, privatisation and the commodification of land on the rights of rural women.[61] It is not apparent, however, which concrete steps the parties to the CEDAW Convention will be required to take in order to achieve these changes.

On the basis of these diagnoses of the underlying causes of gendered inequalities in food security and associated rights to land and resources, the international human rights mechanisms have developed a number of policy and legislative recommendations.[62] These include: ensuring the participation and empowerment of rural women through their involvement in agricultural cooperatives and political groups, the recognition of the specific needs of smallholders and organic farmers, the adoption of mechanisms to prevent, respond to and redress different forms of violence against women, as well as the reform of discriminatory legal provisions.[63] The 'formalisation' of customary land tenure through individualised land titles has also been one of the major mechanisms through which various actors have sought to improve the food security of women in different contexts.[64] Crucially, however, it has been noted that individual titling programmes are also gendered and modelled on forms of land ownership and usufruct rights that do not necessarily correspond to local customs and practices and that these schemes may inadvertently erode women's customary rights to use and access collectively held land and resources.[65]

This article has drawn attention to discourses of international human rights monitoring mechanisms, and the CEDAW in particular, that tend to reinforce a number of 'myths' concerning rural women, land rights, customary norms and food security.[66] The limitations of these stereotypes are that

[60] CEDAW (n 21) para 10.

[61] Ibid, para 11.

[62] Ibid; UNGA, 'Report by the Special Rapporteur on the Right to Adequate Food' (11 August 2010) UN Doc A/65/281; UNHRC, 'Report of the Special Rapporteur on the Right to Adequate Food' (14 December 15) UN Doc A/HRC/31/51.

[63] CEDAW (n 21).

[64] World Bank (n 27); International Development Law Organisation (n 27).

[65] Doss et al (n 2). See also, Mikael Baaz, Mona Lilja, Alison Östlund, 'Legal Pluralism, Gendered Discourses and Hybridity in Land Titling Practices in Cambodia' (2017) 44 (2) *Journal of Law and Society*, 200.

[66] Doss et al (n 2).

they tell only one part of the story of gendered food insecurity and, as a result, they may narrow the scope of potential remedies. Even when the human rights mechanisms have come up with broad explanatory frameworks for gendered inequalities in connection with the rights to food and land, the solutions proposed are restricted in comparison with their far-reaching diagnosis of the problem. There is a tendency by the human rights mechanisms to make passing references to the role of gendered macroeconomic structures and institutions that fuel food and land speculation and then to ignore these thorny political questions in favour of standardised technical recommendations such as individual land titling schemes, women's economic empowerment initiatives, measures to promote access to markets, agricultural inputs, services and technologies or the 'formalisation' of customary inheritance laws.[67] Focusing on local customs as the primary site of gender inequality in this field obscures both the fact that traditional norms are continually being remade by the forces of colonialism and neo-liberal economic development and that these norms might also provide pathways for positive change.[68]

There are structural constraints that limit the capacity of the human rights monitoring mechanisms—treaty bodies, Special Procedures and the Human Rights Council—to engage in detailed ethnographic and economic research. These limitations include a serious lack of resources within the human rights system for research, coordination and monitoring activities, as well as the political difficulties inherent in countering the powerful, standardised and technocratic discourses on agricultural development being produced in fora such as the Bretton Woods institutions. At the very least, however, the Geneva-based human rights bodies should be cognisant of the complexities of gendered power relations in rural communities and be prepared to make recommendations on the right to food that are nuanced, contextualised and informed by quality research.

Disclosure statement

No potential conflict of interest was reported by the author.

Funding

This article is based on research conducted within a six year-long multidisciplinary research project on gender equality, the right to food and agricultural commercialisation (DEMETER), supported by the Swiss National Science Foundation and the Swiss Agency for Development and Cooperation. For further information see: r4d-demeter.info.

67 Susan Marks, 'Human Rights and Root Causes' (2011) 74 (1) *Modern Law Review* 57.

68 Dorothy Hodgson, *Gender, Justice, and the Problem of Culture* (Indiana University Press, 2017).

The UN Committee on World Food Security's break from the agricultural productivity trap

Nadia Lambek

ABSTRACT
In 2008, the price of grain spiked internationally, leading to a series of events commentators began to call the global food crisis. Although low agricultural productivity was not the cause of the crisis or the high rates of food insecurity that followed, intergovernmental agencies fell into old patterns and largely responded with policies geared towards increasing agricultural productivity. The UN Committee on World Food Security (CFS), however, has offered alternatives to this productivity trap, providing a space for dialogue on different approaches. In this paper, I review CFS policy recommendations from 2010 to 2017, and argue that by focusing on small-scale producer livelihood rather than productivity rates and the availability of food on markets, the CFS has contributed to the normative elaboration of alternative paradigms. I argue further, that the CFS's reformed structure and the inclusion of civil society in policy-making facilitated space for the promotion of these alternatives.

In early 2008, the price of grain spiked internationally, leading to a series of events commentators began to call the global food crisis.[1] In the wake of the crisis, the UN estimated that the number of food insecure across the globe increased by 100 million people, to an alarming 1.02 billion.[2] The crisis was precipitated by increased demands for biofuels, rising energy prices, the depreciation of the US dollar, low interest rates and changing investment patterns.[3] At the time of the crisis, small-scale food producers

---

[1] Priscilla Claeys and Nadia Lambek, 'In Search of Better Options: Food Sovereignty, the Right to Food and Legal Tools for Transforming Food Systems' in Nadia CS Lambek, Priscilla Claeys, Adrienna Wong and Lea Brilmayer (eds), *Rethinking Food Systems: Structural Challenges, New Strategies and the Law* (Springer, 2014) 1–25.

[2] Food and Agricultural Organization of the UN (FAO) and World Food Programme (WFP), *The State of Food Insecurity in the World: Economic Crises – Impacts and Lessons Learned* (2009), online: <www.fao.org/3/a-i0876e.pdf>.

[3] Derek Heady and Shengeen Fan, *Reflections on the Global Food Crisis: How Did It Happen? Who Has It Hurt? And How Can We Prevent the Next One?* (IFPRI, 2011) xii–xvi.

made up the majority of the world's food insecure.[4] They continue to make up the majority of the world's food insecure to this day.[5] Their food insecurity is rooted in structural discrimination and a long history of both unfavourable and harmful policies.[6] Although low productivity rates and issues of food availability were not the causes of the crisis or the food insecurity that ensued, leading institutions and intergovernmental agencies as well as major players, such as the Gates Foundation, fell into old patterns, and largely responded with policies geared towards increasing agricultural productivity.[7]

The UN Committee on World Food Security (the CFS), however, has provided a space for the discussion of alternatives. The CFS is one of many international bodies with jurisdiction over food security governance, but in the years preceding the global food crisis it was met with waning interest and possessed little political power.[8] In 2009, at the height of the crisis and with rising rates of global food insecurity and poverty making headlines, the CFS reformed.[9] Initiated by member states and spurred by civil groups, the reform was intended to breathe new life into the CFS, while elevating the body and its role in ensuring food and nutrition security for everyone across the globe.[10] Through the reform, the CFS adopted a mandate to become the 'foremost inclusive international and intergovernmental platform' working towards the 'elimination of hunger and ensuring food security and nutrition for all human beings'.[11]

---

[4] Committee on World Food Security (CFS), 'Reform of the Committee on World Food Security' (October 2009), UN Doc. CFS:2009/2 Rev/2, para 1 [CFS]; FAO & WFP (n 2).

[5] FAO et al, *The State of Food Security and Nutrition in the World: Building Resilience for Peace and Food Security* (2017), online: <http://www.fao.org/3/a-I7695e.pdf>.

[6] Carmen G Gonzalez, 'International Economic Law and the Right to Food' in Lambek et al. (eds), *Rethinking Food Systems: Structural Challenges, New Strategies and the Law* (Springer, 2014) 165–94; FAO & WFP (n 2) 1. ('The increase in food insecurity is not a result of poor crop harvests but because high domestic food prices, lower incomes and increasing unemployment have reduced access to food by the poor. In other words, any benefits from falling world cereal prices have been more than offset by the global economic downturn.').

[7] Eve Fouilleux, Nicolas Bricas and Arlène Alpha, 'Feeding 9 Billion People': Global Food Security Debates and the Productionist Trap' (2017) 24(11) *Journal of European Public Policy* 1658; Jessica Duncan, *Global Food Security Governance: Civil Society Engagement in the Reformed Committee on World Food Security* (Routledge, 2015) 34; Tim Lang and David Barling, 'Food Security and Food Sustainability: Reformulating the Debate' (2012) 178(4) *The Geographic Journal* 313; IPES Food, *The New Science of Sustainable Food Systems* (2015) 16, online: <www.ipes-food.org/_img/upload/files/NewScienceofSusFood.pdf>.

[8] Josh Brem-Wilson, 'La Vía Campesina and the UN Committee on World Food Security: Affected Publics and Institutional Dynamics in the Nascent Transnational Public Sphere' (2016) 43(2) *Review of International Studies* 302, 314.

[9] CFS (n 4)

[10] *Ibid.*

[11] *Ibid*, para 4.

While the reformed CFS has been lauded elsewhere as a model multi-stakeholder platform[12] and participatory space,[13] as well as a response to fragmentation in global food security governance,[14] in this paper, I argue that the CFS is also noteworthy for opening a space for discussing alternatives to the productivity paradigm. The result of this space can be seen in the negotiation and adoption of many policy instruments that address and emphasise food accessibility, inadequate incomes, and the livelihoods of small-scale producers, over questions of food availability and increasing productivity. More specifically, these instruments have focused on the productive resources and the infrastructure needed for small-scale producers to ensure their own food security through small-scale food production, as well as social protection schemes and other government services to ensure food security more broadly. While not all policy recommendations have offered an alternative to productivity paradigm, those that have set an important precedent.

I argue further that the CFS's reform structure provided an enabling environment for discussion of alternatives to the productivity paradigm. The reform led to one of the most robust participatory mechanisms of any global governance body, with mandated inclusion of stakeholders, including small-scale producers, in almost all aspects of its work. In the years following the reform, civil society and social movements promoting food sovereignty were major participants in the CFS space and were able to shape and push agendas, resulting in policy recommendations that in part reflected their perspectives.

The paper begins with a brief description of the productivity paradigm and its relationship to food security. It then outlines how the reform structure of the CFS facilitated a space open to alternative policy approaches. The third section reviews CFS policy recommendations from 2010 (the year following the reform) to 2017, analysing their approach to addressing food insecurity. The paper draws from experience attending the 38th, 43rd, 44th and 45th sessions of the CFS, conversations with actively engaged civil society players at the CFS, participation in two CFS stock taking events on the right to food,[15] and engagement with the ethnographic works of other CFS scholars.[16]

---

[12] Ban Ki-Moon, *Secretary General Address to the 37th Committee on World Food Security*, YouTube, online: <www.youtube.com/watch?v=5ycTZmuAeb4> (accessed 15 March 2018).

[13] Duncan (n 7); Brem-Wilson (n 8).

[14] Olivier De Schutter, 'The Reform of the Committee on World Food Security: The Quest for Coherence in Global Governance' in Lambek et al. (eds), *Rethinking Food Systems: Structural Challenges, New Strategies and the Law* (Springer, 2014) 220.

[15] The first stock taking event was for the 10th anniversary of the *Voluntary Guidelines to support the Progressive Realization of the Right to Adequate Food in the Context of National Food* in 2014, while the second is the Global Thematic Event monitoring national implementation of the same Guidelines in 2018.

[16] This includes the work of Jessica Duncan, Josh Brem-Wilson, and Nora McKeon.

I. The productivity paradigm

Food security is generally defined as existing, 'when all people, at all times, have physical and economic access to sufficient, safe and nutritious food that meets their dietary needs and food preferences for an active and healthy life'.[17] Flowing from this, food security is said to have four dimensions: availability (supply side assessment referring to the existence of sufficient quantities of food through domestic food production, trade or food assistance), accessibility (the ability of individuals to procure adequate resources to acquire food as well as the removal of any physical obstacles in acquiring food), utilisation (the nutritional elements of food), and stability (whether individuals have access to available food that meets nutritional needs on a consistent basis over time).[18] Using the food security lens and measurement, as is most commonly done in international and intergovernmental settings, the causes of food insecurity can be traced to these different dimensions, as can policy prescriptions.

Since the 1930s, the predominant international response to food insecurity has been to increase the availability of food by increasing production.[19] Over the years, the mechanisms for increasing production and the policy prescriptions have differed, but the general mantra that more food to feed a growing population ensures better food security has remained strong.[20] Rather than focus on the ability of food insecure populations to better access what food is available—through improved incomes, better social protection, supports for marginalised groups, etc.—this paradigm looks to increase overall availability of food by both improving agricultural yields (eg, through intensification or synthetic fertilisers) as well as through increasing the quantity of overall food production, with the hopes of a trickle-down effect on accessibility.

A variety of terms have been used to categorise different iterations of this productivity paradigm, including productionism and productivism.[21] Fouilleux, Bricas and Alpha articulate the difference between these terms, noting that while:

> productionism relates to a general discourse focused on the need to increase production without mentioning any technical or social specific agricultural pattern, productivism focuses on the need to increase productivity through

---

[17] This definition was first articulated at the World Food Summit in 1996. World Food Summit, Plan of Action (1996), at para. 1, online: <www.fao.org/WFS/>. This definition is now used by the FAO and other UN bodies, as is the basis for global food security measurements.

[18] FAO, 'An Introduction to the Basic Concepts of Food Security' (2008), online: <www.fao.org/docrep/013/al936e/al936e00.pdf>.

[19] Lang and Barling (n 7) 313.

[20] *Ibid.*

[21] Fouilleux et al. (n 7); Tim Lang, 'The Complexities of Globalization: The UK as a Case Study of Tensions within the Food System and the Challenge of Food Policy' (1999) 16 *Agriculture and Human Values* 169.

> increased use of chemical inputs (fertilizers, pesticides), hybrid seeds (possibly including genetically modified seeds), mechanization and large-scale farms.[22]

Nora McKeon argues that the productivism paradigm remains ever present today, and is often now presented as 'sustainable intensification', GMO promotion, and 'disguising chemical fertilizers and other inputs under epithets like "sustainable crop nutrition"'.[23] The term 'productivity paradigm' is used here to encompass both productionism and productivism.

Following the 2008 food price crisis, key and hegemonic actors in food security governance pursued policies in line with the productivity paradigm as a primary response to rising rates of food insecurity. For example, the Gates Foundation, the G20 and the World Bank, through the Global Agriculture and Food Security Programme and other initiatives, largely pursued policies and projects—like financing access to seeds and fertilisers—aimed at increasing food availability by increasing agricultural production,[24] shying 'away from tackling the broader structural economic dimensions of the food crisis'.[25] Similarly, the G8, along with the African Union, several African governments and the private sector, through the New Alliance for Food Security and Nutrition, sought to address poverty and food insecurity through massive investments in growing Africa's agriculture sector, by promoting *inter alia* 'capital intensive agriculture based on commercial seeds and inputs' intended to spur increased production.[26]

The productivity paradigm has been criticised by a diversity of scholars and civil society actors.[27] In an overarching critique, Olivier De Schutter, former UN Special Rapporteur credits the focus on increasing agricultural production throughout the twentieth century, as moving agriculture systems towards industrial agriculture and input heavy modes of production, and as directly responsible for poor diets and associated health outcomes, as well as for having a severe environmental impact, including a significant loss of ago-biodiversity, accelerated soil erosion and increased greenhouse gas

---

[22] Fouilleux et al. (n 7) 1659–60.

[23] Nora McKeon, *Food Security Governance: Empowering Communities, Regulating Corporations* (Routledge, 2015) 72.

[24] Jennifer Clapp and Sophia Murphy, 'The G20 and Food Security: A Mismatch in Global Governance?' (2013) 4(2) *Global Policy* 129, 130, 132–3; 'Framework Document for a Global Agricultural and Food Security Program' (2009) 13, online: <www.gafspfund.org/sites/default/files/inline-files/GAFSP%20Framework%20Document%20FINAL%20%28external%29_0.pdf>; 'Global Agricultural and Food Security Program, Projects', online: <www.gafspfund.org/projects>.

[25] Clapp and Murphy (24) 130.

[26] FIAN et al., 'G8 New Alliance for Food Security and Nutrition in Africa: A Critical Analysis from a Human Rights Perspective' (2015) 4–5, online: <www.fian.org/fileadmin/media/publications_2015/2014_G8NewAlliance_screen.pdf>.

[27] See Fouilleux et al. (n 7); McKeon (n 23); Clapp and Murphy (n 24). The Civil Society and Indigenous Peoples Mechanism (CSM) to the UN Committee on World Food Security has been particularly critical. For example, in two speeches on the floor during the 2015 session of the CFS, the CSM critiqued approaches to food insecurity focused on production over resilient agriculture. CSM, Civil Society Statements to CFS 42 (2015), 6, 16, online: <www.csm4cfs.org/wp-content/uploads/2016/04/En-CS-contribution-2015-BR.pdf>.

emissions.[28] He notes further that this focus has done little to address alarming rates of food insecurity: 'despite the impressive increase in agricultural output per capita, the number of hungry people has hardly been reduced'.[29] Others have shared this critique, also noting that the productivity paradigm has led to policies and practices that fail to realise the right to food, including ensuring the participation of smallholders in the design of policies,[30] and result in the 'significant expulsion of smallholders from agriculture'.[31]

II. An enabling environment through the reformed CFS

In 2009, following six months of negotiations in which both governments and civil society groups took part, the CFS reform document was adopted by member states reflecting many of the demands of civil society.[32] The reform document details the agreed upon reform structure of the CFS as well as a mandate to become:

> the foremost inclusive international and intergovernmental platform for a broad range of committed stakeholders to work together in a coordinated manner and in support of country-led processes towards the elimination of hunger and ensuring food security and nutrition for all human beings.[33]

The reform structure and the participation dynamics following the reform have created an enabling environment at the CFS for discussions of alternatives to the productivity paradigm.

As a direct result of civil society participation in the reform process, the CFS moved towards increased inclusivity as a multi-stakeholder platform. 'Committed stakeholders'—including civil society organisations, NGOs, private sector associations, private philanthropic organisations and others 'active in the areas related to food security, nutrition, and the right to food'[34]—were not just given observer status (as they are in most UN and international/intergovernmental bodies), but participant status.[35] Within this open space, the reform document left room for new voices, in particular for civil society, including those most impacted by food insecurity to influence

[28] Olivier De Schutter, 'The Specter of Productivism and Food Democracy' (2014) *Wisconsin Law Review* 199, 205–7.

[29] *Ibid.* at 202.

[30] FIAN et al. (n 26).

[31] Nora McKeon, 'The New Alliance for Food Security and Nutrition' (TNI Agrarian Justice Programme: Policy Paper, 2014), 6, online: <www.tni.org/files/download/the_new_alliance.pdf>; Olivier De Schutter, 'The New Alliance for Food Security and Nutrition in Africa' (EU Parliament, Directorate-General for External Policies Study, EP/EXPO/B/DEVE/2015/1, 2015), online: <www.europarl.europa.eu/RegData/etudes/STUD/2015/535010/EXPO_STU(2015)535010_EN.pdf>.

[32] Ingeborg Gaarde, *Peasants Negotiating a Global Policy Space: La Vía Campesina in the Committee on World Food Security* (Routledge, 2017) 49.

[33] CFS (n 4) para 4.

[34] *Ibid,* paras 16–17.

[35] *Ibid,* paras 4, 11–12.

policy agendas, as well as recommendations. The reform document lists 'organisations representing smallholder family farmers, artisanal fisherfolks, herders/pastoralists, landless, urban poor, agricultural and food workers, women, youth, consumers, Indigenous Peoples and International NGOs' as key participants.[36] With participant status, civil society groups were granted rights to intervene in plenary and breakout discussions, to contribute to the preparation of meeting documents and agendas, to submit and present documents and formal proposals, and to engage in intersessional activities of the CFS.[37] Civil society groups were also given space on the CFS Advisory Group, a body set up to provide input to the Bureau, the central governing body of the CFS. However, states remained the only CFS members, and thus the only entities with voting rights.

While the private sector was given participant status, in the years following the reform civil society groups were more active than the private sector in CFS negotiations and processes. For example, in 2010, in the first post-CFS session, the only private sector participants were from Croplife International, while representatives from forty-two civil society organisations and non-governmental organisations were present.[38] Over the years, the private sector presence at the CFS has grown, both during the plenary meetings and intersessional periods. By 2017, the private sector had representatives from 58 private companies and private philanthropic groups, like the Gates Foundation, had become regularly participants.[39]

Following the reform, civil groups self-organised into the Civil Society and Indigenous Peoples' Mechanism (the CSM) to coordinate participation in the CFS.[40] The CSM is composed of participant organisations many of whom actively resist the productivist paradigm, advocating instead for food sovereignty.[41] Food sovereignty, as described by La Vía Campesina, 'is the right of peoples to healthy and culturally appropriate food produced through

[36] *Ibid*, para 11(ii).

[37] *Ibid*, para 12.

[38] CFS, 'Thirty-sixth Session: Final Report' (2010) UN Doc. CFS:2010/final report, para 1 and Appendix C. By 2011, there were forty-three civil society and social movement organizations represented, and the number of private sector and philanthropic organizations, including the Gates Foundation, moved up to thirty-one. CFS, 'Thirty-Seventh Session: Final Report' (2011) UN Doc. CFS:2011/final report, Annex C.

[39] CFS, 'Making a Difference in Food Security and Nutrition: Report' (2017) UN Doc. CFS 2017/44/Report, para 1. See also Pierre-Marie Aubert, 'On the Growing Participation of Multinational Corporations in Food Security Global Governance' (2016), Food Governance Blog, online: <https://foodgovernance.com/2017/01/30/on-the-growing-participation-of-multinational-corporations-in-food-security-global-governance/>.

[40] See generally: ActionAid International et al., *Proposal for an International Food Security and Nutrition Civil Society Mechanism for Relations with the CFS*, (2010) UN Doc. CFS:2010/9.

[41] For example, many member organizations of La Vía Campesina are active members of the CSM. *See generally*, Gaarde (n 32). The CSM gives 'priority to the organizations and movements of the people most affected by food insecurity and malnutrition, recognizing that they are the organizations of rights-holders that are the subjects of their own development and also the most important contributors to food security and nutrition worldwide'. The Civil Society Mechanism, 'What is the CSM?', online: <www.csm4cfs.org/the-csm/> (accessed 14 March 2018).

ecologically sound and sustainable methods, and their right to define their own food and agriculture systems'.[42] It emphasises placing food producers and consumers at the centre of policymaking regarding the food system, and promotes agroecology and sustainable food production over industrial or input heavy food production.[43] In the past nine years, the CSM has made use of the CFS's participatory platform and while it has had to continually struggle to secure its space and voice, it has been frequently successful in influencing the agenda of the CFS and negotiated outcomes.[44]

III. Contributions to an alternative normative elaboration

In the years following the reform, and under the conditions set out above, the CFS has negotiated and endorsed over twenty sets of policy recommendations and voluntary guidelines.[45] Though not exclusively, CFS outputs have focused on the most food insecure globally, namely smallholder food producers, particularly women, Indigenous peoples and other rural inhabitants. Many CFS policy recommendations have offered alternatives to the productivity paradigm, focusing less on the productive capacity of smallholders and their ability to increase food availability on domestic and international markets, and more on smallholder access to the productive resources and infrastructure needed for small-scale food production and achieving food security as well as more broadly securing an income to make food accessible. This is not to say that none of the CFS instruments contain recommendations geared at increasing productivity and availability of food on markets through input intensive or industrial agriculture—indeed, many policy recommendations like the Responsible Investment in Agriculture and Food Systems (CFS-rai) support such an approach. But even these outputs generally emphasise increasing the income of producers through increased production over reducing prices or increasing food security with improved yields through input intensive agricultural, industrialisation, or land consolidation. As such, the CFS, while not dismissing the productivity paradigm, has advanced a set of policy recommendations elaborating the normative development of alternative paradigms. In this section, three trends—a focus on productive resources (like land and water), infrastructure and social protection—within the CFS policy recommendations which break from the productivity paradigm are discussed.

First, CFS negotiated policy instruments over the last decade have contributed to the normative elaboration of steps states should take to ensure small-

42 La Vía Campesina, 'Declaration of Nyéléni' (2007), online: <https://nyeleni.org/spip.php?article290>.

43 *Ibid.*; International Forum for Agroecology, 'Declaration of the International Forum for Agroecology' (2015), online: <www.foodsovereignty.org/wp-content/uploads/2015/02/Download-declaration-Agroecology-Nyeleni-2015.pdf>.

44 Duncan (n 7).

45 Jessica Duncan, 'Governing in a Post-political Era: Civil Society Participation for Improved Food Security Governance' in David Barling (ed), *Advances in Food Security and Sustainability* (Elsevier, 2016).

scale producers' access to productive resources for small-scale production, without resorting to an emphasis chemical inputs or hybrid seeds (often associated with the productivity paradigm[46]). The CFS's most notable work on productive resources concerns land and, in particular, land tenure systems. Negotiated under the backdrop of rising numbers of large-scale land acquisitions, a growing global population, and the impact of environmental degradation and climate change on the availability of land, fisheries and forests, the CFS endorsed *The Voluntary Guidelines on the Responsible Governance of Tenure of Land, Fisheries and Forests in the Context of National Food Security* (the VGGT) in 2012.[47] The VGGT seek to

> provide guidance to improve the governance of tenure of land, fisheries and forests with the overarching goal to achieving food security for all and to support the progressive realization of the right to adequate food in the context of national food security.[48]

The VGGT cover a wide range of issues including tenure rights for producers, fisherfolk, Indigenous peoples and others, and focus on providing the security needed for individuals and communities to earn an income, steward the environment and celebrate and practice their culture. As detailed in the preamble, 'people can be condemned to a life of hunger and poverty if they lose their tenure rights to their homes, land, fisheries and forests and their livelihoods'.[49] To address this, states are to 'recognize that policies and laws on tenure rights operate in the broader political, legal, social, cultural, religious, economic and environmental context', and are to set up tenure systems that ensure fair transfer of land, protection of tenure rights, respect for customary tenure, protection of the commons, non-discrimination, no forced evictions, and remedies for violations of tenure rights.[50] The VGGT recommend legal rules and provisions around displacement and compensation, including for those with customary tenure, that put in place some barriers to land consolidation and acquisitions, and efforts by states or investors to move away from small-scale production to large-scale industrial farming. During the VGGT negotiations, civil society groups won key victories on including a rights-based approach in the Guidelines,[51] protecting customary tenure, ensuring a strong gender-based approach, and giving priority to

[46] Fouilleux et al. (n 7) 1659–60.

[47] CFS, *The Voluntary Guidelines on the Responsible Governance of Tenure of Land, Fisheries and Forests in the Context of National Food Security* (FAO, 2012); Duncan (n 7) 169. ('To say that the VGGT represent a landmark in the evolution of the reformed CFS would not be hyperbole').

[48] CFS (n 47) iv.

[49] *Ibid*, at v.

[50] *Ibid*, at paras 3.1(1), 3.1(2), 3.1(4), 5.9, 8.2, 8.3 and 11.1.

[51] The VGGT recommend that states implement tenure systems in a manner that reflects human rights principles, specifically by ensuring human dignity, non-discrimination, equity and justice, gender equality, holistic and sustainable approaches, consultation and participation, rule of law, transparency, accountability and continuous improvement (which would be understood as progressive realisation in the context of human rights). *Ibid*, para 3B.

restitution and redistributive reforms geared at the most vulnerable.[52] However, they were unsuccessful in securing references to water, an international ban on large-scale land acquisitions, and provisions concerning restitution of ancestral lands for Indigenous peoples.[53]

Rural social movements opposing the productivity paradigm were 'cautiously positive' about the VGGT text as adopted.[54] Many continue to be supportive. In a 2016 exercise to monitor national implementation of the VGGT, the CSM praised the VGGT's holistic approach, recognising the inextricable link between tenure of land, fisheries and forests, and access to and management of other natural resources. They note that this holistic approach:

> is in line with the relationships that people in many parts of the world have with their living environment, according to which land, oceans, rivers, forests and all of nature are much more than a means of production and instead are the very basis of life, culture and identity, and fulfil crucial social, cultural, spiritual and environmental functions.[55]

The holistic approach taken in the VGGT also offers an alternative to the productivity paradigm. By valuing land and the environment as much more than a means of production, the VGGT highlight the importance of policies that deemphasise extraction and high productive rates at any cost and instead prioritise social, cultural, spiritual and environmental functions of land alongside food production.

While implementation of the VGGT may lead to higher productivity rates by ensuring stable access to land over time, they do not promote increased production as the means of ensuring food security. Rather than facilitate land convergence, acquisition by large-scale producers or intensified agriculture that would support the productivity paradigm, the VGGT outline basic protections to ensure that a variety of tenure systems are recognised and protected, and that individuals, families, and communities cannot be removed from land (at least not in an arbitrary manner and without compensation), to make way for large-scale production.

Other CFS outputs have offered alternatives to the productivity paradigm by supporting smallholder access to productive resources.[56] Policy outputs

---

[52] McKeon (n 23) 161. McKeon continues noting that success on redistributive reforms favouring the most vulnerable, was 'affirmation of states' obligations to regulate their corporations' operations beyond their own territorial boundaries.' *Ibid.* Jessica Duncan notes that the participation of civil society groups throughout the negotiation process 'strengthened the rational for their inclusion as official participants in the reformed CFS.' Duncan (n 7) 169.

[53] Philip Seufert, 'The FAO Voluntary Guidelines on the Responsible Governance of Tenure of Land, Fisheries and Forests' (2013) 10(1) *Globalizations* 181, 185.

[54] McKeon (n 23) 161.

[55] Civil Society Mechanism, *Synthesis Report on Civil Society Experiences Regarding the Use and Implementation of the Tenure Guidelines and the Challenge of Monitoring CFS Decisions* (2016), 4.

[56] CFS, 'Fortieth Session: Final Report' (2003) UN Doc. CFS 2013/40, para 32 [CFS 40] (' … particular attention to enabling smallholder access—especially for women—to productive assets, local, national and regional markets, appropriate training, research, technology and farm support services.').

such as *Sustainable Forestry for Food Security and Nutrition* (2017), *Sustainable Agricultural Development for Food Security and Nutrition: What Roles for Livestock?* (2016), and *Water for Food Security and Nutrition* (2015), all address access to resources for smallholders to continue small-scale production through ecological practices in an effort to earn a liveable income and to ensure their own food security. They make policy recommendations that support small-scale production and resource use, instead of industrial animal production, deforestation, and large-scale irrigation.

Of course, the VGGTs and the other CFS outputs could be stronger in providing recommendations that support agroecology, and greater participation of producers and impacted persons in policy-making. Further still, language concerning access to resources is not the same as language guaranteeing rights to resources or food sovereignty.[57] However, in these documents, the producers and their ability to support an income that would ensure their food security, and not overall availability of food on markets, take the centre role. Indeed consumers, the availability of food, and the costs of purchasing food are rarely mentioned in these CFS outputs.

Second, CFS outputs have contributed to the normative development of policy recommendations geared at access to infrastructure for smallholders to assist them in earning an income and ensuring their food security through small-scale production. Infrastructure is understood as broadly covering the basic physical and organisation structures, such as roads, electricity, telecommunication, running water, markets, etc., needed for small-scale production. References to access to infrastructure can be found throughout the CFS's policy recommendations. For example, in 2013, the CFS adopted policy recommendations to support smallholders' own investments in infrastructure, such as 'feeder roads, energy, post-harvest handling infrastructure, rural electrification and telecommunication grids'.[58]

Of particular note, in 2016, the CFS adopted a set of principles entitled *Connecting Smallholders to Markets*. Rather than focus on greater availability of food on markets, the principles address steps states can take to ensure smallholders have access to markets and can maintain their existences as smallholder producers while earning a decent living.[59] Recommendations include: providing smallholders fair and transparent prices, as well as information about pricing; promoting and expanding public procurement of safe, healthy, nutritious and diverse smallholder produced food; facilitating production diversification to increase smallholder 'resilience to climate

---

[57] In December 2018, the UN General Assembly adopted the *Declaration on the Rights of Peasants and Others Working in Rural Rights*, recognizing rights over productive resources (water, land, biodiversity, seeds etc.). *See* the article of Priscilla Claeys in this issue for more information: Priscilla Claeys, 'The Rise of New Rights for Peasants. From Reliance on NGO Intermediaries to Direct Representation' (2019) 9(3–4) *Transnational Legal Theory* 1.

[58] CFS 40 (n 56) para 42.

[59] CFS, 'Connecting Smallholders to Markets' (FAO, 2016), online: <www.fao.org/3/a-bq853e.pdf>.

change, natural disasters and price shocks';[60] promoting smallholder products with 'specific quality characteristics which increase income and can respond to consumer demand while preserving traditional practices and knowledge, and agricultural biodiversity';[61] developing or improving 'smallholder-targeted infrastructure, such as irrigation, small-scale centers for processing and packaging, and infrastructure that links rural areas with urban areas and relevant markets, such as feeder roads, and market places for direct sales; improving access to energy';[62] and numerous references to ensuring income and economic stability for smallholders.[63] Though some recommendations do address availability of food and 'improve[ed] agricultural production', even these are qualified by references to enhancing smallholder integration into territorial markets, as well as food safety and nutritional value.[64]

Third, CFS outputs have contributed to the normative development of tools that address income security with programmes aimed at 'on the farm' support and social protection more broadly. In 2012, the CFS made a number of recommendations to states concerning social protection for food security and nutrition.[65] These recommendations propose that social protection provide 'essential assistance in the short-term while simultaneously protecting or building productive assets and infrastructure that support livelihoods and human development in the long term',[66] and that it be human rights based, supporting the progressive realisation of the right to food, and drawing on the International Labour Organization's social protection floors.[67] Social protection prioritises food accessibility and income security over food availability by providing an income or other transfers to food insecure populations.[68]

The CFS, both in outputs on social protection and elsewhere, has also recommended states provide other services to support smallholders in small-scale production. For example, in 2013, the CFS policy recommendations suggest states support 'health-care, child care, nutrition, education and capacity development, social protection, water and sanitation' with the direct aim of enhancing 'food security and nutrition' and reducing 'smallholder poverty'.[69] In its output on social protection, the CFS does recommend social protection geared directly to support agricultural productivity, through

[60] *Ibid*, Recommendation 5.
[61] *Ibid*, Recommendation 14.
[62] *Ibid*, Recommendation 11.
[63] *Ibid*, Recommendations 2, 14, 15, 16, 18, 19, and 24.
[64] *Ibid*, Recommendations 7 and 9.
[65] CFS, 'Thirty-ninth Session: Final Report' (2012) UN Doc. CFS 2012/39, para 8 [CFS 39].
[66] *Ibid*, para 8b.
[67] *Ibid*, para 8d.
[68] Olivier De Schutter and Magdalena Sepulveda, *Underwriting the Poor: A Global Fund for Social Protection*, Briefing Note 07 (2012) 2.
[69] CFS 40 (n 56) para 43.

extension services and input support, but even those recommendations centre on livelihood concerns, and are bundled with recommendations for weather, crop and livestock insurance and public procurement schemes, such as purchasing from local smallholder farmers for school feeding initiatives.[70]

Beyond access to social protection, productive resources and infrastructure, other CFS recommendations offer alternatives to the productivity paradigm. For example, discussions on food loss and waste at the CFS do not fall into traditional productivity discourse, with limited concerns expressed in policy outputs over overall productivity rates, and instead a focus on the sustainability and resilience of agricultural and food systems, as well as impacts on food security.[71] Solutions to food loss and waste recommended by the Committee included improving data collection and knowledge sharing, encouraging sustainable patterns of consumption and production, investing in infrastructure and public goods, supporting small-scale producers and processors for better access to knowledge and innovations, markets, financial services, logistics, and other services and exploring the impact of short supply chains.[72]

There have, of course, been tensions between the productivity paradigm and other approaches at the CFS, as many states, particularly the G20, still subscribe to the productivity paradigm. This tension was present in debates over whether the CFS should endorse the Principles for Responsible Agricultural Investment that Respect Rights, Livelihoods and Resources (PRAI) developed by UNCTAD, the FAO, IFAD and the World Bank. The PRAI principles were *investor-driven* and did not align with the CFS's structural approach. The CSM pushed against their adoption and instead sought to negotiate principles that were *producer rights-driven*.[73] The CSM was ultimately successful and the PRAI were not endorsed. Instead, the CFS adopted the CFS-rai, which stress the importance of strengthening the capacity of smallholders to make their own investments and promote responsible investment by other stakeholders.[74] The CFS-rai highlight that responsible investment in agriculture and food systems contributes to food security, nutrition and poverty eradication through increasing sustainable production of safe, nutritious, diverse and culturally acceptable food, as well as through improving incomes, enhancing the fairness and transparency of markets, and enhancing food utilisation, through access to clean water, sanitation, energy, technology, childcare, health care, and access to education.[75] While the ultimate negotiation and adoption of the alternative principles

[70] CFS 39 (n 65) para 8b.
[71] CFS, 'Fortieth-first Session: Final Report' (2014) UN Doc. CFS 41/Final Report, para 12 [CFS 41].
[72] *Ibid*, para 13.
[73] Philip McMichael, 'The Right to Food and Politics of Knowledge' (2015) 2(2) *Canadian Food Studies* 52.
[74] CFS 41 (n 71) Appendix D, para 4.
[75] *Ibid*, at Appendix D, para 21.

were not without political contestation, the ability of civil society organisations to block the endorsement of PRAI was a remarkable success in promoting an approach that at least in part supported small-scale producer livelihood and was grounded in the experience of those most impacted by food insecurity.

IV. Conclusion

In this paper, I argue that many of the CFS' policy recommendations have offered an alternative to the productivity paradigm. Through these recommendations, and the negotiation and consensus building processes that led to their adoption, the CFS has created policy outputs that address food accessibility, the livelihoods of small-scale producers, and inadequate incomes as responses to food insecurity. The CFS reform structure has created an enabling environment for these alternatives by allowing alternative voices, particularly from civil society, to influence policy recommendations. This has led the CFS to focus policy outputs on producers and in particular, their standard of living and food security. These outputs address access to productive resources for small-scale production, infrastructure and various forms of social protection and not the availability of food on markets through increased production, chemical inputs, intensive agriculture, monocultures or industrial agriculture.

While CFS recommendations may not represent a radical departure from dominant modes of food security policy-making—for example, they do not recognise food sovereignty, or challenge international economic law and its impact on food security governance—they do offer alternatives to the productivity paradigm. They have also had an impact beyond the CFS. Today CFS outputs have been integrated into or relied upon in other normative elaboration processes at the global level, such as CEDAW General Recommendation No. 24 on the rights of rural women,[76] and the *Declaration on the Rights of Peasants and Other People Working in Rural Areas*,[77] recently adopted by the UN General Assembly, as well as in domestic contexts.[78] In this way, CFS recommendations form a precedence of agreed upon language negotiated through consensus that can work beyond the CFS to challenge the productivity paradigm.

[76] Committee on the Elimination of Discrimination against Women (CEDAW), 'General Recommendation No. 34 on the Rights of Rural Women' (2016) UN Doc. CEDAW/C/CG/34.

[77] For the most recent draft, see: UN Human Rights Council, 'Revised Draft United Nations Declaration on the Rights of Peasants and Other People Working in Rural Areas' UN Doc. A/HRC/WG.15/5/2.

[78] *See for example* lists of countries adopted portions of the VGGTs: CFS, 'Compilation of Experiences and Good Practices in the Use and Application of the Voluntary Guidelines on the Responsible Governance of Tenure of Land, Fisheries and Forests in the Context of National Food Security' (FAO, June 2016), online: <www.fao.org/fileadmin/templates/cfs/Docs1516/OEWG_Monitoring/3rd_Meeting/Compilation_of_VGGT_Submissions_24_June__2016.pdf>.

Today, many scholars and civil society members have identified the CFS as under threat—with a limited budget, concerns for efficiency and cost-control, states rejecting human rights, and challenges to the participatory ethos all threatening to de-politicise the CFS's work, limit participation and weaken its impact.[79] Addressing these threats is essential to ensuring that the CFS can continue to provide space for inter-governmentally negotiated policies that provide alternatives to an outdated paradigm, while ensuring that those most impacted by food insecurity have a voice at the table. The CFS remains an important policy space and one worth defending.

Disclosure statement

No potential conflict of interest was reported by the author.

[79] Nora McKeon, 'Are Equity and Sustainability a Likely Outcome When Foxes and Chickens Share the Same Coop? Critiquing the Concept of Multistakeholder Governance of Food Security' (2017) 14(3) *Globalizations* 379; Civil Society Mechanism, *Civil Society Report: The Use and Implementation of the Right to Food Guidelines* (2018); Jessica Duncan et al., 'The Committee on World Food Security: Politics Under Threat' in Delphine Thivet and Antoine de Raymond (eds), *Un monde sans faim? Gouverner la sécurité alimentaire au 21e siècle* (Presse de Sciences-Po, *forthcoming* 2019).

Index

www.ingramcontent.com/pod-product-compliance
Lightning Source LLC
LaVergne TN
LVHW011120300926
849160LV00008B/459
9781032839257